AN APOSTOLIC GOSPEL

The so-called *Epistula Apostolorum* is an early gospel-like text in which the eleven apostles recount a question-and-answer session with the risen Jesus on Easter morning, intended to equip them for the worldwide mission to which they are now called. The *Epistula* draws selectively from the Gospels of John and Matthew, while disagreeing with its sources at a number of points and claiming definitive status for its own rendering of the apostolic gospel. This book is based on a new translation of this important but neglected text, drawing on the Coptic, Ethiopic, and Latin manuscript evidence and with variants noted in an English-language critical apparatus. Extensive additional notes are provided to clarify issues of text, translation, and exegesis. The central chapters explore major theological themes such as incarnation, resurrection, and eschatology in the light of related texts within and beyond the New Testament.

FRANCIS WATSON has held posts at King's College London and the University of Aberdeen before moving to his present position at Durham University in 2007. His recent publications include *Gospel Writing: A Canonical Perspective* (2013) and a co-edited volume entitled *Connecting Gospels: Beyond the Canonical/Non-Canonical Divide* (2018).

SOCIETY FOR NEW TESTAMENT STUDIES

MONOGRAPH SERIES

General Editor: Edward Adams, *King's College, London*

179

AN APOSTOLIC GOSPEL

An Apostolic Gospel

The 'Epistula Apostolorum' in Literary Context

FRANCIS WATSON

CAMBRIDGE
UNIVERSITY PRESS

CAMBRIDGE
UNIVERSITY PRESS

Shaftesbury Road, Cambridge CB2 8EA, United Kingdom

One Liberty Plaza, 20th Floor, New York, NY 10006, USA

477 Williamstown Road, Port Melbourne, VIC 3207, Australia

314–321, 3rd Floor, Plot 3, Splendor Forum, Jasola District Centre, New Delhi – 110025, India

103 Penang Road, #05–06/07, Visioncrest Commercial, Singapore 238467

Cambridge University Press is part of Cambridge University Press & Assessment, a department of the University of Cambridge.

We share the University's mission to contribute to society through the pursuit of education, learning and research at the highest international levels of excellence.

www.cambridge.org
Information on this title: www.cambridge.org/9781108794619

DOI: 10.1017/9781108884631

© Cambridge University Press & Assessment 2020

First published 2020
First paperback edition 2022

A catalogue record for this publication is available from the British Library

Library of Congress Cataloging-in-Publication data
Names: Watson, Francis, 1956- author.
Title: An apostolic gospel : the "Epistula apostolorum" in literary context / Francis Watson, University of Durham.
Other titles: Epistle of the Apostles. English.
Description: Cambridge, United Kingdom; New York, NY, USA : University Printing House, 2020. | Series: Society for New Testament studies monograph series | Includes bibliographical references and index.
Identifiers: LCCN 2020037672 (print) | LCCN 2020037673 (ebook) | ISBN 9781108840415 (paperback) | ISBN 9781108794619 (paperback) | ISBN 9781108884631 (epub)
Subjects: LCSH: Epistle of the Apostles.
Classification: LCC BS2900.A7 W38 2020 (print) | LCC BS2900.A7 (ebook) | DDC 229/.93–dc23
LC record available at https://lccn.loc.gov/2020037672
LC ebook record available at https://lccn.loc.gov/2020037673

ISBN   978-1-108-84041-5   Hardback
ISBN   978-1-108-79461-9   Paperback

CONTENTS

Contents

ACKNOWLEDGEMENTS

My warmest thanks to Sarah Parkhouse, Madison Pierce, Kelsie Rodenbiker, Henk Jan de Jonge, Darrell Hannah, Isaac Soon, and Christopher Jones, for invaluable and much appreciated help at successive stages of this project. For digital images of the single Coptic and multiple Ethiopic manuscripts, I am indebted to the Bibliothèque nationale (Paris), the British Library (London), the Hill Museum and Manuscript Library (Collegeville, MN), and the Universitätsbibliothek Stuttgart.

INTRODUCTION

In June 1919, exactly a hundred years ago as I write, the great German Coptologist Carl Schmidt published a lengthy monograph entitled, *Gespräche Jesu mit seinen Jüngern nach der Auferstehung: Ein katholisch-apostolisches Sendschreiben des 2. Jahrhunderts*; 'Conversations of Jesus with his Disciples after the Resurrection: A Catholic and Apostolic Epistle of the Second Century'.[1] At the heart of the monograph lies Schmidt's reconstruction and transcription of a damaged and incomplete Coptic manuscript of the fourth or fifth century, containing a translation into the 'Akhmimic' dialect of a work much of whose original Greek vocabulary it preserves in the form of loan-words – around 160 of which are listed in Schmidt's index. The surviving material gave no evidence of the work's title.

In the years after Schmidt first encountered this work, in Cairo in 1895, evidence of a Latin translation came to light in a Vienna palimpsest (1908), and – more significantly – a complete Ethiopic text was published, with French translation, by Louis Guerrier (1912). Guerrier's edition had been based on four Ge'ez manuscripts, none older than the sixteenth century. Evidently dissatisfied with Guerrier's work, Schmidt arranged for the Ethiopic text to be re-edited and translated by the Polish scholar Isaak Wajnberg, and Wajnberg's translation of the Ethiopic and Schmidt's of the Coptic (where available) face each other on opposite pages near the beginning of Schmidt's monograph, with extensive linguistic notes provided by both scholars.[2]

By correlating the surviving Coptic pagination with the full Ethiopic text, it became clear that the Ethiopic preserved not only

---

[1] Carl Schmidt (with Isaak Wajnberg), *Gespräche Jesu mit seinen Jüngern nach der Auferstehung: Ein katholisch-apostolisches Sendschreiben des 2. Jahrhunderts* (Leipzig: J. C. Hinrichs, 1919; repr. Hildesheim: Georg Olms, 1967). The history of the rediscovery of the *Epistula Apostolorum* (*EpAp*) is covered in detail in Chapter 1, below.
[2] Schmidt, *Gespräche Jesu*, 23–155.

1

the lost Coptic opening of the work (now chapters 1–6) but also a long preliminary section of eschatological prophecy that was never part of the Coptic manuscript. This preliminary section is manifestly a secondary addition to the text-form preserved in Coptic. It is included as an integral part of the Ethiopic text in Guerrier's edition, where it forms chapters 1–11, and its Galilean setting accounts in part for the title Guerrier gave the entire work: *Le Testament en Galilée de Notre-Seigneur Jésus-Christ*. The Coptic manuscript in its intact form would have begun at Guerrier's chapter 12 ('What Jesus Christ revealed to his disciples...'), and Schmidt and Wajnberg renumber Guerrier's chapters in the format 'Cap 1 (12)' and so on, relegating the secondary material to an Appendix under the heading 'Apokalyptische Rede Jesu an seine Jünger in Galiläa'.[3]

The synoptic presentation of the two translations makes it clear that variations between the Ethiopic and the extant Coptic are frequent but mostly inconsequential. With a few exceptions, the Ethiopic variants consist in little more than alternative nuances, minor expansions within a limited semantic range, different decisions by the original translators, and errors in transmission – many of which come to light in variants within the Ethiopic manuscript tradition itself.

I

In the title of his monograph, Schmidt characterizes the work as a *katholisch-apostolisches Sendschreiben*, a catholic and apostolic epistle. It is 'apostolic' because its supposed authors are eleven named apostles, it is 'catholic' in that it is addressed to all Christians everywhere, and it is an 'epistle' because it employs the standard epistolary format in which author and addressee are identified and differentiated at the outset, together with the communication of a greeting or blessing (here unusually placed first):

> In the name of God, ruler of all the world, and of Jesus Christ, grace be multiplied to you. John and Thomas and Peter and Andrew and James and Philip and Bartholomew and Matthew and Nathanael and Judas the Zealot and Cephas to the churches of the east and the west, to those in the north and the south...   (*EpAp* 1.5–2.2)

---

[3] Schmidt, *Gespräche Jesu*, 47*–66*.

Schmidt devised the title *Epistula Apostolorum* on the basis of the header 'Epistula' in the Latin palimpsest, and this passage – not known to him at the time – might seem to confirm that he was right.[4] Yet the only other epistolary feature in this text is the consistent use of the first person plural, and the text initially presents itself not as an epistle but as a revelation or apocalypse: 'What Jesus Christ revealed to his disciples and to all', perhaps ὃ ἀπεκάλυψεν Ἰησοῦς Χριστὸς τοῖς μαθηταῖς αὐτοῦ καὶ τοῖς πᾶσιν in the original Greek. This announcement of a revelation with a deferred epistolary opening recalls the *Book of Revelation* (where John is the sole author rather than the lead author): Ἀποκάλυψις Ἰησοῦ Χριστοῦ ἣν ἔδωκεν αὐτῷ ὁ θεὸς δεῖξαι τοῖς δούλοις αὐτοῦ ἃ δεῖ γενέσθαι ἐν τάχει (*Rev* 1.1), followed by the author's greeting to 'the seven churches that are in Asia' (*Rev* 1.4–6). The content of the 'conversations of Jesus with his disciples after his resurrection' is revelatory from beginning to end; Schmidt's term, 'Gespräche', is too casual for the contents of a work that preserves instruction delivered by Jesus 'after he rose from the dead, when he revealed to us what is great and wonderful and true' (*EpAp* 1.2). It is fundamental truths about the heavenly world and the future that 'our Lord and Saviour revealed to us and showed us, as we likewise do to you' (6.1). On three occasions the disciples give voice to the text's own sense of its revelatory significance:

> Lord, great indeed are the things you have now revealed to us! (16.1)
>
> Lord, in everything you have been merciful to us and you have saved us and you have revealed everything to us! (20.1)
>
> Lord, what great things you have spoken to us and announced to us and revealed to us, things never yet spoken, and in everything you have comforted us and been gracious to us! (34.1)

This text is an *Epistula Apostolorum* from the perspective of its communicative intention, but in terms of its content it is an *Apocalypsis Apostolorum* to complement or compete with the *Apocalypsis Iohannis*.

The Johannine apocalypse is delivered by the exalted Lord, a figure of transcendent majesty (cf. *Rev* 1.12–20), and the same is true

---

[4] There is direct address from authors to readers in *EpAp* 7–8, at the start of the extant Coptic.

of a further Johannine text of the second century, the *Apocryphon of John* (cf. *ApocrJn* 2.18–4.20). The apocalypse is concerned with the present situation of the Asian churches and the eschatological events that must soon come to pass whereas the apocryphon is oriented towards primordial origins, contextualizing and correcting the flawed *Genesis* narrative. Neither work has much in common with the gospel genre developed by early Christian authors to record significant aspects of Jesus' human existence (events, acts, teaching, in one combination or another).

Works with this 'biographical' focus all locate themselves within the sequence that runs from Jesus' birth and its antecedents through to his ascension. They may be limited in scope, consisting in birth stories alone in the case of the *Protevangelium of James* or sayings alone in the *Gospel of Thomas*. In other cases they are more comprehensive, influenced in this by Graeco-Roman biographical conventions. The *Gospel of Luke* begins before Jesus' birth and includes a story from his adolescence before recounting his adult ministry and his death, burial, resurrection, appearances, and ascension. The *Gospel of John* lacks either an ascension account or birth stories, but it traces Jesus' existence far back behind the time of the emperor Augustus (cf. *GLk* 2.1) to the beginning of all things (*GJn* 1.1–4). Comprehensiveness of scope does not mean comprehensiveness of detail, however. The Johannine prologue merely sketches an eternal existence, and the Lukan ending reports the fact of the ascension with minimal circumstantial detail (*GLk* 24.50–51). All early gospels or gospel-like texts reflect their authors' choices about which areas to prioritize: the ministry and passion in some cases (e.g. *GMark*), post-Easter events in others (e.g. *GMary*).

The (so-called) *Epistula Apostolorum* fits comfortably within this profile. Its use of the first person is unusual within early gospel literature but not unique (cf. *GPet* 7.26–27; 14.59, 'we, the twelve disciples of the Lord. . .'). The single passage of epistolary discourse in *EpAp* 1–2 serves not as an indicator of overall genre but as an articulation of the text's communicative strategy, which is to make the apostles' collective testimony as accessible to later generations through their writing as it was to their contemporaries through their speech (cf. *EpAp* 2.3). The scope of *EpAp* is unusually comprehensive. Like *GJohn* but at greater length, it acknowledges the role of the pre-existent Son in the creation of the world (*EpAp* 3.1–10). Like *GLuke*, it speaks of the annunciation, the miraculous conception, and the swaddling clothes (*EpAp* 3.13–15; 14.1–7). Like all four canonical gospels it contains a collection of miracle stories (4.1–5.21), then proceeding to speak briefly of Jesus' death and burial (9.1) and at much greater length of his appearance to his female and male disciples on Easter morning (9.2–12.4). After the long dialogue (13.1–50.11), the work concludes with an account of the ascension that is relatively full and entirely independent of *Luke–Acts* (*EpAp* 51.1–4). Setting aside the assumption that the only 'real' gospels are the canonical four and bearing in mind the fluidity of ancient genre boundaries, there is no good reason not to regard this text as a gospel.[5]

II

It is possible that early Greek manuscripts of *EpAp* bore the title εὐαγγέλιον τῶν ἀποστόλων, or some variant of that. Collective apostolic works were in circulation from an early period. Origen refers to 'the Gospel entitled "of the Twelve"' (τὸ ἐπιγεγραμμένον τῶν Δώδεκα εὐαγγέλιον),[6] and the *Didache* was known by the title Διδαχὴ τῶν ἀποστόλων.[7] By the time of the first scribe of the Vienna palimpsest, however, *EpAp* could be identified simply as *Epistula*. Later still, an expanded version of this text circulated in Ge'ez manuscripts under the title 'Testament of our Lord and Saviour Jesus Christ' (a title drawn from the still larger and later work to which it had been annexed). The Ge'ez text opens with the words, 'The discourse [*or* word, *nagar*] that Jesus Christ spoke to his twelve disciples in Galilee after he was raised from the dead…'(*Galilean Discourse [GD]* 1.1).[8] The Coptic title (if any) is unknown, but

---

[5] For the view that early Christian gospels constitute a single literary field retrospectively divided by the canonical boundary, see my *Gospel Writing: A Canonical Perspective* (Grand Rapids, MI: Eerdmans, 2013), esp. 1–9, 609–16; also Francis Watson and Sarah Parkhouse (eds.), *Connecting Gospels: Beyond the Canonical/Non-Canonical Divide* (Oxford: Oxford University Press, 2018), 1–6; Francis Watson, 'A Reply to my Critics', in Catherine Sider Hamilton with Joel Willitts (eds.),*Writing the Gospels: A Dialogue with Francis Watson* (London: T&T Clark, 2019), 227–48.

[6] Origen, *Hom. in Luc.* 1 (text in *Origenes, Homilien zu Lukas in der Übersetzung des Hieronymus und die griechischen Reste der Homilien und des Lukas-Kommentars*, Griechische Christliche Schriftsteller, ed. Max Rauer (Berlin: Akademie-Verlag, 1959²), 4–5).

[7] Kurt Niederwimmer, *The Didache: A Commentary on the Didache* (Minneapolis, MN: Augsburg Fortress, 1998), 56–57.

[8] See the Appendix to this volume. For reasons explained there, my chapter enumeration differs from Guerrier's at this point.

EpAp would have been read as an 'apocryphon' in the context of late antique Egypt within which the Coptic manuscript was produced and read – a member of the category of 'apocrypha', purportedly apostolic or prophetic writings outside the canonical boundary, criticized and rejected as spurious by ecclesial authority yet avidly consumed by ordinary Christian readers.[9]

Following the publication of Schmidt's monograph, *EpAp* was immediately and without question consigned to that same category, as though the qualitative difference asserted and established by the canonical boundary were a mere neutral fact. *EpAp* was made available to modern readers as part of an *Apocryphal New Testament* (M. R. James 1924; J. K. Elliott 1993), or as one more item within an ever-expanding collection of *Neutestamentliche Apokryphen* (Hennecke–Schneemelcher 1959[3], 1990[6]) or *Antike christliche Apokryphen* (Markschies–Schröter 2012).[10] Useful and indispensable as such collections are, they conceal the fact that the distinction between the 'canonical' and the 'apocryphal' is a construct of the early church that should not be anachronistically projected back onto the products of the first hundred years and more of Christian literary activity. The point has been classically formulated by Dieter Lührmann:

> The term 'canonical' does not represent an attribute inherent to the gospels so designated. Rather, it presupposes that this status has in some way been ascribed to them: canonical gospels have *become* such. Until this occurs, however, there can equally be no gospels that lack this quality from the outset. 'Noncanonical' gospels have *become* 'apocryphal' through the canonization of the others.[11]

---

[9] As evidenced by Athanasius's thirty-ninth 'Festal Letter' (367), as preserved in Coptic. On this, see David Brakke, 'Canon Formation and Social Conflict in Fourth-Century Egypt: Athanasius of Alexandria's Thirty-Ninth "Festal Letter"', *Harvard Theological Review* 87 (1994), 394–419; 'A New Fragment of Athanasius's Thirty-Ninth Festal Letter: Heresy, Apocrypha, and the Canon', *Harvard Theological Review* 103 (2010), 47–66 (including a full English translation and the Coptic text of a new fragment).

[10] Christoph Markschies and Jens Schröter (eds.), *Antike christliche Apokryphen in deutscher Übersetzung*, vol. 1: *Evangelien und Verwandtes*, 1–2 (Tübingen: Mohr Siebeck, 2012).

[11] Dieter Lührmann, *Die apokryph gewordenen Evangelien: Studien zum Neuen Texten und Neuen Fragen* (Leiden: Brill, 2004), 2 (my translation). German: '"Kanonisch" ist freilich keine Eigenschaft, die den so bezeichneten Evangelien von sich aus zukommt; vorausgesetzt wird damit vielmehr, dass ihnen ein solcher Rang in

In the case of early gospel literature, ascription of canonical status occurs when a text's claim to authority is validated by a user community – that is, when a text's representation of Jesus' authoritative action and speech is deemed true and reliable and authorized for certain types of communal usage. Ascription of 'apocryphal' status occurs when a text's claim to authority is regarded with caution or rejected outright.

Before the concept of a fourfold gospel achieved dogmatic status, the collective decision about any gospel text remained in principle open. If *EpAp* can be shown to pre-date the canonical dogma, it can take its place within the diverse landscape of early Christian literature as yet undivided by the canon's binary logic. The date and provenance of this text are therefore of more than incidental interest.

III

Schmidt argued that *EpAp* originated in Asia Minor, and his grounds for this are still compelling.[12] Those who favour an Egyptian origin are unduly influenced by the 'gnostic' dialogue gospels known to have circulated in Egypt (e.g. *GMary, ApocrJas, 1ApocJas, SophJesChr, DialSav, Pistis Sophia*) and by the unsubstantiated claim that the author of *EpAp* seeks to refute 'gnostic' users of such texts by turning their own preferred dialogue gospel format against them.[13] In favour of an Asian and perhaps Ephesian origin is the naming of the apostle John first in the list of apostolic authors rather than Peter, relegated to third place (*EpAp* 2.1). The 'false apostles' Simon and Cerinthus are introduced as the occasion for the letter (1.1), although in reality no clear anti-heretical agenda is in evidence. Tradition associates Simon with Peter and Cerinthus with John, and when the heretics are named again it is John's opponent in Ephesus rather than Peter's in Rome who is named first: 'Cerinthus

---

irgendeiner Weise beigemessen worden ist – kanonische Evangelien sind also zu solchen erst geworden. Solange das aber nicht geschehen ist, kann es ebensowenig Evangelien geben, denen diese Qualität von vornherein abgeht, und "nicht kanonische" sind ebenso durch die Kanonisierung der anderen erst "apokryph" *geworden*.' Italics original.

[12] Schmidt, *Gespräche Jesu*, 361–402.

[13] Manfred Hornschuh, *Studien zur Epistula Apostolorum*, Patristische Texte und Studien 5 (Berlin: de Gruyter, 1965), 6–8, 102–15. Hornschuh's arguments are critiqued by Charles E. Hill, 'The *Epistula Apostolorum*: An Asian Tract from the Time of Polycarp', *Journal of Early Christian Studies* 7 (1999), 8–13.

and Simon have gone out, they go around the world, but they are enemies of our Lord Jesus Christ. . .' (7.1–2).[14] The commemoration of Easter at the time of the Jewish Feast of the Passover is typical of Asian 'quartodeciman' practice (15.1–3).[15]

An initial indication of the date of composition is given within *EpAp* itself. Jesus announces his glorious cloud-borne return from heaven to earth, and his disciples ask: 'Lord, after how many years will these things be?' (*EpAp* 17.1). In the Coptic text as it stands, Jesus' reply is mysterious: 'When the hundredth part and the twentieth part are completed, between Pentecost and the Feast of Unleavened Bread, the coming of my Father will take place' (17.2). In the question-and-answer that follows, it becomes clear that Jesus' parousia can also be ascribed to the Father because 'I am in wholly in my Father and my Father is in me' (17.3–4). The reverse sequence of Pentecost and Unleavened Bread may be intended to emphasize the beginning of the fifty-day period as the key eschatological moment. And the Coptic ⲟⲅⲱⲛ (ⲟⲅⲏ̄), 'part', seems to stem from a Greek reading, τὸ ἑκατοστὸν καὶ εἰκοστόν ('the hundred-and-twentieth') which the translator takes as a mysterious pair of fractions, aware that a parousia after 120 years is no longer credible in his own time.[16] A Greek text in which Jesus promises to return after 120 years would seem to suggest a mid-second-century *terminus ad quem* for *EpAp*.

In the Geʻez text Jesus promises to return 'when the hundred-and-fiftieth year is completed'. This is most probably a correction within the early Greek transmission of this text; it cannot plausibly be ascribed to the much later Ethiopic translator. The correction might stem from the non-occurrence of the parousia 120 years after the Easter event (i.e. in or around the year 150 CE). Yet it is also possible that both the original figure and its correction originated at much the same time, *c.*170 CE, with an expected parousia date within the decade, and that the correction is based on more accurate chronological information than the original figure. One might speculate that someone within the author's circle has noticed the chronological information in *GLuke* 3.1, dating the beginning of the ministry of

----

[14] A tradition linking John, Cerinthus, and Ephesus is attested in Irenaeus's story about the endangered bath-house (*Adv. haer.* 3.3.4). Peter, Simon, and Rome are linked in the *Acts of Peter*.

[15] Schmidt, *Gespräche Jesu*, 577–725.

[16] On this passage, see the *Additional Notes* in Part III of the present work.

John the Baptist to 'the fifteenth year of the reign of Tiberius Caesar', and recalculated accordingly.[17]

A reason for regarding the higher figure as a more reliable indicator of the date of composition than the lower is the remarkable emphasis on a worldwide plague in the section on the signs of the end (*EpAp* 34–36). Plagues (that is, epidemics) can feature in stereotypical lists of impending disasters, as in *GLuke* 21.11, where it is predicted that 'there will be great earthquakes and famines and plagues [λοιμοί] in various places, and terrors, and there will be great signs from heaven.' Vague and generic lists of disasters provide no help in dating a text. Similar lists occur in *EpAp*, where warning is given of 'great hailstones like raging fire, and sun and moon fighting together, and constant terror of thunder and lightning...' (34.8–9), along with 'a tumult of clouds, continual drought and persecution of those who believe in me' (35.3). Yet 'a great plague' features here not just as an item in a list but as a significant topic in its own right. A poignant account is given of the intense isolation caused by extreme sickness, even among family members, along with the breakdown of wider social norms:

> And the passing of child and parent will be on a single bed, and the parent will not turn to the child nor the child to the parent, and one person will not turn to another. And those who are bereaved will rise up and see those who had departed from them being carried out. For there will be a plague everywhere, hatred and suffering and jealousy, and they will take from one and give to another. (*EpAp* 34.11–13)

The disciples are particularly concerned about future Christians affected by the plague. Jesus replies that Christian plague victims will not generally die, but they will experience severe suffering as a test of their faith. Their suffering will be short-lived, and if they do die they have the hope of resurrection:

> And we said to him, 'Will their departure from the world be through the plague that torments them?' And he said to us, 'No, but when they are tormented such an affliction will be to test them. If there is faith within them and if they

---

[17] Schmidt, *Gespräche Jesu*, 398. Schmidt draws attention to Justin, *1 Apol.* 46.1, where Justin states that 150 years have passed since the birth of Christ 'under Quirinius' (cf. *GLk* 2.2).

remember these words of mine and obey my commandments, they will be raised. And their situation will be for a
few days, so that the one who sent me may be glorified and
I with him, for he sent me to you.   (*EpAp* 36.3–6)

Underlying this unusual emphasis on a single item from the usual
repertoire of disasters is probably the so-called 'Antonine plague'
that began in the year 165, and that may have been a smallpox
epidemic.[18] Writing around two centuries later, Ammianus
Marcellinus records how, following the Persian campaigns of the
co-emperors Lucius Verus and Marcus Aurelius, an epidemic broke
out 'with the force of an incurable disease' and 'polluted the whole
world from the borders of Persia to the Rhine and Gaul with conta-
gion and death [*contagiis et mortibus*].[19] *EpAp* similarly emphasizes
the extent of the epidemic: 'There will be a plague everywhere'
(34.13). For Galen, a contemporary, this event is not just an ordinary
epidemic but has its own title, 'the great plague', to underline its
uniqueness. Galen recounts how he left Rome 'when the great plague
started [ἀρξαμένου τοῦ μεγάλου λοιμοῦ]', and how, arriving in
Aquileia (168 CE), he found 'the plague still more devastating than
it had been before [κατέσκηψεν ὁ λοιμὸς ὡς οὔπω πρότερον]', with
mass deaths caused by the combination of plague and winter.[20] For
EpAp too, this event is 'a great plague' causing such 'widespread
death' that 'funerals will cease for those who die' (*EpAp* 34.10).
According to another writer, 'thousands were carried off by the
plague', so that 'the dead were removed in carts and waggons',
presumably for disposal in a mass grave.[21] It was said that, on his
deathbed, Marcus Aurelius appealed to his friends to weep not for
him but for the plague victims.[22] The entire period of his rule
(161–80) was remembered long afterwards as the era of 'the great
plague'.

[18] See R. J. Littman and M. L. Littman, 'Galen and the Antonine Plague',
American Journal of Philology 94 (1973), 243–55.
[19] Ammianus Marcellinus, 23.4.24. On the Antonine plague, see R. P. Duncan-
Jones, 'The Impact of the Antonine Plague', *Journal of Roman Archaeology* 9 (1996),
108–36; R. P. Duncan-Jones, 'The Antonine Plague Revisited', *Arctos* 52 (2018),
41–72; Christer Bruun, 'The Antonine Plague and the "Third Century Crisis"', in
O. Hekster, G. de Kleijn, and Daniëlle Slootjes (eds.), *Crises in the Roman Empire*
(Leiden: Brill, 2007), 201–17.
[20] Galen, in C. G. Kühn (ed.), *Galeni Opera Omnia* (Leipzig: Car. Cnoblochii,
1830), 19.15, 18.
[21] *Historia Augusta, Marcus Antoninus*, 13.5, 3.
[22] *Historia Augusta, Marcus Antoninus*, 28.4.

Evidence from tombstones of mortality patterns in Asia Minor suggests that the epidemic caused greatly increased mortality in the years 165–70 although tailing off in 171–81.[23] As their pagan neighbours sought the help of the gods, *EpAp*'s Christian readers are encouraged to view their sufferings as a prelude to Jesus' long-awaited return.[24]

Dating from *c.*170, *EpAp* does not present itself as an 'apocryphon', an edifying adjunct to four gospel texts whose status and authority were already beyond question. This is a 'gospel' supposedly written by the entire apostolic collective, addressed to all Christians everywhere and recording Jesus' definitive utterances in the short interval between his resurrection and ascension. While it is aware of and draws from at least three of the canonical four, *EpAp* is selective in its engagement with its source material and treats it critically and with great freedom. In that respect it is comparable to another early gospel rediscovered during the twentieth century, the *Gospel of Thomas*. The question is why, a century after Schmidt's publication and in contrast to *GThomas*, this text is so little known. As we shall see in the chapter that follows, the answer is that – in spite of its groundbreaking achievements – Schmidt's work is seriously flawed, and its flaws have never been adequately addressed.

[23] Duncan-Jones, 'The Antonine Plague Revisited', 48–50.

[24] Hill refers to the Antonine plague only in order to argue that '[t]he possibility of an earlier epidemic in Smyrna or its vicinity earlier in the century is not at all remote' ('Epistula Apostolorum', 40). Underlying this odd evasion of extant evidence is Hill's inclination towards a much earlier dating, on the unlikely assumption that the 120 years of the Coptic text may be dated from Christ's birth (49–52).

Part I

Recovering the *Epistula*

1

AN AMBIGUOUS LEGACY: THE *EPISTULA APOSTOLORUM* AND ITS EDITORS

Following the publication of the Ethiopic text of the *Epistula Apostolorum* in 1912 and the Coptic text in 1919,[1] two approaches emerged to the task of making it more widely available in translation. One was that of Montague Rhodes James, who included *EpAp* in his 1924 edition of New Testament apocrypha in a section devoted to apocryphal letters such as the *Letter to the Laodiceans* and the correspondence between Paul and Seneca.[2] On the basis of Guerrier's French translation of the Ethiopic and Schmidt's German translation of the Coptic, James produced a composite version that followed the incomplete Coptic where available and used the Ethiopic to fill in larger or smaller lacunae and to provide some variant readings.[3] The existence of a short Latin fragment is also noted. Thus James renders the first part of *EpAp* 9 as follows:

> Concerning whom we testify that the Lord is he who was crucified by Pontius Pilate and Archelaus between the two thieves (and with them he was taken down from the tree of the cross, *Eth.*), and was buried in a place which is called the place of a skull (*Kranion*). And thither went three women, Mary, she that was kin to Martha, and Mary Magdalene

---

[1] Ethiopic: L. Guerrier (with S. Grébaut), *Le Testament en Galilée de Notre-Seigneur Jésus-Christ*, Patrologia Orientalis (Paris: Firmin-Didot, 1912; repr. Turnhout: Brepols, 2003). Coptic: C. Schmidt (with I. Wajnberg), *Gespräche Jesu mit seinen Jüngern nach der Auferstehung: Ein katholisch-apostolisches Sendschreiben des 2. Jahrhunderts* (Leipzig: J. C. Hinrichs, 1919).

[2] M. R. James, *The Apocryphal New Testament* (Oxford: Clarendon Press, 1924), 485–502.

[3] James acknowledged indebtedness to the translations of Guerrier and Schmidt (*Apocryphal New Testament*, 485), but may also have referred to Isaak Wajnberg's retranslation of the Ethiopic within Schmidt's edition of the Coptic.

(Sarrha, Martha, and Mary, *Eth.*), and took ointments to pour upon the body, weeping and mourning over that which was come to pass.   (*EpAp* 9.1–3)

James is selective in his inclusion of Ethiopic material, omitting the statement that Jesus was crucified 'in the days of' Pontius Pilate and Archelaus the Judge'. Variants within the Ethiopic manuscript tradition are hardly ever noted. Thus, 'with them he was taken down from the tree of the cross' occurs in two of the four manuscripts edited by Guerrier but is replaced by 'with them he was numbered, he was taken down from the cross' in a third. Within its limitations, however, James's translation is readable and usable. The decision to prioritize the Coptic where available is appropriate, given that the oldest of Guerrier's Ethiopic manuscripts goes back only to the sixteenth century while the Coptic one may date from the fourth or fifth. Also appropriate is the creation of a single text from the two versions (together with the Latin fragments). The differences between the versions are generally on a small scale, and supplementary material such as the reference to the deposition from the cross is unusual. The major difference between the two versions is that the Ethiopic opens with a long and secondary apocalyptic discourse delivered by the risen Jesus in Galilee (chapters 1–11 in Guerrier's edition), and James leaves this untranslated.

Also in 1924, Edgar Hennecke published the second edition of his New Testament apocrypha collection, but provided only an introduction to *EpAp* and a summary of its contents.[4] The omission was rectified the following year when Hugo Duensing published a translation in the series, 'Kleine Texte für Vorlesungen und Übungen', edited by Hans Lietzmann.[5] Duensing's translation passed largely unaltered into the third edition of Hennecke's collection (1959), re-edited by Wilhelm Schneemelcher,[6] and it remains virtually unchanged in later editions although now credited to C. Detlef

[4] E. Hennecke (ed.), *Neutestamentliche Apokryphen in Verbindung mit Fachgelehrten in deutscher Übersetzung und mit Einleitungen*, 2 vols. (Tübingen: J. C. B. Mohr (Paul Siebeck), 1904[1], 1924[2]).

[5] H. Duensing, *Epistula Apostolorum nach dem äthiopischen und koptischen Texte herausgegeben* (Bonn: A. Marcus & E. Weber, 1925).

[6] E. Hennecke with W. Schneemelcher (eds.), *Neutestamentlichen Apokryphen in deutscher Übersetzung*, vol. 1, *Evangelien* (Tübingen: J. C. B. Mohr (Paul Siebeck), 1959[3]), 126–55.

G. Müller, whose 'careful revision' is in fact minimal at best.[7] Under its new editorial name, Duensing's translation appears in English guise in R. McL. Wilson's translation of the sixth edition of Hennecke–Schneemelcher[8] and also in Keith Elliott's revision of the M. R. James collection, where it is credited to R. E. Taylor – the English translator of the German version attributed to Müller but in reality still largely Duensing's.[9] Müller/Duensing continue to hold sway in the early Christian apocrypha edition of Christoph Markschies and Jens Schröter.[10]

Given its remarkable longevity, it is unfortunate that Duensing's translation is in important respects seriously deficient. While it gives a much fuller account of differences between the Ethiopic and Coptic texts than does M. R. James, its constant recourse to parallel columns makes *EpAp* unintelligible as a single work. Here for example is Duensing's rendering of *EpAp* 8 in its original 1925 formatting, with bold type representing wording common to the Ethiopic (col. 1) and the Coptic (col. 2), roman Ethiopic only, and italics Coptic only:[11]

Sieh also *deswegen* **haben wir nicht gezögert**	
mit dem wahren **Zeugnis von**	*euch zu schreiben betreffs des*
unserm Herrn und **Heiland**	**Zeugnisses von unserm Heiland**
Jesus **Christus**, wie er gehandelt	**Christus**, *dasjenige, was er getan hat,*
hat, **während wir** ihn sahen, und	**während wir** *auf ihn blickten (und?)*
wie er beständig unsere **Gedanken**	*wiederum (noch?) in den* **Gedanken** *und*
bei uns sowohl erklärte als wirkte.	*Werken.*

Here the collective apostolic authors explain why they are writing. Duensing's formatting makes it possible to differentiate the Ethiopic version of their explanation ('Behold *[Sieh]*, we have not delayed with the true testimony...') from the Coptic one ('For this reason *[Deswegen]* we have not delayed to write concerning the testimony...'). Useful though this differentiation is, it should be

---

[7] W. Schneemelcher, *Neutestamentliche Apokryphen*, vol. 1, *Evangelien* (Tübingen: J. C. B. Mohr (Paul Siebeck), 1990[6]), 205–33, 207n.

[8] W. Schneemelcher, *New Testament Apocrypha,* vol. 1, *Gospels and Related Writings*, Eng. trans., rev. ed., ed. R. McL. Wilson (Louisville, KY: WJK, 1991), 249–84.

[9] J. K. Elliott, *The Apocryphal New Testament: A Collection of Apocryphal Christian Literature in an English Translation based on M. R. James* (Oxford: Clarendon Press, 1993[1], 1999[2]), 555–88.

[10] Markschies and Schröter, *Antike christliche Apokryphen in deutscher Übersetzung*, vol. 1: *Evangelien und Verwandtes*, 2, 1062–92.

[11] Duensing, *Epistula*, 8.

preliminary to an editorial decision about which is the older and better reading – a decision that would probably favour the Coptic, where '[f]or this reason' (ⲉⲧⲃⲉ ⲡⲉⲓ) may reflect an original Greek διὰ τοῦτο. Furthermore, the difference between the two versions is exaggerated by the selection of different wording to express the same sense. 'How he acted while we saw him' (Ethiopic) is no different from 'what he did while we observed him' (Coptic), but the identity is concealed by the divergent translation decisions. The major problem, however, is the two-column format – a useful preliminary to a critical translation but inadequate in itself.

This problematic dual column tradition was inherited by Duensing and was not invented by him. To uncover the reasons why the Coptic and Ethiopic texts of *EpAp* have never been satisfactorily co-ordinated, we must piece together the complex story of their discovery.

1.1   The Coptic Text and its Discoverer(s)

In a letter dating from December 1898, Adolf Harnack writes (with some exaggeration) on behalf of his thirty-year-old protégé Carl Schmidt: 'Of the discoveries over the past ten years in the field of ancient Christianity, half are due to him; in his specialty as an expert in Coptic and church history he is unique.'[12] One such 'discovery' was the text that Schmidt would later name the *Epistula Apostolorum*, on which he prepared a report presented by Harnack at a session of the Königlich Preussische Akademie der Wissenschaften in Berlin in June 1895.[13] In this report, prepared while he was still in Egypt, Schmidt noted that the papyrus manuscript was in poor condition; as the pagination showed, the sixteen surviving though damaged folios represented less than half of the original work.[14] While the unfamiliar 'Akhmimic' dialect posed further problems of comprehension, the essential content of the text was clear: it consisted in a conversation between Jesus and his

---

[12] Cited by C. Markschies, 'Carl Schmidt und kein Ende: Aus großer Zeit der Koptologie an der Berliner Akademie und der Theologischen Fakultät der Universität', *Zeitschrift für Antikes Christentum* 13 (2009), 5–28; 15. Translations here and throughout are my own.

[13] C. Schmidt, 'Eine bisher unbekannte christliche Schrift in koptischer Sprache', *Sitzungsberichte der Königlich Preussischen Akademie der Wissenschaften zu Berlin* (June–Dec. 1895), 705–11.

[14] Schmidt, 'Eine bisher unbekannte christliche Schrift', 705–6.

disciples, as indicated by the recurring introductory formulae, 'We said to him' and, 'He answered and said to us'.[15] The conversation occurs in the aftermath of Jesus' resurrection, and Schmidt provides a translation of the new text's account of the events of Easter morning: the women's visit to the grave, their encounter with the risen Lord, their attempts to persuade the unbelieving male disciples who come to faith only when they can see and touch him for themselves.[16] According to Schmidt, the text's hostile reference to the well-known 'Gnostic' figures Cerinthus and Simon indicated that this work was an anti-heretical product of the 'Great Church', employing the *Evangeliengattung* of the post-resurrection dialogue that the Gnostics themselves invented.[17]

In the initial 1895 report Schmidt provided surprisingly vague and inaccurate information about the provenance of his 'previously unknown Christian writing'.

> It is to the great library that Maspero discovered in the early '80s in a monastery at Akhmim, the ancient Panopolis, that we are already indebted for a series of valuable fragments of Coptic writings on papyrus and parchment, which are highly significant for the study not just of the Coptic language but also of ancient Christian literature... This library must have been a veritable treasure-chamber of ancient Christian literature, as the Greek Enoch, the Gospel of Peter, the Apocalypse of Peter, and the Apocalypse of Elijah and of Zephaniah all derive from it... From it also derives the writing I have the honour to bring to the attention of the Royal Academy today.[18]

The intended reference is to the library of the White Monastery (or Monastery of St Shenute), not in Akhmim on the east bank of the Nile but in Sohag, a short distance away on the west bank. The discovery there of around 4,000 parchment leaves was claimed by Gaston Maspero, director of the Service des antiquités égyptiennes (1881–86), who edited the Coptic Old Testament fragments among them in 1892, by which time the collection had been transferred to

---

[15] Schmidt, 'Eine bisher unbekannte christliche Schrift', 707.
[16] Schmidt, 'Eine bisher unbekannte christliche Schrift', 707–8.
[17] Schmidt, 'Eine bisher unbekannte christliche Schrift', 708–10.
[18] Schmidt, 'Eine bisher unbekannte christliche Schrift', 705.

the Bibliothèque nationale in Paris or to other European libraries.[19] The fragments were said to have been found in a cell joined to the choir of the ancient monastic church by a secret passage,[20] although it was alleged that Maspero may have bought them from an antiquities dealer in Akhmim.[21] Schmidt seems to have confused the material from the monastery with the discovery by Urbain Bouriant of a codex containing fragments of *1 Enoch* and the *Gospel* and *Apocalypse of Peter* in Greek, found in a cemetery in Akhmim during the winter of 1886–87, after Maspero's departure from Egypt. From its position in the cemetery Bouriant dates the grave to the eighth to twelfth centuries, while conceding that the manuscript itself may be older; and he claims – without providing evidence – that the grave belonged to a monk.[22] Schmidt's conflation of Bouriant's Greek manuscript with Maspero's Coptic ones betrays a strangely casual attitude to the question of provenance.

Confusion about the White Monastery and the Akhmim cemetery remains in evidence twelve years later. In his initial report of the discovery of a Coptic text of *1 Clement*, Schmidt states:

> During my stay in Egypt in the summer of 1905, I received information that three papyrus manuscripts had been found by natives in an Akhmim cemetery below a monastery, and had passed into the hands of an antiquities dealer there.[23]

In his edition of the Coptic *1 Clement* manuscript, published in 1908, the story changes. Now Schmidt acknowledges that, contrary to his initial report,

---

[19] G Maspero, 'Fragments de manuscrits Copte-Thébains provenants de la bibliothèque du deir Amba-Shenouda', in *Mémoires publiées par les membres de la Mission archéologique française au Caire*, vol. 6/1 (Paris: Leroux, 1892), 1–160.

[20] Maspero, 'Fragments', 1; Maspero speaks of the 'hasard heureux' that led to the 'discovery' but gives no further explanation. For confirmation of the existence of this cell, see W. E. Crum, 'Inscriptions from Shenoute's Monastery', *Journal of Theological Studies* 5 (1904), 552–69.

[21] E. A. Wallis Budge, *By Nile and Tigris: A Narrative of Journeys in Egypt and Mesopotamia on Behalf of the British Museum between the Years 1886 and 1913*, vol. 1 (London: Murray, 1920), 135.

[22] U. Bouriant, 'Fragments Grecs du livre d'Énoch et de quelques écrits attribués à saint Pierre', in *Mémoires publiées par les membres de la Mission archéologique française au Caire*, vol. 9/1 (Paris: Leroux, 1892), 91–147; 93–94.

[23] C. Schmidt, 'Der 1. Clemensbrief in altkoptischer Übersetzung', *Sitzungsberichte der Königlich Preussischen Akademie der Wissenschaften zu Berlin* (Jan.–June 1907), 154–64; 155. Schmidt does not report the content of the other two papyri.

[m]ore recent investigations have shown that all three manuscripts stem from Shenute's famous 'White Monastery' near Sohag and opposite Akhmim, where the old library was discovered during restoration work at the monastery.[24]

Also in 1908 Schmidt published a second report on *EpAp*, in response to the discovery of fragments of a Latin version in a palimpsest in Vienna. Like *1 Clement*, *EpAp* is again confidently assigned to 'the library of the Shenute monastery near Sohag in Upper Egypt'.[25] Equally confidently, Schmidt now claims to have discovered the manuscript himself – not in the White Monastery, however, but in the Institut français in Cairo.[26] A final version of the provenance story is given when Schmidt's edition of *EpAp* was finally published in 1919. Here Schmidt no longer takes credit for the 'discovery' and acknowledges that the attribution to the White Monastery was just an informed guess. The Coptic manuscript

was acquired by Bouriant, but in spite of persistent investigation I have found no evidence as to when or where the fragments were acquired. On the basis of previous purchases of Coptic papyri in Akhmimic dialect, however, we may safely conclude [*wird man den sicheren Schluss ziehen können*] that our manuscript too once belonged to the book collection of the White Monastery, the so-called Shenute monastery, in the neighbourhood of present-day Sohag – a library which has provided us with the *Apocalypse of Elijah* and of *Zephaniah*, the *First Letter of Clement*, and the still unedited *Wisdom of Solomon*, among other valuable manuscripts.[27]

In contrast to the statements in the 1895 and 1908 reports, discovery of the *EpAp* manuscript is now credited not to Maspero or Schmidt himself but to Bouriant. When Schmidt first encountered the manuscript in 1894 or 1895 it was Bouriant who, 'with his customary generosity, allowed me the use and study of the text'.[28] Bouriant

---

[24] C. Schmidt, *Der erste Clemensbrief in altkoptischer Übersetzung* (Leipzig: J. C. Hinrichs, 1908), 5.

[25] C. Schmidt, 'Eine Epistola apostolorum in koptischer und lateinischer Überlieferung', *Sitzungsberichte der königlich Preussischen Akademie der Wissenschaften zu Berlin* (July–Dec. 1908), 1047–56; 1053.

[26] Schmidt, 'Eine Epistola apostolorum', 1047.

[27] Schmidt, *Gespräche Jesu*, 4.

[28] Schmidt, *Gespräche Jesu*, 1.

seems to have been less than generous in providing information about the text's provenance, however. Conversely, the young German scholar failed to obtain basic information about the text from his more senior French colleague – perhaps wishing to preserve his self-image as the 'discoverer' of this text. Thus Schmidt's attribution of the Coptic *Epistula* manuscript to the White Monastery remains a conjecture in spite of his confidence in it.[29]

1.2   The Latin Title

It was in the title of Schmidt's 1908 report that the text ceased to be merely 'eine bisher unbekannte christliche Schrift in koptischer Sprache' and became 'eine *Epistola apostolorum* in koptischer und lateinischer Überlieferung'. (Schmidt may have preferred the spelling 'Epistola' because of its proximity to a hypothetical original Greek ἐπιστολή.) Barely legible fragments of a Latin version were deciphered and identified by Josef Bick, librarian at the royal library in Vienna, on two folios of a palimpsest from the monastery at Bobbio in northern Italy.[30] (As we shall see, the identification was only partially correct.) The original page enumeration of the two folios (60 and 67) was still legible, as was a quire number (VIIII) indicating that the folios were once the outer sheet of a quaternion, trimmed back at its top and left margins so as to fit its new context. The heading 'Epistula' occurred on both verso pages, although nothing remained of any continuation (e.g. 'Epistula/Apostolorum') on the (preceding) recto pages. Bick dated the script to the fifth century (pre-dating the sixth century foundation of the monastery by the Irish monk Columbanus), and he identified the text on the basis of a reference to Schmidt's 1895 report in the first edition of Hennecke's *Neutestamentliche Apokryphen* (1904).[31] In the first of the two

[29] On the White Monastery library, see S. Emmel and C. E. Römer, 'The Library of the White Monastery in Upper Egypt', in H. Froschauer and C. E. Römer (eds.), *Spätantike Bibliotheken: Leben und Lesen in den frühen Klöstern Ägyptens* (Vienna: Phoibos, 2008), 5–14. On the presence of 'apocryphal' books in Egyptian monasteries, see H. Lundhaug and L. Jennott, *The Monastic Origins of the Nag Hammadi Codices* (Tübingen: Mohr Siebeck, 2015), 146–76.

[30] J. Bick, 'Wiener Palimpseste, I. Teil: Codex Palat. Vindobonensis 16 olim Bobbiensis', *Abhandlungen der Sitzungsberichte der k. Akademie der Wissenschaften in Wien: Phil.-hist. Klasse* 159 (1908), 90–99.

[31] E. Hennecke (ed.), *Neutestamentliche Apokryphen: in Verbindung mit Fachgelehrten in deutscher Übersetzung und mit Einleitungen*, 2 vols. (Tübingen: J. C. B. Mohr (Paul Siebeck), 1904[1]), 1.38.

columns on the verso of the second extant folio (67v), Bick was able to read part of an account of the descent of Christ at his incarnation, accompanied by angels whose form he has taken:

Michael et	Michael and
[G]abriel et Uriel et Ra	Gabriel and Uriel and Ra-
[f]ael palam comitati	phael openly accompa-
[s]unt mihi usque ad	nied me to
quintum caelum	the fifth heaven,
[p]utantes me esse unū	thinking me to be one
ex eis talis data est po	of them – such power was
[t]estas mihi a patre	given me by the Father.

(Codex Vindobonensis 16, fol. 67v   (cf. *EpAp*[cop] 13.4)
    col.1 1–8)[32]

As Bick suspected and Schmidt confirmed, the wording here is virtually identical to Schmidt's (still unpublished) Coptic text. Both scholars assumed – wrongly, as we shall see – that the preceding text on folio 60 belonged to the lost opening of *EpAp*, the first eight pages of which were missing from the Coptic manuscript. As initially transcribed by Bick, the text on folio 60r opens as follows:

<. … … …>	
<. … … …>	
<. … …> pruden	
<..>me<. … ….>	
dud<. …>s quia ego	. … … for I
sum filius dei vivi	am the Son of the living and
omnipotentis ego	omnipotent God, I
sum pater omnium	am the Father of all things!
ergo audi a me signa	So hear *[s.]* from me signs
quae futura sunt in	which are coming at
finem saeculi huius	the end of this age,
ut transeat antequā	when it passes away, before
exiant electi de sae	the elect depart from the
culo dicam tibique…	world! I say to you *[s.]*…

Codex Vindobonensis 16, fol. 60r col.1
    1–14 (transcribed by J. Bick)

Here Jesus is speaking to an individual, not to the disciples collectively as in *EpAp*. Schmidt found here a confirmation of the conjecture in his 1895 report that the lost opening of the Coptic text would have contained references to an individual 'I', complementing

---

[32] Schmidt, 'Eine Epistola apostolorum', 1050.

the collective 'we' of the surviving Coptic text – the 'I' in question being Peter. The conjecture was based on the fragments of the Greek *Gospel of Peter* and *Apocalypse of Peter*, published by Bouriant in 1892, where the Petrine narrator speaks both in the first person plural (ἡμεῖς δὲ οἱ δώδεκα μαθηταὶ τοῦ κυρίου [*GPet* 14.59], ἡμεῖς οἱ δώδεκα μαθηταί [*ApPet*^{gk} 5]) and in the first person singular (ἐγὼ δὲ Σίμων Πέτρος [*GPet* 14.60, cf. 7.26; *ApPet*^{gk} 9, 12, 13, etc.]). Schmidt assumed that this must also have been the case with *EpAp*,[33] thus adding a third Petrine text to the two discovered by Bouriant. The second person singular address in the Vienna text seemed to confirm at least part of the earlier conjecture.

Surprisingly, Schmidt failed to calculate how the space available in the Latin manuscript relates to the eight missing pages at the start of the Coptic one. The Latin text is formatted in two columns, and (on the basis that fol. 67v col.1 = Coptic p. 13, line 14–p. 14, line 10) each column corresponds to around eleven lines of Coptic text (allowing for part-lines). Thus the fifteen double-column pages of Latin fols. 60r–67r could in principle have accommodated the equivalent of $15 \times 2 \times 11 = 330$ lines of Coptic text. There are fifteen lines per page in the single-column Coptic manuscript, and a Latin equivalent of Coptic p. 1, line 1–p. 13, line 14 would thus require only $(12 \times 15) + 14 = 194$ lines. If the two Latin fragments on fols. 60 and 67 belong to the same text, the Latin version of *EpAp* must have been considerably longer than its Coptic counterpart. If the two versions were more or less identical in scope and allowing for a margin of error, the Latin equivalent of the first 194 lines of the Coptic manuscript would have required nine Latin pages ($9 \times 2 \times 11 = 198$). The Latin *Epistula* would then have begun on fol. 63r, probably at or near the beginning of the page.[34] The text of folio 60 would be something other than *EpAp*, and, if it began at folio 60r, it would occupy a total of six pages (fols. 60r–62v). Rather than carrying out these straightforward calculations, Schmidt merely

---

[33] '[M]eines Erachtens steckt hinter dem "wir" doch ein "ich", das sich ohne Zweifel am Anfang genannt hatte und der Zahl der Jünger angehörte. Darum liegt die Vermuthung nahe, dass diese Schrift ebenfalls zu den unter dem Namen des Petrus verbreiteten Werken gehört' (Schmidt, 'Eine bisher unbekannte christliche Schrift', 707). For Schmidt's reference back to this conjecture, see 'Eine Epistola apostolorum', 1053.

[34] The Latin version may, however, have been shorter than the Coptic. The Latin fragments correspond to *EpAp* 12.2–13.6 and 17.2–5, with 17.2 following on directly from 13.6 and omitting 14.1–17.1. Similar omissions from earlier chapters cannot be ruled out.

assures his readers that the identity of the Latin and Coptic texts is 'beyond doubt' (*nicht zu zweifeln*).[35]

Shortly after Schmidt's 1908 report, the Vienna fragments were re-edited by Edmund Hauler, who identified the first of them as the *Revelatio quae appellatur Thomae* or *Apocalypse of Thomas* (referred to in the sixth-century 'Gelasian decree' as a work 'not to be received', *non recipiendum*), on the basis of transcriptions of two ninth-century manuscripts, one recently published by Friedrich Wilhelm in 1907[36] and the other transcribed by Ernst von Dobschütz.[37] As a result, Hauler was able to reconstruct the opening of an apocryphal text ascribed to the apostle Thomas:

<...............>
<...............>
<.....> ẹps pruden
<te> mẹ<..........>

Audị, Thomas, quia ego	Hear, Thomas! For I
sum filius dei vivi	am the Son of the living and
omnipotentis ego	omnipotent God, I
sum pater omnium	am the Father of all
sp̣(irituu)m, audi a me signa	spirits. Hear *[s.]* from me signs
quae futura sunt in	which are coming at
finem saeculi huius	the end of this age,
ut transeat antequā	when it passes away, before
exiant electi de sae	the elect depart from the
culo dicam tibique...	world! I say to you *[s.]*...

Codex Vindobonensis 16, fol. 60r col.1, 1–14
(transcribed by E. Hauler)

In the published manuscript used by Hauler, this text is entitled not *Revelatio Thomae* but *Epistula Domini Nostri Ihesou Christi ad Thomam discipulum suum*.[38] The text is already known as an *Epistula* rather than an apocalypse in the Vienna manuscript, where this term serves as the header both for the Thomas text (fol. 60v) and for the

---

[35] Schmidt, 'Eine Epistola apostolorum', 1053.

[36] F. Wilhelm, *Deutsche Legenden und Legendare: Texte und Untersuchungen zu ihrer Geschichte im Mittelalter* (Leipzig: J. C. Hinrichs, 1907), 40*–42*. The manuscript is Munich Clm. 4585, dating from the ninth century, and is a longer form of a text a short form of which is found in Munich Clm. 4563 (eleventh or twelfth century), published by P. Bihlmeyer in 1911 ('Un texte non interpolé de l'Apocalypse de Thomas', *Revue bénédictine* 28 [1911], 270–82).

[37] E. Hauler, 'Zu den neuen lateinischen Bruchstücken der Thomasapokalypse und eines apostolischen Sendschreibens im Codex Vind. Nr. 16', *Wiener Studien* 30 (1908), 308–40; 310–11.

[38] Wilhelm, *Deutsche Legende*, 40*.

text which, on the basis of this header, Schmidt now names as the *Epistula Apostolorum*:

> In the Latin translation our text carries the heading 'Epistula' on both verso sides, and, while the continuation of the title on the recto sides has disappeared owing to the cropping of the upper edge, the Coptic text leaves no doubt as to the identity of the senders... We have before us a writing from the apostles addressed to the catholic congregations under the title, ἐπιστολὴ τῶν ἀποστόλων.[39]

Schmidt is confident in his reconstruction of the work's original title from its Latin header, and it seems not to have been questioned since. There are, however, several problems with this, all related to Schmidt's mistaken identification of the first as well as the second Latin fragment with his Coptic text – an error that should have been avoided and that was exposed almost immediately by Hauler.[40]

(i)   If the header 'Epistula' was used for two distinct texts, then it is possible that it was originally completed on the matching recto with 'ad Thomam' in one case and 'apostolorum' on the other. These titles are by no means certain, however. If the first text was headed 'Epistula Christi', the same header might have been extended to cover the second as well, which presents itself at the outset not as a letter but as a revelation of Jesus to his disciples (*EpAp* 1.1). Indeed, the two texts might have been conflated, with the first serving as a prelude to the second by highlighting the popular theme of the signs of the end. As we shall see, something very similar occurred in the case of the Ethiopic version, where later apocalyptic material with a Galilean setting has been loosely attached to the original text. It cannot be taken for granted that the two texts were given separate titles in the Latin manuscript.

(ii)   It is also possible that the header for both texts was simply 'Epistula', without any specification of the author or addressee. If 'Epistula' on the verso header was completed on the recto by 'ad Thomam' in one case and 'apostolorum' in the other, one would expect both parts of the title to be

---

[39] Schmidt, 'Eine Epistola apostolorum', 1054.

[40] In 1919, Schmidt disingenuously criticizes Bick for insisting on the unity of the Latin fragments in face of his own doubts, passing over the endorsement he claimed in 1908 for his earlier Petrine hypothesis (*Gespräche Jesu*, 20).

located at a uniform distance from the top of the page in its original and cropped forms. It is surprising, then, that the conclusion of the titles is absent from the recto of fols. 60 and 67, at the same level as 'Epistula' on the verso.[41] Hauler's claim that the continuation of the title has been 'almost entirely cut away' (*fast ganz weggeschnitten*)[42] may imply that a few illegible ink-marks could be detected on one or both of the recto pages, but if so it is puzzling that the second part of the title should be located higher up the page than the first part. As a complete heading, 'Epistula' might suggest that the scribe was either unaware of more specific titles or cautious about employing titles that might highlight the text's apocryphal status.

(iii)   It is unlikely that the term *epistula* featured in the original title of either of the two Latin texts. A text that opens with the words, 'Hear, Thomas!' and then proceeds to recount the signs of the end is plausibly identified as an *Apocalypse of Thomas* but can hardly be a 'letter'. In *EpAp* there is a double epistolary preface (chs. 1–2, 6–8) but no indication that the work as a whole is to be read as a letter. There is no further direct address to the readers, even in contexts where it might have been appropriate, and there is no epistolary conclusion. It is doubtful whether the author of such a work would have designated it as an ἐπιστολή when such limited use is made of epistolary conventions.

Schmidt needed a title for his 'previously unknown Christian writing in Coptic', but his title need not have been *Epistula Apostolorum*. If that title might seem to have been vindicated when the Ethiopic text became available, the presence of an epistolary opening is countered by the absence of an epistolary conclusion. The primary affinities of the text as a whole are with the New Testament gospels rather than the New Testament epistles. On the analogy of the recently published *Gospel of Peter*, or the *Gospel of Mary* in the Berlin codex of which he himself was the editor,[43] Schmidt might have selected *Gospel of*

---

[41] The presence of a title (or half-title) on the verso of both an even- and an odd-numbered folio rules out one possibility that the title was only given on alternate openings.

[42] Hauler, 'Zu den neuen lateinischen Bruchstücken', 312.

[43] Schmidt highlighted the title 'Gospel of Mary' in his 1896 report on the 'Berlin Gnostic Codex': 'Ein vorirenäisches gnostisches Originalwerk in koptischer Sprache',

the Apostles as the most appropriate title. Had *EpAp* been designated a gospel rather than an epistle, its significance might have been more widely appreciated.

1.3   Two Ethiopic *Testaments*

As we have seen, Schmidt's response to Bick's initial edition of the Vienna Latin fragments was superseded almost immediately by Hauler's demonstration that the first fragment was unrelated to *EpAp*. All three publications date from 1908. Shortly afterwards Schmidt narrowly avoided a similar experience. The debate about the Latin fragments

> spurred me on to delay no longer with the publication of the Coptic text. Early in 1910 I was able to submit the manuscript to the Press. The typesetting of the Coptic text and the index was already complete and the printing of the translation was about to begin, when there occurred a further unexpected complication. Mr Montague Rhodes James, the celebrated scholar of apocryphal literature, wrote to inform me of a note by Abbé L. Guerrier in the *Revue de l'Orient chrétien* for 1907, entitled 'Un testament (éthiopien) de Notre Seigneur et Sauveur Jésus Christ en Galilée', which had escaped my attention. This described a text in Ethiopic which showed the closest similarities to the one I had treated in the Academy's *Sitzungsberichte*. A correspondence with M. Guerrier immediately confirmed James' assumption.[44]

The substance of James's letter to Schmidt was no doubt included in a two-page note in the *Journal of Theological Studies* for October 1910, where similarities are listed between the Coptic and Ethiopic documents as described by their respective editors.[45] In both, the

---

Sitzungsberichte der Königlich Preussischen Akademie der Wissenschaften zu Berlin (July–Dec. 1896), 839–47; 839. At this stage, damaged pagination led Schmidt to conclude incorrectly that the *Gospel of Mary* was identical to the *Apocryphon of John.*

[44] Schmidt, *Gespräche Jesu*, 3, referring to L. Guerrier, 'Un "Testament (éthiopien) de Notre-Seigneur et Sauveur Jésus-Christ" en Galilée', *Revue de l'orient chrétien* 12 (1907), 1–8. Schmidt omits Guerrier's unprotestant hyphens. The term 'éthiopien' occurs only in the table of contents of the *Revue de l'orient chrétien* volume but is omitted (perhaps accidentally) from the title of the article itself (1).

[45] M. R. James, 'The Epistola Apostolorum in a New Text', *Journal of Theological Studies* 12 (1910), 55–56; 55. In my summary of James's list, references are added by myself.

risen Christ appears first to the women weeping at the tomb (*EpAp* 10.1) and then to the disciples (11.1–12.1), who prostrate themselves and ask forgiveness for their unbelief (12.2). Jesus informs the disciples that it was he who appeared to Mary at the Annunciation, under the form of Gabriel (13.5), and he instructs them to keep the Passover (or Easter) in memory of him (15.1), predicting that at that time one of them will be imprisoned and then released by himself, again under the form of Gabriel (11.2–7; cf. 14.7–8). Jesus says of himself, 'I am wholly in the Father and the Father in me' (13.4). The apostles enquire about the timing of the parousia (17.1), and they are taught about the resurrection of the flesh (19.17–25.9). An exposition is provided of the parable of the wise and foolish virgins (43.1–16). James speculates, rightly, that the fourteen missing pages in the middle of the Coptic text (pages 37–50) may have accommodated the account of the conversion of Paul, preserved in Ethiopic (31.1–33.9).

James's note on *EpAp* may have been the first reference to the newly discovered text in English. In the 1910 *JTS* issue it follows directly after a full-length article, also by James, announcing the discovery of the *Apocalypse of Peter* in Ethiopic translation.[46] This is one of several curious symmetries in the recovery of the two texts. Both were embedded in longer and later texts; both represented intact versions of texts partially extant in another, recently discovered version; and both were to be found, side by side, within the same sixteenth-century Ethiopic manuscript.

The manuscript in question belonged to the collection of Antoine d'Abbadie (1810–97), an explorer and scientist who spent eleven years in Ethiopia (1838–49) and wrote extensively about the country. In 1859, d'Abbadie published a catalogue of 234 of his manuscripts,[47] and a 1912 revision extended the number to 283 and provided further detail about their contents.[48] Following d'Abbadie's death, his manuscript collection was transferred to the Bibliothèque nationale in Paris in 1902,[49] and in the following years several publications recognized the particular importance of MS 51, dating

---

[46] M. R. James, 'A New Text of the Apocalypse of Peter', *Journal of Theological Studies* 12 (1910), 36–54.

[47] A. d'Abbadie, *Catalogue raisonné de manuscrits éthiopiens* (Paris: Imprimerie Impériale, 1859).

[48] M. Chaîne, *Catalogue des manuscrits éthiopiens de la collection Antoine d'Abbadie* (Paris: Imprimerie Nationale, 1912).

[49] Chaîne, *Catalogue*, v.

from the sixteenth century. The volume opens (fols. 1–77) with a work entitled, in Ethiopic, *Sargis Abergawi* and otherwise known as the *Doctrina Iacobi nuper baptizati*, a fictional dialogue between Christian and non-Christian Jews in Carthage following the Emperor Heraclius's decree of 632 CE that all Jews should be baptized.[50] This is followed by the *Testament of our Lord Jesus Christ* (fols. 78–130), familiar to scholars from the publication in 1899 of a Syriac version of this originally Greek work, edited by Ignatius Ephraim Rahmani, patriarch of the Syriac Catholic Church.[51] In its Syriac form, the work is divided into the two books which open the 'Clementine Octateuch', a collection of works relating to church order and attributed to the editorship of Clement, a follower of Peter.[52] A colophon states that the second book (and presumably also the first) was 'translated from the Greek to the Syrian language by the wretched James, in the year 998 of the Greeks', i.e. 687 CE.[53] In the Ethiopian form as represented by d'Abbadie's MS 51 there is no division into two books or attribution to Clement, although the texts are closely related – with the crucial exception that the Ethiopic version conceals within itself a longer recension of the text that Schmidt entitled the *Epistola Apostolorum* and Guerrier the

---

[50] 'Sargis Abergawi' or 'Sargis of Aberga' is 'Sergius the Eparch', the governor of Carthage who enforces Heraclius's decree. On the original Greek version of this work and the early translations, see *Encyclopedia Aethiopica* (ed. Siegbert Uhlig and Alessandro Baussi, 5 vols. [Wiesbaden: Harrasowitz, 2003–14]), 4.540–41; for an outline of its contents, see Robert G. Hoyland, *Seeing Islam as Others Saw It: A Survey and Evaluation of Christian, Jewish and Zoroastrian Writings on Early Islam* (Princeton, NJ: Darwin Press, 1997), 55–61. MS Abbadie 51 is the sole witness to the Ethiopic version of this work, which was edited by Sylvain Grébaut, *Sargis d'Aberga: controverse judéo-chrétienne*, Patrologia Orientalis 3.4, 13.1 (Paris: Firmin-Didot, 1909–19).

[51] I. E. Rahmani, *Testamentum Domini Nostri Iesu Christi* (Mainz: Kirchheim, 1899; repr. Hildesheim: Georg Olms, 1968) (Syriac and Latin); J. Cooper and A. J. Maclean, *The Testament of our Lord, Translated into English from the Syriac with Introduction and Notes* (Edinburgh: T&T Clark, 1902). The Ethiopic version was edited by R. Beylot, *Testamentum Domini éthiopien: Édition et traduction* (Louvain: Peeters, 1984). Latin fragments relating to the Antichrist (*Testament* i.11) and signs of the end (i.6) had earlier been published by M. R. James, *Apocrypha Anecdota: A Collection of Thirteen Apocryphal Books and Fragments* (Cambridge: Clay and Co., 1891), 151–54. Greek fragments from the liturgical material forming the major part of this work have been edited by S. Corcoran and B. Salway, 'A Newly Identified Greek Fragment of the *Testamentum Domini*', *Journal of Theological Studies* 62.1 (2011), 118–35; 127–31.

[52] F. Nau and P. Ciprotti, *La Version syriaque de l'Octateuque de Clément* (Milan: Giuffrè, 1967).

[53] Rahmani, *Testamentum*, 148–49; cf. Cooper and Maclean, *Testament*, 138.

Testament in Galilee of our Lord Jesus Christ.[54] The final two works in this Ethiopic manuscript are related to Clement, though unrelated to the Syriac Clementine Octateuch. They were edited by Sylvain Grébaut under the general heading of 'Littérature éthiopienne pseudo-clémentine',[55] the fourth work in the volume (*The Mystery of the Judgement of Sinners*)[56] being published in 1907–8, and the third (*The Second Coming of Christ and the Resurrection of the Dead*)[57] in 1910. It was within this last text, with its Clementine conclusion removed, that M. R. James recognized the Ethiopic version of the *Apocalypse of Peter*.[58] Almost simultaneously, James also recognized that the text that Guerrier had extracted from within the *Testament* and announced in 1907 was very closely related to the *Epistola Apostolorum* named as such by Schmidt in 1908.

The origins of Louis Guerrier's discovery of the Ethiopic text lie in his unpublished 1903 Lyons PhD thesis, entitled, 'Le Testament de Notre-Seigneur Jésus-Christ: Essai sur la partie apocalyptique'. The 'Testament' in question was the fifth-century work whose Syriac version had been published by Rahmani.[59] The 'apocalyptic section' studied by Guerrier is found in the dialogue between the resurrected Jesus and his disciples that opens this work. Its post-resurrection setting is established in a prologue:

> After our Lord rose from the dead, he appeared to us and was touched by Thomas and Matthew and John. And we were persuaded that our Teacher had truly risen from the

[54] L. Guerrier (with S. Grébaut), *Le Testament en Galilée de Notre-Seigneur Jésus-Christ*, Patrologia Orientalis (Paris: Firmin-Didot, 1913; repr. Turnhout: Brepols, 2003). Unfortunately, Beylot's 1984 edition of the Ethiopic *Testamentum* omits this material, and so passes over the opportunity to update Guerrier's edition with textual information from nine MSS as opposed to Guerrier's five.

[55] S. Grébaut, 'Littérature éthiopienne pseudo-clémentine', *Revue de l'orient chrétien* 12 [1907], 139–51. On Grébaut's career as an Ethiopicist, see *EA* 2.878–79.

[56] S. Grébaut, 'Littérature éthiopienne pseudo-clémentine: Texte et traduction du *mystère du jugement des pecheurs*', *Revue de l'orient chrétien* 12 [1907], 285–97, 380–92; *Revue de l'orient chrétien* 13 [1908], 166–80, 314–20.

[57] S. Grébaut, 'Littérature éthiopienne pseudo-clémentine: Texte et traduction du traité, *La seconde venue du Christ et la résurrection des morts'*, *Revue de l'orient chrétien* 15 (1910), 198–214, 307–23, 425–39.

[58] M. R. James, 'A New Text of the Apocalypse of Peter', *Journal of Theological Studies* 12 (1910), 36–54; 'A New Text of the Apocalypse of Peter, II', *Journal of Theological Studies* 12 (1911), 362–83; 'A New Text of the Apocalypse of Peter, II', *Journal of Theological Studies* 12 (1911), 573–83.

[59] For the dating, see S. Corcoran and B. Salway, 'Newly Identified Greek Fragment', 131–33, who date the Latin fragments they edit to the late fifth century (119–22), no more than a century after the work's composition.

dead, and falling on our faces we blessed the Father of the new world, the God who saved us through Jesus Christ our Lord. And being overcome by very great fear we remained flat on the ground like speechless children. But our Lord Jesus put his hand on each one of us and raised us, saying, 'Why have your hearts failed like this, and why are you so astonished? Do you not know that the One who sent me can perform miracles for the salvation of those who believe in him from the heart? So do not stand astonished and ashamed and idle, but as children of light ask my Father in heaven for the Spirit of counsel and might, and he will fill you with the Holy Spirit and grant you to be with me for ever.'[60]

In response to the disciples' request, Jesus breathes on them and bestows the Holy Spirit (cf. *GJn* 20.22), promising eternal salvation to them and to those who believe through them.[61]

As Peter and John ask about the signs of the end,[62] the text switches from narrative to apocalyptic mode, drawing on the traditional linkage between Easter and eschatology that can be traced back to *1 Corinthians* 15 and to texts such as the *Epistula Apostolorum*, the *Apocalypse of Peter*, and the *Gospel of Mary*. Indeed, the question about the signs of the end appears to echo the *Apocalypse of Peter*, which opens with a similar question (1.2–3). In both cases, the question is motivated by the need to hand down accurate information to later generations of believers so that they remain vigilant. In the *Apocalypse*, the risen Jesus responds in language echoing the eschatological discourse of *GMatthew* 24; in the *Testamentum*, a distinction is drawn between that earlier teaching (given 'in the days of the world before I was glorified')[63] and the new teaching, introduced by the appeal, 'And now, hear, you children of light!'[64] The discourse that follows reproduces motifs familiar from

---

[60] Rahmani, *Testamentum*, 2, 4; cf. Cooper and Maclean, *Testament*, 49–50. The Ethiopic variants (Beylot, *Testamentum*, 1) are few and probably secondary.

[61] Rahmani, *Testamentum*, 4; Cooper and Maclean, *Testament*, 50; Beylot, *Testamentum*, 2–3.

[62] Rahmani, *Testamentum*, 4; Cooper and Maclean, *Testament*, 50–51; Beylot, *Testamentum*, 3.

[63] Beylot, *Testamentum*, 3; cf. Rahmani, *Testamentum*, 6; Cooper and Maclean, *Testament*, 51.

[64] Beylot, *Testamentum*, 4; cf. Rahmani, *Testamentum*, 6; Cooper and Maclean, *Testament*, 51.

the repertoire of early Christian apocalypticism: evil rulers (i.4–5), alarming signs in heaven and on earth (i.6–7), degeneracy within the church (i.8), the arrival of the Antichrist (i.9, 11), oracles against the nations (i.10), an appeal to remain faithful (i.13).[65] At this point in the text, the risen Lord begins to instruct his disciples about issues of church order such as the furnishing of the church building (i.19), the ordination of a bishop (i.20–21), and the eucharistic liturgy (i.23). Only at the conclusion of this lengthy text does the post-resurrection narrative resume as John, Peter, and Matthew worship the ascending Jesus, compose the *Testamentum*, and arrange for copies of it to be circulated to the universal church (ii.26–27).

In studying the Ethiopic version of the *Testamentum* as represented by MS 51 of the d'Abbadie collection, Guerrier noted a crucial difference from Rahmani's Syriac text. Closely related to the *Testamentum*, and following it with only a minimal break is a new text in which the risen Jesus discourses with his disciples in Galilee on some of the same apocalyptic themes as are treated at the beginning of the *Testamentum*, leading to a letter written by the apostles to the universal church recounting their conversations with the risen Lord. The narrative setting of this work is closely related to that of the *Testamentum*, and a literary relationship between the two works is undeniable. Here too, the discourse opens with the appeal, 'Hear, children of light...'; here too, previously unbelieving disciples fall on their faces after touching the risen Lord.[66] This unexpected supplement is seen as part of the *Testamentum* in the d'Abbadie catalogue, where it is listed simply as section 55 and entitled 'Discours de Jésus-Christ'.[67] But Guerrier's belief that this was an independent work was confirmed by the evidence of a second manuscript, held in London at the British Museum, in which the supplementary material has its own title. Confusingly, however, the title is exactly that of the *Testamentum*, which it directly follows: both are headed, 'Testament of our Lord and Saviour Jesus Christ'.[68] The larger work has bestowed its own title on the shorter one, from which, however, it has derived its own narrative framework. The

---

[65] The references follow the Syriac version.

[66] Texts in Guerrier (with S. Grébaut), *Le Testament en Galilée de Notre-Seigneur Jésus-Christ*, 37 (= *GD* 2.1 [see Appendix]), 56 (=*EpAp* 12).

[67] D'Abbadie, *Catalogue*, 62.

[68] The London manuscript is listed as Or. 793 in William Wright, *Catalogue of Ethiopian Manuscripts in the British Museum Acquired since the Year 1847* (London: British Museum, 1877), 270–74. The two titles occur at fols. 1r, 14r.

supplementary work is introduced with the words, 'Discourse spoken by our Lord Jesus to his eleven disciples in Galilee after he rose from the dead', and this enabled Guerrier to differentiate the new work from its neighbour in the Paris and London manuscripts by entitling it 'The Testament *in Galilee* of our Lord Jesus Christ.'[69]

Guerrier published his edition of the *Testament in Galilee* in 1912, basing it on three Paris manuscripts (MSS 51, 90, and 199, labelled A, B, and C respectively) together with the London manuscript (Or. 793, labelled L). The oldest of these are MSS 51 and 90, both dated to the sixteenth century,[70] although Guerrier takes the mid-eighteenth-century London manuscript as his base text. The Ethiopic manuscripts of the *Testament in Galilee* or *Epistula Apostolorum* are thus later than Schmidt's incomplete Coptic manuscript by more than a millennium. With the publication of Guerrier's edition Schmidt felt able to proceed with his own, put on hold following M. R. James's intervention in 1910. This required him to address the crucial question how the two versions were to be co-ordinated.

1.4   The Problem of Co-ordination

Schmidt's response to Guerrier's publication has had serious and negative long-term consequences. Rather than using it constructively to advance his own work, Schmidt subjects Guerrier's edition to severe and largely unjustified criticism and arranges for the Ethiopic text to be retranslated while not allowing it to impinge on his own earlier transcription and reconstruction of the Coptic. No evidence is offered that the Coptic and Ethiopic texts represent significantly different recensions (except in the case of the 'Galilean prelude'),[71] and the possibility of filling the many Coptic lacunae with readings from the Ethiopic – in place of Schmidt's own conjectures – is largely ignored.

Schmidt made contact with Guerrier in 1910 but did not share with him his transcription and translation of the Coptic text. In contrast, Guerrier sent Schmidt a pre-publication copy of his own material, and one would have expected Schmidt to express

---

[69] As explained in Guerrier's 1907 article, 'Un "Testament (éthiopien) de Notre-Seigneur et Sauveur Jésus-Christ" en Galilée', 1. Schmidt later claimed incorrectly that Guerrier provides no justification for this title (*Gespräche Jesu*, 156).

[70] D'Abbadie's catalogue does not date these manuscripts, but datings are provided in the extensive revision by Chaîne, *Catalogue*, 37, 58.

[71] i.e. Guerrier's chapters 1–11, which were never part of the Coptic text.

appreciation of the high value of the complete Ethiopic text for filling in major and minor lacunae in the Coptic. Bizarrely, however, he appeals to the Coptic text as evidence of deficiencies in Guerrier's editing of the Ethiopic. On comparing the two,

> [i]t became clear that the Coptic text necessitates a re-evaluation of the manuscripts used by Guerrier. Guerrier has based his edition on the manuscript L, rejecting variants from the other manuscripts noted in the textual apparatus, although in many cases these represent the original text. For that reason I arranged for a new translation into German by Herr [Isaak] Wajnberg, an expert in Ethiopic...[72]

Schmidt's statements are disingenuous. Not possessing Ethiopic expertise himself, he could have had only limited access to Guerrier's variants and was in no position to judge whether Guerrier's preferred London manuscript (L) deviated further from the Coptic than the Paris ones (A B C). Schmidt probably approached Wajnberg because he needed Guerrier's translation to be independently checked against the Ethiopic, and subsequently claimed that alleged textual problems identified by Wajnberg had been evident to himself all along.

In reality, Schmidt's complaint about Guerrier's choice of a base text simply echoes Wajnberg, who contributed a section on the Ethiopic manuscript tradition as well as an extensively annotated translation to Schmidt's 1919 monograph.[73] In his assessment of the Ethiopic manuscripts, Wajnberg claims that 'in many cases the worst of them seems to be L, precisely the one selected – perhaps at random – by Guerrier as the basis for his edition.'[74] Wajnberg provides seven (untranslated) examples of cases where MSS A B C agree with the Coptic against L,[75] a claim repeated by Schmidt. These examples are, however, either spurious or trivial. In two of the seven cases no Coptic text exists.[76] In four cases Guerrier himself prefers an A B C reading to an L one.[77] An imperfect tense in L is cited, but in reality it is at least as close to the Coptic as the perfect

---

[72] Schmidt, *Gespräche Jesu*, 4.
[73] Schmidt and Wajnberg, *Gespräche*, 6–20, 25–155, 48*–66*.
[74] Schmidt and Wajnberg, *Gespräche*, 11.
[75] Schmidt and Wajnberg, *Gespräche*, 13.
[76] Wajnberg gives page and line numbers in Guerrier: 65,9; 65,11.
[77] Guerrier, 58,2; 65,9, 11; 71,4. Wajnberg acknowledges that Guerrier often rejects L readings but claims that he would have done so more frequently if he had had access to the Coptic text (Schmidt and Wajnberg, *Gespräche*, 12–13).

tense in A B C.[78] That leaves just two cases where Guerrier's
Ethiopic text could be adjusted in the light of the Coptic. At *EpAp*
13.5, L reads 'fulfil the ministry of the Father', where A B C agree
with the Coptic in omitting 'of the Father'.[79] At *EpAp* 29.5, A B
C agree with the Coptic against L in reading, 'We said, Lord, blessed
are we. . .', where L omits 'Lord'.[80] While Guerrier's reliance on L is
open to criticism, Schmidt's claim that this leaves his edition fundamentally flawed is unwarranted.

Schmidt systematically undervalues the Ethiopic version, as
though he were determined to preserve the integrity of his Coptic
text from alien influences emanating from Ethiopia – or France.
Thus, both his Coptic text and his German translation follow the
page and line divisions of the Coptic manuscript but fail to incorporate Guerrier's chapter or paragraph divisions, which are dismissed as
'highly arbitrary'.[81] Navigating between the two versions is thus
made needlessly complicated. While Schmidt's translation from the
Coptic does on occasion fill lacunae from Wajnberg's translation
from the Ethiopic, his edition of the Coptic text – still the only one
available – was evidently completed before he became aware of
Guerrier's work and remains uncorrected in the light of it. In addition, chapters 1–11 of the Ethiopic text – the 'Galilean prelude' – are
buried in an appendix;[82] the chapter enumeration in Wajnberg's
translation from the Ethiopic begins from the likely opening of the
Coptic text, so that what was chapter 12 for Guerrier is now chapter
1 – a precedent followed by later translations even when they claim
to be based exclusively on the Ethiopic.[83] It is clear that the Galilean
apocalyptic material is secondary and that it was absent from the
extant incomplete Coptic and Latin manuscripts. In both cases,
surviving pagination indicates that there was enough space for the

[78] Guerrier, 70,12.
[79] Guerrier, 57,6.
[80] Guerrier, 71,4–5.
[81] Schmidt, *Gespräche Jesu*, 24.
[82] These chapters are also placed in an Appendix in the present work, which (unlike
Schmidt-Wajnberg's) does not include an independent translation of the Ethiopic text.
In the introduction to the Appendix, it is suggested that chapters 1–11 of the so-called
Testament in Galilee are secondary to the *Testamentum Domini*, which would be
compatible with a date in the second millenium.
[83] Cf. Jacques-Noël Pérès, *L'Épître des Apôtres et le testament de notre sauveur
Jésus-Christ: Présentation et traduction de l'éthiopien* (Turnhout: Brepols, 1994), where
EpAp and the *Testament* (= Guerrier's chapters 1–11) are translated from Ethiopic as
separate works. The New Testament apocrypha editions of Hennecke–Schneemelcher,
Elliott, and Markschies–Schröter omit the Galilean material altogether.

material designated as chapters 1–6 in modern editions, beginning from 'What Jesus Christ revealed to his disciples...' (ch. 1) and continuing with the epistolary opening (ch. 2), a confession of faith and a catena of miracle stories (chs. 3–5), and an apostolic exhortation (ch. 6). On the other hand, there is no evidence that *EpAp* ever circulated in Ethiopia without its Galilean supplement. If there is to be a translation exclusively from the Ethiopic, it should include the whole of the Ethiopic text.

Setting aside the issue of the supplementary material, the question is how the Ethiopic and Coptic textual evidence is to be co-ordinated. Schmidt's determination to safeguard the integrity of his Coptic text takes its most damaging form in the decision that Wajnberg's translation from the Ethiopic should be printed separately from his own translation of the Coptic, on facing pages but without any other attempt to co-ordinate the two. As a result, *EpAp* has repeatedly been published in two parallel translations, evidently closely related but always kept apart. That this is entirely unnecessary may be demonstrated from an analysis of the Wajnberg/Schmidt translations of *EpAp* 7.1–2, the passage that opens the extant Coptic text:[84]

EpAp 7.1–2 Eth (Wajnberg)	*EpAp 7.1–2 Cop (Schmidt)*
Cerinth und Simon sind gekommen, um die Welt durchzuwandern. Sie sind die Gegner des Herrn Jesu Christi, sie, die in der Wirklichkeit diejenigen verführen, die an das wahre Wort und an die Tat, das ist an Jesum Christum glauben.	Kerinthos und Simon sind gekommen, um <zu wandeln> in der Welt. Diese aber sind <Feinde> unseres Herrn Jesu Christi, denn sie verkehren die <Worte> und den Gegenstand, d. h. Jesum Christum.

(i)   Wajnberg selects the form 'Cerinth', Schmidt 'Kerinthos'. Since both translators agree that a reference is intended to the heretic Cerinthus, the difference is unnecessary. In fact, *Eth* manuscripts read Qerentos, while *Cop* reads Korinthos, presumably an error which might be corrected from the Ethiopic.

(ii)   Wajnberg and Schmidt agree that the two heretics 'have come' (*sind gekommen*), although *Eth* actually reads 'have gone out' and should have been translated, *sind ausgegangen*. In Schmidt's rendering there is an uncertain letter

---

[84] Schmidt and Wajnberg, *Gespräche*, 32–35. Angled brackets represent lacunae with Schmidt's reconstructions.

followed by a lacuna at the end of the first line of *Cop*, ⲁⲩⲉⲓ
ⲁⲛ[.....]. In deference to Schmidt, Wajnberg actually cor-
rects *Eth waṣ'u* (= *waḍ'u*, have gone out) to *maṣ'u* (have
come).[85] This is exactly the opposite of the appropriate
procedure: reconstructed *Cop* needs to be adjusted to extant
Eth, not the reverse. The letter-trace Schmidt reads as a
possible ⲛ is more likely to represent a ⲃ, suggesting ⲁⲩⲉⲓ
ⲁⲃ[ⲁⲗ], 'have gone out', as in *Eth*. The reference to heretics
going out into the world finds a close parallel in *2 John* 7,
πολλοὶ πλάνοι ἐξῆλθον εἰς τὸν κόσμον.

(iii)   Cerinthus and Simon go out *um die Welt durchzuwandern*
(Wajnberg), *um <zu wandeln> in der Welt* (Schmidt). The
translations are almost identical in sense but not in wording,
leaving the reader uncertain how far *Eth* and *Cop* actually
agree. If the *Cop* lacuna is again completed from *Eth*, their
agreement is clear: *Eth* here reads, 'they go around the
world' (without the purpose clause), which would correspond to *Cop* [...ⲥⲉⲛⲁ]ⳍⲉ ⳍⲛ̄ ⲡⲕⲟⲥⲙⲟⲥ] with both versions
perhaps deriving from *Gk* διοδεύουσιν ἐν τῷ κόσμῳ.[86]
Thus *EpAp* 7.1 should be translated, 'Cerinthus and Simon
have gone out, they go around the world', rather than
'Cerinthus and Simon have come to go through the
world'.[87]

(iv)   In *EpAp* 7.2, Wajnberg reads, *Sie sind die Gegner des Herrn
Jesu Christi*; Schmidt, *Diese aber sind <Feinde> unseres
Herrn Jesu Christi*. There is no need to differentiate between
'opponents' and 'enemies' when the common underlying *Gk*
is most likely ἐχθροί. Here Guerrier's *Eth* manuscripts read
either 'enemies of Jesus Christ' (B) or 'enemies of the God
Jesus Christ' (A C L), but Wajnberg's translation includes
readings from an additional manuscript (S) which here
agrees with *Cop* in reading 'enemies of our Lord Jesus
Christ'. While noting this, Wajnberg's translation omits
the possessive 'our', ignoring the likelihood that an agreement of one or more Ethiopic manuscripts with the Coptic

---

[85] Schmidt and Wajnberg, *Gespräche*, 32.
[86] See Crum, 203b, 204b; Dillmann, 999.
[87] Müller, *NTApoc*, 254.

and against other Ethiopic manuscripts will represent the original Ethiopic reading.[88]

(v)   Wajnberg continues, ... *sie, die in der Wirklichkeit diejenigen verführen, die an das wahre Wort und an die Tat, das ist an Jesum Christum glauben*; Schmidt, *denn sie verkehren die* <*Worte*> *und den Gegenstand, d. h. Jesum Christum.* Cerinthus and Simon lead astray those who believe the true word and deed, that is Jesus Christ; or, they distort the words and the object, i.e. Jesus Christ. There are minor difficulties with the sense here, but there is no justification for several of the deviations in wording (*verführen/verkehren, Tat/Gegenstand, das ist/d.h.*). Here the shorter text represented by *Cop* is expanded by *Eth*: 'They <[Eth]utterly> pervert [Cop]the words {[Eth]those who believe in the true word} [Cop+Eth]and the work, which is Jesus Christ.' A single translation would require a choice between the two readings, of which the shorter is probably preferable.

As this analysis indicates, there are multiple methodological problems in the *editio princeps* of the Coptic text. Some of these problems are mitigated by Duensing and Müller, whose formatting does bring to light convergences of wording by presenting short passages of closely similar wording in a single column. Yet here too the presentation is dominated by the two-column format. The Ethiopic evidence has not been adequately exploited to restore lacunae in the Coptic text; there has been little concern to establish the common Greek terminology that may underlie both versions; attempts to differentiate primary and secondary readings have been lacking; and the common basis of the two versions has often been concealed by unnecessary differences of phraseology. What is evident in all this is the enduring influence of Schmidt's decision that the Coptic *EpAp* is to be viewed as a free-standing object existing in parallel with its Ethiopic counterpart, and that the two versions (along with the Latin fragment) are *not* to be presented as witnesses to a *single* early Christian text. More than any other factor, it is this confusing dual existence that explains the continuing neglect of an early gospel-like text, potentially at least as important as the *Gospel of Thomas*, more than a century after it was first brought to light.

---

[88]   See n. 91, below.

In the translation that follows, *EpAp* is presented in a single-column format with the Ethiopic text used to fill larger or smaller gaps in the Coptic and with a critical apparatus indicating variations between the Ethiopic and the Coptic and/or within the Ethiopic textual tradition. In the absence of an adequate critical edition of the Ethiopic text, the presentation of the Ethiopic textual evidence is selective, based on just eight of the sixteen or more accessible manuscripts of *EpAp*. Variants from Guerrier's collation of four sixteenth- to nineteenth-century manuscripts (A B C L) are given in translation, and to these are added readings from four further manuscripts (E G K S). S is Wajnberg's Stuttgart manuscript, here re-collated, K is a second London manuscript known to Guerrier but not used by him, while E and G are significant in view of their early, possibly fifteenth century, dates. In a number of cases G agrees with the Coptic against most or all of the other Ethiopic manuscripts studied here, suggesting that many of the minor deviations from the Coptic may have entered the Ethiopic textual tradition at a relatively late stage.[89] A collation of a larger number of manuscripts might have resulted in a few changes to the main text; but it would also have overloaded an already complicated critical apparatus and focused attention on the ongoing Ethiopic textual tradition rather than on the recovery of the text of *EpAp* in an approximation to its original second-century form. A representative selection of the available manuscripts seems adequate for the purpose in hand.[90]

---

[89] Nineteen agreements are noted in the textual apparatus between the Coptic and G (+) and against most or all of the other Ethiopic manuscripts collated here. These occur at *EpAp* 7.2 (G K S), 10.3 (G), 10.6 (G), 10.7 (G K), 10.9 (G K), 11.7 (E G), 14.6 (G), 15.3 (A C G), 15.4 (G), 18.5 (A G S), 24.2 (E G K), 30.1 (E G), 39.3 (G), 39.10 (G), 39.13 (E G), 41.4 (G K), 45.4 × 2 (G, G L), 48.1 (A C E G). Only nine agreements are noted between the Coptic text and Ethiopic manuscripts excluding G: *EpAp* 13.4 (F), 15.5 (E K), 24.3 (E), 25.5 (S), 27.3 (L), 30.1 (C), 30.3 (E K), 43.12 (B K), 47.6 (L S). These 19 + 9 = 28 agreements include nine that feature E. It is also noteworthy that G does not include the *Testamentum Domini* and thus presents *EpAp* with its Galilean prelude as a free-standing text. While this may suggest that the linkage with the *Testamentum Domini* is a late development within the Ethiopic textual tradition, G has already taken over the title of the longer work ('Testament of our Lord and Saviour Jesus Christ') and thus already presupposes awareness of the linkage.

[90] Textual evidence from fourteen Ethiopic manuscripts (including A B C K L S but not E or G) is found in Julian V. Hills, *The Epistle of the Apostles*, Early Christian Apocrypha 2 (Santa Rosa, CA: Polebridge Press, 2009), 6–8 and *passim*. For formatting and other reasons, it was not possible to incorporate information derived from Hills in the textual apparatus here. While Hills's translations are independent of Duensing's, the conventional separation of the Ethiopic and Coptic versions is maintained.

The Coptic manuscript that preserves around 60 per cent of this text is dated to the fourth or fifth centuries and is thus at least a millennium older than the available Ethiopic manuscripts. As a general rule, the Coptic should be prioritized over the Ethiopic textual witnesses, where expansion, paraphrase, and scribal errors result in a degree of indeterminacy – although for the most part within a limited semantic range. Each case should be considered on its merits, however. Like the Coptic, the Ethiopic was almost certainly translated directly from the original Greek. The earlier assumption that it is based on a hypothetical Arabic version and dates from the second millennium has no merit.[91] Other than the Ethiopic version itself, there is no evidence that *EpAp* was in circulation during the second millennium, in contrast to the clear evidence of its early circulation prior to about the sixth century – in the form of the Coptic and Latin versions, together with the *Testamentum Domini* and a remarkably clear allusion in the voluminous post-resurrection dialogue known as *Pistis Sophia.*[92] If both the Coptic and the Ethiopic texts go back to early and independent translations from shorter or longer Greek exemplars, then they are in principle of equal value as witnesses to the original text.

---

[91] According to Wajnberg, the Ethiopic text derives from the Coptic, 'wahrscheinlich durch das Medium einer arabischen Übersetzung' (Schmidt and Wajnberg, *Gespräche*, 6). The sole basis for this claim is the assumption that 'Übersetzungen unmittelbar aus dem Griechischen sind in der abess[inischen] Literatur wohl sehr selten' (18). Subsequent research has made this assumption untenable: see, for example, Rochus Zuurmond, *Novum Testamentum Aethiopice: The Synoptic Gospels, General Introduction/Edition of the Gospel of Mark* (Stuttgart: Franz Steiner, 1989), 37–133; James C. VanderKam, *Textual and Historical Studies in the Book of Jubilees* (Missoula, MT: Scholars Press, 1977), 12–17; Michael A. Knibb, *Translating the Bible: The Ethiopic Versions of the Old Testament* (Oxford: British Academy/Oxford University Press, 1999), *passim*. Yet Wajnberg's assessment continues to be repeated. According to Judith Hartenstein (citing Wajnberg/Schmidt, Müller and Vielhauer), '[D]ie äthiopische ist wahrscheinlich über den Umweg des Koptischen und Arabischen entstanden' (*Die zweite Lehre: Erscheinungen des Auferstandenen als Rahmenerzählungen frühchristlicher Dialoge,* Texte und Untersuchungen zur Geschichte der altchristlichen Literatur 146 [Berlin: Akademie Verlag, 2000], 98). Müller's unthinking repetition of Wajnberg's assessment lives on in the Markschies–Schröter collection, where we read that 'die koptische Tradition auf dem üblichen Wege über die Arabische bis Äthiopien kam' (*Antike Christliche Apokryphen in deutscher Übersetzung,* 1/2, 1063).

[92] Compare *Pistis Sophia* 1.7.12 with *EpAp* 13.2–14.5 (Jesus' descent from heaven disguised as the angel Gabriel).

2

TRANSLATION

Main Text

<COP>	Translation of Coptic text, from the manuscript IFAO Copte inv. 413-433, Bibliothèque nationale, Paris, ed. Schmidt, checked against digitized images
<ETH>	Translation of Ethiopic (Ge'ez) text in major sections where Coptic is lacking[1]
<+LAT>	Text from Latin palimpsest begins at this point
<–LAT>	Text from Latin palimpsest ends at this point
[ⲥⲱⲙⲁ]	Greek loanwords in Coptic text
italics	words in Coptic fragments corresponding to Ge'ez text
1.1...	Verse enumeration derived from the translation by Julian V. Hills, modified in the case of chapters 3, 4, 9, 13, 19, 36
[ⲁ], ⲁ...	Original reconstructed or extant pagination of Coptic manuscript[2]
I, II...	Pagination of extant manuscript (Schmidt, omitting his enumeration of fragments as **XV** and **XVI**)

---

[1] Major passages missing from the Coptic manuscript are *EpAp* 1.1–6.3 (MS pp. 1–8), 18.5b–19.8 (MS pp. 19–20), 21.3b–22.3b (MS pp. 25–26, except for fragments), 31.1–38.3a (MS pp. 37–50, except for fragments), 49.1–51.5 (MS pp. 65–68?). Thus thirty out of (probably) sixty-eight pages are entirely or almost entirely missing. All extant pages have suffered more or less significant damage.

[2] Original pagination survives at MS pp. 15, 16, 18, 23, 27, 28, 51–55, 57–64.

Textual Apparatus

Cop	Coptic reading
Eth	Ethiopic manuscripts A B C L (collated by Guerrier), E G K S (collated from digital images)[3]
(Eth)	other Ethiopic manuscripts (in contrast to the one(s) just cited)
Lat	Latin reading
A	Ethiopic manuscript A (Guerrier, 163), Fonds d'Abbadie no. 51 (Chaîne, 34), Bibliothèque nationale, Paris, sixteenth cent.
B	Ethiopic manuscript B (Guerrier, 163), Fonds d'Abbadie no. 90 (Chaîne, 58), Bibliothèque nationale, Paris, sixteenth cent.
C	Ethiopic manuscript C (Guerrier, 163), Fonds d'Abbadie no. 199 (Chaîne, 119), Bibliothèque nationale, Paris, nineteenth cent.
E	Ethiopic manuscript EMML 8744, Lake Tana (Six 1999, 233–37), ?fifteenth cent.
G	Ethiopic manuscript GG 00072 (HMML C3-IV-167), Gunda Gundē, ?fifteenth cent.
K	Ethiopic manuscript K, Or. 795 (Wright, 275–77), British Library, London, mid-eighteenth cent.
L	Ethiopic manuscript L (Guerrier, 163), Or. 793 (Wright, 270–75), British Library, London, eighteenth cent.
S	Ethiopic manuscript S, Cod. orient. fol. Nr. 49, Universitäts-bibliothek, Stuttgart (Six 1994, 461–66), ?seventeenth cent.
and... truth]	First and last words of passage in main text where a variant is to be noted
|	break between variants
< >	additional wording within variant

---

[3] Hills assigns the fourteen Ethiopic manuscripts he has collated to one of two groups: family 1 is said to include A B C K, while L S belong to family 2 (*Epistle*, 6–12). The readings collected in the present textual apparatus do not appear to support this analysis. Of 14 L S agreements noted here, all but three also agree with one or more family 1 manuscript (including A × 3, B × 6). Thirteen agreements of L + one or more family 1 manuscript against S are noted, and eight agreements of S + one or more family 1 manuscript against L. The family 1 and 2 distinction is not used in the present work.

{ }	alternative wording within variant
{– }	absence from specified MS(s) of preceding word(s) within variant
*	emendation

For *Additional Notes*, see Part III, *ad loc.*

1.1 <**ETH**> What Jesus Christ revealed to his disciples and* to all: 2 on account of Simon and Cerinthus the false apostles this has been written, so that no one should associate with them, for there is in them a venom by which they kill people; 3 so that you may be strong and not waver or be disturbed or depart from what you have heard, the word of the gospel. 4 What we have heard and remembered and written for the whole world we entrust to you, our sons and daughters, in joy. 5 In the name of God, ruler of the whole world, and of Jesus Christ, grace be multiplied to you.

2.1 John and Thomas and Peter and Andrew and James and Philip and Bartholomew and Matthew and Nathanael and Judas the Zealot and Cephas 2 to* the churches of the east and the west, to those in the north and the south: 3 proclaiming and declaring to you our Lord Jesus Christ, as we heard so have we written; and we touched him after he rose from the dead, when he revealed to us what is great and wonderful and true.

1.1 What... revealed] Christ A, Testament that Jesus Christ spoke and revealed S | his disciples] + the book A B K L | and*] *Eth* + how Jesus Christ revealed a book about {through B E L S} the company of the apostles, disciples of Jesus Christ | and to all] this concerning S | *See Additional Notes*
2 Simon] Semon A B C | Cerinthus] Qerenotos K S, Qelentos A L, Qelonotos B C G this... written] –A | venom G] deceit *(Eth)* | *See Additional Notes*
3 *See Additional Notes*
4 What] As S | we entrust to] I entrust to B L, we greet you E K, we suffer for S *See Additional Notes*
5 God] + the Father B L S | the whole] –L | to you] among you E K | *See Additional Notes*

2.1–2 John] We, John S | Thomas and Peter] Peter and Thomas E K | Nathanael... Zealot] Nathanael the Zealot and Judas S | to*] *Eth* we have written to | churches G L] church A B C | to those in E G K] above *(Eth)* | *See Additional Notes*
3 as... written G] as we have seen so we have written and we have heard him C, as we have written so we have heard him *(Eth)* | *See Additional Notes*

Confession of Faith

3.1 This we declare, that our Lord and Saviour Jesus Christ is God, the Son of God,

2 who was sent from God, ruler of the whole world, maker of every name that is named;

3 who is above all authorities, Lord of lords and King of kings, Power of the heavenly powers;

4 who sits above the Cherubim at the right hand of the throne of the Father;

5 who by his word commanded the heavens and founded the earth and what is in it, and established the sea, and it did not cross its boundary, and depths and springs to gush forth and flow into the earth day and night;

6 who established the sun and moon and stars in heaven;

7 who separated light and darkness;

8 who summoned Gehenna, and summons rain in the twinkling of an eye for the winter time, and mist and frost and hail, and the days each in its time;

9 who shakes and makes firm;

10 who made humankind in his image and likeness;

11 who spoke with the forefathers and prophets in parables and in truth;

12 whom the apostles preached and the disciples touched.

13 And God the Son of God do we confess, the Word who became flesh of Mary,* carried in her womb through the Holy Spirit. 14 And not by the desire of the flesh but by the will of God was he born;

3.1 we... that] we know, that E G, + God A, –S | and Saviour] – A C | God] –C S, the Lord E | the... God] + God G | *See Additional Notes*

2 maker G] + and creator *(Eth)*

3 *See Additional Notes*

4 who sits E G K] who is *(Eth)* | Cherubim A] + and Seraphim *(Eth)* | at E G K] and who sits at *(Eth)* | *See Additional Notes*

5 his word] a word E | established ... not E G] bounded the sea so that it might not *(Eth)* | into the earth] –C | *See Additional Notes*

6 who established] –K | and stars] the stars E

8 and frost] for frost E

11–12 who ... apostles] of whom the forefathers and the prophets spoke in parables and the apostles in truth S | *See Additional Notes*

13 And God A] God E, + the Lord *(Eth)* | confess] E G K know | the Word] from the Word E K | Mary*] + the virgin E G K, from the holy virgin *(Eth)* | carried] –E G | *See Additional Notes*

14 he] God E | *See Additional Notes*

15 and he was swaddled in Bethlehem and manifested and nourished and grew up, as we saw.

The Miracle Cycle

4.1 This is what our Lord Jesus Christ did when he was taken by Joseph and Mary his mother to where he was to be taught letters. 2 And his teacher said to him as he taught him, 'Say, Alpha'. 3 He answered and said to him, 'You tell me first what Beta is, and then I will trust you and say Alpha!'*

5.1 And then there was a wedding in Cana of Galilee, and they invited him with his mother and his brothers, and water he made wine. 2 And the dead he raised, and paralytics he made to walk, and the man whose hand was withered he restored.

3 And a woman who suffered her periods twelve years touched the hem of his garment and was immediately well. 4 And as we considered and wondered at the glorious things he had done, he said to us, 'Who touched me?' 5 And we said to him, 'Lord, the press of the crowd touched you!' 6 And he answered and said to us, 'I felt that power came forth upon me.' 7 Immediately that woman came before him and answered him and said to him, 'Lord, I touched you.' 8 And he answered and said to her, 'Go, your faith has made you well.' 9 And then the deaf he made to hear and the blind to see and those with demons he exorcized and those with leprosy he cleansed.

10 And the demon Legion, who dwelt in a man, met Jesus and cried out and said, 'Before the day of our destruction have you come

15 and manifested and nourished B L S] he was killed who was nourished *(Eth)* | *See Additional Notes*

4.1 our Lord Jesus B C L] he {our Lord A} did, that is, our Lord Jesus *(Eth)* | Christ] –K | letters] –A

3 then S] is this C E K, when *(Eth)* | I... Alpha*] truly <and E S> really the work that was done {he did S} *Eth* | *See pp. 94–97*

5.1 *See Additional Notes*

2 paralytics] the paralytic E K S | *See Additional Notes*

3 woman] + whose blood was flowing A

4 And as] And then E G | he[2]... us] –G

5 Lord] our Lord E K | the... you] the crowd pressed you and handled you and touched you S

6 upon B] from L, from upon *(Eth)* | *See Additional Notes*

7 and answered him] –A C | you] –S

8 *See Additional Notes*

10 Before] + the time and | drive us out] destroy us C | *See Additional Notes*

to drive us out?' 11 And Jesus rebuked him and said to him, 'Go out of this man and do nothing to him!' 12 And he went into the pigs and plunged them into the sea and they were drowned.

13 And then he walked on the sea, and the winds blew and he rebuked them, and the waves of the sea he stilled.

14 And when we his disciples had no *denarii*, we said to him, 'Teacher, what shall we do about the tax-collector?' 15 And he answered and said to us, 'Let one of you cast a hook* into the deep and draw out a fish, and he will find *denarii* in it. 16 Give them to the tax-collectors for myself and for you.'

17 Then when we had no food except five loaves and two fishes, he commanded the men to recline. 18 And their number was found to be five thousand besides women and children, and to these we brought pieces of bread. 19 And they were satisfied and there was some left over, and we removed twelve basketfuls of pieces. 20 If we ask and say, 'What do these five loaves mean?', they are an image of our faith as true Christians; 21 that is, in the Father, ruler of the whole world, and in Jesus Christ and in the Holy Spirit and in the holy church and in the forgiveness of sins.

6.1 And these things our Lord and Saviour revealed to us and showed us, as we likewise do to you, 2 so that you may be partakers in the grace of the Lord and in our ministry and our praise, as you think of eternal life. 3 Be strong and do not waver in the knowledge and certainty of our Lord Jesus Christ, and he will be merciful and gracious and save constantly, to the end of the age.

11 Jesus E] the Lord Jesus *(Eth)*
12 And] + the demon came out immediately and A C | went] + immediately A
13 blew] + upon him A | he stilled] were stilled A L
14 Teacher] –L | tax-collectors E G K S] tax-collector A B C L
15 hook*] *Eth* + a trap of the throat | *See Additional Notes*
16 tax-collectors G K S] tax-collector *(Eth)* | myself] the Teacher S
17 *See Additional Notes*
18 women and children E K] children and women *(Eth)* | pieces] our pieces E
19 *See Additional Notes*
20 and say] –A | as true Christians] in true Christianity K L S
21 Jesus Christ] + our Saviour B L S | the Holy Spirit] + the Paraclete L, the Spirit the Paraclete S

6.1 showed] taught B K S | to you] –L
2 so... may] you will be E | partakers] established B E K S | *See Additional Notes*
3 our Lord] –C | be... gracious G] be gracious L, teach and be gracious *(Eth)* | to... age E G] and to the age of the age without end B L S, and to the end of the age, the age without end A C | *See Additional Notes*

Recapitulation: Reasons for Writing

7.1 <COP> ([ө] I) Cerinthus and Simon have gone out, they go around the world [ᴋᴏᴄᴍᴏᴄ], 2 but they are enemies of our Lord Jesus Christ [ⲓ̅ⲥ̅ ⲡ̅ⲭ̅ⲥ̅], for they pervert the wo[rd]s and the work, that is, Jesus Christ [ⲓ̅ⲥ̅ ⲡ̅ⲭ̅ⲥ̅]. 3 So beware of them, for [ⲅⲁⲣ] in them there is death and a great defilement of corruption. 4 [Their] end will be judgement [ᴋⲣⲓⲥⲓⲥ] and eternal perdition.

8.1 For this reason we have not delayed to write to you about the testimony of our Saviour the Christ [ᴍⲁⲣⲧⲩⲣⲓⲁ, ⲥ̅ⲧ̅ⲣ̅, ⲭ̅ⲣ̅], 2 the things he did as we watched him and that are still [ⲉⲧⲓ] in our thoughts and deeds.

The Dawn of Easter Faith

9.1 This we confess, that the Lord was crucified [ⲥⲧⲁⲩⲣⲟⲩ] by Pontius Pilate and Archelaus between the two thieves [ⲗⲏⲥⲧⲏⲥ], and he was buried in a place [ⲧⲟⲡⲟⲥ] called ([ı] II) 'The Skull' [(ⲕⲣⲁⲛⲓ)ⲟⲛ]. 2 There came to that place three women, Mary and Martha and Mary Magdalene. 3 They took ointment to pour over his body

7.1 Cerinthus] *Cop* Corinthos, *Eth* For Cerinthos | *See Additional Notes*

1–2 they go around... Christ[1]] they have gone out, they go around the world, to God and our Lord Jesus Christ they are enemies E

2 our Lord *Cop* G K S] –B, God A C L | pervert the words] *Eth* utterly pervert those who believe in the true word | *See Additional Notes*

3 So beware] *Eth* Take heed and beware | in them] – B L S, in him E K | death... corruption] *Eth* affliction and defilement and death {death and defilement S} | *See Additional Notes*

4 Their... perdition] *Eth* His end {To the end K, The end S} will be destruction and judgement | *See Additional Notes*

8.1 For this reason] *Eth* Behold | delayed] neglected S, neglected or delayed E G K | to write... testimony] *Eth* the true testimony | of... Christ] *Eth* of our Lord and our Saviour A C G, of our Saviour and our Lord B E K S, of our Lord Jesus Christ and our Lord L

2 as... him] + and were present A E, as we watched with him C, as we were considering L | and... deeds] *Eth* and how our {–E} thoughts are still with us and <he spoke with us and G> he explained {the explanation K, his explanation S} and he made us to be his witnesses {it to be a testimony A B L}.

9.1 confess] believe S | the Lord] *Eth* he | by] *Eth* in the days of | Pontius Pilate] *Eth* Pilate the Pontian {the Pontian Pilate E G K} | Archelaus] *Eth* + the Judge | two thieves, and] *Eth* + he was crucified and with them <he was numbered, C> they took him down from <the tree of B E K L> the {his G} cross | buried] crucified A | <ⲕⲣⲁⲛⲓ>ⲟⲛ] *Eth* qarānǝyo (= κρανίου) | *See Additional Notes*

2 three women] *Cop* a third woman | Mary and Martha] *Cop* Mary [sister] of Martha, *Eth* Sarah and Martha | *See Additional Notes*

3 to pour] *Cop* they poured it | *See Additional Notes*

[ⲥⲱⲙⲁ], weeping and grieving [ⲗⲩⲡⲉⲓ] over what had happened. 4 But [ⲇⲉ] when they reached the tomb [ⲧⲁⲫⲟⲥ] and looked inside they did not find the body [ⲥⲱⲙⲁ].

10.1 And as [ⲱⲥ] they were grieving [ⲗⲩⲡⲉⲓ ⲇⲉ] and weeping the Lord appeared to them and said to them, 'For whom do you weep? Weep no longer! I am the one you seek. 2 But [ⲁⲗⲗⲁ] let one of you go to your brothers and say, "Come, the Teacher has risen from the dead!"'

3 Martha came and told us. 4 We said to her, 'What do you want with us, O [ⲱ] woman? One who died and is buried, can he live?' 5 We did not believe [ⲡⲓⲥⲧⲉⲩⲉ] her that the Saviour [ⲥⲧⲣ] had risen from the dead. 6 ([ⲓⲁ] **III**) Then [ⲧⲟⲧⲉ] she returned to the Lord and said to him, 'None of them believed [ⲡⲓⲥⲧⲉⲩⲉ] me that you are alive.'

7 He said, 'Let another of you go to them to tell them again.' 8 Mary came, she told us again, and we disbelieved [ⲡⲓⲥⲧⲉⲩⲉ] her. 9 She returned to the Lord, and she too told him.

11.1 Then [ⲧⲟⲧⲉ] the Lord said to Mary and her sisters, 'Let us go to them.' 2 And he came and found us within. 3 He called us forth, but [ⲇⲉ] we thought it was a phantasm [ⲫⲁⲛⲧⲁⲥⲙⲁ] and we did not believe [ⲡⲓⲥⲧⲉⲩⲉ] that it was the Lord. 4 Then [ⲧⲟⲧⲉ] he said to us, 'Come, fear not, I am your teacher whom you, Peter, denied three times, and now do you deny [ⲁⲣⲛⲁ] again?' 5 And [ⲇⲉ] we came to

---

4 the tomb] his tomb G | and... inside] *Eth* they found the stone where it had been rolled from the tomb and they opened the door {the door open A} and | the body] *Eth* his body

10.1 Lord] our Lord G | For... weep?] –*Eth* | *See Additional Notes*
2 say, Come, the Teacher] *Eth* say to them, Come {Behold G}, the {our A B L} Teacher {Lord C} <is with us, he is calling you, he G>
3 Martha *Cop* G] *(Eth)* Mary
4 What... us?] *Eth* What to us and to you...? | One... live] *Cop* The one who died is buried, and can he live? | *See Additional Notes*
5 the Saviour] *Eth* our Saviour
6 the Lord *Cop* G] our Lord A C E L, the Lord Jesus B K S | that... alive] *Eth* concerning your resurrection | *See Additional Notes*
7 He said *Cop* G K] we said C, + to her *(Eth)* | to them] –*Eth*
8 Mary] *Eth* Sarah | *See Additional Notes*
9 the Lord *Cop* G K] *(Eth)* our Lord | him] *Eth* + like Mary {Martha G}

11.1 and her sisters] and her brothers and sisters A, and Martha B K S
2 within] veiled B L, fishing *(Eth)* | *See Additional Notes*
3 He... was] *Eth* And we doubted and did not believe, <and A E G> he seemed to us <as B C L> | and we... Lord] and it was indeed he E, and we did not believe that it was he and it was indeed he *(Eth)* | *See Additional Notes*
4 times] *Eth* + before the cock crowed | do... again?] do not deny again! A, do you deny him again? S | *See Additional Notes*
5 doubting... hearts] *Eth* considering and doubting

him doubting [ⲁⲓⲥⲧⲁⲍⲉ] in our hearts whether it was he. 6 Then he said to us, ([ⲓⲃ] **IV**) 'Why do you still doubt [ⲁⲓⲥⲧⲁⲍⲉ ⲉⲧⲓ], you disbelieving ones? I am he who spoke to you about my flesh [ⲥⲁⲣⲝ] and my death and my resurrection. 7 That you may know that it is I, Peter, thrust your fingers into the nail-marks of my hands; and you, Thomas, thrust your fingers into the spear [ⲗⲟⲅⲭⲏ] wounds in my side; and [ⲁⲉ] you, Andrew, look at my feet and see if they are not in contact with the ground. 8 For [ⲅⲁⲣ] it is written in the prophet [ⲡⲣⲟⲫⲏⲧⲏⲥ], "As for an appearance of a demon [ⲫⲁⲛⲧⲁⲥⲓⲁ, ⲇⲁⲓⲙⲱⲛ], its foot is not in contact with the ground."'

12.1 <+**LAT**> And [ⲁⲉ] we touched him, that we might know that he had truly risen in flesh [ⲥⲁⲣⲝ]. 2 And we fell on our faces, confessing [ⲉⲍⲟⲙⲟⲗⲟⲅⲉⲓ] our sins, because we had been unbelieving.

3 Then [ⲧⲟⲧⲉ] the Lord our Saviour [ⲥⲧⲣ̄] said to us, 'Rise ([ⲓⲅ] **V**) and I will reveal to you what is above the heavens and what is in the heavens and your rest in the kingdom of the heavens. 4 For [ⲅⲁⲣ] my Father gave me authority [ⲉⲍⲟⲩⲥⲓⲁ] to take you up and those who believe [ⲡⲓⲥⲧⲉⲩⲉ] in me.'

The Descent through the Heavens

13.1 And [ⲁⲉ] what he revealed are these things that he said to us: 'It came to pass that when I came from the Father of all and passed through [ⲡⲁⲣⲁⲅⲉ] the heavens, I put on the wisdom [ⲥⲟⲫⲓⲁ] of the Father and clothed myself in the power [ⲇⲩⲛⲁⲙⲓⲥ] of his

6 still] –*Eth* | you. . . ones] and why do you not believe {confess K} E G, and which [of you] does not believe A C, and what are you saying? Do you not know that L S

7 your fingers[1] *Cop* E G] your hand A L S, your hand and your fingers B K, and your fingers C | and. . . side] *Eth* and you, Thomas, into my side | look. . . ground] *Eth* see if my feet tread on the ground and are in contact with it. | *See Additional Notes*

8 its. . . ground] *Eth* it does not connect with the ground

12.1 that. . . know] –*Eth Lat* | that. . . truly risen] *Cop* truly that he had risen | *See Additional Notes*

1–3 *See Additional Notes*

2 faces] *Eth* + before him | our sins] *Eth* and entreating him | been unbelieving] *Eth* not believed him | *See Additional Notes*

3 the . . . Saviour] *Eth* our Lord and our Saviour <Jesus Christ S> | said to us] *Cop* said | what is above. . . in the heavens] *Eth* what is of the heavens {earth L S} and what is above the heavens | rest] *Eth* resurrection

4 For. . . authority] *Eth* For this reason {For A} my Father {he E} sent me | *See Additional Notes*

13.1 *Cop* revealed] *Eth* + to us | It. . . that] –*Eth Lat* | came] *Cop* + coming | from] to B L S | passed. . . heavens] we passed the heavens K, he did not pass S | I put on] we put on K, *Cop* I clothed myself in | of the Father] *Eth* + and his power | the power. . . might] *Eth* his power | *See Additional Notes*

might. 2 I was in the heavens, and archangels [ΑΡΧΑΓΓΕΛΟC] and angels [ΑΓΓΕΛΟC] I passed [ΠΑΡΑΓΕ] in their likeness as though [ωC] I were one of them. 3 Among the powers and rulers [ΑΡΧΗ] and authorities [ΕϨΟΥCΙΑ] I passed, having the wisdom of the one who sent me. 4 And [ΔΕ] the commander [ΑΡΧΙCΤΡΑΤΗΓΟC] of the angels [ΑΓΓΕΛΟC] is Michael, with Gabriel and Uriel and Raphael, and [ΔΕ] they ([ΙΛ] **VI**) followed me down to the fifth firmament [CΤΕΡΕωΜΑ], for [ΓΑΡ] they were thinking in their hearts that I was one of them – such was the power given me by the Father. 5 And on that day I prepared the archangels [ΑΡΧΕΑΓΓΕΛΟC], in a voice of wonder, so that they might go in to the altar [ΘΥCΙΑCΤΗΡΙΟΝ] of the Father and serve [ΥΠΗΡΕΤΕΙ] and fulfil the ministry [ΔΙΑΚΟΝΙΑ] until I returned to him. 6 This is what I did in the wisdom [COΦΙΑ] of the likeness, for [ΓΑΡ] I became all in all so that I might fulfil the will [ΟΙΚΟΝΟΜΙΑ] of the Father of glory who sent me <–**LAT**> and return to him.

14.1 'For [ΓΑΡ] you know that the angel [ΑΓΓΕΛΟC] Gabriel brought the good news to Mary?'

2 We answered, (ΙΕ **VII**) 'Yes, Lord.'

3 Then [ΤΟΤΕ] he answered and said to us, 'Do you not [ΜΗ] remember that I told you a moment ago that I became an angel [ΑΓΓΕΛΟC] among angels [ΑΓΓΕΛΟC] and all in everything?'

4 We said to him, 'Yes, Lord.'

---

2 I... heavens] *–Lat* | and[1]] *Eth* when | archangels and angels] angels S, angels and archangels *(Eth)* | *See Additional Notes*

3 *Lat* powers and] *–Cop, Eth* orders and | rulers and authorities] *Eth Lat* authorities and rulers | having... one] *Eth* having <put on A C> the measure of the wisdom of the {my E} Father {the one K} <and clothed with the power of the one G> | *See Additional Notes*

4 the commander... followed me] *Eth* the archangels Michael and Gabriel, Raphael and Uriel {Seraphim and Cherubim G} followed me, *Lat* the archangel Michael and Gabriel and Uriel and Raphael openly accompanied me | *Cop Lat* E Uriel and Raphael] *(Eth)* Raphael and Uriel | firmament] heaven C | for... was] *Eth* as it {I A C E G} seemed to them <as C> | the Father *Eth Lat* my Father *Cop* | *See Additional Notes*

5 on... day] *Eth Lat* then | in... wonder] *Eth* to wonder at the voice, *Lat* in astonishment of voice | and serve... ministry *Cop Lat*] *Eth* and serve <the Father L S> in their ministry | *See Additional Notes*

6 in... likeness] *Eth* in the likeness of his wisdom | *Lat* all in all] *Cop* in all in everything, *Eth* <all B E G L> in all <to him K> with them {you A} | I might... him] *Eth* having fulfilled the merciful will of the Father and the glory of him who sent me I might return to him, *Lat* I might praise the will of my Father who sent me | *See Additional Notes*

14.1 brought] *Eth* came and brought | Mary] *Cop* Maria, *Eth* Māryām

3 a moment ago] *Eth* earlier | I became... angels] *Eth* to {as S} the angels I was like an angel | and ... everything] *–Eth*

5 Then [тотє] he answered and said to us, 'When I took the form [морфн] of the angel [аггєλoc] Gabriel, I appeared to Mary and I spoke with her. 6 Her heart received me, she believed [пιcтєγє], sh[e moul]ded me, I entered into her, I became flesh [cарҳ]. 7 For [єрєι] I became my own servant [ΔιακοΝοc] in the appearance [аιcєнcιc] of the likeness of an angel [аггєλoc]. 8 I will do likewise after I have returned to the Father.'

Pascha and Parousia

15.1 'And as for you, celebrate the memorial of my death when [отан] the Feast of the Pascha [пасха] comes.* 2 Then [тотє] one of you (ις **VIII**) will be thrown into prison for the sake of my name. 3 And he will be grieved [λγпєι] and distressed that you celebrate Pascha [пасха] while he is in prison and away from you, for he will be grieved [λγпєι гар] that he does not celebrate Pascha [пасха] with you. 4 And [гар] I will send my power [Δγναμιc] in the form of the angel [аггєλoc] Gabriel, 5 and the doors of the prison will open, and he will go out and come to you, 6 he will keep vigil with you and stay with you until the cock [аλєктωр] crows. 7 And when [отан Δє] you have completed my Memorial and my Agape [агапн], he will again [паλιΝ] be thrown into prison as a testimony, until he comes out from there and preaches what I have given you.'

8 And [Δє] we said to him, 'Lord, is it [мн] again [паλιΝ] necessary [анагкн] for us to take the cup [потнрιοΝ] and drink?'

---

5 Then . . . said] *Eth* And he said | when] *Cop* For on that day that | I took] *Eth* in | angel Gabriel] *Eth* archangel {angel S} Gabriel <the archangel K S> | Mary] Mary the virgin L, the holy virgin S | *See Additional Notes*
    6 she moulded me] *Eth* and she laughed | I entered *Cop* G] *(Eth)* I the Word entered *See Additional Notes*
    7 my own servant (lit. a servant to myself)] his servant to myself C | *Eth* servant] *Cop* + to Mary | of the likeness] –A L S | angel] servant E | *See Additional Notes*
    8 the Father] *Eth* my Father

    15.1 when. . . comes*] *Eth* which is the Pascha | *See Additional Notes*
    2 you *Cop*] *Eth* + who stand beside me
    3 grieved] *Eth* greatly grieved | while. . . from you] *(Eth)* he who is in prison {in my death for the sake of my name G} | grieved[2]] + and distressed C | that[2]] *Eth* for | celebrate Pascha *Cop* A C G] *(Eth)* celebrate
    4 the angel Gabriel *Cop* E G K] *(Eth)* an angel {my angel L S}
    5 doors *Cop* E K] *(Eth)* door | go out and] –L S
    6 he will] *Eth* so that he may | until] *Eth* And when
    7 Memorial. . . Agape] *Eth* Agape. . . Memorial | be] *Eth* + taken and | thrown] brought A B | what. . . given] *Eth* as I commanded
    8 is it. . . drink?] *Eth:* have you not completed drinking of the Pascha, for us to do it again? | *See Additional Notes*

9 He said to us, 'Yes, it is necessary [ⲁⲛⲁⲅⲕⲏ ⲅⲁⲣ] ([ⲓⲍ] **IX**) until the day when I come with those who were put to death for my sake.'

16.1 And [ⲇⲉ] we said to him, 'Lord, great indeed [ⲅⲁⲣ] are the things you have now revealed to us! 2 But in what power or [ⲏ] likeness [ⲁⲓⲥⲑⲏⲥⲓⲥ] will you come?'

3 And [ⲇⲉ] he answered and said to us, 'Truly [ⲅⲁⲙⲏⲛ ⲅⲁⲣ] I say to you, I shall surely [ⲅⲁⲣ] come like the rising sun, shining seven times more than it [ⲡⲁⲣⲁ] in my glory. 4 On the wings of clouds I shall be borne in glory, the sign [ⲥⲏⲙⲉⲓⲟⲛ] of the cross [ⲥⲧⲁⲩⲣⲟⲥ] before me. 5 And [ⲇⲉ] I will come down to the earth and judge the living and the dead.'

17.1 And [ⲇⲉ] we said to him, 'Lord, after how many years will these things be?'

2 <+**LAT**> He said to us, 'When the hundred and ~~twentieth~~* fiftieth year is completed, between Pentecost [ⲡⲉⲛⲧⲏⲕⲟⲥⲧⲏ] and the Feast of Unleavened Bread, the coming [ⲡⲁⲣⲟⲩⲥⲓⲁ] of my Father will take place.'

3 (ⲓⲏ **X**) And [ⲇⲉ] we said to him, 'Just now did you not say to us, "I will come"? So how [ⲡⲱⲥ] can you say to us, "The one who sent me will come"?'

4 Then [ⲧⲟⲧⲉ] he said to us, 'I am wholly in my Father and my Father is in me.'

The Interim

5 Then we said to him, 'Will you really leave us until your coming? Where <–**LAT**> will we find a teacher?'

6 And he answered and said to us, 'Do you not know that I am already both here and there, with the one who sent me?'

---

9 it is necessary] *–Eth* | until. . . sake] *Eth* until I come from the Father with my wounds

16.1 revealed. . . us] *Eth* you tell us {do A C} and reveal to us | *See Additional Notes*
2 *See Additional Notes*
3 answered and] *–Eth* | seven . . . it] in humanity A C E S | my glory] *Eth* glory | *See Additional Notes*
4 the sign. . . me] *Eth* and my cross will go before me {with me A}

17.1 Lord] + Lord K | years] ages G | will . . . be] *–Eth*
2 When . . . completed] *Cop* When the hundredth part and the twentieth part are completed, *Eth* When the hundred and fiftieth year is completed, *Lat* . . . year being completed | between. . . Bread] *Eth* between {at the time of B E L S} Pentecost and Pascha | *Eth Lat* my Father] *Cop* the Father | *See Additional Notes*
3 to him] *Eth, Lat* + Lord | Just now] –S | will come²] –A C E K
5–8 Then we said. . . is in me] *–Cop* | *See Additional Notes* on 17.4, 8a.

7 And we said to him, 'Lord, is it possible that you should be both here and there?'

8 And he said to us, 'I am wholly in the Father and the Father is in me, by likeness of form [ΜΟΡΦΗ] and power and fullness and light and the full measure and the voice.

18.1 'I am the Word [ΛΟΓΟΣ], I became a reality to him – that is, [I am the thou]ght fulfilled in the type [ΤΥΠΟΣ], 2 I came into being on the eighth day, which is the Lord's Day [ΚΥΡΙΑΚΗ]. 3 And [ΔΕ] the fulfilment of all fulfilment you will see through the redemption which has come to pass in me. 4 And you will see me go to heaven to my Father who is in heaven. 5 But [ΑΛΛΑ] behold, I give you a new commandment [ΕΝΤΟΛΗ]: love one another, and <**ETH**> that there may be continual peace among you. 6 Love your enemies, and what you do not wish them to do to you, do not do to another, or that one to you.

19.1 'Preach and teach those who believe in me, and preach about the kingdom of my Father. 2 And as he has given me authority, I have given it to you so that you may bring his children near to my heavenly Father. 3 Preach and they will believe, you who are to bring the children to the kingdom of heaven.'

4 And we said, 'Lord, it is possible for you to do what you have told us, but how is it possible for us?'

5 And he said to us, 'Truly I say to you, preach and proclaim, as I will be with you. For I am pleased to be with you; you will be heirs

8 by . . . voice] *Eth* that is, {from G} his likeness and from his form and from his power and from his fullness and from his <perfect S> light

18.1–2 I am. . . Lord's Day] *Eth* And I am {from A C E K} his perfect Word, that is, when he was crucified and died and rose, as {this G} he said, and the work that was accomplished in flesh, when he was crucified {killed E G K}, and his {the E K} ascension | *See Additional Notes*

3 And. . . see] *Eth* And this is the fulfilment of the number, and wonders and his {their E G K S} likeness and all fulfilment you will see in me | *See Additional Notes*

4 you. . . me] *Eth* when I | my Father] *Eth* the Father

5 love] that you love A S | one another *Cop* A G S] *(Eth)* + and obey one another

6 to you¹] –K

19.1 Preach E G K] And preach *(Eth)* | me] my name S | about] –C | kingdom] + of heaven L S

2 he] my Father L | I. . . to you C] –*(Eth)* | bring. . . to E G K S] bring near the children of *(Eth)*

3 the children] his children, –C | the kingdom of G] –*(Eth)*

4 for . . . do] that we should do G | told] reminded C

5 heirs] my heirs K

of the heavenly kingdom of the one who sent me. 6 Truly I say to you, you will be brothers and companions, for my Father is pleased with you and with those who believe in me through you. 7 Truly I say to you, such and so great a joy has my Father prepared, which angels and authorities longed to behold,* and it will not be permitted them.'

8 And we said to him, 'Lord, what is this that you are saying?'

9 And <COP> ([κλ] XI) he said to us, 'You will surely [ΓλΡ] see a light from shining light, the perfect perfected i[n the perfe]ct. (10 And the Son will be perfected by the Father, the light – for the Father who perfects is perfect... death and resurrection, and the perfection will surpass perfection.) 11 I am wholly the right hand of the Father, in the one who is the fullness.'

12 And [Δε] we said to him, 'Lord, in everything you have become to us salvation and life, proclaiming such a hope to us!'

13 And he said to us, 'Have confidence and be content! 14 Truly [ϩλΜΗΝ] I say to you, such will be your rest [λΝλπλΥCIC], where there is [ΓλΡ] no eating or [ΟΥΤε] drinking and no anxiety or grief and no corruption for those who are above. 15 For [ΓλΡ] you will participate [ΚΟΙΝΩΝεΙ] not in the lower creation but in that which is incorruptible, that of my Father; you yourselves will be incorruptible. 16 As I am always in him, so are ([κΒ] XII) you in me.'

The Resurrection of the Flesh

17 And again [πλΛΙΝ] we said to him. 'In what form? That of [ειΤε] angels or [λΓΓεΛΟC Η] flesh?'

---

6 and with... believe] –C, and with those A | through you] –K S

7 has... prepared] has God <my Father> prepared K <for you S> | which... longed A] + and long B G L, which you longed and angels and archangels long S, who sent me and angels and authorities are sent C | behold*] *Eth* + and see | and... them A] –C, they saw B, + to see the greatness of my Father *(Eth)* | *See Additional Notes*

8 saying E G K] + to us *(Eth)*

9 us] them G | perfect ... perfect] *Eth* and the perfect from {of B E G K} the perfect

10 And the Son... surpass perfection] –*Cop* | death] the Father K | *See Additional Notes*

11 is the fullness] *Eth* fulfils | *See Additional Notes*

12 And ... him] *Eth* And we the twelve {The twelve and we E K} said to him | proclaiming ... us] such a hope is proclaimed to us K

13 content] *Eth* steadfast

14 grief] *Eth* + and no earthly clothing | for... above] –*Eth* | *See Additional Notes*

16 in him] *Eth* in my Father

18 And he answered and said to us, 'Behold, I have put on your flesh [ⲥⲁⲣⲍ], in which I was born and in which I was crucified [ⲥⲧⲁⲩⲣⲟⲩ] and raised by my heavenly Father, 19 that the prophecy [ⲡⲣⲟⲫⲏⲧⲓⲁ] of David the prophet [ⲡⲣⲟⲏⲧⲏⲥ] might be fulfilled, concerning what was proclaimed about me and my death and my resurrection [ⲁⲛⲁⲥⲧⲁⲥⲓⲥ], say[ing]:

20 "Lord, many are those who afflict me, and many have risen against me!

21 "Many there are who say of my soul [ⲯⲩⲭⲏ], 'There is no salvation for you with God.'

22 "But you, Lord, are my support, my glory and the lifter of my head.

23 "With my voice I cried to (ⲕⲅ **XIII**) the Lord, and he heard me.

24 "I lay down and slept, I was raised, for you, Lord, are my support.

25 "I will not be afraid of tens of thousands of people [ⲗⲁⲟⲥ] who oppose me round about.

26 "Rise, Lord, save me, my God, for you have struck all those who are my enemies without cause, the teeth of sinners you have broken.

27 "Salvation is the Lord's, and his love is upon his people [ⲗⲁⲟⲥ]."

28 'And [ⲇⲉ] if all the words spoken by the prophets [ⲡⲣⲟⲫⲏⲧⲏⲥ] are fulfilled in me – for [ⲅⲁⲣ] I was in them – then how much more [ⲡⲟⲥⲱ ⲙⲁⲗⲗⲟⲛ] what I say to you! 29 Truly [ⲟⲛⲧⲱⲥ] what I say to you will come to pass, so that the one who sent me will be glorified by you and by those who believe [ⲡⲓⲥⲧⲉⲩⲉ] in me!'

---

18 answered] *Eth* + us on this matter | and said to us] –G K | Behold] *–Eth* | crucified] *Eth* put to death and buried

19 the prophecy of] *Eth* what was said by | what... me and] *–Eth* | death] + and what was done E K | saying] *–Eth*

20–27 *See Additional Notes*

20 many[1]] *Eth* how many

21 my soul] + Your God will not save you, and S | for... God] *Eth* of his God

23 me] *Eth* + from the mountain of his sanctuary

24 I was raised] *Cop* I rose | for ... support] *Eth* for God raised me

25 who... about] *Eth* who surrounded me and rose against me

26 Rise... my God] *Eth* Rise, Lord my God, and save me | struck] destroyed C E G all those] all of them and destroyed those S

27 and ... people] *Eth* and upon your people be your blessing

28 And if... fulfilled] *Eth* All therefore that was said by the prophets was accomplished and came to pass {was spoken and accomplished A} and was fulfilled | I was] *Eth* I spoke | say to you] *Eth* made known to you, made known S

29 what... you[1]] *Eth* it | by you] by me L

20.1 And [ⲇⲉ] when he had said these things to us, we said to him, 'Lord, in everything you (ⲕⲁ **XIV**) have been merciful to us and you have saved us and you have revealed everything to us. 2 Once again [ⲉⲧⲓ] we wish to inquire of you, if you permit us.'

3 He answered and said to us, 'I know indeed [ⲅⲁⲣ] that you will bear it and that your heart is pleased to hear me. 4 So [ⲇⲉ] ask about what you wish, and I will gladly [ⲕⲁⲗⲱⲥ] speak with you.

21.1 'Truly [ⲅⲁⲙⲏⲛ ⲅⲁⲣ] I say to you, as my Father raised me from the dead, so you too will rise and they will take you up above the heavens to the place of which I spoke to you in the beginning, to the place prepared for you by the one who sent me. 2 And thus will I fulfil every dispensation [ⲟⲓⲕⲟⲛⲟⲙⲓⲁ], being unborn yet born among humans, without flesh [ⲥⲁⲣⲝ] yet I have borne flesh [ⲫⲟⲣⲉⲓ, ⲥⲁⲣⲝ]. 3 For this is why I came, so that you <**ETH**> who were born in flesh* might be raised in your flesh as in a second birth, a garment that will not perish, with all who hope and believe in the one who sent me. 4 For so it has pleased my Father, that to you and to those whom I will I should give life, the hope of the kingdom.'

5 And then we said to him, 'Great is the hope you give, of which you speak!'

6 He answered and said to us, 'Do you believe* that everything I say to you will come to pass?'

7 And we answered him and said to him, 'Yes, Lord!'

8 And he said to us, 'Truly I say to you that I have received all authority from my Father so that those *in darkness I* may turn to light and those in corruption to incorruption and those in error to truth and those in death to life, and that those in prison should be

20.2 Once again] *Eth* One more thing | if] so that K

3 that you... me] *Eth* that you will bear witness {will be thirsty G} and long to hear
4 wish] *Eth* + behold {–S}, you will ask me and remember <his testimony B K S, Hear E L>

21.1 my Father] *Eth* the Father | rise... they] *Eth* be raised <from the dead B K> in the flesh and he {they E K} | for you] –*Eth* | *See Additional Notes*
2 will... dispensation] *Eth* have I fulfilled every {–A} mercy | borne flesh] *Eth* + and grew up
3 For... came] –*Eth* | in flesh*] *Eth* + <and B L> the resurrection | be raised] rise A C E
4 give] + you G | life] –L S
6 Do you believe*] *Eth* Believe | *See Additional Notes*
6–8 believe that ... received] Believe that I have received S
8 See *Additional Notes*

released. 9 For what is impossible for humans is possible for the Father. 10 I am the hope of the despairing, and the helper of those who have no helper, the wealth of the needy, the physician of the sick, the resurrection of the dead.'

22.1 And when he said this to us, we said to him, 'Lord, is the *flesh* [ⲥⲁⲣⲝ] really to be judged with the soul and the spirit? 2 And will some [ⲙⲉⲛ] find rest in the kingdom of heaven *and others* [ⲇⲉ] be condemned for ever *while liv[ing]*?'

3 *And* [ⲇⲉ] *he said* <**COP**> (ⲕⲍ **XVII**) to us, 'How long will you question and seek?'

23.1 Again [ⲡⲁⲗⲓⲛ] we said to him, 'Lord, it is necessary [ⲁⲛⲁⲅⲕⲏ ⲅⲁⲣ] for us to question you, for you command us to preach; 2 so that we ourselves may know with certainty through you and be useful preachers, and [that] those who will teach through us may believe [ⲡⲓⲥⲧⲉⲩⲉ] in you. 3 That is why we question you so much!'

24.1 He answered us, saying, 'Truly [ϩⲁⲙⲏⲛ] I say to you that the resurrection [ⲁⲛⲁⲥⲧⲁⲥⲓⲥ] of the flesh [ⲥⲁⲣⲝ] will occur with the soul [ⲯⲩⲭⲏ] and spirit [ⲡⲛⲁ] within it.'

2 And we said to him, 'Lord, is it [ⲙⲏ] possible for what is dissolved and destroyed to be saved? 3 Not that as [ⲟⲩ, ⲱⲥ] unbelieving [ⲁⲡⲓⲥⲧⲟⲥ] do we ask you, or [ⲏ] as if it were impossible for you, but [ⲁⲗⲗⲁ] we truly believe [ⲟⲛⲧⲱⲥ, ⲡⲓⲥⲧⲉⲩⲉ] that what you say (ⲕⲏ **XVIII**) will come to pass.'

4 And he was angry with us, saying to us, 'O [ⲱ] you of little faith [-ⲡⲓⲥⲧⲓⲥ], how long will you question? But [ⲁⲗⲗⲁ] what you wish, say

9 the Father] God A
10 the helper... helper] their helper a helper K | the needy] the poor A C | the physician (keeper of medicine)] the medicine S

22.1 Lord] –C | with the soul] our soul, the soul K
2 some] *Eth* it | others] *Eth* part | *See Additional Notes*
3 How long] Why A

23.1 to preach] *Eth* + and proclaim and teach {and be taught K}
1–2 *See Additional Notes*
2 *Cop* we... preachers] *Eth* so that having heard with certainty {in truth G} from you we may be good {and K} preachers | those... us] *Eth* we may teach them so that they
3 so much] –*Eth*

24.1 the flesh... it] *Eth* the flesh of every man will be raised with his <living B C L > soul and <his G> spirit
2 dissolved and destroyed *Cop* E G K] destroyed and dissolved *(Eth)*
3 do... you[1]] –E, and that we ask you K, or belittle S | or... for you *Cop* E] –*(Eth)* | say] *Eth* + has come to pass and
4 will[1] ... unreservedly] *Eth* will you disbelieve {–A B}? You ask me and inquire, unreservedly you wish to hear {and unreservedly you hear K}

to me, and I will tell you unreservedly [-ⲫⲑⲟⲛⲉⲓ. 5 Only [ⲙⲟⲛⲟⲛ] keep my commandments [ⲉⲛⲧⲟⲗⲏ] and do what I tell you, and do not turn your face from anyone so that I would turn my face from you. 6 But [ⲁⲗⲗⲁ] without delay or shame or partiality, serve [ⲇⲓⲁⲕⲟⲛⲉⲓ] in the way that is straight and narrow and difficult. 7 This is the way of my Father himself, and he will rejoice over you.'

25.1 Again [ⲡⲁⲗⲓⲛ] we said to him, 'Lord, ([ⲕⲑ] **XIX**) we are now [ⲏⲇⲏ ⲅⲁⲣ] ashamed that we are questioning you so much and are wearying [ⲃⲁⲣⲉⲓ] you.'

2 Then [ⲧⲟⲧⲉ] he answered and said to us, 'I indeed [ⲅⲁⲣ] know that in faith [ⲡⲓⲥⲧⲓⲥ] and with your whole heart you ask of me – therefore I rejoice over you! 3 Truly [ϩⲁⲙⲏⲛ ⲅⲁⲣ] I say to you, I am glad, and my Father who is in me, that you ask me, for your shamelessness brings me joy and gives you life.'

4 And [ⲇⲉ] when he said this to us, we were glad that we were questioning him. 5 And we said to him again, 'Lord,* in everything you grant us life and show us mercy. For you will tell us what we ask!'

6 Then [ⲧⲟⲧⲉ] he said to us, 'Which is it that perishes, the flesh [ⲥⲁⲣⲝ] or the spirit?'

7 We said to him, 'It is the flesh [ⲥⲁⲣⲝ] that perishes!'

8 ([ⲗ] **XX**) Then [ⲧⲟⲧⲉ] he said to us, 'Indeed [ⲁⲣⲁ], what has fallen will rise and what is lost will be found and what is weak will recover, so that in this the glory of my Father may be revealed. 9 As he has done to me, so I will do to all of you who believe [ⲡⲓⲥⲧⲉⲩⲉ].

5 Only] –*Eth* | and do not... from you] –*Eth*

6 delay... partiality] delay or shame A, delay or partiality B C G | straight and narrow] *Eth* narrow and straight | *See Additional Notes*

7 This... you] *Eth* And thus the Father <he E> will rejoice over you in everything

25.1 we are now... wearying you] *Eth* behold, with so many questions we are talking foolishly to you | *See Additional Notes*

2 answered and] –*Eth* | you ... therefore] –S | therefore] *Eth* and {–E S}

3 I[2...] in me] *Eth* my Father is glad and rejoices in me | that you ask me] *Eth* that you inquire and ask like this | brings me joy] is proper for us G

4 that... him] –C E G K, that he spoke to us graciously *(Eth)*

5 again, Lord*] again, our Lord A B G L, our Lord <again S> C E K | you grant... mercy] *Eth* you show us mercy and grant us life | what] *Eth* everything that

6 *Eth* which ... spirit] *Cop* Does the flesh perish that is in the Spirit? | *See Additional Notes*

7 It ... perishes] The flesh that has fallen will be raised G, The flesh! *(Eth)*

8 Then ... Indeed] –G | and... found] –*Eth*, And he said to us G | the glory ... revealed] *Eth* my Father may be glorified

9 all... believe] you and to all you <those L> who believe in me

26.1 'Truly [ẑⲀⲘⲎⲚ Ⲇⲉ] I say to you that the flesh [ⲤⲀⲢⲌ] will rise with the soul [ⲮⲨⲬⲎ] alive, so that they may be judged [ⲀⲠⲟⲖⲟⲅⲓⲀ] on that day for what they have done, whether [ⲉⲓⲧⲉ] good or [ⲉⲓⲧⲉ] evil, 2 so that there may be a selection [ⲉⲕⲖⲟⲅⲎ] of believers [ⲠⲓⲤⲧⲟⲤ] who have performed the commandments [ⲉⲚⲧⲟⲖⲎ] of my Father who sent me. 3 Thus the judgement [ⲔⲢⲓⲤⲓⲤ] will take place in severity. 4 For [ⲅⲀⲢ] my Father said to me, "My Son, ([ⲖⲀ] **XXI**) on the day of judgement [ⲔⲢⲓⲤⲓⲤ] you shall neither [ⲟⲨⲧⲉ] be ashamed before the rich nor [ⲟⲨⲧⲉ] pity the poor, but according to [ⲀⲖⲖⲀ ⲔⲀⲧⲀ] the sin of each you shall deliver [ⲠⲀⲢⲀⲆⲓⲆⲟⲨ] them to eternal punishment [ⲔⲟⲖⲀⲤⲓⲤ]." 5 But [Ⲇⲉ] to my beloved, who have performed the commandments [ⲉⲚⲧⲟⲖⲎ] of my Father who sent me, I will give rest [ⲀⲚⲀⲠⲀⲨⲤⲓⲤ] of life in the kingdom of my Father in heaven. 6 And they will see what he has granted [ⲬⲀⲢⲓⲌⲉ] me: he has given me authority [ⲉⲌⲟⲨⲤⲓⲀ] to do as I will, and to give what I promised and what I willed to give them and grant them.'

The Descent into Hell

27.1 'For [ⲅⲀⲢ] this is why I descended to the place of Lazarus and preached to your fathers and the prophets [ⲠⲢⲟⲫⲎⲧⲎⲤ] that they would go forth from the rest [ⲀⲚⲀⲠⲀⲨⲤⲓⲤ] below and ascend to that which is in heaven. 2 ([ⲖⲂ] **XXII**) And with my right hand I poured* over them the baptism of life and forgiveness and deliverance from all evil, as I have done for you and for those who believe in me. 3 But

26.1 the soul] its soul S | be... done] *Eth* confess and that the works they did may be judged in righteousness | *See Additional Notes*

2 selection] *Eth* + and manifestation

3 Thus... severity.] *Eth* Then the righteous judgement will take place.

4 For my Father] *Eth* For thus my Father wills, and he

5 my beloved] *Eth* those who loved me <and will love me B E G L> | the commandments... me] *Eth* <my will and K> my commandments <and my will S> | of life... kingdom] *Eth* in <eternal C> life {–S} in the <heavenly C> kingdom <in life S>

6 And they... grant them] *Eth* Behold, see what authority he has granted me, and he has given me what I will and what I willed for those to whom I promised | *See Additional Notes*

27.1 to... Lazarus] *–Eth* | and preached... prophets] *Eth* to <and conversed with B L S> Abraham, Isaac, and Jacob, and your fathers <and E K> the prophets {–G}, and announced {granted A} to them | and ascend] *–Eth* | *See Additional Notes*

2 And... life] *Cop*... right [ha]nd over them... of life, *Eth* And I gave them the right hand, the baptism of life | and forgiveness... all evil] and all forgiveness and deliverance from evil G | for you and] *Eth* + from now on | *See Additional Notes*

3 in me *Cop* L] *–(Eth)* | has... course] they have run their course E

[ⲇⲉ] if anyone believes [ⲡⲓⲥⲧⲉⲩⲉ] in me and does not do my commandments [ⲉⲛⲧⲟⲗⲏ] after confessing [ϩⲟⲙⲟⲗⲟⲅⲉⲓ] my name, he receives no benefit [ⲱⲫⲉⲗⲉⲓ] at all and has run his course in vain. 4 For [ⲅⲁⲣ] such people will incur loss and punishment, because they have transgressed [ⲡⲁⲣⲁⲛⲟⲙⲉⲓ] my commandments [ⲉⲛⲧⲟⲗⲏ].

28.1 'But I have granted you to be children of life, I have delivered [you] from all evil [ⲕⲁⲕⲟⲛ] and from the power of the rulers [ⲁⲣⲭⲱⲛ], with everyone who believes in me through you. 2 For what I have promised you I shall also give them, so that they may come forth from the prison and chains of the rulers [ⲁⲣⲭⲱⲛ] ([ⲗⲅ] **XXIII**) and the terrible fire.'

3 We [answered and] said to him, 'Lord, you have surely [ⲅⲁⲣ] given us rest [of life] and you have given us joy with signs to [confirm] faith [ⲡⲓⲥⲧⲓⲥ]. Will you now preach to us what you preached to our fathers and the prophets [ⲡⲣⲟⲫⲏⲧⲏⲥ]?'

4 Then he said to us, 'Truly [ϩⲁⲙⲏⲛ ⲅⲁⲣ] I say to you, everyone who believes [ⲡⲓⲥⲧⲉⲩⲉ] in me and who believes [ⲡⲓⲥⲧⲉⲩⲉ] in the one who sent me I will lead up to heaven, the place which my Father prepared for the elect. 5 And I will give you the kingdom that is chosen in rest [ⲁⲛⲁⲡⲁⲩⲥⲓⲥ] and eternal life.'

Other Teachings

29.1 'But [ⲇⲉ] those who transgress [ⲡⲁⲣⲁⲛⲟⲙⲉⲓ] my commandments [ⲉⲛⲧⲟⲗⲏ] and teach teachings other [than] what is written, and who add to th[em] and establish ([ⲗⲇ] **XXIV**) their own glory,

4 such… incur] –S, his end is *(Eth)* | punishment… transgressed] *Eth* punishment of great torment because he has {they have E K} transgressed

28.1 life] God A B E G, light and children of God C, light in God L S | I have delivered you] *Eth* and to be cleansed | the power… you] *Eth* all the power of condemnation, and to you who believe in me, likewise I shall do for them

2 For… rulers] *Eth* And I have told you and promised you that he will come forth from prison and be released from chains and condemnation

3 answered and] –*Eth* | you have surely… joy] *Eth* in everything you have given us joy and rest | with… faith] *Eth* for {–A} in faith and in truth | Will… prophets] *Eth* You have announced them to our fathers and the prophets, and likewise to us and to all {–A} | *See Additional Notes*

4 everyone… and who believes] *Eth* and all who believe and {–E} who are going to believe | to heaven] above the heavens E K {heaven G} | elect] + and for the elect of the elect B L

5 And… rest] *Eth* And he will give the rest that he promised

29.1 teachings… written] *Eth* other teachings | who] *Eth* + take away and | teaching… words] *Eth* they turn aside | if… punishment] –*Eth* | *See Additional Notes*

teaching with different words those who believe [ⲡⲓⲥⲧⲉⲩⲉ] in me rightly – if they fall away through such people, they will receive an eternal punishment [ⲕⲟⲗⲁⲥⲓⲥ].'

2 And we said [ⲇⲉ] to him, 'Lord, will there [ⲙⲏ] come teachings other than what you have told us?'

3 He said to us, 'It is indeed [ⲅⲁⲣ] necessary for them to come, so that [ⲓⲛⲁ] those who do evil and those who do good may be revealed.

4 And in this way the judgement [ⲕⲣⲓⲥⲓⲥ] will reveal those who do these works, and according to [ⲕⲁⲧⲁ] their works they will be judged and delivered [ⲡⲁⲣⲁⲇⲓⲇⲟⲩ] to death.'

Mission

5 Again [ⲡⲁⲗⲓⲛ] we said to him, 'Lord, blessed [ⲙⲁⲕⲁⲣⲓⲟⲥ] are we that we see you and hear you as you say such things, for our eyes have seen these ([ⲇⲉ] **XXV**) great signs that you have done.'

6 He answered and said to us, 'Blessed [ⲙⲁⲕⲁⲣⲓⲟⲥ ⲅⲁⲣ] rather are those who have not seen and yet believed [ⲡⲓⲥⲧⲉⲩⲉ], for such will be called sons of the kingdom, and they will be perfect [ⲧⲉⲗⲉⲓⲟⲥ] in the perfect one [ⲧⲉⲗⲉⲓⲟⲥ], and I will be life to them in the kingdom of my Father.'

7 Again [ⲡⲁⲗⲓⲛ] we said to him, 'Lord, how will they believe, when you are to go and leave us behind? For you say to us, "There comes a day and an hour when I shall ascend to my Father."'

30.1 And he said [ⲇⲉ] to us, 'Go and preach to the twelve tribes [ⲫⲩⲗⲏ] and preach also to the Gentiles [ⲉⲑⲛⲟⲥ] and to the whole land

---

2 teachings... us] *Eth* other teachings and sufferings

3 It... come] *–Eth* | so ... good] so that the good and {so that A E} those who do <peace and B K S> good and evil

4 And in... these works] *Eth* And then there will be a righteous judgement in their works | judged and] *–Eth*

5 Lord] *–L* | hear you] receive E

6 seen and yet believed] *Eth* seen me and yet believed <me B C L> | the kingdom[1]] heaven E, + of heaven B K, + and sons of God S | they will be] *–Eth* | life] *Eth* eternal life

7 will ... believe] *Eth* is it possible <Lord K S> to believe | go and] *–Eth* | to us] *– Eth* | There... Father] *Eth* that there comes a time and an hour when you will ascend to your Father

30.1 said] *Eth* answered and said | tribes] *Eth* + of Israel | and preach also... Gentiles *Cop* E G] *–S*, to the Gentiles and to Israel *(Eth)* | and... Israel] and to the land of Israel A C E G, and teach Israel {them K S} B L | believe *Cop* C] *(Eth)* + in me

of Israel [ⲓ̄ⲏ̄ⲗ̄] ([ⲗ̄ⲥ̄] **XXVI**) from east to west and from south to north, and many will believe [ⲡⲓⲥⲧⲉⲩⲉ] in the Son of God.'

2 We said [ⲇⲉ] to him, 'Lord, who will believe [ⲡⲓⲥⲧⲉⲩⲉ] us, or [ⲏ] who will listen to us or who will then teach the mighty works and signs you have done, and the wonders?'

3 Then [ⲧⲟⲧⲉ] he answered and said to us, 'Go and preach the mercy of my Father, and what he has done through me I will do through you, since I will be in you. 4 And I will give you my peace [ⲉⲓⲣⲏⲛⲏ] and by my Spirit [ⲡ̄ⲛ̄ⲁ̄] I will give you power, and you will prophesy [ⲡⲣⲟⲫⲏⲧⲉⲩⲉ] to them their eternal life. 5 And to others also I will give my power [ⲇⲩⲛⲁⲙⲓⲥ], and they will teach the rest of the Gentiles [ⲉⲑⲛⲟⲥ].'

Paul the Persecutor and Confessor

31.1 <**ETH**> 'And behold, you will meet a man whose name is Saul (which being interpreted is Paul), who is a Jew, circumcised by the commandment of the law, and he will hear my voice from heaven with astonishment and fear and trembling. 2 And he will be blinded, and by your hand shall his eyes be sealed with saliva. 3 And do everything for him that I have done for you, and pass him on to others. 4 And immediately this man's eyes shall be opened and he will praise God, my heavenly Father. 5 And he will be strong among the people, and he will preach and teach many, and they will be glad to hear him, and many will be saved. 6 And then they will hate him

---

2 believe us] believe you E | or who will then... wonders?] *Eth* and how can we do {tell G K} and teach and tell {–S, do E G K} as you have done, the wonders and signs and mighty works?

3 Then] *Eth* And | go and] –E | preach *Cop* E K] *(Eth)* + and teach about <the coming of G, the coming and B L S> | he] *Eth* my Father | I will do] + for you K | in you] *Eth* with you | *See Additional Notes*

4 by... life] *Eth* my Spirit and <love and C> power so that they may believe

5 And to others... Gentiles] *Eth* To them shall be given and bestowed this power so that they may give it <it may be given K> to the Gentiles | *See Additional Notes*

31.1 a Jew] of Judah C | from... fear] with astonishment and fear from heaven G

2 he] his eyes A L S | sealed with saliva] sealed in hope S, guarded L

3 for him... done] –K

4 this... opened] this man will open his eyes S

5 people] Gentiles K | many... him] and many will be glad when they hear them A B C L | many[2...] saved] they will be saved A B C L

6 they will hate him] he will be hated B | into the hand of] to B | his enemy] sinful men A, enemies B | confess] + me B | transitory kings] mortal and transitory kings A, victorious kings L, victorious and transitory kings E, transitory ones C

and deliver him into the hand of his enemy, and he will confess before transitory kings. 7 And the fulfilment of his confessing me will come upon him, so that instead of persecuting me and hating me he confesses me. 8 And he will preach and teach, and he will be with my elect an elect vessel and a wall that shall not fall. 9 The last of the last shall be a preacher to the Gentiles, perfected by the will of my Father. 10 As you have learnt from the scriptures that the prophets* spoke about me and in me it is truly fulfilled, so you must provide guidance in them. 11 And every word that I have spoken to you and that you write about me, that I am the Word of the Father and the Father is in me, you also must pass on* to that man, as is fitting for you. 12 Teach him and remind him what is said in the scriptures about me and is now fulfilled, and then he will be the salvation of the Gentiles.'

32.1 And we said to him, 'O Master, do we have one hope of inheritance with them?'

2 He answered and said to us, 'Are the fingers of the hand alike, or the ears of corn in the field? Or do fruit-bearing trees give the same fruit? Do they not bear fruit each according to its kind?'

3 And we said to him, 'Lord, you are again speaking with us in parables!'

4 And he said to us, 'Do not be troubled! Truly I say to you, you are my brothers, participants in my Father's kingdom, for so it pleased him. 5 Truly I say to you, to those whom you teach and they believe in me, I will give that hope.'

33.1 And we said to him again, 'Lord, when shall we meet that man? And when will you go to your Father and ours, our God and our Lord?'

2 And he answered and said to us, 'That man will go out from the land of Cilicia to Damascus in Syria in order to tear apart the church

---

7 upon him] upon me G | and²··· confesses me] –L

8 my elect] the elect L

10 the prophets*] *Eth* your fathers the prophets | about me] about you A | truly fulfilled G] fulfilled, <this E K> they spoke truly and it was fulfilled A E K, + and he said <to us B C L> S | *See Additional Notes*

11 you write B E K] I have written G, I have written to you A C L S | the Word of] the Word in B E, my Word in C | pass on*] *Eth* be | *See Additional Notes*

12 and remind him] –A

32.2 alike] forgiven S | according ... kind] its own cluster A K

4 my... kingdom] in the kingdom of the heavens with my Father L | for... him] –C

5 to those whom] when S

33.1 Lord] –L | our God... Lord] our God and our Saviour A C, our Lord and our Saviour G

2 go out] come A | tear apart C] hand over A E G K, turn away B, kill L

that you are to found. 3 It is I who will speak through you, and it will happen soon. 4 In this faith he will be strong, so that what the prophetic voice said might be fulfilled: 5 "Behold, from the land of Syria I will begin to call a new Jerusalem, and Zion I will subdue to myself and it will be captured." 6 And the barren one who has no children will have a child; and she will be called the daughter of my Father, and to me she will be my bride – for so it has pleased the one who sent me. 7 And that man I will turn aside so that he may not come and fulfil his evil intention, and his shall be the glory of my Father. 8 For when I have gone and am with my Father, I will speak with him from heaven. 9 And all that I have predicted to you about him will take place.'

The Time of Trial

34.1 And we said to him again, 'Lord, what great things you have spoken to us and announced to us and revealed to us, things never yet spoken, and in everything you have comforted us and been gracious to us! 2 For after your resurrection you revealed all this to us, so that we might truly be saved. 3 But you have told us only that there will be signs and wonders in heaven and on earth before the end of the world comes – so teach us, that we may know.'

4 And he said to us, 'I will teach you what will happen not only to you that this will happen but also those whom you teach and who believe, and those who hear this man and believe in me. 5 In those years and in those days it will happen.'

6 And we again said to him, 'Lord, what is it that will happen?'

3 it will happen B L S] I will come *(Eth)* | *See Additional Notes*
4 strong C] –*(Eth)*
4–5 *See Additional Notes*
5 from... of] after **B E K**
6 will... she] –E | called G] –*(Eth)*
7 he... intention] his evil intention may not come about G | come and] –A | his^2] there E G K
8 him] them G

34.1 and announced to us] –L
2 all this] –G
4 what ... believe^1] you will teach and they will believe, what will happen to you but also to those you K *(two lines transposed)* | and those ... believe] –A S | *See Additional Notes*
5 In... and] –B K S
6 And ... happen] And we said to him, What is it that will happen, Lord, again S

7 And he said to us, 'At that time believers and unbelievers will perceive the sound of a trumpet from heaven and the sight of great stars that appear during the day, 8 and a sign from heaven that reaches the earth, and stars falling like fire, and great hailstones like raging fire, 9 and sun and moon fighting together, and constant terror of thunder and lightning and thunderbolt and an earthquake following, 10 and cities shall fall and people shall die in their ruins, and there will be constant drought from lack of rain, and a great plague and widespread death and many trials, so that funerals will cease for one who dies. 11 And the passing of child and parent will be on a single bed, and the parent will not turn to the child nor the child to the parent, and one person will not turn to another. 12 And those who are bereaved will rise up and see those who had departed from them being carried out. 13 For there will be a plague everywhere, hatred and suffering and jealousy, and they will take from one and give to another. 14 And what follows will be worse than this.

35.1 'And then my Father will be angry because of human evil, for many are their transgressions and the abomination of their uncleanness is greatly against them in the corruption of their life.'

The Fate of the Elect

2 And we said to him, 'Lord, what then of those who hope in you?'
3 And he answered and said to us, 'How long are you still slow of heart? 4 Truly I say to you, as the prophet David spoke about me and about those who are mine, so likewise he [God] wills for those who believe in me. 5 And there will be in the world deceivers and enemies of righteousness, and there shall come to pass David's prophecy about them which says:

7 from] in L | sight ... stars] great sight of stars G S
7–8 that ... stars] –E
8 sign B L] dragon A C G K S | like] – K | like... fire] –A C
9 and thunderbolts... earthquake] –A | following] –L S
10 widespread... trials] *See Additional Notes*
11 will be] + despairing A | to the child] –B L | nor... parent] –A
12 *See Additional Notes*
13 jealousy B L S] + and murder *(Eth)*

35.2 Lord] –L
4 about me E G K] about them A B C, about you L S | wills for] + them and for K | those who... me] you <and those S> who believe in me K L S, + and who are in me K
5 enemies B C G] slanderers A L

6 "Swift are their feet to shed blood, and their tongue weaves deceit, and the venom of snakes is under their lips.

7 "And I see you as you go about with a thief, and with an adulterer is your portion.

8 "And while you sit you slander your brother and set a stumbling-block for your mother's son. What do you think, that I am like you?"

9 'And behold, see how the prophet spoke about everything, so that everything may be fulfilled that was said before.'

36.1 And we said to him again, 'Lord, will the Gentiles not say, "Where is their God?"'

2 And he answered and said to us, 'By this the elect will be made known, that they depart after enduring such torment.'

3 And we said to him, 'Will their departure from the world be through the plague that torments them?'

4 And he said to us, 'No, but when they are tormented such an affliction will be to test them. 5 If there is faith within them and if they remember these words of mine and obey my commandments, they will be raised. 6 And their situation will be for a few days, so that the one who sent me may be glorified and I with him, for he sent me to you. 7 This I tell you, and you must tell it to Israel and to the Gentiles, that they may hear and be saved and believe in me and depart out of the affliction of the plague. 8 And whoever survives the affliction of death will be taken and kept in prison, punished like a thief.'

9 And we said to him, 'Lord, will they be like those who do not believe? And will you punish those who survive the plague in the same way?'

---

6 deceit] arrogance A | on] under A L S
6–8 See *Additional Notes*.
7 go about] pursue L S | with a thief] as a thief B | is] you bring E, you set K S
9 prophet] + David B K S, + of God L

36.2 the elect] my elect A
3 their] the G | departure from] coming out of A C
4 when they] as for those who E | them A G] him B C L
4–5 See *Additional Notes*
5 be raised] rise A
6–7a *See Additional Notes*
7 in me] –A B C
7b–8 *See Additional Notes*
9 And will … plague] Will those who come out of the plague similarly be punished? A | survive] + the torment of C

10 And he said to us, 'If they believe in my name but acted as sinners, they have behaved like unbelievers.'

11 And we said to him again, 'Lord, so this is the fate of those who survive, that they fail to attain life?'

12 And he answered and said to us, 'Whoever glorifies my Father will dwell* with my Father.'

37.1 And we said to him, 'Lord, teach us what will happen after this.'

2 And he said to us, '*In th*ose years and *days* there will be war upon war, and the four corners of the world will be shaken and will *war* [ⲡⲟⲗⲉⲙⲟⲥ] on one another. 3 And then, a tumult of clouds, darkness, drought, and persecution of those who believe in me and of the elect! 4 And then, dissension, strife, and evil conduct among them, and there are some of those who believe in my name but follow evil and teach *vain* teaching. 5 And people will follow them and obey their wealth, their wickedness, their drunkenness, and their bribery; and there will be *partiality* among them.

38.1 '*And* [ⲇⲉ] those who de*sire* to see the face of God, and *who do* not show partiality to rich *sinne*rs, and who are not ashamed before the men who go astray but rebuke them, these will be crowned* in the presence of the Father. 2 So too those who rebuke *their neighbour* will be saved. This is a son *of wisdom* [ⲥⲟⲫⲓⲁ] and faith. 3 But [ⲇⲉ] *if* he is not *a son* of wisdom *he will hate* and persecute and not turn to <COP> (ⲛⲁ **XXVII**) his neighbour but will despise and reject him. 4 Those who conduct themselves [ⲡⲟⲗⲓⲧⲉⲩⲉⲥⲑⲁⲓ] in truth and in the knowledge of faith [ⲡⲓⲥⲧⲓⲥ] having love [ⲁⲅⲁⲡⲏ] for me endured [ⲩⲡⲟⲙⲉⲓⲛⲉ ⲅⲁⲣ] abuse [ⲩⲃⲣⲓⲥ]; and they will be despised as they walk

---

11 And ... Lord] And the Lord said to us again C | *See Additional Notes*

12 answered and] –A | will dwell* with] *Eth* is the dwelling-place of {with A C E G K} | *See Additional Notes*

37.1 Lord] –B C E | what... happen] –A, what E G

37.2–38.4 Italics = words wholly or partly attested in *Cop* fragments.

2 years and days] years of days G | world] earth A

3 clouds] *Cop* air | darkness] trembling A, falling G, great falling C, continual E K | the elect] my elect G

4 conduct] deeds L, deeds and conduct S

5 wickedness] rites A C

38.1 God] + the Father E G K | go astray] lead them astray L | but] who B C K | crowned*] *Eth* <with E> the wounded | in... Father] –E | *See Additional Notes*

3 neighbour] *Eth* brother | but will] + not K | him] them E

4 faith] *Eth* + in me | having... abuse] *Eth* having knowledge of wisdom {wisdom of knowledge E G} and endurance for righteousness' sake | as... in] *Eth* who pursue | those... hate them] *Eth* great is their reward | torment them] *Eth* + and persecute them

in poverty and endure [ϒⲡⲟⲙⲓⲛⲉ] those who hate them, who mock them and torment them; 5 destitute, since men were arrogant against them as they walk in hunger and thirst. 6 Yet because [ⲁⲗⲗⲁ ⲉⲡⲉⲓ] they have endured [ϒⲡⲟⲙⲉⲓⲛⲉ] for the blessedness [-ⲙⲁⲕⲁⲣⲓⲟⲥ] of heaven, they will be with me for ever. 7 But woe [ⲟϒⲁⲓ ⲇⲉ] to those who walk in arrogance and boasting! For their end (ⲛⲃ **XXVIII**) is perdition.'

Divine Justice

39.1 And [ⲇⲉ] we said to him, 'Lord, it is in your power not to allow these things* to befall them!'

2 He answered and said to us, 'How will the judgement [ⲕⲣⲓⲥⲓⲥ] take place for either the righteous [ⲏ ⲇⲓⲕⲁⲓⲟⲥ] or the unrighteous [ⲏ ⲁⲇⲓⲕⲟⲥ]?'

3 And [ⲇⲉ] we said to him, 'Lord, in that [ⲅⲁⲣ] day they will say to you, "You did not separate righteousness [ⲇⲓⲕⲁⲓⲟⲥϒⲛⲏ] and unrighteousness [ⲁⲇⲓⲕⲓⲁ], light and darkness, evil [ⲕⲁⲕⲟⲛ] and good [ⲁⲅⲁⲑⲟⲛ]!"'

4 Then [ⲧⲟⲧⲉ] he said, 'I will answer them, saying: "Adam was given the power [ⲉⲍⲟϒⲥⲓⲁ] to choose one of the two. 5 And [ⲇⲉ] he chose the light and stretched out his hand for it, but [ⲇⲉ] the darkness he rejected and cast it from him. 6 So all people have the power [ⲉⲍⲟϒⲥⲓⲁ] to (ⲛⲅ **XXIX**) believe [ⲡⲓⲥⲧⲉϒⲉ] in the light, which is the life of the Father who sent me." 7 Everyone who believes and does the

5 men] *Eth* they | as... in] *Eth* when they
6 for... heaven] *Eth* they will be blessed {–A C} in <the kingdom of S> heaven
7 who... boasting] *Eth* who {for they E} hate them and despise them

39.1 to him] + again A | it is... them] *Eth* (–A) Will this befall all of {–E G K} them? | *See Additional Notes*
1–2 it is... unrighteous] Will the righteous judgement befall the unrighteous and the righteous? A
2 answered and] –*Eth* | How... unrighteous] *Eth* (–A) How will the righteous judgement take place for sinners and the righteous?
3 Lord] – B L | they ... you] *Eth* will they not say to you {will you not say L} | did... unrighteousness] *Eth* showed righteousness and sin | light and darkness] *Eth* and you separated {created L} darkness and light {light from darkness G} | *See Additional Notes*
4 Then... saying] *Eth* Then he said to us | Adam] He K | to choose... two] *Eth* to choose which of the two {them L S} he wanted
5 hand] *Eth* hands | for it] –A, and took B C E L | and cast... him] and fell from it A, and kept away from it *(Eth)*
6 the life of] –A | of] *Cop* and which is
7 believes] *Eth* + in me | through them] –*Eth*

works of light will live through them. 8 But [Ⲇⲉ] if there is someone who confesses [ⲅⲟⲙⲟⲗⲟⲅⲉⲓ] that he belongs to the light while doing the works of darkness, such a person has no defence [ⲁⲡⲟⲗⲟⲅⲓⲁ], nor [ⲟⲩⲧⲉ] will he lift up his face to look at the Son of God, which is I myself. 9 For [ⲅⲁⲣ] I shall say to him, "As you sought you have found, and as you asked [ⲁⲓⲧⲉⲓ] you have received! 10 Why did you condemn [ⲕⲁⲧⲁⲅⲓⲛⲱⲥⲕⲉ] me, O [ⲱ] man? Why did you proclaim me and deny [ⲁⲣⲛⲁ] me? And why did you confess [ⲅⲟⲙⲟⲗⲟⲅⲉⲓ] me and deny [ⲁⲣⲛⲁ] me?" 11 Therefore [ⲁⲣⲁ ⲟⲩⲛ] every person has the power [ⲉⲝⲟⲩⲥⲓⲁ] to live or to die, and so the one who keeps (ⲛⲁ **XXX**) my commandments [ⲉⲛⲧⲟⲗⲏ] will become a son of light, that is, of the Father who is within me. 12 And [Ⲇⲉ] because of those who corrupt my words I have come down from heaven, I the Word [ⲗⲟⲅⲟⲥ] who became flesh [ⲥⲁⲣⲝ] and suffered, 13 teaching that these who are called will be saved and that those who are lost will be lost eternally and tormented alive and punished [ⲕⲟⲗⲁⲍⲉ] in their flesh [ⲥⲁⲣⲝ] and their soul [ⲯⲩⲭⲏ].'

40.1 And [Ⲇⲉ] we said to him, 'Lord, truly we are concerned for them!'

2 And [Ⲇⲉ] he said to us, 'You do well [ⲕⲁⲗⲱⲥ ⲅⲁⲣ] for the righteous [Ⲇⲓⲕⲁⲓⲟⲥ ⲅⲁⲣ] are concerned for sinners and pray for them, interceding with my Father.'

3 Again [ⲡⲁⲗⲓⲛ] we said to him, 'Lord, so does no one intercede with you yourself?'

---

8 confesses] does not confess B E L S | while doing] and remains in B L S | the Son of God] *Eth* the Son

9 received] + the kingdom G

10 Why... me *Cop* G] Why did you reject me {–S, us A C} E K, What did you not receive B L | O man] –*Eth* | Why... deny me[1]] *Eth* Why did you depart from <me and from A> my {the E G K} kingdom? | And why... deny me[2]] *Eth* You confessed me and denied me

11 Therefore] *Eth* Behold, see how | or to die] and to believe {–K} B L S | keeps] *Eth* does and keeps | who... me] –A L

12 And... words] *Eth* And for those who keep and do {–A C} my {the E} commandments {–L}, and because of this | suffered] *Eth* died

13 teaching] *Eth* + and warning | who... called] who are saved G, –*(Eth)* | who are lost *Cop* E G] –*(Eth)* | and tormented alive] –*Eth* | in... soul] *Eth* with fire in flesh and spirit

40.1 Lord] –A, + and we said K

1–2 *See Additional Notes*

2 for them] –*Eth* | my Father] *Eth* God the Father {–B K L S} and beseeching him <and the Father K>

3 Again] *Eth* And | Lord... yourself] –Lord B, *Cop* Lord, why then is no one ashamed before you? | *See Additional Notes*

4 And [ⲇⲉ] he said (ⲛⲉ **XXXI**) to us, 'Yes, and I will hear the prayer the righteous [ⲇⲓⲕⲁⲓⲟⲥ] make for them.'

Ministry

5 And [ⲇⲉ] when he had said this to us we said to him, 'Lord, [ⲅⲁⲣ] in everything you have taught us and pitied us and saved us so that we may preach [ⲕⲏⲣⲩⲥⲥⲉ] to those who are worthy of salvation – and do we gain a reward with you?'

41.1 And [ⲇⲉ] he answered and said to us, 'Go, preach, and you will be good workers [ⲉⲣⲅⲁⲧⲏⲥ] and servants [ⲇⲓⲁⲕⲟⲛⲟⲥ].'

2 And [ⲇⲉ] we said to him, 'It is you who will preach through us.'

3 Then [ⲧⲟⲧⲉ] he answered us, saying, 'Will you not all be fathers? Will you not all be teachers?'*

4 We said to him, 'Lord, you said to us, "Do not call anyone your father on earth, for [ⲅⲁⲣ] there is one who is your Father who is ([ⲛϭ] **XXXII**) in heaven and your teacher." 5 Why do you now say to us, "You will be fathers of many children, and servants [ⲇⲓⲁⲕⲟⲛⲟⲥ] and teachers"?'

6 And [ⲇⲉ] he answered and said to us, 'It is as [ⲕⲁⲧⲁ] you have said. 7 For truly [ϩⲁⲙⲏⲛ ⲅⲁⲣ] I say to you, whoever hears you and believes [ⲡⲓⲥⲧⲉⲩⲉ] in me will receive [from y]ou the light of the seal [ⲥϕⲣⲁⲅⲓⲥ] throu[gh me]. You will [be fath]ers and servants [ⲇⲓⲁⲕⲟⲛⲟⲥ] and teachers.'

42.1 And [ⲇⲉ] we said to him, 'Lord, how can each of us be these three?'

5 when... to us] –*Eth* | Lord] Yes, Lord G | taught us] been merciful to us E | pitied... saved us] *Eth* saved us and pitied us | so ... may] *Eth* and we will | of salvation] –*Eth*

41.1 answered and] – *Eth* | you... workers] *Eth* you will be {judge the E} good <and E G S> apostles

2 It... us] *Eth* <Our A> Lord, you are {–K} our father

3 Then ... saying] *Eth* And he {You S} said to us | Will... teachers?*] *Cop* Do not all be a father, and do not [ⲟⲩⲇⲉ] all be a teacher, *Eth* Are all fathers, and are all servants, and are all teachers? <And he said to us, Yes S> | *See pp. 171–72*

4 you ... us *Cop* G K] you said A, did you not say *(Eth)* | call ... earth] say, <We have a A> father on earth and teacher *Eth* | in... teacher] *Eth* your teacher who is in heaven

5 You will... teachers] *Eth* that we will be fathers of many children and teachers and servants

7 in me] –A | from you] –*Eth* | through me] *Cop* + and baptism [ⲃⲁⲓⲧⲓⲥⲙⲁ] through me | You... teachers] *Eth* and in me you will be fathers and good {–A G L} teachers

42.1 each... three] *Eth* three be one

2 And [Ⲇ̅ⲉ] he said to us, 'Truly [ϩⲁⲙⲏⲛ] I say to you that you will indeed [ⲙⲉⲛ] be called fathers, because [ⲉⲣⲉⲓ] with a willing heart and love [ⲁⲅⲁⲡⲏ] you have revealed to them the things of the king- ([ⲛⲍ] **XXXIII**) dom of heaven. 3 And you will be called servants [Ⲇⲓⲁⲕⲟⲛⲟⲥ] because they will receive the baptism [ⲃⲁⲡⲧⲓⲥⲙⲁ] of life and the forgiveness of their sins by my hand through you. 4 And you will be called teachers because you have given them the word [ⲗⲟⲅⲟⲥ] without envy [-ⲫⲑⲟⲛⲉⲓ]. 5 You admonished [ⲛⲟⲩⲑⲉⲧⲉⲓ] them, and when you rebuked them they separated themselves. 6 You were unafraid of their wealth and their person, but [ⲁⲗⲗⲁ] you kept the commandments [ⲉⲛⲧⲟⲗⲏ] of my Father and did them. 7 There will be a great reward for you with my Father who is in heaven, and for them there will be forgiveness of sins and eternal life, and they will share [ⲕⲟⲓⲛⲱⲛⲉⲓ] in the kingdom of heaven.'

8 And we said to him, 'Lord, if [ⲕⲁⲛ] each of us had ([ⲛⲏ] **XXXIV**) ten thousand tongues for his speech, we would not be able to give thanks [ⲉⲩⲭⲁⲣⲓⲥⲧⲉⲓ] to you that you promise us such things!'

9 Then [ⲧⲟⲧⲉ] he answered, saying to us, 'Just [ⲙⲟⲛⲟⲛ] do what I tell you, the things I myself have done.'

Parable of the Virgins

43.1 'And you will be like the wise virgins [ⲡⲁⲣⲑⲉⲛⲟⲥ] who watched and did not sleep but [ⲁⲗⲗⲁ] went out to meet the Lord and entered with him into the wedding-chamber. 2 But [Ⲇⲉ] the foolish ones were unable to watch but [ⲁⲗⲗⲁ] slept.'

2 And] + he answered and A L | Truly] *Eth* Truly, truly | with... love] *Eth* in love and compassion

3 you... because] –*Eth*

4 you... called] –*Eth* | given... envy] *Eth* interpreted my word without suffering {judging A}

5 separated themselves] *Eth* turned aside from that for which you reproved them

6 You... their wealth] And I will say to them, Do not be afraid L | and their person] *Eth* and you did not show partiality | my Father] *Eth* the Father

7 great] –*Eth* | share] + in the Holy Spirit and E | of heaven] –*Eth*

8 if each ... we] *Eth* if there were ten thousand tongues, they | that... things] *Eth* as is fitting

9 Just] –*Eth* | done] *Eth* + for you

43.1 And... be] *Eth* And be | watched] *Eth* lit their lamps | went out] *Eth* + with their lamps | Lord] *Eth* + <and E> the bridegroom | and... wedding-chamber] –A

1–2 *See Additional Notes*

2 foolish] *Eth* + who spoke with them

3 And [Ⲇⲉ] we said to him, 'Lord, who are the wise and who are the foolish?'

4 He said to us, 'There are five wise. Of them [ⲄⲀⲢ] the prophet [ⲡⲢⲟⲫⲏⲦⲏⲤ] said, "They are children of God." Hear their names!'

5 But [Ⲇⲉ] we were weeping and (Ⲛⲉ **XXXV**) distressed at heart about those who slept.

6 He said to us, 'The five wise [ⲄⲀⲢ] are Faith [ⲡⲓⲤⲦⲓⲤ] and Love [ⲀⲄⲀⲡⲏ] and Grace [ⲬⲀⲢⲓⲤ], Peace [(ⲉⲓ)ⲢⲎⲚⲎ] and Hope [ⲅⲉⲗⲡⲓⲤ]. 7 Those who possess these [Ⲇⲉ] among those who believe [ⲡⲓⲤⲦⲉⲨⲉ] will be guides to those who believe in me and in the one who sent me. 8 For [ⲄⲀⲢ] I am the Lord and I am the bridegroom whom they received, and they entered the bridegroom's house and reclined with me in my wedding-chamber and rejoiced. 9 But [Ⲇⲉ] as for the five foolish ones who slept, they awoke and came to the door of the wedding-chamber and knocked, for [ⲄⲀⲢ] it had been shut against them. 10 Then [ⲦⲞⲦⲉ] they wept and grieved [ⲡⲉⲚⲐⲉⲓ] that they did not open to them.'

11 And [Ⲇⲉ] we said to him, 'Lord, those wise sisters of theirs who were in the bridegroom's house, (ⲍ **XXXVI**) did they fail to open to them? And did they not grieve [ⲗⲨⲡⲉⲓ] for them or [ⲏ] did they not plead with the bridegroom on their behalf to open to them?'

12 He answered, saying to us, 'They were not yet able to find grace on their behalf.'

13 We said to him, 'Lord, when will they enter for their sisters' sake?'

14 Then [ⲦⲞⲦⲉ] he said to us, 'Whoever is shut out is shut out.'

---

4 wise] *Cop* + and five foolish | children] *Eth* daughters
5 weeping... slept] *Eth* sorrowful and grieving and weeping over those who were shut out
6 five] –G | Grace] *Eth* Joy
7 believe[1]] + in my name C, + in me and in the one who sent me *(Eth)*
8 and I am] –B L | entered] *Eth* + with me | house] wedding-chamber E | with... wedding-chamber] *Eth* with the bridegroom | *See Additional Notes*
9 to the door... knocked] *Eth* to the house of the bridegroom and knocked at the door
10 and grieved] –*Eth* | they... them] *Eth* they were shut out
11 bridegroom's] –*Eth* | or did they not ... them] –*Eth*
11–12 *See Additional Notes*
12 He ... us] *Eth* (–A) And he said to us, Yes, they were sorrowful and they grieved for them, (+A) and they pleaded with the bridegroom, and | yet *Cop* B K] –*(Eth)* find grace] agree E
13 Lord] God B K | when... sake] when will their sisters enter B L
14 Then] And *Eth*

15 And [ⲗⲉ] we said to him, 'Lord, is this matter decided? Who then are the foolish?'

16 He said to us, 'Hear their names: Knowledge [ⲅⲛⲱⲥⲓⲥ], and Wisdom, Obedience, Patience, and Mercy. 17 For [ⲅⲁⲣ] it is these that slept among those who believe [ⲡⲓⲥⲧⲉⲩⲉ] and confess [ⲉⲟⲙⲟⲗⲟⲅⲉⲓ] me.

44.1 'Since those who slept did not fulfil my commandments [ⲉⲛⲧⲟⲗⲏ], they will [ⲅⲁⲣ] remain outside the kingdom (ⲍⲁ **XXXVII**) and the fold [ⲁⲩⲗⲏ] of the shepherd and his flock. 2 And [ⲗⲉ] whoever remains outside the sheepfold [ⲁⲩⲗⲏ] the wolves will eat, and he will hear [th]em; he will die in great pain, and distress and endurance [ⲉⲩⲡⲟⲙⲟⲛⲏ] shall come upon him. 3 And he will be terribly [ⲕⲁⲕ(ⲱⲥ)] tortured and lacerated and torn apart with a great punishment [and he will] be in agony [ⲃⲁⲥⲁⲛⲟⲥ].'

45.1 And [ⲗⲉ] we said to him 'Lord, you have revealed all things to us well [ⲕⲁⲗⲱⲥ].'

2 Then [ⲧⲟⲧⲉ] he answered, saying to us, 'Do you not understand [ⲛⲟⲓⲉ] these words?'

3 And we said to him, 'Yes, Lord, through the five they will enter your kingdom. 4 Yet [ⲙⲉⲛⲧⲟⲓⲅⲉ] those who watched and were with you, the Lord and bridegroom, surely they do not rejoice over those who slept?'

(ⲍⲃ **XXXVIII**) 5 And he said to us, 'They indeed [ⲙⲉⲛ] rejoice that they entered with the bridegroom, the Lord, and they grieved [ⲗⲩⲡⲉⲓ]

---

15 Lord] –A B | is … decided?] What is decided? A, + And he said to us, Yes! And we said to him G | *See Additional Notes*

16 their names] and I will tell you G, –*(Eth)* | Knowledge and Wisdom] *Eth* Wisdom, Knowledge

44.1 Since] *Cop* And | commandments] + so *Cop* | the kingdom and] –A | and his] *Eth* of the | *See Additional Notes*

2 he… them] –A K | die] be judged and die C | endurance] lack of endurance A | him] them L S | *See Additional Notes*

3 be terribly tortured] find comfort K | with… agony] and with a long punishment he will be punished and with an evil death he will die G, with a long punishment and evil, and he will be unable to die quickly *(Eth)*

45.2 Do … understand] *Eth* Understand and comprehend

3 Yes, Lord… kingdom] *Eth* Lord, those {we E K} five are to come into your kingdom, and the five who were shut out, they will be outside your kingdom

4 were… bridegroom] *Eth* came with the Lord <and G> the bridegroom | do not rejoice *Cop* G L] rejoiced A C

5 the bridegroom] –*Eth*

over those who slept, for [ⲅⲁⲣ] they are their sisters. 6 For the ten are daughters of God the Father.'

7 And we said to him, 'Lord, it is in your power to be gracious to their sisters!'

8 He said to us, 'That is not your affair but [ⲁⲗⲗⲁ] his who sent me, and I myself agree [ⲥⲩⲛⲉⲩⲇⲟⲕⲉⲓ] with him.'

Discipline

46.1 'But [ⲇⲉ] as for you, preach and teach uprightly and well [ⲕⲁⲗⲱⲥ], showing partiality to no one and fearing no one, especially [ⲇⲉ] the rich, for [ⲅⲁⲣ] they do not do my commandments [ⲉⲛⲧⲟⲗⲏ] but [ⲁⲗⲗⲁ] delight in their wealth.'

(ⲝⲅ **XXXIX**) 2 And [ⲇⲉ] we said to him, 'Lord, do you speak to us only of the rich?'

3 He answered, saying, 'If one who is not rich, having [a little] property [ⲃⲓⲟⲥ], gives to the [poor and] needy, people will call him a benefactor.

47.1 'But [ⲇⲉ] if one should fall, bearing a burden because of the sins he has committed, let his neighbour reprove him for [ⲁⲛⲧⲓ] what he did to his neighbour. 2 And when his neighbour has reproved him and he returns, he will be saved and the one who reproved him will be awarded eternal life. 3 But [ⲅⲁⲣ] if a man who is in need sees his benefactor sinning and does not reprove him, he will be judged (ⲍⲁ **XL**) with an evil judgement [ⲕⲣⲓⲙⲁ]. 4 And if a blind man leads a blind man, both will fall into a pit. 5 And whoever shows partiality and whoever receives partiality will both be judged with a single judgement. 6 As [ⲕⲁⲧⲁ] the prophet [ⲡⲣⲟⲫⲏⲧⲏⲥ] said, "Woe [ⲟⲩⲁⲉⲓ] to

---

6 the Father] –L
7 it ... be] *Eth* it is {we praise G} your greatness, that you are

46.1 you] *Eth* + go | uprightly and well] *Eth* truly and uprightly | the rich... not do] *Eth* the rich who are found among those who do not do {opposing those who do A}
2 do... us] –A C G
3 He answered, saying] *Eth* And he said to us | having ... property] –*Eth* | gives... needy] *Eth* when he gives and becomes proud to the one who has not

47.1 because of] *Eth* that is | committed] + before his neighbour <if one should fall, bearing a burden because of the sins he has committed B K>,
2 and he returns] –A [|] will be awarded] *Eth* will find
3 a man... need] *Eth* he | does... him] *Eth* shows partiality | an evil] *Eth* a great
5 And] *Eth* + likewise | whoever[2]] –C, those who L
6 Woe to those *Cop* L S] and he said to them <Woe to those B> *(Eth)* | *See Additional Notes*

those who show partiality, who justify the sinner for a bribe [ⲁⲱⲣⲟⲛ], whose stomach is their god." 7 Consider how it is with the judgement [ⲕ(ⲣ)ⲓⲥⲓⲥ]! 8 For truly [ⲅⲁⲙⲏⲛ ⲅⲁⲣ] I say to you, in that day I will neither [ⲟⲩⲧⲉ] fear the rich nor [ⲟⲩⲧⲉ] have pity on the poor.

48.1 'If you see a sinner, reprove him between yourself and him. 2 But [ⲁⲉ] if he does not listen to you take up to three others with you and teach your brother. 3 If he again [ⲡⲁⲗⲓⲛ] does not listen to you, set him before you as a gentile and a tax-collector.

49.1 <ETH> 'If you hear of a matter, do not believe anything against your brother and do not slander and do not love the word of slander. 2 For as it is written, "Let your ear not listen to anything against your brother." 3 But only if you have seen, reprove him, instruct him, and convert him.'

4 And we said to him, 'Lord, you have taught us and warned us in every way. 5 But, Lord, among the believers, those among them who truly believe the preaching of your name, will there really be division and strife and jealousy and quarrelling and hatred and slander among them? 6 For you have said, "They will reprove one another, and they shall show no partiality to those who sin and who hate the one who reproves them."'

7 And he answered and said to us, 'Why then will the judgement take place? 8 So that the wheat may be put into its barns and its chaff put onto the fire!'

50.1 'So they hate the one who loves me and who reproves those who do not keep my commandments, and they will be hated and persecuted and despised and mocked. 2 And they will speak what is untrue, taking counsel and conspiring together against those who love me. 3 And these will reprove them so that they may be saved,

---

48.1 see] *Eth* + with your eyes | sinner] (one) sinning L, those who sin *(Eth)* | and him] + If he listens to you, you have gained him B K L S | *See Additional Notes*
2 take... you] *Eth* let there be two or up to three
2–3 *See Additional Notes*

49.1 the word of G] *(Eth)* to listen to
5 slander G] *(Eth)* distress
6 no] –S | them] + Lord S
8 So that... may] For the wheat will A | its... fire] your barns and the chaff put in K | *See Additional Notes*

50.1 hate E G K] + and *(Eth)* | who do not keep E K S] who keep *(Eth)* | persecuted] –B, be persecuted L | *See Additional Notes*
3 so... reprove them] –C | but those... instruct them] –B

but those who reprove them and instruct them and warn them they will hate and ostracize and scorn, and those who wish to do good to them will be prevented. 4 But those who endure will be witnesses before the Father, for they were zealous for righteousness, and it was not with a zeal for corruption that they were zealous.'

5 And we said to him, 'So will this happen among us?'

6 And he said to us, 'Do not fear what will not happen to many but to a few.'

7 And we said to him, 'Tell us how!'

8 And he said to us, 'There will be strange teaching and strife, and they will desire their own glory, putting forward unprofitable teaching, and there will be a deadly stumbling-block within it. 9 And they will teach and turn those who believed in me from my commandments and deprive them of eternal life. 10 But woe to those who falsify this my word and my commandments, and also to those who listen to them and who are far from the life of the teaching! 11 With them they will be eternally punished.'

Ascension

51.1 And when he had said this and finished speaking with us, he said to us again, 'Behold, on the third day, at the third hour, the one who sent me will come so that I may go with him.' 2 And as he spoke there was thunder and lightning and an earthquake, and the heavens were torn asunder, and a bright cloud came and took him. 3 And we heard the voice of many angels as they rejoiced and blessed and said, 'Gather us, O priest, into the light of glory!' 4 And when he drew near to the firmament of heaven, we heard him saying, 'Go in peace!'

5 In the name of our Lord Jesus Christ.

---

5 So] + Lord L
8 There will be] –A K
9 believed] believe L S
10 falsify A C G] desire E, use as a pretext B L S | of the teaching] and the teaching A, in their teaching C, + to those who are far from the commandments of life L

51.1 on… hour] at the third hour, on the third day S
3 we heard C G] –(*Eth*) | glory] his glory B C K
4 he B L] they A C

Part II

Themes

3

THE MIRACLE SEQUENCE

Following a complex epistolary opening and a passage of credal confession, the *Epistula Apostolorum* has its collective apostolic authors narrate a series of seven miracle stories from Jesus' earthly life, before proceeding to the events of Easter Day, a long question-and-answer session with the risen Lord, and a concluding ascension narrative. Of the seven miracle stories, one is paralleled in *GJohn* alone (turning water into wine), another in *GMatthew* alone (the fish with coins in its mouth). Two stories occur in all three synoptic gospels (the haemorrhaging woman, Legion), one in *GMatthew, GMark,* and *GJohn* (walking on the water), and one in all four canonical gospels (the feeding of the five thousand). The story about the child Jesus' first day at school has parallels in Irenaeus and the *Infancy Gospel of Thomas.*

The sequence of seven stories is as follows.

(1) Jesus' alphabet lesson
(2) Water into wine
(3) The haemorrhaging woman
(4) Legion
(5) Walking on water
(6) The coins in the fish's mouth
(7) The feeding of the five thousand[1]

---

[1] A different analysis of *EpAp* 4–5 is offered by Hills, who argues that its narrative components are expansions of a list of miraculous actions whose basic form is preserved in *EpAp* 5.2, 9. Julian V. Hills, *Tradition and Composition in the Epistula Apostolorum* (Cambridge, MA: Harvard University Press, 2008[2]), 37–48. Hills identifies a miracle list genre from texts such as the *Acts of Paul,* the *Pseudo-Clementine Homilies,* and the *Teaching of Addai,* and he views these lists as 'differing in both form and function from the canonical miracle *stories*' (38; italics original). Given the prominence in *EpAp* of stories closely related to canonical counterparts, this emphasis on difference seems exaggerated.

The placing of item (2) reflects the Johannine claim that the miracle at Cana was 'the beginning of the signs' (*GJn* 2.11), although here it is preceded by a story implying the child Jesus' possession of supernatural knowledge. Items (3) to (7) are all present in *GMatthew*, though the sequence is out of step with the canonical evangelists.[2] The haemorrhaging woman is placed before the encounter with Legion, not immediately after (*GMark, GLuke*)[3] or after several intervening episodes (*GMatthew*).[4] The feeding of the five thousand is preceded by the walking on the water rather than being followed by it, as in *GMatthew, GMark*, and *GJohn*,[5] and the incident of the coins in the fish's mouth is inserted between them. While the author of *EpAp* shows signs of familiarity with *GMatthew, GLuke*, and *GJohn*, he does not feel himself bound by editorial decisions made by his predecessors.[6] For this author there is no pre-existing canonical sequence of miracle stories, nor is there a canonical limit to the number of sources on which to draw – as the inclusion of the childhood story indicates.

The new sequence is not constructed at random. Setting aside the first story for the moment, the second (water into wine) has to do with Jesus' power over the material creation, and specifically over water. The liquid theme continues into the story of the haemorrhaging woman: from water to wine to blood. In the Legion story, the water is that of the Sea of Galilee: the demon Legion 'went into the

---

[2] (3) *GMt* 9.20–22 (haemorrhaging woman); (4) *GMt* 8.28–34 (Legion); (5) *GMt* 14.22–27 (walking on water); (6) *GMt* 17.24–27 (coins in fish's mouth); (7) *GMt* 14.13–21 (feeding of the five thousand).

[3] *GMk* 5.1–20, 25–34; *GLk* 8.26–39, 42b–48.

[4] Legion (*GMt* 8.28–34), the paralytic (*GMt* 9.1–8), the call of Matthew (*GMt* 9.9–13), fasting (*GMt* 9.14–17), Jairus/haemorrhaging woman (*GMt* 9.18–31). The first and last of these episodes are drawn from *GMark* 5.1–43, and between them the evangelist has inserted material from *GMark* 2.1–22. See my *Gospel Writing: A Canonical Perspective* (Grand Rapids, MI: Eerdmans, 2013), 148–51.

[5] *GMt* 14.13–21, 22–33; *GMk* 6.30–44, 45–52; *GJn* 6.1–15, 16–21.

[6] For the author's knowledge of earlier gospel material, see Schmidt, *Gespräche Jesu*, 213–29; J. Hartenstein, *Die zweite Lehre: Erscheinungen des Auferstandenen als Rahmenerzählungen frühchristlicher Dialoge*, Texte und Untersuchungen zur Geschichte der altchristlichen Literatur 146 (Berlin: Akademie Verlag, 2000), 119–26. Knowledge of gospels that were to be included in the New Testament does not mean that, for this author, 'the authoritative sources are fixed and now closed' (C. Hill, *The Johannine Corpus in the Early Church* [Oxford: Oxford University Press, 2004], 368; cf. Darrell D. Hannah, 'The Four-Gospel "Canon" in the *Epistula Apostolorum*', *Journal of Theological Studies* 59 [2008], 598–633). To adapt material from a text for one's own purposes is not at all to regard it as part of an already established and complete New Testament canon. Hill wrongly assumes that the author of *EpAp* does both, which 'seems... like a complete and utter contradiction' (371).

pigs and plunged them into the sea, and they were drowned' (*EpAp* 5.12). The sea also features in the episodes that follow: Jesus 'walked on the sea, and the winds blew and he rebuked them, and the waves of the sea he stilled' (5.13). When the disciples can find no money to pay off the tax-collector, Jesus responds: 'Let one of you cast a hook into the deep and draw out a fish, and he will find *denarii* in it' (5.15). Finally, the fish with coins in its mouth provides a link to the 'five loaves and two fish' of the miraculous feeding story with which the sequence ends (5.17). The chain of verbal or thematic links begins with water and ends with fish, taking in wine, blood, and the sea along the way.

The miracle sequence demonstrates Jesus' power over water and its derivatives. This in turn creates a connection with the credal or hymn-like passage that immediately precedes the miracle sequence. There Jesus is referred to as the one

> who sits above the Cherubim at the right hand of the throne of the Father, who by his word commanded the heavens and founded the earth and what is in it, and established the sea, and it did not cross its boundary, and depths and springs to gush forth and flow into the earth day and night. (*EpAp* 3.4–5)

While it is initially unclear whether it is the Father or the pre-existent Jesus 'who by his word commanded the heavens', the sequence of *who*-formulations begins with a confession of 'our Lord Jesus Christ, the Son of God, who was sent from God...' and ends with a reference to the one 'who spoke with the forefathers and prophets in parables and in truth, whom the apostles preached and the disciples touched' (3.11–12). The identity of Jesus seems here to be assimilated to that of the Father, and the earthly Jesus who turned water into wine and calmed the sea is thus the same as the pre-existent Jesus who restrained the sea and caused springs to gush forth. As we shall see, the first story in the miracle sequence – the child Jesus' lesson in the alphabet – may have been intended as a conceptual link between the confession or hymn and the miracle sequence.

3.1   The Question of Genre

If the *Epistula* is classified as a 'post-resurrection dialogue' alongside such texts as the *Apocryphon of James* (NHC I,2), the *Gospel of*

Mary (BG 8502,1), or the *Sophia of Jesus Christ* (NHC III,4; BG 8502,3), the miracle sequence may seem an anomaly, leading one to speculate that it might be a later addition to a text with an originally exclusive post-resurrection setting. If, however, the miracle sequence turns out to be integral to the structure of *EpAp*, that would draw this text closer to the earlier 'ministry gospels' of which its author was clearly aware – most obviously *GMatthew* and *GJohn*.[7] Affinities with post-resurrection dialogues would remain, but these would not necessarily represent the primary literary context within which the *Epistula* is to be interpreted.

Post-resurrection dialogues typically lack even an account of the events of Easter morning, focusing instead on the epiphanic appearance of the risen Lord that occasions the dialogue and the revelations it contains.[8] In the *Apocryphon of James*, the Lord appears to his disciples as they write their respective gospels, 550 days after he had risen from the dead, and also, apparently, at an unspecified interval after his ascension – an event that must therefore be repeated at the end of this text.[9] Here and elsewhere, Jesus' resurrection is the presupposition of his appearance, but Easter Day itself remains in the background. Still less is the earthly life emphasized, present only in the negative form represented by the 'parables', impenetrable mysteries no longer appropriate in a situation of post-resurrection clarity.[10] Similarly, the *Sophia of Jesus Christ* opens by recounting how

> After he rose from the dead, the twelve disciples and seven women continued as disciples, coming to Galilee onto the Mountain called Divination and Joy.[11]

---

[7] On the problems of classifying this text, see my article, 'A Gospel of the Eleven: The *Epistula Apostolorum* and the Johannine Tradition', in Watson and Parkhouse, *Connecting Gospels*, 189–215; 190–201.

[8] The absence of an Easter story in these texts is rightly noted by Judith Hartenstein, *Die zweite Lehre*, 99–100. Along with the *Epistula*, Hartenstein discusses the *Sophia of Jesus Christ*, the *Apocryphon of John*, the *Gospel of Mary*, the *Letter of Peter to Philip*, the *First Apocalypse of James*, and the *Letter* (or *Apocryphon*) *of James* (34–246).

[9] The pseudonymous James tells how 'the Saviour appeared, having left us as we gazed after him, and [this was] five hundred and fifty days after he rose from the dead' (*ApocrJas* 2,17–21). Coptic text in *Nag Hammadi Codex I (The Jung Codex): Introductions, Texts, Translations, Indices* (Nag Hammadi Studies 22, ed. Harold W. Attridge [Leiden: Brill, 1985]).

[10] *ApocrJas* 7,1–6; cf. 8,1–10.

[11] *SophJesChr*, NHC III 90,14–91,1. Text in *Nag Hammadi Codices III,3–4 and V,1* (Nag Hammadi Studies 27, ed. Douglas M. Parrott [Leiden: Brill, 1991]).

The overwhelming post-resurrection clarity may be signified by the Lord's glorious appearance, in explicit or implicit contrast to the lowly human form he had earlier assumed. In the *Sophia of Jesus Christ*, 'the Saviour appeared not in his previous form but in the invisible spirit, and his likeness was like a great angel of light...'[12] In the *Apocryphon of John*, the apostle John retreated to the desert to contemplate, when suddenly 'the heavens opened and the whole creation below heaven shone and the world was shaken.'[13]

In such texts as these, there is no place for accounts of Jesus' pre-Easter ministry. The same might in principle have been true of *EpAp* in its original form; the miracle sequence might be a later addition. Yet, rather than forcing *EpAp* into the mould of texts with which it may have little in common beyond its post-resurrection setting and dialogical form, there is good reason to think that the miracle sequence is an integral part of this text.

The sequence is only extant in Geʿez translation, but it was almost certainly part of the Coptic version as well. Where they can be compared, deviations between the two versions are slight. Page I of the present incomplete and damaged Coptic text must originally have been page 9, as is clear from the first extant page number on what was originally page 18 (now page X).[14] A Coptic manuscript page of 15 lines corresponds to 7–9 lines in the modern printed Geʿez text, in which chapters 1–6 of *EpAp* occupy a total of 61 lines,[15] and a Coptic text corresponding closely to the Geʿez version of these chapters could therefore be accommodated within the missing first 8 pages.

While the Coptic text must have included an equivalent of the Geʿez version of *EpAp* 1–6, with no more than the usual range of minor variants, this is a relatively self-contained section in which the summary and closing exhortation of chapter 6 form an *inclusio* with chapter 1:

> And these things our Lord and Saviour revealed to us and showed us, as we likewise do to you... Be strong and do not waver...   (6.1, 3)

---

[12] NHC III 91,10–13.

[13] NHC II 1,30–33. Text in *The Apocryphon of John: Synopsis of Nag Hammadi Codices II,1; III,1; and IV,1 with BG 8502,2* (Nag Hammadi and Manichaean Studies 33, ed. Michael Waldstein and Frederik Wisse [Leiden: Brill, 1995]).

[14] Schmidt, *Gespräche Jesu*, 7*, confirmed from digital images. Schmidt's Roman numerals refer only to (partially) extant pages.

[15] Guerrier, *Le Testament en Galilée*, 188–93.

> What Jesus Christ revealed to his disciples and to all... so
> that you may be strong and not waver...   (1.1, 3)

The self-contained character of *EpAp* 1–6 might seem to strengthen
the suspicion that this section and the miracle sequence it includes
may have been an originally independent composition. Incorporated
into the present larger work, the initial warning against the heresy of
Cerinthus and Simon (1.2) would then be the model for the similar
warning when the text makes a new start in chapter 7. The contents
of *EpAp* prior to the beginning of the dialogue (chapters 13–50) may
be set out as follows.

EpAp 1	Epistolary introduction (1): Warning against heresy – blessing
EpAp 2	Epistolary introduction (2): Authors and addresses identified – content
EpAp 3	Confession of faith in Christ as creator and as incarnate
EpAp 4–5	Miracle sequence
EpAp 6	Summary and exhortation
EpAp 7–8	Warning against heresy
EpAp 9	Easter morning: women visit the tomb
EpAp 10	Women's unsuccessful mission to male disciples
EpAp 11–12	The disciples touch the risen Lord and are convinced

In *EpAp* 1 the apostolic authors warn their readers against the false
apostles Simon and Cerinthus before they name themselves and
identify their readers as 'the churches of the east and the west, the
north and the south' (2.1–2). The warning against Simon and
Cerinthus is repeated in *EpAp* 7–8. In both cases it is the ostensible
reason for writing, although these figures and their dangerous teaching play no role in the rest of the text.[16] In chapter 1 the authors
promise to communicate 'what we have heard and remembered and
written for the whole world' (1.4), a promise of which the miracle
sequence of chapters 4–5 might be the fulfilment, summed up in the
words: 'And these things our Lord and Saviour revealed to us and
showed us, as we likewise do to you' (6.1). In contrast, chapter 2

---

[16] This text is aware of the general concept of false teaching (29.1–4; 37.4; 50.8–11)
but says nothing about wrong doctrinal content; rather, the focus is on inappropriate
conduct (cf. 29.1, and chapters 38–50, *passim*, on which see Chapter 7, below). It is
therefore inappropriate to 'mirror-read' heretical views from *EpAp* on such topics as
resurrection (see Hartenstein, *Die zweite Lehre*, 102–7).

specifically refers to the resurrection: the apostolic authors 'touched him when he rose from the dead, when he revealed to us what is great and wonderful and true' (2.3). This statement corresponds precisely to the Easter narrative of chapters 9–12 and the revelatory dialogue of chapters 13–50.

One might therefore envisage a development in which a revelatory dialogue with an exclusively post-resurrection setting (chapters 2, 7–51) is conflated with a shorter text focusing on the miracle sequence (chapters 1, 3–6). This is very unlikely, however. In reality there is a skilfully constructed symmetry between two narrative components of similar length (the miracle sequence and the Easter account) and the passages of warning and confession that introduce them. The symmetry is evident at three points.

(i)   *Warnings against False Apostles as Reason for Writing*

What Jesus Christ revealed to his disciples and to all: on account of Simon and Cerinthus the false apostles this has been written, so that no one should associate with them... (1.1–2)

Cerinthus and Simon have gone out, they go around the world, but they are enemies of our Lord Jesus Christ... For this reason we have not delayed to write to you about the testimony of our Saviour the Christ... (7.1–2; 8.1)

More positively, the apostles write about 'what we have heard and remembered' (1.4), 'what he did as we watched him, things still in our thoughts and deeds' (8.2). The later passage does not derive from a different source but recapitulates the opening of this text.

(ii)   *Confession of Faith*

And God the Son of God do we confess [*na'ammən*], the Word who became flesh of Mary, carried in her womb through the Holy Spirit. And not by the desire of the flesh but by the will of God was he born; and he was swaddled in Bethlehem, and manifested and nourished and grew up as we saw. (3.13–15)

This we confess [ⲡⲉⲓ (ⲉⲧⲛ̄ⲣ̄)ⲙ̄ⲛ̄ⲧⲣⲉ] / *zanta na'ammən*], that the Lord was crucified by Pontius Pilate and Archelaus between the two thieves, and he was buried in a place called 'The Skull'... (9.1)

The miracle sequence of chapters 4–5 fits precisely between these two confessional statements, filling the interval between Jesus' birth and his death. The link has been partially obscured by the summary of chapter 6 and the recapitulation of the anti–heretical warnings in chapters 7–8, but it remains evident nonetheless.

(iii)   Narrative Section (Miracle Sequence/Easter Day)

> This is what our Lord Jesus Christ did when he was taken by Joseph and Mary his mother to where he was to be taught letters. . .   (4.1)

> There came to that place three women, Mary and Martha and Mary Magdalene. . .   (9.2)

The two narrative sections (*EpAp* 4–5, 9–12) are of similar length, and the first should not be seen as merely preparatory for the second. The second section is anticipated in the apostles' claim to have 'touched him after he rose from the dead' (2.3). The first section is summarized in their statement that 'these things our Lord and Saviour revealed to us and showed us, as we likewise do to you' (6.1).

In view of this carefully constructed symmetry, it is clear that the miracle sequence is as deeply embedded in the text of *EpAp* as is the Easter narrative.[17] Further insights into its complex frame may be gained by comparison with Johannine literature – a category that may already have been known to the author, who lists John as the first of the apostles (2.1).[18] The work opens with the phrase, 'What Jesus Christ revealed to his disciples' (*EpAp* 1.1), which recalls the 'revelation of Jesus Christ' announced in *Revelation* 1.1. A further parallel may be seen in the deferred identification of author and readers: 'John and Thomas and Peter. . . to the churches of east and west, north and south' (*EpAp* 2.1–2); 'John to the seven churches that are in Asia' (*Rev* 1.4). In *EpAp* 1.4, 'What we have heard and

---

[17] Contrast Hartenstein's view that the miracle sequence belongs to the 'Einleitungskapiteln' that precede 'die eigentliche Rahmenerzählung für den Dialog', i.e. chapters 9–12 (*Die zweite Lehre*, 99). In view of the continuous narrative thread through *EpAp* 3.13–5.21 + 9.1–12.4, it is arbitrary to claim that the 'real narrative frame' is provided by the Easter story alone.

[18] The apostle John is identified as the author of the Book of Revelation by Justin (*Dial.* 81.4). Irenaeus also attributes to him the Gospel (*Adv. haer.* 3.1.1), *1 John* (*Adv. haer.* 3.16.5), and *2 John* (*Adv. haer.* 3.16.3).

remembered and written... we entrust to you... in joy', an echo of *1 John* 1.3–4 is perceptible: 'What we have seen and heard we announce to you... And we write these things so that our joy may be fulfilled in you.'[19] In the confession that introduces the miracle sequence (*EpAp* 3.13–14), echoes of the Johannine prologue are unmistakable: 'the Word... became flesh of Mary' (cf. *GJn* 1.14), 'And not by the desire of the flesh but by the will of God was he born' (cf. *GJn* 1.13).[20] Finally, the summary that explains the purpose of the miracle sequence seems to parallel the original ending of the *Gospel of John*.

> But <u>these things</u> are written <u>so that</u> you may believe that Jesus is the Christ, the Son of God, and <u>so that</u> believing you may have <u>life</u> in his name.   (*GJn* 20.31)

> And <u>these things</u> our Lord and Saviour revealed to us and showed us, as we likewise do to you, <u>so that</u> you may be partakers in the grace of the Lord and in our ministry and our praise, as you think of eternal <u>life</u>.   (*EpAp* 6.1–2)[21]

Both passages speak of the soteriological significance of the seven miracles that have been selected in each case, and both do so in a primarily post-resurrection context (*GJn* 20; *EpAp* 9–51). Indeed, the Johannine passage seems out of place in its present context, referring as it does to a series of signs that concluded with the raising of

---

[19] Noted by Hans-Josef Klauck, *Apocryphal Gospels: An Introduction* (London and New York, T&T Clark, 2003), 154. But there is little reason to follow Klauck in concluding from this that 'the author intends to fight against a docetic dissolution of Jesus' true human nature and of the reality of his bodily resurrection', or that he 'sometimes adopts gnostic elements in the course of his battle against gnosis' (154). In spite of the references to Simon and Cerinthus, no such 'battle against gnosis' [*sic*] is evident in this text.

[20] The *EpAp* passage corresponds closely to the well-known Latin variant, *qui non ex sanguinibus neque ex voluntate carnis nec ex voluntate viri sed ex deo natus est* (Codex Veronensis [b, sixth century]; cf. Tertullian, *De Carn. Chr.* 19.1–5, where there is an extended defence of the singular against the plural reading). While the singular reading might seem to have been occasioned by the ambiguity of the Latin *qui* (masc. sing. or masc.pl., contrast Greek ὅς, οἵ), Irenaeus's allusions to this passage in connection with Jesus' conception suggest that this reading may also have been current in early Greek manuscripts (*Adv. haer.* 3.16.2, 19.2; 5.1.3). Ge'ez *ba-fətwata śəgā* probably represents *Gk* οὐκ ἐξ ἐπιθυμίας τῆς σαρκός, however, rather than the Johannine οὐδὲ ἐκ θελήματος σαρκός (cf. *1 Jn* 2.16; Dillmann, 1369).

[21] The author's knowledge of *GJohn* 20 is confirmed by *EpAp* 11.7, which elaborates the Johannine invitation to Thomas to confirm the bodily reality of the risen Lord (*GJn* 20.27), and by *EpAp* 29.5–6, the blessing of those who have not seen (cf. *GJn* 20.29).

Lazarus back in chapter 11. *GJohn* 20.30–31 is one of several pieces of evidence that make the hypothesis of a pre-Johannine signs source plausible and attractive.[22] On that hypothesis, *GJohn* 20.30–31 would originally have rounded off a pre-Johannine miracle sequence, suggesting a still closer analogy to *EpAp* 6.

These Johannine affinities raise questions about genre, creating difficulties for the view that *EpAp* can be straightforwardly classified as a 'post-resurrection dialogue', differing from its companions only in its 'proto–orthodoxy'. In this text eleven apostles record what they have 'heard and remembered' (1.4), perhaps representing an original ὡς ἑωράκαμεν καὶ ἐμνήσθημεν. Thus *EpAp* recalls Justin's references to early gospel literature as ἀπομνημονεύματα τῶν ἀποστόλων αὐτοῦ, 'memoirs of his [Christ's] apostles'.[23] While there is nothing to suggest that Justin was familiar with *EpAp*, his claim that gospels known to him derive from collective apostolic memory corresponds closely to this text. For Justin, these gospels embody apostolic memory even when they speak of Jesus' birth and childhood.[24] Similarly, in *EpAp*,

---

[22] On the Johannine signs source, see Rudolf Bultmann, *The Gospel of John: A Commentary* (Eng. trans. [Oxford: Blackwell, 1971]), 6–7, 113–15, and *passim*; Robert T. Fortna, *The Gospel of Signs: A Reconstruction of the Narrative Source Underlying the Fourth Gospel*, Society for New Testament Studies Monograph Series 11 (Cambridge: Cambridge University Press, 1970); Robert T. Fortna, *The Fourth Gospel and its Predecessor: From Narrative Source to Present Gospel* (Edinburgh: T&T Clark, 1989); H.-P. Heekerens, *Die Zeichen-Quelle der johanneischen Redaktion: Ein Beitrag zur Entstehungsgeschichte des vierten Evangelium* (Stuttgart: Katholisches Bibelwerk, 1984); John Ashton, *Studying John: Approaches to the Fourth Gospel* (Oxford, Clarendon Press, 1994), 90–113. Ashton rightly cautions that, while 'the arguments in favour of the *existence* of a signs source are overwhelming', we should not suppose 'that it can be *reconstructed* with equal certainty in the form in which the author left it' (*Studying John*, 103; italics original).

[23] The full phrase occurs in *Dial.* 100.4; 101.3; 102.5; 104.1; 106.4, abbreviated versions in 103.6; 105.1, 5, 6; 106.1, 3; 107.1, and an expanded version in 103.8. Cf. also *1Apol* 66.3.

[24] For an analysis of Justin's use of canonical gospel material, see my *Gospel Writing: A Canonical Perspective*, 473–77. In *Dial.* 103.8, Justin cites passages from the Lukan and Matthean Gethsemane narratives (sweat like blood, *GLk* 22.44; 'Remove this cup...', *GMt* 26.39), introducing them with the fullest of his references to the apostolic memoirs: ἐν γὰρ τοῖς ἀπομνημονεύμασιν, ἅ φημι ὑπὸ τῶν ἀποστόλων καὶ τῶν ἐκείνοις παρακολουθησάντων συντετάχθαι. It is likely that Justin sees *GMatthew* not as the product of an individual apostle but as collective apostolic memoirs, and *GLuke* as the prime example of memoirs by apostolic followers. Justin's language here may be influenced by *GLuke* 1.1–3, where the evangelist differentiates the apostolic eyewitnesses from writers of gospels such as himself. Justin's καὶ τῶν ἐκείνοις παρακολουθησάντων συντετάχθαι may echo Luke's κἀμοὶ παρηκολουθηκότι...γράψαι. Text in Miroslav Marcovich (ed.), *Iustini Martyris Apologiae pro Christianis, Dialogus cum Tryphone* (Berlin and New York: de Gruyter, 2005).

the apostles can collectively claim that Jesus 'was swaddled in Bethlehem and manifested and nourished and grew up *as we saw*' (3.15). The apostles' participation in the events of Jesus' ministry is also strongly emphasized in the miracle sequence by the continuing use of the first person plural.

> And as *we* considered and wondered at the glorious things he had done, he said *to us*, 'Who touched me?' And *we* said to him, 'Lord, the press of the crowd touched you!' And he answered and said to *us*, 'I felt that power came forth upon me.' Immediately that woman came before him and answered him and said to him, 'Lord, I touched you.' (5.4–7)

> And when *we* his disciples had no *denarii, we* said to him, 'Teacher, what shall we do about the tax-collector?' And he answered and said to *us*, 'Let one of you cast a hook into the deep and draw out a fish, and he will find *denarii* in it. Give them to the tax–collectors for myself and for you *[pl.]*.' (5.14–15)

> Then when *we* had no food except five loaves and two fishes, he commanded the men to recline. And their number was found to be five thousand besides women and children, and to these *we* brought pieces of bread. And they were satisfied, and there was some left over, and *we* removed twelve basketfuls of pieces. (5.17–19)

In each case the first person plural has been added to the author's probable sources (on this see further below). It continues on into the Easter narrative and beyond.

> Martha came and told *us. We* said to her, 'What do you want with us, O woman? One who died and is buried, can he live?' *We* did not believe her that the Saviour had risen from the dead. (*EpAp* 10.3–5)

This thread of collective first person plural references remains unbroken through the dialogue section (*EpAp* 13–50) and to the ascension narrative with which it concludes.

> And when he had said this and finished speaking with *us*, he said to *us* again, 'Behold, on the third day, at the third hour, the one who sent me will come so that I may go with him.' And as he spoke there was thunder and lightning and an

earthquake, and the heavens were torn asunder, and a bright cloud came and took him. And *we* heard the voice of many angels as they rejoiced and blessed and said, 'Gather us, O priest, into the light of glory!' And when he drew near to the firmament of heaven, *we* heard him saying, 'Go in peace!'   (*EpAp* 51.1–4)

Thus the extensive narrative frame for the central dialogue is similar in scope to that of *GLuke*, incorporating Jesus' birth in Bethlehem, his childhood, the mighty works of his ministry, and his crucifixion, burial, resurrection, and ascension. In other dialogue-centred texts such as the *Apocryphon of James* and the *Sophia of Jesus Christ*, the narrative setting is confined to the post-Easter sequel to Jesus' earthly life. The collective nature of the dialogue between Jesus and his disciples is a further link between *EpAp* and canonical gospel literature. The introductory formula, 'And we said to him. . .' occurs fifty-one times in this text, and echoes canonical phraseology such as, 'And his disciples came and said to him. . .' (*GMt* 13.10), 'His disciples said to him. . .' (*GMt* 19.10), 'And the apostles said to the Lord. . .' (*GLk* 17.5), 'His disciples said. . .' (*GJn* 16.29). Collective address is also the norm in *GThomas*: 'His disciples asked him. . .' (*GTh* 6), 'The disciples said to Jesus. . .' (*GTh* 12), 'His disciples said to him. . .' (*GTh* 52).[25] At no point in *EpAp* does an individual disciple pose a question, as Peter, Thomas, Philip, and 'Judas not Iscariot' do in the opening section of the Johannine Farewell Discourses (*GJn* 13.36; 14.5, 8, 22).

When this Johannine individuation of the disciples and their questions is extended across a whole text, the result is to fragment the previously collective apostolic testimony. In the *Dialogue of the Saviour* and the *Sophia of Jesus Christ*, individual questions are put to Jesus by privileged disciples: Matthew, Judas, and Mary in the first case, Philip, Matthew, Thomas, Mary, and Bartholomew in the second. The *Apocryphon of James* tells how 'the twelve disciples [were] all sitting together and recalling [ⲉⲩⲉⲓⲣⲉ ⲙ̄ⲡⲙⲉⲉⲩⲉ] what the Saviour had said to each one of them, whether secretly or openly, and arranging it in books.'[26] In the *Apocryphon of John* an extended revelation is communicated to John alone, and the work closes by

---

[25] Questions or proposals put to Jesus by individual disciples occur in *GTh* 21 (Mary), 61 (Salome), and 114 (Peter).

[26] *ApocrJas* 2,8–14.

describing how 'he went to his fellow disciples [ⲛⲉϥϣⲃⲣ ⲙⲁⲑⲏⲧⲏⲥ] and told them what the Saviour had said to him.'[27] A similar expectation of individual revelation is expressed in *GMary*, where Peter asks Mary to 'tell us the words of the Saviour that you remember [ⲉⲧⲉⲉⲓⲣⲉ ⲙⲡⲉⲩⲙⲉⲉⲩⲉ], the ones that you know and we do not…'[28]

These gospels or gospel-like texts all present themselves as the product of apostolic memory, but *EpAp* is distinctive in assuming that apostolic memory is collective rather than individual. That is still the view of Justin, as it had earlier been of Luke, for whom the 'many' written gospels to which he is to add his own contribution conform to what has been handed down by 'those who from the beginning were eyewitness and ministers of the word' (*GLk* 1.3). This further Lukan link confirms that *EpAp* straddles the boundary between the narrative gospel and dialogue gospel genres. It also serves as a reminder that ancient literary genres are not fixed categories but loose, overlapping, interacting, and constantly shifting sets of conventions that must be renegotiated by authors and readers of every new work.[29] The author of the *Epistula* is both an innovator and one among the Lukan 'many' who created a literary embodiment for the authentic apostolic teaching as they understood it. The miracle sequence is one of several features that establish this text's credentials as a contribution to narrative gospel literature.

3.2   Tradition and Redaction

Most of the stories recounted in the miracle sequence of *EpAp* appear to be derived from one or more of the canonical gospels. From *GJohn* there is the wedding at Cana, here briefly summarized;[30] from the

---

[27] *ApocrJn* 83.4–6.

[28] *GMary* 10, 4–6, cf. POxy 3525 14–17. The expectation of individual revelation here is a generic feature and should not be reduced to an issue of characterization. Cf. Christopher Tuckett (ed.), *The Gospel of Mary*, Oxford Early Christian Gospel Texts (Oxford: Oxford University Press, 2007), 168–69.

[29] On these now widely recognized points, see John Marincola, 'Genre, Convention, and Innovation in Greco-Roman Historiography', in C. S. Kraus (ed.), *The Limits of Historiography: Genre and Convention in Ancient Narrative Texts* (Leiden: Brill, 1999), 281–324; David L. Smith and Zachary L. Kostopoulos, 'Biography, History, and the Genre of Luke–Acts', *New Testament Studies* 63 (2017), 390–410; and, with specific reference to dialogue gospels, Sarah Parkhouse, *Eschatology and the Saviour: The Gospel of Mary among Early Christian Dialogue Gospels*, Society for New Testament Studies Monograph Series 176 (Cambridge: Cambridge University Press, 2019), 31–51.

[30] *EpAp* 5.1; cf. *GJn* 2.1–11.

three synoptists, the haemorrhaging woman and the exorcism of the demon named Legion;[31] from *GMatthew, GMark*, and *GJohn*, the walking on the water;[32] from *GMatthew*, the story of the coins in the fish's mouth;[33] and from all four canonical evangelists, the feeding of the five thousand.[34] In tracing this material back to canonical sources, it should not be assumed that those sources were already 'canonical' for the author. All that can safely be deduced is that they were available to him, just as *GMark* was available to Matthew and Luke.[35] If the *EpAp* version of the fish with coins in its mouth is secondary to Matthew, Matthew's version of the haemorrhaging woman is equally secondary to *GMark*. In other words, the *EpAp* miracle sequence belongs within a single ongoing process of writing and rewriting the traditional stories about Jesus. There are not two processes of gospel writing, one canonical and the other apocryphal; there is a single process retrospectively divided by the canonical decision for the fourfold gospel.

(1) With the fourfold gospel securely in place, Irenaeus can attack a popular story about the child Jesus' first day at school as a 'fabrication' (ῥᾳδιούργημα) illustrating his opponents' use of 'an unspeakable multitude of apocryphal and spurious writings' (ἀμύθητον πλῆθος ἀποκρύφων καὶ νόθων γραφῶν).[36] In the absence of a fourfold canonical gospel, however, the author of *EpAp* feels free to include the story as a miracle of precocious supernatural knowledge to open his miracle sequence. With the corrupt Ge'ez version of its ending emended, the story reads as follows.

> This is what our Lord Jesus Christ did when he was taken by Joseph and Mary his mother to where he was to be taught letters. And his teacher said to him as he taught him, 'Say,

---

[31] *EpAp* 5.3–12; cf. *GMt* 9.20–22, *GMk* 5.25–34, *GLk* 8.43–48; *GMt* 8.28–34, *GMk* 5.1–20, *GLk* 8.26–39.

[32] *EpAp* 5.13; cf. *GMt* 14.22–33, *GMk* 6.45–52, *GJn* 6.15–21.

[33] *EpAp* 5.14–16; cf. *GMt* 17.24–27.

[34] *EpAp* 5.17–21; cf. *GMt* 14.15–21, *GMk* 6.35–44, *GLk* 9.12–17, *GJn* 6.1–12.

[35] The distinction between the use of a source and recognition of its ongoing authority is rightly emphasized by David C. Sim, 'Matthew's Use of Mark: Did Matthew Intend to Supplement or Replace his Primary Source?', *New Testament Studies* 57 (2011), 176–92. See also my article, 'How Did Mark Survive?', in K. A. Bendoraitis and N. K. Gupta (eds.), *Matthew and Mark across Perspectives: Essays in Honour of Stephen C. Barton and William R. Telford*, Library of New Testament Studies (London: T&T Clark/Bloomsbury, 2016), 1–17.

[36] Irenaeus, *Adv. haer.* 1.20.1.

Alpha!' He answered and said to him, 'You tell me first what Beta is, and then *I will trust you and say Alpha!' (*EpAp* 4.1–3)[37]

In the Ge'ez manuscripts, the sequel to 'You tell me first what Beta is...' reads, 'and when {*vars.* then, is this} truly <and> really the work that was done {*var.* he did}'. This seems to be an attempt at an *inclusio* with the opening ('This is what the Lord did...'), yet it is virtually meaningless.[38] With minor emendations, the opening three words, *wa-'əmza 'amān* ('And when truly') can be read as *wa-'əmzə 'a'ammən* ('And then I will trust'). Indeed, 'and then' is already the reading of at least one manuscript.[39] This suggests a link with the longer version of the story in the *Infancy Gospel of Thomas*, where the child Jesus dutifully repeats the letter Alpha but objects to the hasty transition to Beta with Alpha still unexplained: 'First teach me Alpha, and then I will trust you and say Beta' (πρῶτον δίδαξόν με τὸ ἄλφα καὶ τότε πιστεύσω σοι λέγειν τὸ βῆτα).[40] The *EpAp*[gk] version of the second part of this saying may therefore have read, ... καὶ τότε πιστεύσω σοι λέγειν τὸ ἄλφα.

The story as told in *EpAp* is also closely related to the version recorded by Irenaeus. With probable equivalences to *EpAp*[gk] underlined, Irenaeus's version runs as follows.

> ὡς τοῦ κυρίου τὰ διὰ τοῦ διδασκάλου αὐτῷ φήσαντος, καθὼς ἔθος ἐστιν, εἰπὲ ἄλφα, ἀποκρίνασθαι τὸ ἄλφα, πάλιν τε τὸ βῆτα τοῦ διδασκάλου κελεύσαντος εἰπεῖν, ἀποκρίνασθαι τὸν κύριον σύ μοι πρότερον εἰπὲ τί ἐστι τὸ ἄλφα, καὶ τότε σοι ἐρῶ τί ἐστι τὸ βῆτα.

> When the Lord's teacher said to him, as was his custom, 'Say Alpha!', the Lord answered, 'Alpha'. And when again

---

[37] The asterisk marks the beginning of a textual emendation.

[38] As Hills acknowledges, the concluding phrase 'is probably corrupt in all mss.' (*The Epistle of the Apostles*, 24).

[39] S, '*and then* truly and really the work that he did'. It is not clear whether 'and then' here is a true vestige of an originally correct reading or a later attempt to correct 'and when' by emending it to the linking phrase used in the next verse (*EpAp* 5.1). 'And then' seems secondary to 'and when' (= 'and as') at 5.4 E G.

[40] *IGTh* 6.9. Text in Reidar Aasgaard, *The Childhood of Jesus: Decoding the Apocryphal Gospel of Thomas* (Eugene, OR: Cascade, 2009), 224. Aasgaard draws the Greek text from Codex Sabaiticus 259, an eleventh-century manuscript in which the episode of the alphabet lesson has been much elaborated (19–22). Comparison with Irenaeus and *EpAp* indicates that an early version of the alpha/beta saying remains intact in late manuscripts.

the teacher told him to say Beta, the Lord <u>answered</u>, 'You
<u>first tell me what</u> Alpha <u>is, and then</u> I will tell <u>you</u> what
Beta is!'   (Irenaeus, *Adv. haer.* 1.20.1)[41]

As in the *Infancy Gospel of Thomas*, the child does say 'Alpha', as
requested, but refuses to pronounce 'Beta' until the esoteric significance of the first letter of the alphabet has been explained. In the
more succinct *EpAp* version, there is no initial compliance from the
child, and the teacher is challenged to explain Beta. *EpAp*[gk] may here
have read: σύ μοι πρότερον εἰπὲ τί ἐστι τὸ βῆτα καὶ τότε πιστεύσω
λέγειν τὸ ἄλφα. In the *IGTh* and hypothetical *EpAp*[gk], the apodosis
of Jesus' response is a conditional promise to fulfil the teacher's
instruction to pronounce a letter: '...and then I will trust you and
say Alpha [*EpAp*[gk]] / Beta [*IGTh*].' In the Irenaean version, the child
Jesus promises an ontological explanation of 'what Beta is' if the
teacher can prove himself worthy by explaining Alpha. In *EpAp* the
concern with Beta points towards something subsequent to beginnings or origins.

In the *Book of Revelation*, Christ is the Alpha and the Omega, the
First and the Last (*Rev* 22.13). In *EpAp* 4 he is Alpha and Beta, the
First and the Second. An explanation may be found in the two
articles of the christological confession immediately preceding the
miracle sequence:

> This we declare, that our Lord and Saviour Jesus Christ is
> God, the Son of God, who was sent from God, ruler of the
> whole world, maker and creator of every name that is
> named...; who sits above the Cherubim at the right hand
> of the throne of the Father; who by his word commanded
> the heavens and founded the earth and what is
> in it...   (*EpAp* 3.1–2, 4–5)

> And God the Son of God do we confess, the Word who
> became flesh of Mary, carried in her womb through the
> Holy Spirit. And not by the desire of the flesh but by the
> will of God was he born; and he was swaddled in
> Bethlehem, and manifested and nourished and grew up, as
> we saw.   (*EpAp* 3.13–15)

---

[41] Text from Adelin Rousseau and Louis Doutreleau (eds.), *Irenée de Lyon: Contre
les Hérésies*, Libre 1, Tome 2, Sources chrétiennes 264 (Paris: Éditions du Cerf, 1979).
Irenaeus's Greek is preserved in Epiphanius, *Pan.* 34.18.7–9.

Christ is Alpha as the divine creator who is one with his Father in the work of creation, and he is Beta as the Word made flesh and born of Mary. If his teacher recognizes who he is in his present Beta form, he will be worthy to learn of his pre-existence as Alpha. Understood in this way, the alphabet story provides an important conceptual link between the confession and the miracle sequence. In his Alpha capacity as creator, the Lord 'established the sea and it did not cross its boundary' (3.5). As Beta, the incarnate Lord walked on the Sea of Galilee and stilled its waves (5.13). As Alpha, the Lord makes 'depths and springs to gush forth and flow into the earth' (3.5). As Beta, he caused water made wine to gush forth at the wedding but stopped the flow of blood within the woman's body (5.1, 3–7). While for Irenaeus the alphabet story is utterly false, for the author of *EpAp* it encapsulates his christology.[42]

(2) The miracle sequence continues with a brief version of the Johannine water-into-wine story: 'And then there was a wedding in Cana of Galilee, and they invited him with his mother and his brothers, and water he made wine' (*EpAp* 5.1).[43] The first phrase is closely related to *GJohn* 2.1a, καὶ τῇ ἡμέρᾳ τῇ τρίτῃ γάμος ἐγένετο ἐν Κανὰ τῆς Γαλιλαίας. The third phrase, summarizing the miracle itself, corresponds exactly to *GJohn* 4.46, ἐποίησεν τὸ ὕδωρ οἶνον.[44] However, the second phrase diverges from *GJohn* 2.1b–2, καὶ ἦν ἡ μήτηρ τοῦ Ἰησοῦ ἐκεῖ, ἐκλήθη δὲ καὶ ὁ Ἰησοῦς καὶ οἱ μαθηταὶ αὐτοῦ. In *EpAp* Jesus' disciples are absent from this scene and their place is taken by his brothers, in spite of the emphasis on the disciples' presence in the miracle sequence as a whole (cf. *EpAp* 3.15; 5.4–5, 14–17). In *GJohn* 2 Jesus is already accompanied by his first disciples (cf. *GJn* 1.35–51), and their presence at the wedding is necessary for the coherence of the narrative. In *EpAp* 5.1 the story of

[42] That the author of *EpAp* can find theological content in his selected miracle stories is evident from his interpretation of the five loaves of the feeding miracle (5.20–21), on which see below. The alphabet story does not merely demonstrate 'that Jesus is superior to all other teachers' (Hills, *Tradition and Composition*, 51).

[43] 'Water he made wine' (*EpAp* 5.1c) is followed in 5.2 by 'and the dead he raised, and paralytics he made to walk, and for the man whose hand was withered he restored it'. Hills suggests that the reference to the wedding and the guest-list in 5.1ab is a later addition, the removal of which produces a structure of miracle story + four reports (4.1–3 + 5.1c–2) which is repeated in 5.3–8 + 9 (Hills, *Tradition and Composition*, 48–49, cf. 46). Hills overlooks the family context that links the alleged gloss to the preceding alphabet story and argues unconvincingly that 'his brothers' means 'his disciples' (49).

[44] So, rightly, Hills, *Epistle*, 25.

the wedding at Cana is self–contained and belongs to the period of Jesus' youth when he is still living with his family.[45]

That Jesus' brothers were among the wedding-guests in a pre-Johannine version of the story, but were later supplanted by his disciples, is suggested by the story's conclusion in *GJohn* 2.12 as attested in Greek, Latin, and Coptic witnesses.[46] Here, those who journey with Jesus from Cana to Capernaum after the wedding are his mother and brothers but not his disciples: μετὰ τοῦτο κατέβη εἰς Καφαρναοὺμ αὐτὸς καὶ ἡ μήτηρ αὐτοῦ καὶ οἱ ἀδελφοὶ αὐτοῦ καὶ ἐκεῖ ἔμειναν οὐ πολλὰς ἡμέρας (ℵ, cf. it$^{a\,b\,e}$, cop^{ly}). Among manuscripts that add the disciples here, there is difference of opinion about where to place them.

1a αὐτὸς καὶ ἡ μήτηρ αὐτοῦ καὶ οἱ ἀδελφοὶ αὐτοῦ (ℵ)[47]

1b ipse et mater eius et fratres [eius b] (it$^{a\,b\,e}$)[48]

1c [ⲚⲦⲀϤ] ⲘⲚ̅ⲦⲈϤⲘⲀⲀⲨ ⲘⲚ̅ⲚⲈϤⲤⲚⲎⲨ (cop^{ly})[49]

2a αὐτὸς καὶ ἡ μήτηρ αὐτοῦ καὶ οἱ ἀδελφοὶ <καὶ οἱ μαθηταὶ> αὐτοῦ (𝔓$^{66*\,75}$)

2b αὐτὸς καὶ ἡ μήτηρ αὐτοῦ καὶ οἱ ἀδελφοὶ αὐτοῦ <καὶ οἱ μαθηταὶ αὐτοῦ> (𝔓^{66c} A)

3 αὐτὸς καὶ ἡ μήτηρ αὐτοῦ <καὶ οἱ μαθηταὶ αὐτοῦ> καὶ οἱ ἀδελφοί (K Π *f*^{13})

4 αὐτὸς καὶ <οἱ μαθηταὶ αὐτοῦ> καὶ ἡ μήτηρ καὶ οἱ ἀδελφοὶ αὐτοῦ (W^{sup})

---

[45] *EpAp* 5.1 is rightly cited by Bultmann as confirmation that the disciples have displaced Jesus' brothers in the present text of *GJohn* 2.1 (*John*, 114–15n.).

[46] Without reference to the text-critical evidence, Wellhausen rightly notes that 'nach 2, 12 darf man vermuten, das οἱ μαθηταὶ αὐτοῦ in Vers 2 für οἱ ἀδελφοὶ αὐτοῦ cingesetzt sei' (*Das Evangelium Johannis* [Berlin: Georg Reimer, 1908], 13).

[47] The Greek textual evidence is conveniently presented in Reuben Swanson (ed.), *New Testament Greek Manuscripts: Variant Readings Arranged in Horizontal Lines against Codex Vaticanus: John* (Sheffield and Pasadena, CA: Sheffield Academic Press/William Carey International University Press, 1995).

[48] Latin textual evidence in Adolf Jülicher (ed.), *Itala: Das Neue Testament in altlateinischer Überlieferung*, IV. *Johannes-Evangelium* (Berlin: de Gruyter, 1963); P. H. Burton, J. Balserak, H. A. G. Houghton, and D. Parker (eds.), *Vetus Latina, The Verbum Project: The Old Latin Manuscripts of John's Gospel* (2007), www.iohannes.com/vetuslatina.

[49] Sir Herbert Thompson (ed.), *The Gospel of St. John According to the Earliest Coptic Manuscript* (London: British School of Archaelogy in Egypt, 1924). The manuscript opens with the words from John 2.12 cited here: '[he] and his mother and his brothers' (xxii, 1, 53).

The sequence of these readings from the third to the ninth centuries shows how the disciples were introduced into a text from which they were previously absent, and subsequently promoted above Jesus' brothers and, in one case, above his mother. In the form attested in Codices Sinaiticus, Vercellensis (a), Veronensis (b), Palatinus (e), and the Coptic Qau Codex (ly), *GJohn* 2.12 coheres with *EpAp* 5.1 as vestiges of a pre-Johannine version of the water-into-wine story.[50]

(3) The brief *EpAp* account of the wedding at Cana leads directly into a general summary of Jesus' miracle-working activity: '… and the water he made wine, and the dead he raised, and paralytics he made to walk, and for the man whose hand was withered he restored it' (5.2). The author is familiar with synoptic miracle stories and probably has in mind Jairus' daughter,[51] the paralytic let down through the roof,[52] and the sabbath healing in the synagogue.[53] The last of these references still refers to an individual event, but the author sees the raising of the dead and the healing of paralytics as typical of Jesus' activities and refers to them in the plural. Thus the story of the haemorrhaging woman that follows is set against a broader background of restorative activity.

In the analysis below, redactional material introduced by the author of *EpAp* is italicized,[54] and the relationship to synoptic versions is indicated for convenience by reference to the Eusebian canons (**II** Matthew–Mark–Luke, **V** Matthew–Luke, **VIII** Luke–Mark, **X₂** Mark only, **X₃** Luke only).[55] The prominence of material

---

[50] For a more elaborate attempt to find text-critical evidence for early Johannine text-forms, see Elizabeth Schrader, 'Was Mary of Bethany Added to the Fourth Gospel in the Second Century?', *Harvard Theological Review*, 110 (2017), 360–92.

[51] *GMt* 9.18–19, 23–26; *GMk* 5.22–24, 35–43; *GLk* 8.40–42, 49–56.

[52] *GMt* 9.1–8; *GMk* 2.1–12; *GLk* 5.17–26.

[53] *GMt* 12.9–14; *GMk* 3.1–6; *GLk* 6.6–11.

[54] That there are redactional elements in the miracle sequence is denied by M. Hornschuh, who writes: 'Vergleicht man den vorliegenden Abriss der synoptischen Wunder mit den kanonischen Darstellungen, so sieht man, dass der Verfasser auf eine knappe, das Wesentliche zusammenraffende Art der Darstellung bedacht ist, um schnell zu den Fragen und Themen überzugehen, um die es ihm eigentlich geht. So hätte der Verfasser also den Zusatz kaum geboten, wenn er ihn nicht in irgendeiner Quelle – es kann aber auch eine mündliche Tradition gewesen sein – vorgefunden hätte' (Manfred Hornschuh, *Studien zur Epistula Apostolorum*, Patristische Texte und Studien 5 [Berlin: de Gruyter, 1965], 11). It is, however, implausible to postulate a source on the basis of the author's lack of interest in its contents.

[55] On the Eusebian canons, see Matthew R. Crawford, 'Ammonius of Alexandria, Eusebius of Caesarea, and the Beginnings of Gospel Scholarship', *New Testament Studies* 61 (2015), 1–29; Matthew R. Crawford, *The Eusebian Canon Tables: Ordering Textual Knowledge in Late Antiquity*, Oxford Early Christian Studies (Oxford: Oxford

shared by *GLuke* and *GMark* (cf. *GLk* 8.43–48; *GMk* 5.25–34) is the result of Matthew's tendency to abbreviate the longer stories he inherits from Mark (cf. *GMt* 9.20–22).

> [II]And a woman who suffered her periods twelve years touched [V]the hem of [II]his garment [VIII]and was immediately well. *And as we considered and wondered at the glorious things he had done,* [VIII]he said *to us,* 'Who touched me?' [X2]And *we* said to him, [X3]'Lord, the press of the crowd *touched you!' And he answered and said to us,* 'I felt that power *came forth upon me.' Immediately* [VIII]that woman came *before him and answered him saying, 'Lord, I touched you.'* [II]And he *answered and* [II]said to her, [VIII]'Go, [II]your faith has made you well.'   (*EpAp* 5.3–7)

The distinction here between tradition and redaction is straightforward, although the wording of the traditional elements – motifs drawn from the synoptics – has been adapted to the new context. The redaction consists mainly in *(i)* the insertion of a passage in which the disciples testify to Jesus' miracle-working in general ('As we considered and wondered at the glorious things he had done') and *(ii)* the rewriting of the sequel to the healing as a dialogue between Jesus and the disciples ('he said *to us.* . .', '*we* said to him. . .', '*And he answered and said to us.* . .'). As a result, the woman's confession ('I touched you') answers a question actually addressed to the disciples ('Who touched me?').[56] Thus this passage initiates the dialogue format that predominates in this work as a whole. Also to be noted is the reference to power coming upon Jesus from above, rather than going out from him.[57]

One general statement about Jesus' miracle-working immediately precedes the story of the haemorrhaging woman (5.2), another occurs in first person form within it (5.4), and yet another follows it: 'And then the deaf he made to hear and the blind to see and those with demons he exorcized and those with leprosy he cleansed' (5.9).

University Press, 2019); Anthony Grafton and Megan Williams, *Christianity and the Transformation of the Book* (Cambridge, MA: Harvard University Press, 2006), 194–98; Francis Watson, *The Fourfold Gospel: A Theological Reading of the New Testament Portraits of Jesus* (Grand Rapids, MI: Baker, 2016), 109–23. The Eusebian apparatus is concerned with parallel contents, not identical wording.

[56] Contra Hills (*Tradition and Composition,* 55), there is no more need to find an anti-docetic polemic here than in the synoptic versions of this story.

[57] For the text here, see the *Additional Note* on 5.6.

The point is to suggest that the seven events narrated in the miracle sequence are a selection from a much wider range. A similar point was made in the conclusion of *GJohn* and the signs source that may have preceded it: 'Many other signs Jesus performed before his disciples that are not written in this book...' (*GJn* 20.31, imitated in the Johannine 'Longer Ending' at 21.25). In both the Johannine signs source and *EpAp*'s miracle sequence, the presence of the disciples as witnesses is emphasized.

(4) The next individual story is that of 'the demon Legion' (cf. *GMt* 8.28–34; *GMk* 5.1–20; *GLk* 8.26–39). Here a distinctively Matthean element emerges for the first time in the miracle sequence $(\mathbf{X_1})$.[58]

> *And the demon* ^{VIII} Legion, *who dwelt in a man,* ^{II}met *Jesus* and cried out and said, ^{XI}"Before the day *of our destruction* have you come *to drive us out?' And the Lord Jesus rebuked him and said to him, 'Go out of this man and do nothing to him!' And he* ^{II}went into the pigs *and plunged them* into the sea, ^{VIII}and they were drowned.   (*EpAp* 5.10–12)

Here conflation or assimilation has taken place, although on a very small scale: the name 'Legion' occurs in *GLuke* (and *GMark*) but not in *GMatthew*, while the demon's anticipation of final judgement is exclusively Matthean. The conflation should not be seen as a 'harmonization', negotiating the difference between two or more sources of acknowledged canonical authority.[59] The incorporation here of distinctively Matthean and Lukan elements into the new version of the story is comparable to Luke's incorporation of Matthean elements into the opening of his *GMark*-based retelling of the story of the paralytic. Luke follows Matthew in introducing the story with ἰδού and in having the paralyzed man brought ἐπι

---

[58] In this story and the stories of the haemorrhaging woman and the feeding miracle the wording corresponds in several places to the Old Geʻez version of *GMatthew*, dating perhaps to the fourth century, at points where this differs from the *Eth* text-form that supplanted it several centuries later. See the *Additional Notes* on *EpAp* 5.8, 10, 17, 19; 41.4.

[59] That the author's undoubted knowledge of *GMatthew* and *GLuke* does not amount to recognition of their canonical authority is rightly pointed out by Hornschuh, *Studien*, 9, 12.

κλίνης (*GLk* 5.18, *GMt* 9.2; cf. *GMk* 2.3).[60] Luke 'knows' *GMark* and *GMatthew* just as the author of *EpAp* 'knows' *GLuke* and *GMatthew*, but knowledge and use of a text need not entail recognition of its established canonical authority. In this case, the relative independence of the *EpAp* version of the Legion story is more apparent than its dependence on earlier versions.

(5) The sequel to the demon-possessed pigs drowning in the sea is that Jesus walks on the sea, underlining his triumph over the demon Legion by trampling on his grave. The introductory 'And then' links this episode to the preceding one.

> And he [Legion] went into the pigs and plunged them into the sea, and they were drowned. And then he [Jesus] walked on the sea, and the winds blew and he rebuked them, and the waves of the sea he stilled.   (*EpAp* 5.12–13)

In the canonical gospels Jesus' walking on water is accompanied by a wind strong enough to make rowing difficult (*GMk* 6.48; *GJn* 6.18) and the waves threatening (*GMt* 14.24). The wind ceased when Jesus enters the boat (*GMt* 14.32; *GMk* 6.51); alternatively, the boat arrives instantly at its destination (*GJn* 6.21). The *EpAp* passage introduces the motif of Jesus' rebuke, which also occurs in the synoptic stilling of the storm narrative – where, however, the rebuke is addressed to both winds and waves (*GMt* 8.26; *GMk* 4.39; *GLk* 8.24).

(6) Absent from the previous two episodes, the disciples reappear in the story that follows (cf. *GMt* 17.24–27).

> *And when we his disciples had no denarii, we said to him, 'Teacher, what shall we do about the tax–collector?' And he answered and said to us, 'Let one of you* [X]'cast a hook into *the deep and draw out a fish, and he* will find *denarii in it.* Give *them to the tax–collectors* for myself and for *you* [pl.]'   (*EpAp* 5.14–16)

---

[60] On this 'minor agreement', see Mark Goodacre, *The Case against Q: Studies in Markan Priority and the Synoptic Problem* (Harrisburg, PA: Trinity Press International, 2002), 156–57. Luke subsequently reduces the Matthean κλίνη (a substantial piece of furniture, under which one might in principle place a lamp) to a κλινίδιον (*GLk* 5.19) when faced with the problem – posed by Mark but absent from Matthew – of getting it lowered through a hole in the roof.

In the Matthean version, tax-collectors ask Peter whether the Teacher pays tax, to which Peter answers in the affirmative. Jesus is aware of this conversation, and claims on theological grounds that he and his disciples are in principle exempt from taxation. The production of the coin-bearing fish is a concession intended to pre-vent any trouble. In the *EpAp* version Peter is replaced by the collective 'we' that was earlier prominent in the story of the haemor-rhaging woman. It is again emphasized that knowledge of the events of Jesus' ministry is dependent on the disciples' collective testimony.

(7) The final episode in the miracle sequence contributes a fifth account of the feeding of the 5,000 to the four contained in the canonical gospels (**I** *GMt* 14.13–21; *GMk* 6.30–44; *GLk* 9.10–17; *GJn* 6.1–13). As we have seen, the author of *EpAp* has already shown his independence of his sources by detaching its Matthean, Markan, and Johannine sequel – Jesus' walking on the water – and connecting it to the story of Legion. In the following analysis, **VI** = *GMt* + *GMk*.:

> *Then when we had no food except* **I**five loaves and two fishes, he commanded the men to recline. *And their number was found to be* **X**five thousand besides women and children, *and to these we brought pieces of bread.* **II**And they were satisfied, *and there was some left over, and we* **VI**removed **I**twelve basketfuls of pieces. *If we ask, 'What do these five loaves mean?', they are an image of our faith as true Christians; that is, in the Father, ruler of the whole world, and in Jesus Christ and in the Holy Spirit and in the holy church and in the forgiveness of sins.* (*EpAp* 5.17–21)[61]

This interpretation of the five loaves may be compared with that of Origen, for whom the five loaves represent the five senses and thus the plain meaning of scripture, while the two fishes represent the two sides of the spiritual sense, expressed in scripture and immanent within the divine mind. Alternatively, the two fishes are the word of the Father and the Son.[62] Earlier analogies to *EpAp*'s interpret-ation of the five loaves may be found in Irenaeus's summaries of post-Valentinian expositions of gospel passages as referring to heav-enly realities. In one such exposition, the haemorrhaging woman represents the erring aeon Sophia, who risked dissolution by striving

---

[61] For the translation, 'true Christians', cf. Hills, *Tradition and Composition*, 62–64.
[62] Origen, *In Matth.* 11.2.

for union with the unknown Father, and who was healed from her passion by touching the garment of the Son (Aletheia, consort of Monogenes) and by the power that went out from him (Horos).[63] Irenaeus later remarks sarcastically on the lack of a correlate to the five loaves in the Valentinian pleroma, expressing his disdain for this method of exegesis – although he himself practises something not dissimilar when he links the fourfold gospel to the four living creatures around the divine throne.[64] Like Origen and Irenaeus but unlike the Valentinians, the author of *EpAp* believes that there are just three primary occupants of the heavenly realms, the Father, the Son, and the Spirit. The five loaves fulfil their symbolic intent with the addition of the holy church and the forgiveness of sins.

Thus the sequence reaches its climax in a miracle that contains within itself the sum total of Christian faith, a *regula fidei* reduced to a minimum. A certain analogy may be seen with the dogmatic content of the first story, where the child Christ is the incarnate form (Beta) of the eternal creative word (Alpha). If so, the rule of faith places the christological claim in a larger context that encompasses the heavenly community of Father, Son, and Spirit as well as the earthly community of the holy church, where there occurs the forgiveness of sins. It is the number of the loaves that lies at the heart of this symbolism, rather than the bread itself as in the Johannine parallel. In the Johannine version of the story there are 'five barley loaves', πέντε ἄρτους κριθίνους (*GJn* 6.9, cf. v. 13), but as the interpretation gets under way the plural loaves ('... you ate from the loaves and were satisfied', *GJn* 6.26) are replaced by the singular 'food' (βρῶσις, v. 27) and then by the scriptural reference to 'the bread from heaven' (v. 31), finally identified with Jesus himself: 'I am the bread of life...' (v. 35).

In *EpAp*, in contrast, Jesus is represented not by the totality of the bread but by just one loaf among the five. This interpretation of the story directs us not to an all-important encounter with a single life-giving object but to a more spacious field marked out by a plurality of co-ordinates. Thus the collective apostolic authors establish their status both as participants in the event and as guarantors of proto-orthodox faith.

---

[63] Irenaeus, *Adv. haer.* 1.3.3.
[64] Irenaeus, *Adv. haer.* 2.24.4; 3.11.8.

4

RESURRECTION AND ESCHATOLOGIES

EpAp's collection of miracle stories does not lead directly to a summary account of Jesus' death and resurrection, as the precedent of the canonical gospels might lead us to expect. Surprisingly, the miracle sequence is rounded off with what looks very like an epistolary conclusion:

> And these things our Lord and Saviour revealed to us and showed us, as we likewise do to you, so that you may be partakers in the grace of the Lord and in our ministry and our praise, as you think of eternal life. Be strong and do not waver in the knowledge and certainty of our Lord Jesus Christ, and he will be merciful and gracious and save constantly, to the end of the age. (*EpAp* 6.1–3)

Here the miracles that have just been narrated are viewed as a series of revelations granted to the disciples and, through them, also to their addressees. With their faith strengthened by the apostolic recollections of Jesus' mighty works, readers will be 'partakers in the grace of the Lord' (*Gk* perhaps ἵνα ἦτε κοινωνοί ἐν τῇ χάριτι τοῦ κυρίου), along with the apostles themselves. The thought here is close to that of *1 John* 1.3: 'What we have seen and heard we also proclaim to you, so that you too may have fellowship [κοινωνία] with us.' A retrospective reference to Jesus' 'signs' as the basis for faith and the hope of eternal life also occurs in the original ending of *GJohn*, where the importance of the disciples' eyewitness testimony is again emphasized ('... in the presence of his disciples', *GJn* 20.30) and where its ultimate purpose is again introduced with a ἵνα-clause: ἵνα πιστεύοντες ζωὴν ἔχητε... (*GJn* 20.31b), ἵνα καὶ ὑμεῖς κοινωνίαν ἔχητε... (*1Jn* 1.3), ἵνα ἦτε κοινωνοί... (*EpAp* 6.2). The Johannine reference to Jesus' signs is positioned after the evangelist's Easter narrative, rather than before (as in the case of *EpAp*). Yet Jesus' resurrection does not belong to the sequence of Johannine signs, which are acts carried out by Jesus himself.[1] The original conclusion – the Johannine Shorter Ending – seems to point back to the account of Jesus' public ministry that concludes in chapter 12 where the transition from public to private is carefully noted:

> Jesus said these things and going out he was hidden from them. Although he had done such great signs before them, they did not believe in him, so that the word of the prophet Isaiah might be fulfilled... *(GJn* 12.36b–38a)[2]

Faith, then, is the intended outcome of Jesus' public performance of 'signs'. These events have their own distinct significance quite apart from his passion and resurrection. Following this Johannine lead, *EpAp* takes a similar view: the collective apostolic authors pause to underline the significance of the miracles they have witnessed and recounted before proceeding to speak briefly of Jesus' death and burial and at length of the sequel. The imitation of an epistolary conclusion in *EpAp* 6 serves to emphasize that Jesus' mighty works already represent a sufficient foundation for faith.

At *EpAp* 7–8 the recapitulation and elaboration of the letter opening continues to emphasize 'the things that he did as we watched him' (8.2), although the author's purpose from now on is to demonstrate the supreme importance of Easter morning as the occasion of Jesus' resurrection and his instruction of the disciples in preparation for their worldwide mission. This focus on Jesus' resurrection is anticipated in the reference to 'touch' near the opening of the work:

> Proclaiming and declaring to you our Lord Jesus Christ, as we heard so have we written; and we touched him after he was raised from the dead, when he revealed to us what is great and wonderful and true.   *(EpAp* 2.3)

---

[1] Contra the claim of Raymond Brown that the evangelist 'must mean also to include the appearances to the disciples in xx 1–28 that led them to confess Jesus as Lord' (*The Gospel According to John*, Anchor Bible Series, 2 vols. [New York: Doubleday, 1966], 2.1058). *GJohn* 20.30 speaks of 'the signs *that Jesus did...*' and in spite of 10.18 it seems unlikely that the Johannine evangelist understands Jesus' resurrection as his own act (cf. *GJn* 17.2–3). In 2.19–22 Jesus' apparent reference to a self-resurrection ('I will raise it up', referring to 'the temple of his body') is superseded by a more conventional passive form (ὅτε οὖν ἠγέρθη ἐκ νεκρῶν, v. 22).

[2] The close relationship between the two passages is pointed out by R. Bultmann, who argues that in both cases 'the Evangelist is taking over the formulation of the σημεῖα-source' (*The Gospel of John: A Commentary*, Eng. trans. [Oxford: Blackwell, 1971], 698).

Among the canonical Easter narratives it is only in *GJohn* that the issue of touch plays a significant role, initially in connection with Mary Magdalene ('Do not touch me. . .', *GJn* 20.17) but above all in the physical examination demanded by and offered to Thomas (*GJn* 20.24–29). Yet sight alone finally proves to be sufficient. When Jesus displays his hands and his side, Thomas immediately acclaims him as 'my Lord and my God' without needing to take up the invitation to touch him: 'Because you have *seen* me do you believe?' (*GJn* 20.29a). In *EpAp* actual touch is necessary as a precondition of faith in the physically risen Lord (cf. *1 Jn* 1.1, '. . . and our hands have handled'). Here and elsewhere, a motif is appropriated from the Johannine Easter story but developed in new directions. There is no acknowledgement of the superior authority of the source text. On the contrary, the source stands in need of correction and supplementation.[3]

4.1   Rewriting *GJohn* 20

In *GJohn* it is a single disciple who disbelieves his colleagues' claim to have seen the risen Lord and who demands to put this claim to the text through touch. In *EpAp* the disbelief is general and the three disciples invited to participate in a test involving both touch and sight are representative of the entire group. The intertextual relationship between *EpAp* and the Johannine parallels is close but complex, and may be formatted as follows, with **A**, **B**, **C**, and **D** differentiating the four main components of the Johannine passage and underlining indicating the terminology taken over by *EpAp*:

> *GJn* 20.25: [A]Unless I see in his hands the nail-marks [B]and thrust [βάλω] my finger into the nail-marks [C]and thrust [βάλω] my hand into his side, [D]I will not believe.
>
> *GJn* 20.27: [B]Put [φέρε] your finger here [A]and see my hands [C]and take [φέρε] your hand and thrust [βάλε] into my side, [D]and do not be unbelieving but believing.

Here **A**, **B**, **C** represent the testing of Jesus' bodily identity by sight (**A**) and touch (**B**: wounds to hands, **C**: wound to side), while **D**

---

[3] This unusually close relationship to *GJohn* helps to explain the difference between the narrative framework of *EpAp* and that of other dialogue gospels – noted by Judith Hartenstein, *Die zweite Lehre: Erscheinungen des Auferstandenen als Rahmenerzählungen frühchristlicher Dialoge*, Texte und Untersuchungen zur Geschichte der altchristlichen Literatur 146 (Berlin: Akademie Verlag, 2000), 112.

represents the appropriate responses in the event of confirmation or disconfirmation.[4] In *EpAp* the testing is distributed between three disciples, acting on behalf of the entire group since they are all unbelieving, and not only Thomas.[5] Seeing is focused on Jesus' feet rather than his hands, where touch is sufficient.

> *EpAp* 11.7–12.2: 'That you may know that it is I, [B]Peter, thrust your fingers into the nail-marks of my hands; [C]and you too, Thomas, thrust your fingers into the spear wounds in my side; [A]and you, Andrew, look at my feet and see if they are not in contact with the ground. For it is written in the prophet, "As for an appearance of a demon, its foot is not in contact with the ground."' And we touched him, that we might know that he had truly risen in flesh. And we fell on our faces, confessing our sins, [D]because we had been unbelieving.[6]

The relationship between *EpAp* and *GJohn* in the first part of this passage may also be represented as follows, with square brackets enclosing *EpAp* additions and angled brackets identifying wording drawn from *GJn* 20.27 rather than 20.25:

> [B][Peter] thrust <your> finger[s] into the nail-marks <of my hands> [C]and [you too Thomas] <thrust [your fingers] into [the spear wounds in] my side>

---

[4] Gregory Riley suggests that the Johannine Thomas 'requires a distasteful, even repulsive, method of proof of the physical nature of the risen Jesus', and that this reflects the evangelist's hostility towards a community in which 'Thomas called the Twin' plays a beloved-disciple role: cf. *GJn* 11.16, 20.24, 21.2; *GTh* incipit; *AcTh* 9; *BkTh* 138, 7–8 (NHC II) (*Resurrection Reconsidered: Thomas and John in Controversy* [Minneapolis, MN: Fortress Press, 1995], 115). If this is correct, the author of *EpAp* remains ignorant of or uninterested in this polemical context. For critique of Riley, see Ismo Dunderberg, *The Beloved Disciple in Conflict? Revisiting the Gospels of John and Thomas* (Oxford: Oxford University Press, 2006), 52–67.

[5] According to Hills (*Tradition and Composition*, 88), the sequence Peter–Thomas –Andrew reflects the leading positions of these disciples in the list in *EpAp* 2.1 (John–Peter–Thomas–Andrew in some MSS followed by Hills; Thomas–Peter–Andrew in other MSS followed here). The explanation is more likely to be drawn from the immediate context in the case of Peter, the unbelieving disciple *par excellence* as a result of his denials: 'I am your teacher, whom you, Peter, denied three times, and now do you deny again?' (11.4). Thomas's participation obviously stems from the author's Johannine source, in which Andrew too is given a distinct profile (cf. *GJn* 1.40, 44; 6.8; 12.22).

[6] See the Additional Notes on text-critical issues in *EpAp* 11.7–12.1.

The reference to the 'spear wounds' confirms the author's knowledge of the Johannine passion narrative, which tells how a spear was thrust into Jesus' side immediately after his death (*GJn* 19.34–37). Nevertheless, the clear links with *GJohn* provide the occasion for significant differences – notably the emphasis on the crucial importance of touch, with the implication that sight alone could still be deceptive.

This rewriting of the Johannine post-Easter appearance story sheds light on three distinctive themes or features of *EpAp*'s Easter narrative: *(i)* the personnel present or absent at the tomb (three women, no angels, the risen Jesus); *(ii)* the male disciples' initial disbelief; *(iii)* the role of Jesus' feet in the confirmation of his resurrection in flesh.

4.1.1 The Personnel at the Tomb

As we have seen, the confirmation of Jesus' resurrection in the flesh is distributed between three disciples acting on behalf of the entire group and is no longer assigned to Thomas alone, acting on his own behalf. A similar substitution of three for one occurs in the case of the solitary Johannine Mary Magdalene, who discovers the empty tomb and encounters the risen Lord there (*GJn* 20.1–2, 11–18). In *EpAp* she is accompanied by two other named women, Mary and Martha of Bethany (*EpAp* 9.2). With the exception of the list of eleven apostolic authors near the beginning of this work (*EpAp* 2.1), it is only here and in the confirmation-by-touch passage that individual followers of Jesus are named; elsewhere the collective 'we' predominates. There is a symmetry between the transformation of episodes involving Mary and Thomas alone into new versions in which they share their complementary roles with two companions: Mary and Martha of Bethany in the one case, Peter and Andrew in the other. Indeed, in *EpAp* the two Johannine figures both lose their primacy: Mary Magdalene is named in third place, and Thomas' role in the confirmation scene is subordinated to Peter's and – as we shall see – is less significant than Andrew's.

There is a textual problem to be addressed.[7] Jesus is buried 'in a place called "Skull"' (*EpAp* 9.1; cf. *GJn* 19.41, where he is buried in a 'garden' located 'in the place where he was crucified'). At *EpAp* 9.2, following the reference to Jesus' burial, the Coptic reads:

---

[7] See also the Additional Note on 9.2.

> There came to that place a third woman, Mary [sister] of Martha and Mary Magdalene.

The Ethiopic reads:

> There came to that place three women, Sarah and Martha and Mary Magdalene.[8]

The original reading was probably as follows (angled brackets represent the selection of an Ethiopic variant and braces a Coptic one):

> There came to that place <three women>, {Mary} <and> Martha and Mary Magdalene.

This would account for the variants in both textual traditions, as translators or scribes address the perceived problem of a double reference to an individual named Mary. The Coptic text assumes that 'Mary and Martha' should read 'Mary belonging to Martha' (ⲙⲁⲣⲓⲁ ⲧⲁⲙⲁⲣⲑⲁ, i.e. Mary [sister] of Martha). This ancient conjectural emendation results in two women rather than three, and 'three women' is therefore emended to 'a third woman', with this anonymous figure strangely still mentioned first rather than last. The Ethiopic text adopts a simpler solution, replacing the first 'Mary' with 'Sarah', although the choice of a scriptural name rather than one already associated with the gospel tradition (e.g. 'Salome', *GMk* 15.40, 16.1) is striking.[9]

---

[8] Not 'Mary Magdalene, Martha and Sara', as cited by Jane Schaberg (*The Resurrection of Mary Magdalene: Legends, Apocrypha, and the Christian Testament* [London and New York: Continuum, 2004], 111–12). The 'Mary' who is sent with a message for the disciples (10.8) is Mary Magdalene in the Ethiopic version only. In the Coptic and probably the original Greek Mary Magdalene's only role is to be present with Jesus at the tomb.

[9] See the *Additional Note* on 9.2. According to Darrell Hannah, the underlying Greek text may originally have read 'Salome and Martha and Mary Magdalene', with ΣΑΛΩΜΗ later miscopied as ΣΑΡΩΜΗ and identified as 'Sarah' by the Ethiopic translator ('The Four-Gospel "Canon" in the *Epistula Apostolorum*', *Journal of Theological Studies* 59 [2008], 598–633; 617–22). Hannah is here attempting to show that *EpAp* is familiar with *GMark*, the only canonical gospel to mention Salome. Yet neither Greek nor Ge'ez scribes appear to have any difficulty with the name 'Salome' at *GMark* 15.40, 16.1, with the single exception of the *f*[13] reading Σαλώνη. See Reuben Swanson (ed.), *New Testament Greek Manuscripts: Variant Readings Arranged in Horizontal Lines against Codex Vaticanus: Mark* (Sheffield and Pasadena, CA: Sheffield Academic Press/William Carey International University Press, 1995), 261, 265; Rochus Zuurmond, *Novum Testamentum Aethiopice: The Synoptic Gospels, General Introduction/Edition of the Gospel of Mark* (Stuttgart: Franz Steiner, 1989), 289, 292. While it is true that the *Testamentum Domini* refers to 'Martha and Mary and Salome' (*TestDom* i. 16[syr] = 8[eth]), and that this text is closely related to *EpAp*, the

Also striking is the fact that, in the original text, it is the Johannine Mary and Martha of Bethany who deprive Mary Magdalene of her Easter primacy, unchallenged in the four canonical accounts and *GPeter* 12.50–51, reasserted in the face of male resistance in the *Gospel of Mary* and still perceptible in texts such as the *Dialogue of the Saviour*, the *Sophia of Jesus Christ*, and *Pistis Sophia*, where Mary questions Jesus on equal terms with the male disciples.[10] Mary and Martha have been transplanted from one resurrection story – in which the resurrected individual is their brother Lazarus (*GJn* 11) – to another far more important one in which it is Jesus who is raised. Mary and Martha are promoted just as Mary Magdalene is downgraded. In a further echo of the Bethany tradition, it is not spices (ἀρώματα) but ointment (ⲥⲁϬⲛⲉ = μύρον) that the three women bring to the tomb (*EpAp* 9.3) – the ointment which the Johannine Mary used to anoint the feet of Jesus (*GJn* 11.2, 12.3; cf. *GMt* 26.7). In transferring the bearer of the ointment and her sister into the Easter narrative, the author of *EpAp* exploits the ambiguity of the Johannine passage, where Jesus is anointed and yet suggests 'that she keep it [the ointment] for the day of my burial' (*GJn* 12.7).[11] Indeed, *EpAp* 9.3 may attest a proto-Johannine story in which Jesus declined to be anointed at Bethany, ordering that the ointment be reserved for his burial.[12]

The author of *EpAp* ignores or does not know the secondary Johannine account of the race to the tomb of Peter and the beloved disciple (*GJn* 20.2–10), which breaks into the earlier account of Mary's single visit to the tomb:

links do not extend to the naming of disciples: the later text has Thomas, Matthew, and John touching Jesus (*TestDom* prologue) rather than *EpAp*'s Peter, Thomas, and Andrew.

[10] In differentiating Mary of Bethany from Mary of Magdala, *EpAp* follows Johannine precedent and avoids the later confusions discussed by Mark Goodacre, 'The Magdalene Effect: Misreading the Composite Mary in Early Christian Works', in Mary Ann Beavis and Allysin Kateusz (eds.), *Rediscovering the Marys: Maria, Mariamne, Miriam*, Library of New Testament Studies (London: T&T Clark/ Bloomsbury, 2020).

[11] ἄφες αὐτήν… ἵνα τηρήσῃ αὐτό probably means 'let her keep it' rather than 'let her alone in order that she may keep it', but either way *GJn* 12.7 raises the question, 'In what sense can the woman "keep" the ointment which she has already used?' (C. K. Barrett, *The Gospel According to John: An Introduction with Commentary and Notes on the Greek Text* [London: SPCK, 1978²], 414).

[12] Compare the pre-Johannine form of the water-into-wine story in *EpAp* 5.1, discussed in the previous chapter.

> And on the first day of the week, Mary Magdalene came
> early to the tomb, while it was still dark, and saw the stone
> removed from the tomb. [ ] And <she> stood outside
> the tomb weeping, and as she wept she looked into
> the tomb. . .   (*GJn* 20.1, 11)[13]

In *EpAp* similarly, the three women arrive at the tomb

> weeping and grieving over what had happened. But when
> they reached the tomb and looked inside they did not find
> the body. . .   (*EpAp* 9.3–4)[14]

In other gospels there is no weeping, and the women do not merely
'look inside' the tomb but enter it (cf. *GMk* 16.5; *GLk* 24.3; *GPet*
13.55). Here the Ethiopic text reads, '. . . when they reached the tomb
<they found the stone where it had been rolled from the tomb and
they opened the door> and looked inside. . .' The reference to the
stone and the additional door is clearly secondary, and its absence
from the Coptic is symptomatic of this text's omission of incidental
details in order to focus on what is essential, the actuality of Jesus'
resurrection.

Also omitted is the Johannine encounter with angels (*GJn*
20.12–13), since angels only have a genuine role in the Easter traditions where the risen Jesus himself is absent (cf. *GMk* 16.5–7; *GLk*
24.4–8; *GPet* 13.55–56). If the risen Jesus is represented as appearing
at or near the tomb, angels are not necessary: thus in both *GMatthew*
and *GJohn* the initial angelic address is repeated and superseded by
Jesus himself (*GMt* 28.5–7, 10; *GJn* 20.12–13, 15). This redundancy
is especially clear in *GJohn*, where two angels merely mark the place
where Jesus' body had lain and ask Mary why she is weeping. Their
question ('Woman, why do you weep?') anticipates Jesus', although
now a second question is added ('Woman, why do you weep? Whom

---

[13] When the text in its present form presents her as standing weeping outside the
tomb, 'it seems to be forgotten that Mary has left the tomb' (v. 2) – a problem created
by 'the imperfect interweaving of two separate traditions' (Barnabas Lindars, *The
Gospel of John*, New Century Bible Commentary [London: Marshall, Morgan &
Scott, 1972], 603). Here too *EpAp* reflects a pre- or proto-Johannine Mary tradition
as yet untouched by the concern that the tomb should be visited by one or more
leading male disciples (cf. *GLk* 24.12, 24; *GJn* 20. 3–10).

[14] ⲛ̄ⲡⲟⲩϭⲛ̄ ⲡⲥⲱⲙⲁ = οὐχ εὗρον τὸ σῶμα, *GLk* 24.10 (so Hartenstein, *Die zweite
Lehre*, 121).

do you seek?').[15] *EpAp*, uninterested in vivid detail or literary effect, dispenses altogether with the services of angels:

> But when they reached the tomb and looked inside they did not find the body. And as they were grieving and weeping the Lord appeared to them and said to them, 'For whom do you weep? Weep no longer! I am the one you seek. But let one of you go to your brothers and say, "Come, the Teacher has risen from the dead!"'   (*EpAp* 9.4–10.1)

Thus Jesus identifies himself and, without waiting for a response, calls for a volunteer to bring the news of his resurrection to the male disciples.[16] They are to be invited to meet Jesus at the tomb, where he awaits them with his two remaining female companions.

4.1.2   Apostolic Unbelief

As we have seen, *EpAp* elaborates the role assigned to Thomas in *GJohn* 20 in the confirmation of Jesus' resurrection, distributing it between Peter, Thomas, and Andrew. Similarly, the role of Mary Magdalene in *GJohn* 20 is shared with the equally Johannine figures of Mary and Martha of Bethany. There is a difference between the two groups, however, in that the female trio is complete in itself whereas the male one is representative of the larger apostolic group. While in *GJohn* Thomas speaks and acts on his own behalf, in *EpAp* Peter, Thomas, and Andrew perform the act of confirmation on behalf of the apostles collectively. Thus, although only Peter and Thomas are invited to touch Jesus, it can still be said that '*we* touched him, that *we* might know that he had truly risen in flesh' (*EpAp* 12.1, cf. 11.7). In *GJohn* it is Thomas alone who is told, 'Do not be unbelieving [ἄπιστος] but believing [πιστός]' (20.27), and no criticism of the other disciples is implied. In *EpAp* the unbelief has spread to all the male disciples,

---

[15] 'Die beiden Engeln [haben] für unsere Erzählung so gut wie keine Bedeutung... Die Frage der Engel erscheint um so überflüssiger, als der, wie Mt 28 9. 10, persönlich eingreifende Herr sie erneuert' (Walter Bauer, *Das Johannes-Evangelium*, Handbuch zum Neuen Testament 6 [Tübingen: J. C. B. Mohr (Paul Siebeck), 1925²], 224). The author of *EpAp* might have sympathized with Bauer's comments on the Johannine presentation.

[16] Hartenstein rightly notes the oddity of the author's depiction of the women at the tomb, where nothing is said about their reaction to the unexpected reunion with Jesus despite the previous emphasis on their grief (*Die zweite Lehre*, 114–15).

and their unbelief is overcome collectively: after the act of confirmation, 'we fell on our faces, confessing our sins, because we had been unbelieving' (*EpAp* 12.2).

If the apostles' unbelief is general and is only overcome by touching and seeing the risen Lord when he appears in person, the earlier announcement of the resurrection by Jesus' women disciples must have been disbelieved and rejected. This initial disbelief is a logical requirement of the author's reworking of the Johannine 'doubting Thomas' story, and this theme is strongly emphasized. When Martha comes to the male disciples with news of the resurrection,

> we said to her, 'What do you want with us, O woman? One who died and is buried, can he live?' We did not believe her that the Saviour had risen from the dead. Then she returned to the Lord and said to him, 'None of them believed me that you are alive.'   (*EpAp* 10.4–6)

Following Martha's failure to convince, a second attempt is made by Mary of Bethany but with the same outcome: 'We disbelieved her' (*EpAp* 10.8). Other early gospel texts attest this tradition of initial disbelief. In *GLuke*, the announcement to the apostles is made by a large group of women, but their claim 'seemed nonsense in their sight and they disbelieved them' (*GLk* 24.11). A closer parallel to *EpAp* occurs in the Markan Longer Ending, where, after the risen Lord has appeared to Mary,

> she went and told those who were with him as they mourned and wept. And, hearing that he was alive and had been seen by her, they disbelieved.   (*GMk* 16.10–11)

Here a second announcement – from the two who encounter the Lord 'in another form' as they travel into the country – is also disbelieved (*GMk* 16.12–13). As in *EpAp*, the bare message of the resurrection is not enough. It takes an appearance by the risen Lord to dispel unbelief, and when he does appear he is sharply critical:

> Finally, as the eleven were reclining, he appeared and rebuked their unbelief and hardness of heart, because they had not believed those who had seen him alive.   (*GMk* 16.14)

> And we came to him doubting in our hearts whether it was he. Then he said to us, 'Why do you still doubt, you disbelieving ones? I am he who spoke to you about my flesh and my death and my resurrection.'   (*EpAp* 11.5–6)

In *EpAp* doubt and disbelief persist even in the risen Lord's presence, for initially 'we thought it was a phantasm and did not believe that it was the Lord' (11.3; cf. *GLk* 24.36–43; Ignatius, *Smyr* 3.1–3).[17]

Explicit references to disbelief occur six times in *EpAp*'s Easter narrative (10.5, 6, 8; 11.3, 6; 12.2), and this raises the question why this motif is so important for the author. The paradoxical answer is that the apostles' initial disbelief in Jesus' resurrection helps to create confidence in its veracity. The repeated references to disbelief are intended to show that the apostles are not simply credulous. Confronted with Martha's announcement that 'the Teacher has risen from the dead' (10.2), they respond with a question reflecting universal human experience: 'One who died and is buried, can he live?' (10.4).[18] One who is dead and buried can, however, appear in the form of a ghost, a visible and perhaps audible manifestation of the deceased, terrifying in its insubstantiality. Thus, when Jesus appears in person, 'we thought it was a phantasm' (11.3). What the apostolic authors now regard as their 'unbelief' reflects the sober judgement that there is no way back from death to embodied existence, and that any appearance to the contrary can only be an illusion. These apostolic authors are the individuals to whom Jesus entrusted the task of preaching the word and establishing communities of fellow-believers, and it is crucially important to the believing reader that the apostles became convinced of the resurrection not in a moment of misguided enthusiasm but on the strongest possible evidence. Irrefutable evidence was needed to dispel their deeply entrenched scepticism. They believed on the basis of absolute proof, they communicated their faith to 'us', and 'our' faith is therefore based on the same proof that convinced them. We too know that, if the dead can return at all, it is in spectral rather than embodied form – yet if sceptical apostles were convinced from firsthand experience that Jesus rose in the flesh, what reason have we to doubt?

---

[17] For the threefold repetition of the motif of the announcement to the male disciples (first by Martha, then her sister Mary, finally Jesus himself), compare the Matthean/Lukan temptation narrative, the prayer in Gethsemane, and Peter's denials: so R. Bultmann, *The History of the Synoptic Tradition*, Eng. trans. (Oxford: Blackwell, 1963), 314. Peter's threefold denial is one of the few details of the passion tradition to be included in *EpAp* (11.4; cf. 9.1, 11.7).

[18] See the Additional Note on 10.4 for the selection of *Eth* ('One who died and is buried, can he live?') rather than *Cop* ('The one who died is buried, and can he live?').

4.1.3   Jesus' Feet

In *GJohn* Thomas demands to test the reality of Jesus' resurrection in
flesh by physical contact with the marks of his crucifixion: the holes
in his hands caused by the nails, the post mortem gash in his side
caused by the spear. The resurrected Jesus remains the crucified
Jesus. This is also implied when the Lukan Jesus seeks to persuade
his disciples of who he is by displaying his hands and feet – presumably identifiable as his by the marks of the nails (*GLk* 24.39–40).
Jesus' feet also play a role in the equivalent scene in *EpAp*, not
because of any nail-marks but because they bear his weight. As a
being of flesh and blood – or flesh and bones according to Luke
(24.39) – Jesus has his feet on the ground, and they are weight-
bearing feet:

> '... You, Andrew, look at my feet and see if they are not in
> contact with the ground. For it is written in the prophet, "As
> for an appearance of a demon, its foot is not in contact with
> the ground."'   (*EpAp* 11.7–8)

The Ethiopic text elaborates the point: 'See if my feet tread on the
ground and are in contact with it.' In *EpAp* as in other Easter
traditions (though not *GJohn*), the test of Jesus' bodily reality must
rule out an alternative hypothesis, that he has appeared only in the
illusory form of a 'spirit' (*GLk* 24.37, 39), a 'disembodied demon'
(Ignatius, *Smyrn* 3.2), or a 'phantasm' (*EpAp* 11.3) – evidently a
synonym for 'demon' (*EpAp* 11.8). To underline the point, the
apostolic authors cite an alleged scriptural criterion for identifying
a demonic manifestation: its appearance of substantial humanity
may be exposed as illusory by close observation of the feet, which
will be seen to hover a little above the ground. The apostle Andrew is
invited to see if this is so in the case of Jesus, and the unstated
outcome is that it is not. Jesus' feet perform the same function as
any other human feet, maintaining contact with the ground so as to
enable actions such as standing or walking.[19]

Not all early Christians agreed with *EpAp* and its invented scriptural testimony that non-contact with the ground should be assessed
negatively. In the *Acts of John* the apostle John tells an audience in
Ephesus how,

---

[19] As Hartenstein points out, the test carried out by Peter and Thomas and by
Andrew have different functions: to ensure from his wounds that it is really Jesus who
has appeared, and from his feet that he is not a ghost (*Die zweite Lehre*, 118).

> when I was walking with [Jesus], I often wanted to see if his
> footprint appeared on the ground – for I saw him raising
> himself up from the ground – but I never did see it.
>
> (*AcJn* 93.10–13)[20]

According to this apostolic testimony, Jesus is habitually elevated a
little above the ground, like the prophetic demon. The elevation is
very slight, imperceptible to casual observation, yet, walking at his
side, John notices that the ground beneath Jesus' feet receives from
them no imprint of any kind. It was presumably this same capacity
for frictionless locomotion that enabled the canonical Jesus to walk
on water. John reports his remarkable discovery to his Ephesian
audience 'for the encouragement of your faith' (93.14–15), their faith
not that Jesus is a ghost or demon but that he is divine, his divinity
masked by the appearance of humanity. From the standpoint of
credal orthodoxy and conventional modern scholarship, this is a
'docetic' claim that can be contrasted sharply with the insistence in
EpAp on Jesus' genuine fleshly humanity, even post-resurrection.
Yet for *EpAp* as for *AcJohn*, Jesus' humanity is the *disguise* he has
adopted in order to conceal his true divine identity. In his descent
towards incarnation, Jesus adopts the angelic form appropriate to
the heavens through which he passes, deceiving even archangels in
doing so (*EpAp* 13.2–4). His fleshly disguise is the end-point of this
process of transformation and adaptation. In *AcJohn* the conceal-
ment is not so complete. Symptoms of his true nature may be
detected in his human appearance, and the apostle's testimony to
them is an important aid to faith. Why would one be concerned with
the humanity when it is the divinity that brings salvation?

Nevertheless, in spite of this shared emphasis on Jesus' divinity,
the two texts do part company over the issue of his feet. The question
is whether *EpAp* should therefore be seen as 'anti-docetic', intention-
ally countering the christological conceptions of texts such as
AcJohn.[21] That seems not to be the case. In spite of its double
reference to the heretics Simon and Cerinthus (1.2; 7.1), *EpAp* does

---

[20] Greek text with French translation in Eric Junod and Jean-Daniel Kaestli (eds.),
Acta Iohannis, Corpus Christianorum Series Apocryphorum, 2 vols. (Turnhout:
Brepols, 1983), 1.188–217. The cited passage occurs in the context of an extended
reminiscence by the apostle John (*AcJn* 87–105, which Junod and Kaestli rightly place
between chapters 36 and 37, as there is a backward reference to *AcJn* 87 in chapter 63).

[21] As asserted most recently by Markus Bockmuehl, *Ancient Apocryphal Gospels*
(Louisville, KY: WJK Press, 2017), 219.

not appear to have any specific heretical positions in view. While the risen Jesus does identify 'other teaching' as a future problem (29.1–4; 50.8), nothing is said about its content. As it progresses, this text is far more preoccupied with inappropriate conduct than with incorrect belief.[22]

The significance of Jesus' feet and their contact with the ground lies elsewhere. Having waited outside his own tomb for the return first of Martha then of her sister Mary from their failed announcements to the male disciples,

> the Lord said to Mary and to her sisters, 'Let us go to them.' And he came and found us within, he called us out...   (*EpAp* 11.1–2)

In this text, Jesus' tomb is located 'in a place called "The Skull"' (9.1) and the disciples are presumably thought to be in a house somewhere in Jerusalem, in line with other early traditions (cf. *GMk* 16.14; *GLk* 24.33; *GJn* 20.19, 26).[23] Like *GLuke*, this text knows nothing of post-resurrection appearances in Galilee; Johannine Easter tradition is drawn exclusively from *GJohn* 20, and there is no awareness of the Johannine Longer Ending with its Galilean setting (*GJn* 21). Thus, 'Let us go to them' implies that Jesus undertakes a shorter or longer walk, with his three female companions, from his tomb to a location

---

[22] According to Schmidt – followed here by most subsequent scholarship – the anti-docetic tendency of this Easter narrative is obvious: '[A]lle doketischen Vorstellungen, die sich an die Person des Gekreuzigten und Auferstandenen knüpfen, sollen durch diesen authentischen Bericht der Apostel für immer aus der Welt geschafft werden' (*Gespräche*, 222). Yet scepticism about a physical resurrection following a death and a burial need not be motivated by any specific ideology. Elsewhere Schmidt rightly remarks that *EpAp* 'soll durchaus keine Apologie zur Widerlegung der Gnostiker sein, es ist vielmehr auf die Bestätigung des Glaubens der Katholikern berechnet' (198).

[23] The 'place called "the Skull"' (*Eth* qarānǝyo, *Cop* ⲕⲣⲁⲛⲓⲟⲛ) is the only topographical indication in the entire text, and is derived from the κρανίου τόπον referred to as the site of Jesus' crucifixion in *GJn* 19.17 (cf. *GMt* 27.33, *GMk* 15.22) together with the uniquely Johannine claim that Jesus' tomb was located 'in the place where he was crucified', where there was also a 'garden' (*GJn* 19.41). *EpAp* 9.1 seems to exclude any reference to a garden, possible evidence that the Johannine evangelist has combined two originally distinct traditions about the site of Jesus' burial (though failing to mention that the garden belonged to Joseph of Arimathea). Compare R. H. Fuller's suggestion that an alternative tradition to the 'Joseph legend' is attested in *Acts* 13.27–28, where it is said that 'those who lived in Jerusalem and their rulers... took him down from the tree and laid him in a tomb' (*The Formation of the Resurrection Narratives* [London: SPCK, 1980[2]], 54–55). Such a tradition may also be echoed in *EpAp* 9.1[eth], '... and he was crucified between two thieves, and with them <he was numbered>, and they took him down from <the tree of> the cross, and he was buried in the place named "Skull".'

somewhere in the city. His feet are on the ground, and he uses them not only to stand but also to walk.

In other early Easter traditions, the risen Jesus does very little walking. Rather, he appears and disappears. The Lukan Emmaus road story is a partial exception, although the travelling companion of the two disciples on the journey to Emmaus remains unrecognized and anonymous, appearing in his true identity only in the breaking of bread – before immediately vanishing (*GLk* 24.30–31). In the deutero-Markan parallel, 'he was revealed in another form [ἐφανερώθη ἐν ἑτέρᾳ μορφῇ] to two of them as they walked, going into the country' (*GMk* 16.12). It is not said here that Jesus walked with the two disciples or that he was unrecognized as he did so: on the contrary, *they* were walking whereas *he* appeared to them in another form, as on the earlier occasion of his transfiguration when he was trans-formed (μετεμορφώθη, *GMk* 9.2).[24] Similarly, in the first Matthean appearance story, Jesus 'meets' the women as they run from the tomb (*GMt* 28.8–9). While it can be said that 'Jesus *came* and said to them…' (*GMt* 28.18) or '*came* and stood among them' (*GJn* 20.26), on other occasions he makes himself present without any prior movement, as if appearing from nowhere (cf. *GLk* 24.36; *GJn* 20.14, 21.4). As he appears so he also disappears, whether for a few hours (*GLk* 24.33–36), for a week or more (*GJn* 20.26), or for a year and a half (*ApocrJas* 2, 17–22).[25] The character of the early Easter narratives is essentially *episodic*, and the episodes can even be enumerated: 'This was now the third time that Jesus was revealed to his disciples after he was raised from the dead' (*GJn*

---

[24] On this see Sarah Parkhouse, *Eschatology and the Saviour: The Gospel of Mary among Early Christian Dialogue Gospels*, Society for New Testament Studies Monograph Series 176 (Cambridge: Cambridge University Press, 2019), 87–91.

[25] *ApocrJas* recounts how, as the apostles are writing their gospels, 'Behold, the Saviour appeared, after he had gone from us as we gazed after him, and five hundred and fifty days after he rose from the dead' (NHC II, 2, 17–22, following the punctuation adopted by Judith Hartenstein and Uwe-Karsten Plisch in Hans-Martin Schenke, Hans-Gebhard Bethge, and Ursula Ulrike Kaiser (eds.), *Nag Hammadi Deutsch*, 2 vols. [Berlin and New York: de Gruyter, 2001], I, 19). It later becomes clear that Jesus spent the first eighteen days after his suffering and resurrection interpreting his parables to his disciples (*ApocrJas* 8, 1–10). The emphasis on a discrete appearance is traditional, as is the terminology used to introduce it: 'Behold, the Saviour appeared', where ⲉⲓⲥ = ἰδού (cf. *GMt* 28.9; *GLk* 24.13) and ⲁϥⲟⲩⲱⲛϩ̄ = ἐφανερώθη (cf. *GMk* 16.12, 14; *GJn* 21.1, 14) or ὤφθη (cf. *1 Cor* 15.5–8.) The 550-day or 18-month tradition is also attested in Irenaeus, *Adv. haer.* 1.3.2, 1.30.14, and *AscIs* 9.16 (545 days), and it is arguably closer to 'mainstream' early resurrection traditions than *EpAp*.

21.14). Discrete episodes remain in place even as Luke tries to connect them, referring back to the empty tomb from the Emmaus road (*GLk* 24.22–24) and to the manifestation at Emmaus after the return to Jerusalem (24.35), and then having Jesus 'lead them out as far as Bethany' (late that same night?), from where he ascends into heaven (24.50–51). Discrete appearances are already envisaged in the Pauline or pre-Pauline traditions preserved in *1 Corinthians* 15.3–8.

EpAp departs from this conventional format, maintaining a seamless continuity from the scene at the tomb through the reunion with the male disciples and the dialogue to the ascension. Here there are no discrete episodes and no repeated appearances and disappearances. In presenting Jesus as walking with the women from the tomb to Jerusalem, the author signals that the risen Jesus is no different from his pre-Easter self, still subject to the constraints of space and time as before.

Thus, at the conclusion of the dialogue, Jesus announces that 'on the third day, at the third hour, the one who sent me will come so that I may go with him' (*EpAp* 51.1). Since this announcement is immediately followed by his ascension, the third hour of the third day must already have arrived. The third day is the day of Jesus' resurrection, in line with other early traditions from Paul onwards (cf. *1 Cor* 15.4), and the third hour must represent the time that has elapsed between his rising and the end of the dialogue, i.e. less than three hours. That figure may represent the author's estimate of the time it would take to read the main Easter-related part of his text – in which case readers experience the Easter events in a close approximation to the real time in which they actually occurred. There are no gaps in this telling of the story.

Nor are there any ambiguities.[26] Earlier traditions show a certain ambivalence about the nature of the Lord's risen body. In *GLuke* Jesus offers the clearest possible demonstration that he is not an insubstantial spirit (24.39–43), yet he behaved very like one shortly before when he vanished the moment he was recognized (24.31). He has a visible and tangible body that is capable of taking nourishment, yet he can appear and disappear at will. In *GJohn*, Thomas is invited to confirm Jesus' resurrection through touch (20.27), whereas Mary is told not to touch because Jesus has not yet ascended; she is

---

[26] On this see my article, 'A Gospel of the Eleven: The *Epistula Apostolorum* and the Johannine Tradition', in Watson and Parkhouse, *Connecting Gospels*, 189–215; 210–15.

sent to announce not that Jesus is risen but that he is ascending or about to ascend (20.17). In *EpAp* all such ambiguities have been eradicated. In the resurrection, Jesus resumes the life he temporarily lost in his crucifixion. There is no transformation into a polymorphic identity that can be solid flesh-and-bone at one moment and ghost-like at another. Jesus remains with his feet firmly on the ground for between two or three hours, long enough to answer his disciples' questions, and he then ascends through the heavens to take his place at the right hand of the Father who sent him.

4.2 Contexts of Resurrection

Johannine echoes are heard at numerous points throughout *EpAp*. In both texts God is typically referred to as 'the one who sent me',[27] and Jesus is 'the Word' who 'became flesh'.[28] The Father and the Son indwell each other,[29] and this relationship of mutual indwelling extends also to believers.[30] The Johannine new commandment is repeated and extended.[31] The author shares the Johannine use of participial forms of the verb πιστεύειν,[32] and direct dependence on specific passages is sometimes perceptible:

> Jesus cried out and said, 'The one who believes in me does not believe in me but in the one who sent me.' (*GJn* 12.44)
>
> Then he said to us, 'Truly I say to you, everyone who believes in me and who believes in the one who sent me I will lead up to heaven, the place which my Father prepared for the elect. (*EpAp* 28.4; cf. 43.7)

---

[27] *EpAp* 13.3; 17.3, 6; 19.5; 20.29; 21.1, 3; 28.4; 36.6; 43.7; 45.8; 51.1 (× 12, cf. *GJn* 4.34; 5.24, 30; 6.38, 39; 7.16, 18, 33; 8.29; 9.4; 12.44, 45; 13.16, 20; 15.21; 16.5: ὁ πέμψας με, × 16). Also, 'the Father who sent me' (*EpAp* 39.6; cf. 13.6; 26.2, 5; *GJn* 6.44; 8.16, 18; 12.49; 14.24).

[28] *EpAp* 3.13 ('the Word which became flesh of Mary'); 18.1 ('I am the Word'); 31.11 ('I am the Word of the Father'); 39.12 ('I am the Word who became flesh and suffered'). Cf. *GJn* 1.14.

[29] *EpAp* 17.4 ('I am wholly in my Father and my Father is in me'; cf. 17.8, 31.11). Cf. *GJn* 14.10, 11; 17.21.

[30] *EpAp* 19.16 ('As I am always in him {my Father}, so are you in me'). Cf. *GJn* 17.21, 23.

[31] *EpAp* 18.5 ('But behold, I give you a new commandment: love one another, and that there may be continual peace among you'). Cf. *GJn* 13.34.

[32] Normally 'those who believe in me' in the case of *EpAp* (12.4; 19.1, 6, 29; 27.2; 29.1; 32.5; 33.4; 43.7 (cf. 43.19); 50.9), 'the one who believes in me' in the case of *GJohn* (3.18; 6.35, 40; 7.38; 11.25, 26; 12.44; 14.12).

In *EpAp* the predominant plural usage 'those who believe in me' always refers to those who believe as a result of the future apostolic testimony, reflecting this text's intense concern with the theme of mission. Here the inspiration appears to be *GJohn* 17.20, where Jesus prays no longer for his disciples alone but also for 'those who believe in me through their word'. In addition, there is a further echo of the post-resurrection encounter with Thomas:

> Jesus said to him, 'Have you believed because you have seen? Blessed are those who have not seen and yet have believed.' (*GJn* 20.29)

> Again we said to him, 'Lord, blessed are we that we see you and hear you as you say such things, for our eyes have seen these great signs that you have done.' He answered and said to us, 'Blessed rather are those who have not seen and yet have believed, for such will be called sons of the kingdom, and they will be perfect in the perfect one, and I will be life to them in the kingdom of my Father. (*EpAp* 29.5–6)

In spite of clear indications that the author of *EpAp* was able to draw from *GJohn* 1–20, he deviates from his source in replacing an Easter narrative in which Jesus has relatively little to say (cf. *GJn* 20.15–17, 19, 21–23, 26–27, 29) with an extended series of questions and answers in which the apostles receive the instruction they need to equip them for their future worldwide mission. The Johannine Jesus speaks briefly about the basis of their mission ('As the Father sent me, so I send you', *GJn* 20.21) and bestows the Holy Spirit and the authority to forgive sins (20.22–23). But that is all. Even if these instructions are supplemented by the Matthean 'great commission' (*GMt* 28.18–20, cf. *EpAp* 30.1), the author of *EpAp* views them as quite inadequate.[33] The Johannine narrative reflects the limited scope of early Easter traditions, and *EpAp* should be seen as an ambitious attempt to rectify this deficiency alongside more modest

---

[33] Here as elsewhere *EpAp* stands in a critical relationship to earlier gospel tradition, which it seeks to develop and to correct. There is no justification for Bockmuehl's claim that *EpAp* is 'founded on the authorized apostolic witness explicitly understood to reside in the four New Testament gospels' (*Ancient Apocryphal Gospels*, 223). Selective and free recycling of some Johannine, Matthean, and (to a lesser extent) Lukan material does not amount to a recognition of 'the singular and unquestioned authority of the fourfold gospel' (223) – as though this pan-apostolic catholic epistle was only ever intended to be 'epiphenomenal' (229).

interventions such as the Longer Endings added to *GMark* (16.9–20) and *GJohn* (chapter 21).

The Johannine Jesus leaves the further instruction of his disciples to the Paraclete, who 'will lead you into all the truth' and 'proclaim to you the things that are to come [τὰ ἐρχόμενα]' (*GJn* 16.13). In contrast, *EpAp* has almost nothing to say about the role of the Holy Spirit[34] and it is the risen Jesus who guides 'those in error to truth' (21.8), not least the truth about τὰ ἐρχόμενα, the impending eschatological events: the great tribulation (34.1–38.7), the parousia (16.1–17.4), the resurrection of the flesh (19.17–25.9), and the judgement (26.1–6; 39.1–40.4). In the earlier part of the dialogue it is the resurrection of the flesh that most concerns the author, closely related as it is to Jesus' own resurrection. The distinctive character of the treatment of this theme in *EpAp* can be investigated by way of a comparison with the *Treatise on the Resurrection* (NHC I, 4), perhaps a roughly contemporaneous text with links to the early Valentinian tradition.[35] Each text in its own way reflects the Pauline insistence that the future resurrection is inextricably linked to the resurrection of Jesus (cf. *1 Cor* 15) – a linkage that is missing in the canonical Easter stories.

---

[34] But cf. *EpAp* 5.21; 30.4.

[35] Coptic text, with introduction, translation, and commentary by Jacques É. Ménard, *Le Traité sur la résurrection*, Bibliothèque Copte de Nag Hammadi 12 (Quebec: Les presses de l'université Laval, 1983); Malcolm L. Peel, in Harold Attridge (ed.), *Nag Hammadi Codex I* (*The Jung Codex*), Nag Hammadi Studies 22–23, 2 vols. (Leiden: Brill, 1985), 1.123–57, 2.137–215 (*NHC* I). Translations here are my own. Peel advocates a late second-century date (1.146); Schenke suggests somewhat earlier (*Nag Hammadi Deutsch*, I, 46–47). The possibility of a fourth-century dating is raised by Mark Edwards on the grounds of affinities with the Valentinian *Gospel of Truth* (NHC I, 3), which has in turn been seen by one scholar as a polemic against Arianism ('The *Epistle to Rheginus*: Valentinianism in the Fourth Century', *Novum Testamentum* 37 (1995), 76–91; 77–78). That the *Gospel of Truth* shares the same polemical agenda as Athanasius stretches credulity, and Edwards himself is not committed to this untenable claim. Equally unpersuasive is his appeal to a passage in Epiphanius, where the Valentinians are said to hold that 'it is not this body that rises but another that comes out of it, the one they call spiritual' (*Pan.* 31.7.6). While some such belief might indeed be found in the *Treatise on the Resurrection*, the echoes of *1 Cor* 15.44–46 indicate an origin within debates about resurrection that long pre-date Epiphanius – debates in which exegesis of Pauline passages especially from the Corinthian correspondence played a key role: see Irenaeus, *Adv. haer.* 5.9.1–12.4 and Tertullian, *De Res. Car.*, 40.1–54.5. The *Treatise on the Resurrection* too fits this context (so Ménard, *Traité*, 8). The fact that it shares *EpAp*'s lack of awareness of competing Christian views on this topic (in contrast to *GPhil* 56, 27–57, 22; 73, 1–8) suggests an early date for both texts.

Both these very different texts take the form of a letter; on the one hand a 'catholic' letter from the apostles to all Christians everywhere, on the other, a quasi-philosophical treatise by an unnamed individual addressed to 'my son Rheginus' and the community he represents. The epistolary format is consistently maintained in *TrRes* but is abandoned in *EpAp* after chapter 8. The apostles write in their capacity as leaders of a worldwide missionary movement, whereas the anonymous author of *TrRes* presents himself as a Christian philosopher who has found in the resurrection the answer to the all-encompassing philosophical question of the meaning and nature of existence. Christ

> has come forth as the solution, so as to leave nothing hidden but to reveal all things clearly as regards existence – both the dissolution of evil and the revelation of the elect.
> (*TrRes* 45,4–11)[36]

> The resurrection... is the truth that stands firm and the revelation of existence and the transformation of entities and a transition into newness.   (*TrRes* 48,31–38)

EpAp too views Jesus' resurrection as the key revelatory moment, although in less abstract language. When the apostles have finally come to faith in the risen Lord and lie prostrate on the ground,

> the Lord our Saviour said to us, 'Rise and I will reveal to you what is above the heavens and what is in the heavens and your rest in the kingdom of the heavens.'   (*EpAp* 12.3)

Here too, faith in Jesus's resurrection is the key that unlocks the mysteries of existence, disclosing the teleological movement of 'all things' towards the goal of salvation for the elect. Both texts are written to persuade their readers that resurrection is 'essential' [ⲁⲛⲁⲅⲕⲁⲓⲟⲛ] (*TrRes* 44,7) and that its significance can hardly be over-estimated. Both texts follow the Pauline precedent in defining

---

[36] 'As' = ⲉⲧ<ⲃ>ⲉ, corrected from ⲉⲧⲣⲉ (MS): so Ménard, *Traité*, 44, and others. Peel deletes and translates, 'Since the Solution appeared' (*NHC* I, 2.157). 'Solution' and 'dissolution' = ⲃⲱⲗ... ⲁⲃⲁⲗ × 2 (cf. *2 Pet* 1.20[sah], 3.12[sah]), the first occurrence of which answers to ⲃⲱⲗ in 45,1 ('I know that I am explaining the solution in difficult terms'). ⲙⲡⲉⲧⲥⲁⲧⲣ̄ ('the elect') probably represents *Gk* ἡ ἐκλογή, a collective noun as at *Rom* 11.7, but it might also be translated 'the better part' (cf. 47,9, 21–22) in reference to the soul or spirit; so B. Layton, *The Gnostic Treatise on Resurrection from Nag Hammadi*, Harvard Dissertations in Religion 12 (Missoula, MT: Scholars Press, 1979), 37; rejected by Peel, *NHC* I, 2.158.

resurrection as eschatological salvation grounded in the resurrection of Jesus[37] – in contrast to early patristic discussions of resurrection, in which Jesus' resurrection plays only a limited role if it is mentioned at all.[38] These neglected texts deserve to be regarded as classic expressions of early Christian resurrection faith.

Given this shared Christian conviction, the question is how far the similarities extend, or, otherwise expressed, at what points significant differences come to light. In view of *TrRes*'s Nag Hammadi provenance, one might expect to see in these two texts a confrontation between the 'gnostic' orientation of the one and the 'proto-orthodoxy' of the other. Yet this distinction merely reproduces patristic assumptions about orthodoxy and heresy in a lightly modernized form. As we shall see, it would be wrong to see in these texts any simple binary divide. Instead, they represent two of the diverse ways in which a key primitive Christian belief was interpreted.[39]

---

[37] The prominence of Pauline conceptuality in *TrRes* is emphasized by Outi Lehtipuu, *Debates over the Resurrection of the Dead: Constructing Christian Identity*, Oxford Early Christian Studies (Oxford: Oxford University Press, 2015), 98–102. See also Christine Jacobi, '"Dies ist die geistige Auferstehung": Paulusrezeption im Rheginusbrief und im Philippusevangelium', in Jens Schröter, Simon Butticaz, and Andreas Dettwiler (eds.), *Receptions of Paul in Early Christianity: The Person of Paul and his Writings through the Eyes of his Early Interpreters* (Berlin: de Gruyter, 2018), 355–75.

[38] Tertullian's arguments for the resurrection of the flesh include appeals to the divine origin of the flesh (*De Res. Car.*, 5–7), analogies from nature (12–13), the link with the final judgement (14–17, 56), the semantics of 'resurrection' (18), the testimony of Christ's words and deeds (34–38), but not the resurrection of Jesus. Text and Eng. trans. in E. Evans, *Tertullian's Treatise on the Resurrection* (London: SPCK, 1960). Compare also Athenagoras (Eng. trans., ANF II, 149–62): divine power (*De Res. Car.*, 3), the purposive nature of God's creation of humanity (12–13), the analogy with sleep (16), judgement (18–23). Excerpts of a treatise on resurrection attributed to Justin do, however, mention Jesus' resurrection (Eng. trans., ANF I, 298). In the three books of his anti-Origenistic treatise on resurrection, Methodius turns to the topic of Jesus' risen body only once, in order to refute Origen's claim that the gospels' emphasis on Jesus' post-resurrection physicality (*GLk* 24.39; *GJn* 20.27) was a mere accommodation to his disciples' spiritual immaturity (*De Res. Car.*, 3.12.1–14.7; German translation of the Slavonic text in G. Nathanael Bonwetsch (ed.), *Methodius*, Griechische Christliche Schriftsteller [Leipzig: J. C. Hinrichs, 1917]). Proclus, the Origenist character in Methodius's dialogue, earlier refutes the 'orthodox' appeal to passages such as *Col* 1.18, *1 Cor* 15.20, and *1 Thes* 4.14 to argue that Jesus' physical resurrection is the prototype of our own (1.26.1–2 = Epiphanius, *Pan.* 64.18.1–5).

[39] Alastair Logan argues that Nag Hammadi Codex I (which contains *TrRes*) belongs to a group of codices (I, VII, and XI) comprising texts of a diverse character that stand apart from the 'gnostic' mainstream of the library as a whole, which is centred on Sethian texts such as *ApocrJohn* and *GEgyp* (*The Gnostics: Identifying an Early Christian Cult* [London: T&T Clark, 2006], 22–23).

4.2.1   Resurrection of the Flesh

As we have seen, *EpAp* depicts the risen Jesus as restored to his previous form of life. He walks into Jerusalem with his female disciples, and there is no episodic appearing and disappearing. Jesus' resurrection in the flesh is paradigmatic for those who believe in him, even though their eschatological destiny lies 'not in the lower creation but in that of my Father which does not perish' (19.15). This promise of a transcendent future naturally raises the question of the mode of human existence that will participate in it – so the disciples ask whether the redeemed will exist in flesh or in the form of angels (19.17). In response, Jesus simply points to himself:

> Truly I say to you, as my Father raised me from the dead, so you too will rise and be taken up above the heavens to the place of which I spoke to you in the beginning, to the place prepared for you by the one who sent me. And thus will I fulfil every dispensation, being unborn yet born among humans, without flesh yet I have borne flesh. For this is why I came, so that you who were born in flesh might be raised in your flesh as in a second birth, a garment that will not perish, with all who hope and believe in the one who sent me.   (*EpAp* 21.1–3)

.The pre-existent Jesus existed as pure spirit, without flesh, but he has become flesh and will remain flesh in order to secure and reveal the final salvation of the flesh. Resurrected flesh will be immune from mortality, but it remains flesh, a garment to clothe the human soul and spirit.

This text acknowledges that belief in the resurrection of the flesh is counter-intuitive. In response to Martha's announcement of Jesus' resurrection, the male disciples ask sceptically, 'One who died and is buried, can he live?' (10.4). In spite of the risen Jesus' presence, scepticism returns as the disciples ask, 'Lord, is it possible for what is dissolved and destroyed to be saved?', although here they try to pre-empt a negative response by adding, 'Not that as unbelieving do we ask you, or as if it were impossible for you, but we truly believe that what you say will come to pass' (24.2–3). Jesus is angry with them all the same: 'O you of little faith, how long will you question?' (24.4). The disciples apologise for wearying him with their questioning, Jesus now pronounces himself pleased with their sincerity, and discussion of the resurrection of the flesh resumes (25.1–5).

There is here no apologetic argument – in the form perhaps of an appeal to analogies within the natural order or to the death and rebirth of the phoenix[40] – but pure credal assertion:

> What has fallen will rise and what is lost will be found and what is weak will recover, so that in this the glory of my Father may be revealed. (*EpAp* 25.8)

Hard to believe when considered in the abstract, the resurrection of the flesh is presented as a dogma, a *credendum* which it is the duty of all believers to accept on pain of provoking divine displeasure.

Similarly, the author of *TrRes* acknowledges that to grasp that resurrection is the answer to questions about human existence and destiny is 'difficult' (ⲁⲩⲥⲕⲟⲗⲟⲛ), and that 'there are many disbelieving [ⲁⲡⲓⲥⲧⲟⲥ] in it and few who find it' (*TrRes* 45,2; 44,8–10). One cannot be persuaded into faith by way of rational philosophical arguments, for it is of the essence of resurrection faith to accept without question the dogmatic assertion that 'the one who is dead shall arise' (46,3–8). Such a counter-intuitive claim is exposed to the threat of doubt, and the addressee must be warned against this: 'Do not doubt [ⲁⲓⲥⲧⲁⲍⲉ] concerning the resurrection, Rheginus my son' (47,1–3).

Resurrection hope is grounded in the resurrection of Jesus, and this in turn is grounded in the fact that as the pre-existent Son of God he became incarnate and 'existed in flesh [ϩⲛ̄ ⲥⲁⲣⲝ̄]' (44,14–15). Thus he

> possessed humanity and divinity, so as to overcome death in his identity as Son of God, and so that through the Son of man the restoration [ⲁⲡⲟⲕⲁⲧⲁⲥⲧⲁⲥⲓⲥ] to the Pleroma might take place. (*TrRes* 44,25–32)[41]

---

[40] Cf. *1 Clem* 24.1–26.3. Clement echoes *1 Cor* 15.20 in speaking of Jesus' resurrection as the ἀπαρχή of the future resurrection (*1 Clem* 24.1), and cites day and night, sowing and reaping, and especially the self-regeneration of the phoenix as indications that resurrection is credible: 'Should we consider it so great and extraordinary if the creator of everything [ὁ δημιουργός τῶν ἁπάντων] will accomplish the resurrection of those who have served him in holiness and in the confidence of good faith, when he has shown us the greatness of his promise through a bird?' (26.1). As in *EpAp*, the argument is directed against doubt rather than docetism (cf. δίψυχοι, 23.3). On the reception of *1 Corinthians* 15 in *1 Clement* and on the phoenix, see Clare Rothschild, *New Essays on the Apostolic Fathers*, Wissenschaftliche Untersuchungen zum Neuen Testament 375 (Tübingen: Mohr Siebeck, 2017), 58–59, 97–110.

[41] The Son of God/Son of man parallel occurs in Ignatius *Eph* 20.2, Justin, *Dial. Try.* 100.3–4, and frequently in Irenaeus (e.g. *Adv. haer.* 3.10.2, 16.3, 7, 17.1, 18.3–4, 19.1–2). It is not clear that the use of terms such as ⲡⲗⲏⲣⲱⲙⲁ (*TrRes* 44,33; 46,36; 49,4)

This restoration to the Pleroma corresponds to what is described in *EpAp* as 'your rest in the kingdom of heaven' (12.3). However they conceive of the relation of the redeemed to their earthly embodied selves, the two authors would agree that this is a place or state 'where there is no eating or drinking and no anxiety or grief and no decay' (*EpAp* 19.14). While for *EpAp* the heavenly body is still fleshly, it has ceased to perform normal bodily functions or to be subject to normal bodily constraints. If it still possesses a digestive tract or sex-specific reproductive organs, these have lost their functionality.[42] This body is not subject to ageing, for it is ageless, transfigured by 'the light of glory' in which it now dwells (cf. *EpAp* 51.3). However strongly the author insists on the resurrection of the flesh, that flesh is necessarily transformed when relocated to a heavenly environment.

The difference between *EpAp* and *TrRes* is not that one text affirms what the other text denies, but rather that *TrRes* explicitly reflects on the difference between the present and future body whereas *EpAp* does not. In both texts Christ is with us now and will lead us up to heaven, but only in *TrRes* is the attempt made to identify continuities and discontinuities between now and then. In this text, unlike *EpAp*, resurrection is confined to the elect and occurs immediately after death:

> While we are visible in this world and clothed with it, we are that one's [Christ's] beams, held fast by him until our setting (that is, our death in this life), then drawn by him to heaven like beams by the sun, held back by nothing. This is the spiritual resurrection which swallows up the psychic element and likewise the fleshly.   (*TrRes* 45,28–46,2)[43]

and προβολη (45, 12) 'révèlent chez l'auteur une connaissance de la symbolique et du mythe valentiniens' (Ménard, *Traité*, 3), if what is meant is the developed post-Valentinian myths found in the *Tripartite Tractate* (NHC I, 5) or Irenaeus, *Adv. haer.* 1.1–7. For a sceptical view of the relation between Valentinus and the heresiologists' 'Valentinian school', see Christoph Markschies, *Valentinus Gnosticus? Untersuchungen zur valentinianischen Gnosis mit einem Kommentar zu den Fragmenten Valentins*, Wissenschaftliche Untersuchungen zum Neuen Testament 65 (Tübingen: J. C. B. Mohr (Paul Siebeck), 1992), 392–402. While Markschies rejects the suggestion that Valentinus may have been the author of *TrRes* (356–61), it may still be possible to locate it within a proto-Valentinian milieu.

[42] An issue discussed by Tertullian, *De Res. Car.*, 60– 61.

[43] 'Clothed with it' is preferable to 'wearing him' (contra Peel, *NHC* I, 163; Ménard, *Traité*, 66), which would result in a confusing mixed metaphor. Cf. Schenke, 'Wenn wir aber sichtbar in dieser Welt existieren, tragen wir sie (wie ein Gewand)' (*Nag Hammadi Deutsch*, I, 50). 'Swallows up' alludes to *1 Cor* 15.54 (citing *Is* 25.8); *2 Cor* 5.4. According to *Exc. Theod.* 7.5, Christ's raising of dead people to life

Clothed in an earthly body, we are nevertheless one with Christ and sustained by him, as sunbeams are by the sun. As the sun retracts its rays when it sets, so Christ draws us up to heaven. While the metaphor of the setting sun conflates our death with Christ's action in our death, the general sense is clear. The question is how this 'spiritual resurrection' can be said to 'swallow up' the soul and the flesh. It is also said that 'the Saviour swallowed up death' (45,14–15), that is, he destroyed it, so it is possible that the spiritual resurrection represents the destruction of soul and flesh and their replacement by a body composed of pure spirit. Yet the swallowing up of soul and flesh might also refer to their incorporation and transformation within the new spiritual body. In that case, flesh would somehow be preserved even as the old fleshly body perishes.

The fleshly body is unredeemable insofar as it is subject to mortality, programmed to decay as it ages until it becomes an object of disgust and is discarded:

> The afterbirth of the body is old age and you exist in corruption, so that leaving it behind is to your advantage. You do not surrender the better part when you go!
> (*TrRes* 47,17–22)

The worn out body is left behind at death, but beyond death the elect will not enter into a disembodied state but will experience bodily resurrection, the reintegration of the 'living members' that existed within the old fleshly ones:

> While the visible members which are dead will not be saved, the living members which exist within them will indeed rise. (*TrRes* 47,38–48,3)

The fleshly body has been discarded, yet the living members of the resurrected body receive a new mode of fleshly existence. We entered into fleshly existence at the start of our natural life, and from that point on flesh – earthly or heavenly – is our appointed condition and our permanent possession:

> For if you were not in flesh yet received flesh when you came into this world, why would you not receive flesh when you ascend into the aeon? That which is better than the flesh is

during his earthly ministry is an εἰκόνα τῆς πνευματικῆς ἀναστάσεως (cited by Peel, *NHC* I, 2.167).

the source of life for it. That which came into being for your
sake, is it not yours? Does that which is yours not exist
with you?   (*TrRes* 47,4–13)[44]

In his own way this author too believes in a resurrection of the flesh.
His explanation and defence of it is different from anything in *EpAp*,
yet the two texts represent variant forms of the same fundamental
Christian belief. They do not stand confronting one another on the
two sides of a chasm separating early orthodoxy from heretical
counterparts.

4.2.2   Individual and Cosmos

In *2 Timothy* 2.16–18, the fictive Pauline author complains bitterly
about the distorted and damaging views of Hymenaeus and Philetus,
who teach, perversely and shockingly, that 'the resurrection is
already past [τὴν ἀνάστασιν ἤδη γεγονέναι]' (v. 18). According to
these false teachers, true Christians must live the resurrection life
already in the present.[45] Some decades later, Tertullian will reject a
similar claim. There are some, he reports, who insist on interpreting
allegorically the clear scriptural statements on resurrection.

They claim that even 'death' is to be understood spiritually
[*spiritaliter*], and that this term does not (as commonly
supposed) refer to the separation of flesh and soul but rather
to that ignorance of God in which a person is no less dead to
God than if they were in the grave. So it is also to be
regarded as 'resurrection' when someone is endowed by

---

[44] Bentley Layton ascribes the affirmation of fleshly resurrection in this passage to a
hypothetical objector, and translates it as follows: 'Now (you might wrongly suppose),
granted you did not preexist in flesh – indeed you took on flesh when you entered this
world – why will you not take your flesh with you when you return to the realm of
eternity?' (*The Gnostic Scriptures* [New York: Doubleday, 1987], 322); *Treatise*, 77–85.
Layton's view is rightly rejected by Outi Lehtipuu (*Debates*, 191–92).
[45] The *2 Timothy* passage 'is one of the earliest pieces of evidence for the way
resurrection beliefs were used as a dividing line between different kinds of Christians'
(Lehtipuu, *Debates*, 67). Also relevant here is *3 Corinthians*, another deutero-Pauline
text from the second century in which Paul polemicizes against 'those who say there is
no resurrection of the flesh', citing his own seed imagery from an earlier letter (*1 Cor*
15) and scriptural proofs from the careers of Jonah (cf. *GMt* 12.40) and Elisha (*3 Cor*
3.24–32; discussed in Lehtipuu, *Debates*, 130–33). (The letter is embedded in the
Philippi episode of the *Acts of Paul*.) In contrast to this use of resurrection to create
an inner-Christian boundary, the examples of *EpAp* and *TrRes* show that resurrection
could be variously articulated without reference to any such boundary.

God with new life as they acquire the truth and the ignorance of death is dispelled – as if they burst forth from the grave of their former self [*de sepulchro veteris hominis*]. (*De Resurrectione Carnis*, 19.2–4)

What is criticized here is a particular application of an allegorical hermeneutic rather than 'realized eschatology' as such. Yet advocates of this hermeneutic would no doubt have appealed to Pauline statements to the effect that we participate already in the risen life of Christ. God 'made us alive with Christ... and raised us with him [συνήγειρεν] and installed us with him in the heavenly realms in Christ Jesus' (*Eph* 2.5–6). *TrRes* alludes to this passage when it cites on the authority of 'the apostle' the statement that 'we suffered with him and rose with him and went to heaven with him' (45,23–28). The author seems to approximate the position attributed to Hymenaeus and Philetus when he advises Rheginus that, if he avoids living according to the flesh, 'already [ϩⲎⲆⲎ] you have the resurrection' (49,15–16).

What does that mean? It is not the author's intention to encourage Rheginus to pretend that he has already entered a world of light and glory from which all evil has been banished. Rather, Rheginus is to live in the light of the resurrection *hope*, the only death that matters being safely behind him in his baptism (cf. *Rom* 6.1–11). As ordinary mortals pass their lives in the uncanny awareness that the day of their death is advancing towards them, so the elect must pass their lives in the certainty of their coming salvation:

> If one who is to die knows that he will die (for even if he lives many years in this life it will finally come to that), why do you not regard yourself as risen and already come to that? But if you have the resurrection but continue as if you were still to die (while knowing that you have died already), how could I overlook your lack of discernment?
>
> (*TrRes* 49,16–30)

Rheginus already possesses the resurrection insofar as his life is dominated and determined by the resurrection hope.[46] Resurrection means salvation, and salvation is certain.

---

[46] Lehtipuu finds in *TrRes* a 'strong emphasis on resurrection as a present, spiritual process' (*Debates*, 190). Yet the present reality of resurrection is not independent of or distinct from the future reality, as Lehtipuu's language suggests.

Such a claim would be impossible for the author of *EpAp*. At no point is it suggested that the disciples or those who believe through their testimony already participate in the life of the redeemed. The absence of this theme is not accidental, and the primary reason is that it is not a foregone conclusion that those who believe will gain eternal life at all. Correct belief is a necessary but not sufficient condition for salvation, for belief entails the commitment to observe the divine commandments. The parousia (expected to take place shortly) will coincide with a resurrection of the dead, and this confrontation between the returning Jesus and humanity will herald a day of judgement presided over by Jesus himself. Unusually, Jesus is warned by his Father to avoid undue leniency, as though his performance of his judicial function could in principle be liable to error:

> Truly I say to you that the flesh will rise with the soul alive, so that they may be judged on that day for what they have done, whether good or evil, so that there may be a selection [ekλorн] of believers who have performed the commandments of my Father who sent me. Thus the judgement will take place in severity. For my Father said to me, 'My Son, on the day of judgement you shall neither be ashamed before the rich nor pity the poor, but according to the sin of each you shall deliver them to eternal punishment.' But to my beloved, who have performed the commandments of my Father who sent me, I will give rest of life in the kingdom of my Father in heaven.   (*EpAp* 26.1–5)

The possibility of a belief unaccompanied by obedience is all too real: 'If anyone believes [пicтeve] in me and does not do my commandments after confessing [ромoλorei] my name, he receives no benefit [ωчeλei] at all and has run his course in vain' (27.3). The act of faith does not enable participation in Christ's risen life, for that life is for the present exclusively his own.

In *EpAp* resurrection is not an all-encompassing reality (as in *TrRes*) but belongs within a sequence of eschatological events – parousia, resurrection, judgement – heralded by signs of the end. Thus there is extended description of the preceding times of trial characterized by signs of cosmic catastrophe in heaven and disease, drought, wars, persecution, and dissension on earth (*EpAp* 34.6–37.5). Believers will not be immune from these events (35.2–36.8), which form the backdrop against which they must prove their obedience to the commandments and thus their loyalty to God and his Son. In these circumstances, enjoying eschatological benefits here and now is not an option. Even the future general resurrection is related to the resurrection of Jesus only in that it is he who instantiates and reveals it; this event does not in itself communicate salvation. The general resurrection is the precondition for a judgement according to works and ensuing rewards and punishments – for both of which fleshly embodiment is necessary so that joy or pain may be fully experienced, as intended.

In *EpAp* Jesus' resurrection plays a central part within a wider eschatological scenario. Although the disciples come to acknowledge it with joy, its soteriological significance is indirect. The risen Jesus promises participation in the kingdom of heaven to those who believe and obey, but his resurrection is not soteriologically significant in itself. Rather, it inaugurates a train of events – continuing with the disciples' forthcoming mission and culminating in parousia and universal resurrection and judgement – through which those who truly believe and observe the commandments will gain their heavenly reward. In contrast, *TrRes* views Jesus' resurrection as itself the definitive and inclusive saving event and shows no interest in the cosmic dramas projected by its literary neighbour.

5

NARRATIVES OF INCARNATION

Immediately before the Miracle Sequence, the collective apostolic authors of *EpAp* confess their faith in 'God the Son of God... the Word who became flesh of Mary, carried in her womb through the Holy Spirit', adding that he was born 'not by the desire of the flesh but by the will of God' and that he was 'swaddled in Bethlehem, and manifested and nourished and grew up, as we saw' (*EpAp* 3.13–15). Echoes of the Johannine prologue (*GJn* 1.13–14) and the Lukan infancy narrative (*GLk* 1.35; 2.4, 7) combine to create a credal affirmation that anticipates the Nicene confession of the divine Son as the one who 'came down from heaven and became flesh by the Holy Spirit and Mary the virgin'.[1] Similar affirmations already occur in the summaries of the 'rule of truth' or 'rule of faith' in Irenaeus and Tertullian. According to Tertullian, the Word who is also the Son of God was 'brought down by the Spirit and power of God the Father into the Virgin Mary, made flesh in her womb and born of her'.[2] In such statements, the link between the incarnation or enfleshment of the divine Word and Mary's miraculous conception by the Holy Spirit is taken for granted. The *dramatis personae* of this event include three divine agents: the Father who sends, the Son who is sent, and the Spirit who brings about the act of union between the divine Son and the flesh. Additionally, there is a human agent, Mary the virgin, whose willing participation in the event is secured by a fifth figure whose role is always presupposed even

---

[1] κατελθόντα ἐκ τῶν οὐρανῶν καὶ σαρκωθέντα ἐκ πνεύματος ἁγίου καὶ Μαρίας τῆς παρθένου. Text in Philip Schaff (ed.), *Creeds of Christendom*, 3 vols. (repr. Grand Rapids, MI: Baker, 1977), 2.57.
[2] *De Praescr. Haer.* 13.3: *delatum ex spiritu patris Dei et uirtute in uirginem Mariam, carnem factum in utero eius et ex ea natum.* Text in R. F. Refoulé and P. de Labriolle (eds.), *Tertullien: Traité de la prescription contre les hérétiques*, Sources chrétiennes 46 (Paris: Éditions du Cerf, 1957). For Irenaeus, cf. *Adv. haer.* 1.10.1.

where not made explicit: the angel Gabriel, who appears to Mary at the annunciation.

If *GLuke* is read from a Johannine perspective, the virginal conception is the outward form of the supreme miracle of the incarnation itself. The event is anticipated by the evangelist, but it is not narrated: 'The Holy Spirit will come upon you and the power of the Most High will overshadow you. . .' (*GLk* 1.35). In the Lukan birth narrative, the event is referred to as future or presupposed as having already occurred (cf. 1.41–45; 2.5). There is here no dove-like descent as at the baptism. An angel is sent to Mary from heaven to announce the event of the incarnation, but no canonical evangelist narrates the descent of the Son from heaven or his transformation into a human embryo in Mary's womb. For the author of *EpAp* the lack of a narrative of descent and incarnation represents a deficiency in the older gospel literature, and the risen Jesus addresses himself to this issue as soon as he has convinced his disciples that he is truly risen and is not a ghost. Of the five *dramatis personae* of the credal affirmations, the role of the Holy Spirit is eliminated altogether in this incarnational narrative, and the mission of the angel Gabriel is conflated with that of the divine Son. Gabriel does, however, retain a role within the densely populated heavens through which the Son must descend on his journey towards enfleshment.

5.1 Angelic Transformations (1): The Self-Incarnation of the Logos

Convinced now that Jesus has truly risen from the dead, the disciples are ready to hear the story of his descent through the heavens to take human form. Jesus tells them how his descent fulfils the will of the Father and involves his taking on the appearance of an angel:

> When I came from the Father of all and passed through the heavens, I put on the wisdom of the Father and clothed myself in the power of his might. I was in the heavens, and archangels and angels I passed in their likeness as though I were one of them. Among the powers and rulers and authorities I passed, having the wisdom of the one who sent me. (*EpAp* 13.1–3)

The repeated references to 'passing' imply a descent through a graded series of heavens, from the highest, that of the archangels, to lower levels occupied by subordinate angelic beings; 'angels' seems to be a comprehensive category that incorporates the 'powers and rulers and authorities'. This threefold differentiation is attested primarily by the Latin *EpAp* fragment (*vir[tutes] et pot[es]tates et principes*), with some support from the Ethiopic, where, however, the order of the second and third categories is that of the Coptic: ⲁⲣⲭⲏ (pl.) corresponds to *principes*, ⲉⲝⲟⲩⲥⲓⲁ (pl.) to *potestates*. These are the 'powers' (δυνάμεις) of *Romans* 8.38 together with the 'rulers' (ἀρχάς) and 'authorities' (ἐξουσίας) of *Ephesians* 6.12, although unlike the Pauline texts *EpAp* does not view them as hostile. Malevolent spiritual powers play almost no role here.[3] Nor is there any concern to assign the powers, rulers and authorities to distinct spheres such as the sixth, fifth, and fourth heavens – although that may perhaps be implied. Thus the descending Christ takes on the appearance of archangels and angels in general, rather than subjecting himself to a series of transformations into the appearance first of an archangel, then a power, and so on downwards. As we shall see, this text is concerned with a twofold act of self-transformation, beginning in heaven and ending on earth – a significant modification to an earlier schema in which the descending Christ disguises himself in order to pass unrecognized through increasingly hostile heavenly terrain.[4] Here the angelic appearance is a prelude to the event of the incarnation itself, and the whole process embodies the wisdom and power of the Father even though the agent of the descent is Jesus.

As Jesus proceeds to explain to his disciples, his descent in angelic appearance was intended to deceive not lower and hostile spiritual powers but the leading archangels themselves:

---

[3] The one exception is at *EpAp* 28.1–2, where Jesus promises to deliver his disciples and the righteous dead from the power of the archons.

[4] See below on the *Ascension of Isaiah*, probably the earliest extant version of this schema. Underlying it is the Pauline tradition of the 'principalities and powers' (the terminology varies: cf. *Rom* 8.38–39; *1 Cor* 2.6–8; *Gal* 4.2–3, 8–9; *Eph* 6.12; *Col* 1.16). Later versions of the schema include *2TrSeth* 56,21–57,7 (NHC VII,2) and *PistSoph* 1.7 (C. Schmidt and Violet Macdermot, *Pistis Sophia*, Nag Hammadi Studies 9 [Leiden: Brill, 1978]), both of which appear to be dependent on *EpAp* 13–14. In *2TrSeth* as in *EpAp*, the descending Jesus is said to 'pass' (ⲡⲁⲣⲁⲅⲉ) the various gradations of angels or archons in 'their likeness' (*2TrSeth* 56,27–28; *EpAp* 13.1–3), doing so in order to fulfil the Father's will (*2TrSeth* 57,3–7; *EpAp* 13.6). In *PistSoph* 1.7 (Schmidt and Macdermot, 12) the descending Jesus takes the form of Gabriel as in *EpAp* 14.5, on which the later text is here dependent. In all three accounts, Jesus narrates his own descent.

And the commander [ᴀⲣⲭⲓⲥⲧⲣᴀⲧⲏⲅⲟⲥ] of the angels is Michael, with Gabriel and Uriel and Raphael, and they followed me down to the fifth firmament, for they were thinking in their hearts that I was one of them – such was the power given me by the Father. (*EpAp* 13.4)[5]

As yet, there is no explanation given of an act of deception which leads the four named figures to assume that the one they accompany on the first stages of his downward journey is just another archangel. The disguise motif also seems in tension with the account that follows of the appointment of deputies to ensure that heavenly worship continues while Jesus is unavailable to perform his usual high priestly activity:

And on that day I prepared the archangels, in a voice of wonder, so that they might go in to the altar of the Father and serve and fulfil the ministry until I returned to him. This is what I did in the wisdom of the likeness, for I became all in all so that I might fulfil the will of the Father of glory who sent me and return to him. (*EpAp* 13.5–6)

The priesthood theme returns at the end of the work, where the ascending Jesus is acclaimed by angels with the words, 'Gather us, O priest, into the light of glory!' (*EpAp* 51.3). Here Jesus' high priestly work takes place exclusively in heaven and has nothing to do with his self-sacrificial death on earth as in *Hebrews*. In order to fulfil his vocation as 'Saviour' (× 5 in this text),[6] Jesus must

---

[5] The concept of the angelic ἀρχιστράτηγος derives from *Joshua* 5.14 LXX, where the ἀρχιστράτηγος δυνάμεως κυρίου appears to Joshua with a drawn sword, evidently promising the assistance of heavenly armies in the forthcoming capture of Jericho. The angelic ἀρχιστράτηγος is identified as Michael at *TestAbr* 1.4, 2.2 and *passim* (A recension); further references in Hills, *Epistle*, 35. The archangelic quartet of Michael, Gabriel, Uriel, and Raphael derives from *1 Enoch* 9.1[gk], where the order is Michael, Uriel, Gabriel, Raphael (Aramaic: Michael, Sariel, Raphael, and Gabriel [4QEnoch[a] iv 6 + 4QEnoch[b] iii 7, 13]; Ethiopic: Michael, Gabriel, Suriel [*var.* Suryan], Uriel [*var.* Uryan]). Ethiopic and Greek texts in Michael A. Knibb, *The Ethiopic Book of Enoch*, 2 vols. (Oxford: Clarendon Press, 1978), 1.22–23. Cf. also *1 Enoch*[gk] 10.1[syn] (Uriel), 10.4 (Raphael), 10.9 (Gabriel), 10.11 (Michael). The tradition of four archangels may derive from the throne vision of *Ezekiel* 1 (cf. also *1 Enoch* 40.2–10): see George W. E. Nickelsburg, *1 Enoch 1: A Commentary on the Book of Enoch, Chapters 1–36; 81–108* (Hermeneia, Minneapolis, MN: Fortress Press, 2001), 207.

[6] *EpAp* 3.1; 6.1; 8.1; 10.5; 12.3. Schmidt notes that the usage of 'Saviour' in this text does not imply a Pauline emphasis on the soteriological significance of Jesus' death: 'vergebens suchen wir nach einem Worte des Auferstandenen, in welchem er auf sein Leiden und Sterben im Zusammenhang mit der dadurch bewirkten Versöhnung der

temporarily delegate his primary role as high priest in the heavenly sanctuary.[7]

In taking on his new role as Saviour, Jesus must assume the appearance of an archangel, a companion of Michael chief of angels, Gabriel, Uriel, and Raphael. Such was the will of the Father, and such was the power granted to him so as to fulfil that will. Why? The explanation lies in the author's reading of the Lukan annunciation account. His familiarity with Luke's birth story is already evident in the earlier reference to the infant Jesus as 'swaddled in Bethlehem' (*EpAp* 3.15; cf. *GLk* 2.7, ἐσπαργάνωσεν αὐτόν), and he assumes that his readers – like the disciples themselves – will already know of the annunciation to Mary through the angel Gabriel (cf. *GLk* 1.26–38). In *GLuke*, it is Gabriel who announces the conception and the Holy Spirit who accomplishes it. There is here no pre-existent Logos to be the agent of his own incarnation, as implied perhaps in *GJohn* 1.14, 'the Word became flesh'. The author of *EpAp* reduces these three agencies – the angel, the Spirit, the Logos – to just one. The Spirit is absent altogether, and the angel Gabriel is himself the Logos – the pre-existent Jesus – who announces his own birth and then enters the womb of Mary. Jesus assumed angelic form in heaven in order to appear to Mary *as if* he were Gabriel:

> 'For you know that the angel Gabriel brought the good news to Mary?' We answered, 'Yes, Lord.' Then he answered and said to us, 'Do you not remember that I told you a moment ago that I became an angel among angels...?' We said to him, 'Yes, Lord.' Then he answered and said to us, 'When I took the form of the angel Gabriel,

sündigen Menschheit mit Gott hinweist' (*Gespräche Jesu*, 305; followed by Hornschuh, *Studien*, 52). Hornschuh finds this absence to be at odds with the paschal celebration of 'the memorial of my death' in *EpAp* 15, an indication that the author is 'kein Systematiker' (52). Yet, aside from Paul and prior to Athanasius's *De Incarnatione*, a soteriology focused on the cross plays only a limited role in early Christian literature, canonical or otherwise. Cf. Melito's *Peri Pascha*, where the cross is significant primarily for typological rather than soteriological reasons. S. G. Hall (ed.), *Melito of Sardis, On Pascha and Fragments: Texts and Translations* (Oxford: Clarendon Press, 1979).

[7] The altar (θυσιαστήριον, *EpAp* 13.5) at which Jesus or his angelic deputies minister is presumably the golden 'altar of incense' (θυσιαστήριον θυμιάματος) of *Exodus* 30.1, which the author to the Hebrews locates within the Holy of holies rather than outside the veil (*Heb* 9.3–4). Angelic ministry at this 'golden altar before the throne' is envisaged in *Revelation* 8.3–4, where incense conveys the prayers of the saints to God. In *EpAp* the altar serves the worship of God in heaven without reference to human concerns.

I appeared to Mary and I spoke with her. Her heart received me, she believed; sh[e mou]lded me, I entered into her, I became flesh [ϲⲁⲣⲍ]. For I became my own servant in the appearance of the likeness of an angel. . .' (*EpAp* 14.1–7).[8]

Here an established tradition of an annunciation by Gabriel stemming from *GLuke* is reinterpreted under the influence of an incarnational theology echoing *GJohn*: 'I became flesh.'[9] The likeness of an angel proves to be a transitional stage between disembodied divine sonship and human embodiment.[10] While the reference to Mary's positive response to the pseudo-angelic annunciation again recalls Luke, the earlier evangelist's claim that 'the angel left her' (*GLk* 1.38b) is rejected. On the contrary, Mary's believing response allows the angelically disguised Logos to enter her womb, to take up residence there, and to be 'moulded' within her body so that a being of spirit is transformed into flesh. Here as elsewhere it is characteristic of this text to select traditions later recognized as 'canonical' and to use them freely for its own ends. In doing so, this 'proto-orthodox' text also creates a tension with its earlier credal claim that 'the Word who became flesh of Mary' was 'carried in her womb through the Holy Spirit' (*EpAp* 3.13). The role of the Holy Spirit in the incarnation may be confessed, but there is no place for such a role when the incarnational transformations are narrated.

---

[8] For 'she moulded me' rather than Schmidt's 'ich formte mich' (*Gespräche Jesu*, 51), followed by subsequent translators, see the Additional Note on 14.6. As explained there, the Ethiopic reading ('she laughed') is probably the result of a misreading by an Ethiopic scribe. Attempts to make sense of Mary's laughter (e.g. Hills, *Epistle*, 88) are therefore not relevant to the earliest accessible text-form.

[9] As Hornschuh notes, the identification of Gabriel as the Logos means that annunciation and conception are the same event (*Studien*, 41). While Jesus does not identify himself as the Logos in the present context, he does so on three occasions elsewhere: *EpAp* 18.1 ('I am the Word [ⲗⲟⲅⲟⲥ]'), 31.11 ('I am the Word of the Father'), 39.12 ('I the Word [ⲗⲟⲅⲟⲥ] who became flesh [ϲⲁⲣⲍ] and suffered'); cf. also 3.13.

[10] The author's understanding of the event of incarnation reflects his fusion of two early Christian traditions, and it is unnecessary to follow Hornschuh in postulating here an anti-gnostic polemic itself influenced by gnostic themes. Hornschuh writes: 'Das spekulative Interesse, das sich in diesem Bericht ausspricht, ist genuin altkirchlich-frühchristlichem Denken fremd. Wir erkennen hier, wie sehr der Verfasser, der sich die Kampf gegen die Gnosis vorgenommen hat, seinerseits von gnostischen Denken beeinflusst ist' (*Studien*, 40). Hornschuh's assessment is severe: 'Die ausser- und unbiblischen Einflüsse prägen die Ep. Ap. in seiner Grundsubstanz' (51).

5.2   Angelic Transformations (2): The Hiddenness of the Lord

A parallel to the *EpAp* motif of the descent in disguise is to be found in the *Ascension of Isaiah*.[11] This is an early Christian text once assumed to be composite[12] although its integrity has more recently been strongly advocated[13] and had its supporters even in the early twentieth-century heyday of source-criticism.[14] It may date from as early as the late first century and was apparently already known to the author to the Hebrews.[15] The first part of the work recounts how Isaiah was persecuted and martyred under King Manasseh in an act of satanic revenge for an earlier vision of the future coming of Christ

---

[11] The various witnesses to *AscIs* have been edited (with Italian translations) by Paulo Bettiolo, et al. (eds.), *Ascensio Isaiae*, Corpus Christianorum Series Apocryphorum 7 (Turnhout: Brepols, 1995). There is broad agreement between the complete Ge'ez text (44–129), a Greek fragment of 2.4–4.4 (Amherst Papyrus 1, 136–45), fragments from two Coptic versions (154–87), and Latin fragments of 2.14–3.13 + 7.1–19 (Vat. Lat. 5750, 193–209). A second Latin translation (211–33 [de Fantis, 1522]) and a Slavonic version (234–319) cover only Isaiah's vision (*AscIs* 6–11), and a further Greek manuscript represents a free rewrite of this text (321–51). See M. A Knibb, 'Martyrdom and Ascension of Isaiah', in J. H. Charlesworth (ed.), *The Old Testament Pseudepigrapha*, 2 vols. (London: Darton, Longman, and Todd, 1985), 2.143–76; 2.147–49.

[12] So R. H. Charles, *The Ascension of Isaiah* (London: A&C Black, 1900), xxxvi–xlv. Charles's source-analysis was accepted (with modifications) by M. A. Knibb, 'Martyrdom and Ascension', 143, 147–49, although Professor Knibb informs me that his view on this has since changed. On his earlier view, '[I]t is obvious that chapters 6–11 are Christian in origin, and that chapters 1–5… include a good deal of Jewish material' (147). In reality, there is nothing to suggest a Jewish origin as opposed to a Christian one in the narrative of events leading up to Isaiah's martyrdom; the overtly Christian material in 3.13–4.22 need not be seen as interpolated. Nor is there any reason to suppose that the composition of this text extended over a period of 500 years, from the second century BCE to the fourth century CE (143, 149–50). The separate circulation of chapters 6–11 demonstrates not that Isaiah's vision of the incarnation, earthly life, and ascension of Christ was originally independent but that this section of the two-part work was of more interest to some readers than the account of the prophet's martyrdom.

[13] See Jonathan Knight, *Disciples of the Beloved One: The Christology, Social Setting and Theological Content of the Ascension of Isaiah* (Sheffield: Sheffield Academic Press, 1996), 28–32; Darrell D. Hannah, 'Isaiah's Vision in the Ascension of Isaiah and the Early Church', *Journal of Theological Studies* 50 (1999), 80–101; 84; Jan Dochhorn, 'Ascensio Isaiae', in G. Oegema (ed.), *Jüdische Schriften aus hellenistisch-römischer Zeit*, vol. 6 part 1, *Unterweisung in erzählender Form* (Gütersloh: Gütersloher Verlaghaus, 2005), 1–45.

[14] Notably F. C. Burkitt, *Jewish and Christian Apocalypses* (London: British Academy, 1914), 45–48. Referring no doubt to R. H. Charles, Burkitt writes: 'I sometimes fancy that the spirit of Beliar must be dwelling in some of my friends when they use the wooden saw to dissect the *Ascension of Isaiah*' (45).

[15] Compare *Heb* 11.37–38 with *AscIs* 2.8b–10, and *Heb* 11.39–40 with *AscIs* 9.7–12.

seen during the reign of Hezekiah (*AscIs* 1.1–3.12; 5.1–16). Although the content of the prophet's earlier vision is already anticipated here at some length (3.13–4.22), a more comprehensive account is reserved for the second part (6.1–11.39). This results in an unusual but effective chronological structure. The narrative opens in the twenty-sixth year of Hezekiah, towards the end of his reign, as the king tries to pass on to Manasseh written accounts of revelations earlier received by himself in the fifteenth year of his reign (1.1–5a) and by Isaiah in the twentieth year (1.5b–6a). To the king's grief, the prophet warns of Manasseh's future apostasy and his own martyrdom (1.6b–13). The narrative proceeds to tell how these prophetic warnings were fulfilled after Hezekiah's death. In response to Manasseh's apostasy Isaiah and his prophetic companions are forced to take refuge in the mountains (2.1–11) until the false prophet Belkira secures his arrest (2.12–3.12) and has him put to death by being publicly sawn in two (5.1–16). Within this straightforward narrative sequence, there are constant backward references to Isaiah's earlier vision from the time of Hezekiah (1.5b–6a; 3.13–4.22; 5.1, 15–16).[16] Belkira is said to act at the instigation of Samael, the hostile angelic ruler of this world otherwise known as Beliar (4.1–5.1, *passim*) or Satan (5.16): 'for Samael was very angry with Isaiah from the days of Hezekiah king of Judah because of the things he had seen concerning the Beloved [i.e. Christ]...' (5.15; cf. 3.13, 5.1). A full account of that earlier vision is given in the second half of the work (6.1–11.43), which thus ends at a point that pre-dates the narrative with which it opens. The sophisticated structure of this two-part work is already implicit in chapter 1, in the reference to Isaiah's earlier vision (1.4–6a) and the prophecy of the martyrdom (1.6b–9). The vision follows the martyrdom because it includes an anticipatory account of the commissioning, descent, incarnation, crucifixion, resurrection, and ascension of 'the Beloved' (10.7–11.33).[17]

---

[16] While these passages contain eschatological themes that are not covered in the fuller account of the vision in chapters 6–11, it is misleading to differentiate a 'First Vision' (3.13–4.22) from a 'Second Vision', as Jonathan Knight does (*Disciples of the Beloved One*, 14–15); 3.13–20 corresponds closely to 9.17–11.32, which it summarizes in advance.

[17] The logic of this presentation was overlooked by earlier scholarship, with its orientation towards source criticism. Thus, according to E. Schürer, '[t]he Vision is quite unconnected with the Martyrdom. Indeed, it is attached very clumsily to it, for it should have preceded the prophet's death. In general, the chronology of the events is given in a most haphazard manner' (*The History of the Jewish People in the Age of*

Isaiah experiences his vision in Hezekiah's palace in the presence of his son Josab, a group of forty prophets led by Micah, Ananias, and Joel, and trusted royal officials (6.1–4, 16–17).[18] After Isaiah has been enabled by the Holy Spirit to address 'the words of righteousness and faith' to a wider audience, he becomes silent and his mind finds itself in the presence of a glorious angel who has descended from the seventh heaven, while his body remains on earth, breathing but unconscious (6.6–13). The main focus of his vision will be the descent of Christ through the heavens to take human form and to be born, die, rise, and reascend to his Father (10.7–11.32), but in order to view these events Isaiah himself is taken up to the seventh heaven and provides an elaborate account of all that he sees and hears on his upward journey (7.9–9.41). This culminates in the vision of 'the Great Glory' with 'the Beloved' and 'the Angel of the Holy Spirit' (9.27–42).[19] Thus the heavenly terrain through which Christ must descend is already familiar to the reader who has followed Isaiah's prior ascent.

As they begin their journey, Isaiah and the angel pass first through the 'firmament' inhabited by Samael, who (as the reader already knows) will later bring about the prophet's martyrdom through his earthly representative, the false prophet Belkira (5.15–16). Samael is described by the narrator as 'the archon of this world' (2.4) and by the angel as 'the god of that world' (9.14).[20] His hosts are constantly

---

Jesus Christ, vol. III.1, rev. and ed. G. Vermes, F. Millar, and M. Goodman [Edinburgh: T&T Clark, 1986], 337).

[18] Robert G. Hall finds in *AscIs* 6 and elsewhere a reflection of the author's situation as a member of an early Christian prophetic community struggling to establish its legitimacy; 'The Ascension of Isaiah: Community Situation, Date, and Place in Early Christianity', *Journal of Biblical Literature* 109 (1990), 289–306; 293–98. Extrapolations from a narrative text to a present communal situation are questionable, however.

[19] As Darrell Hannah has shown, this trinitarian passage is based on *Isaiah* 6, with the Beloved and the Angel of the Holy Spirit representing the Seraphim ('Isaiah's Vision in the Ascension of Isaiah and the Early Church', *Journal of Theological Studies* 50 [1999], 80–101; 86–90). Note also the clear identification of the vision of *AscIs* 7–11 with that of *Is* 6 in the accusation that leads to Isaiah's martyrdom: 'Isaiah himself has said, "I see more than Moses the prophet." But Moses said, "No one shall see the Lord and live." But Isaiah has said, "I have seen the Lord, and behold, I am alive!"' (*AscIs* 3.8–9, cf. *Is* 6.1, 5; *Ex* 33.20).

[20] Samael is also known as Beliar (3.11, 13 Greek [Amherst Papyrus 1], Ethiopic × 12), Belial (3.11, 13, Latin [Vat. Lat. 5750]), or Satan (2.1–2, Ethiopic; 7.9, Latin [Vat. Lat. 5750] and Ethiopic). In the Greek Legend (Paris, Cod. Fr. 1534), the replacement of both Belial/Beliar and Samael by Satan is obviously secondary (1.9; 11). Texts in Bettiolo, et al., *Ascensio Isaiae*.

at war with one another, and their warfare is the counterpart of all earthly strife (7.9–12). Samael is the (deutero-)Pauline 'archon of the power of the air' (*Eph* 2.2), and he and his hosts are the 'world-rulers of this darkness, spiritual powers of evil in the heavenly realms' (*Eph* 6.12). The latter passage from *Ephesians* is also used to introduce the figure of Samael in the *Hypostasis of the Archons* (NH II,4), where his name is interpreted as 'god of the blind' (II 86,20–27; 87,3–4; 94,25–26). In *AscIsaiah* as in *HypArch*, Samael boasts that he is the only God: 'I am God, and there is none other besides me' (*HypArch* II 94, 21–22; cf. 86, 30–31), 'I am God, and before me there has been none' (*AscIs* 4.6, cf. 10.13). While *AscIsaiah* does not follow *HypArch* in identifying Samael with the creator deity of *Genesis*, Samael has ruled the world since it came into existence (4.2; 7.12). In both cases, Samael is wilfully ignorant of the existence of heavenly realms above his own, culminating in the being of 'the Holy One, the God of all things' (*HypArch* 92, 34), 'the Holy One, who rests among the holy ones' (*AscIs* 6.8). In both cases, the destruction of the archons will be achieved by Christ (*HypArch* 96, 28–97,13; *AscIs* 5.15–16).[21]

Isaiah and the angel pass through the realm of Samael at the start of their upward journey, traversing five heavens of ever-increasing glory in which, however, God is worshipped at a distance, before attaining the presence of God, Christ, and the Holy Spirit as they arrive in the sixth and seventh heavens: 'When I was in the sixth heaven I thought the light that I saw in the five heavens to be darkness' (*AscIs* 8.21). For the descending Christ, the realm of Samael and the world he presides over are the goal of his journey, not its starting-point as for Isaiah. Christ descends into enemy-occupied territory, and he must therefore come in disguise. The culmination of Isaiah's prophetic vision is 'the transformation and descent of the Lord' (10.18; cf. 3.13), as he is enabled to see 'the Lord of all these heavens and thrones being transformed until he resembles your appearance and likeness' (8.9–10). Thus Christ is commissioned by his Father:

---

[21] These parallels in no way show that *AscIs* is to be regarded as a 'Christian-Gnostic' text and thus as 'semi-Christian', as argued by Andrew K. Helmbold, 'Gnostic Elements in the "Ascension of Isaiah"', *New Testament Studies* 18 (1972), 222–27; 227. It is equally problematic to argue (in opposition to Helmbold) that *AscIs* 'stands its distance from the belief system of Gnosticism' (Knight, *Disciples of the Beloved*, 170). Parallels between *AscIs* and *HypArch* show that these texts share common (though not universal) Christian concerns.

Go and descend through all the heavens. And you shall descend through the firmament and that world, to the angel who is in Sheol shall you descend, but to Perdition you shall not go. And you shall liken yourself to the likeness of all who are in the five heavens, and conform to the appearance of the angels of the firmament, and liken yourself to the angels of Sheol. And none of the angels of that world shall know that you are Lord with me of the seven heavens and their angels... And afterwards you shall ascend from the gods of death to your place, and you shall not be transformed in each heaven but in glory you shall ascend and sit at my right hand. And then the princes and powers of that world will worship you.   (*AscIs* 10.8–11, 14–15)[22]

In the sixth heaven, Christ retains his true form and continues to be the object of angelic praise (10.19). As we have seen, the sixth heaven shares the proximity to God of the seventh. In the fifth and fourth heavens, everything is different: Christ 'made his form like that of the angels there, and they did not praise him, for his form was like theirs' (10.20). In the third, second, and first heaven, the gate-keepers 'demanded the password, and the Lord gave it to them so that he should not be recognized... for his form was like their form' (10.24). As we have learned during Isaiah's ascent, the angels of the five heavens all worship the true God, although the extent of their glory and praise correspond to their place in the heavenly hierarchy. The descending Christ thus passes through the realm of the first heaven, where the glory is least and the praises faintest, and then enters the hostile sphere of the archons: 'And again he descended into the firmament where the prince of this world dwells', a chaotic place where Samael's hosts 'were fighting one another' (10.29). Here too Christ takes the form of the local inhabitants and remains unrecognized. The goal of the successive transformations into ever lowlier forms is that Christ should appear on earth as human, but the transformations are not just a quasi-natural assimilation to different levels of the ontological hierarchy – as perhaps in the opposite case of Isaiah himself, whose face was transformed from one degree of glory to another as he ascended from heaven to heaven (7.25). The

---

[22] The translation follows the Ethiopic text in Bettiolo, et al., *Ascensio Isaiae*. For 'you shall liken yourself to the likeness...', a Coptic fragment reads 'you shall change your form [ⲙⲟⲣⲫⲏ] to the likeness...' (Knight, *Disciples of the Beloved*, 185); the underlying Greek is probably the same.

transformations of the descending Christ are intentional rather than natural: they are a disguise, intended to deceive, and – as we shall see – this is also the case with his humanity.

The elaborate descent-and-transformation narrative of the *Ascension of Isaiah* is echoed in the succinct version given in the *Epistula Apostolorum*, where it is the risen Christ who speaks to his disciples rather than Isaiah to King Hezekiah and the prophets: 'I was in the heavens, and archangels and angels I passed in their likeness as though I were one of them' (*EpAp* 13.2). Here too Christ takes on the likeness of angels, and here too the transformation has the adoption of human likeness as its goal. In both cases the author's intention is not just to confess the incarnation as an element in the rule of faith but to *narrate* it and thereby to interpret it. On closer inspection, however, the two interpretations are very different. The Christ of *EpAp* takes on the specific form of archangels, inhabitants of the seventh heaven at the summit of the heavenly hierarchy, and it is they who are deceived by his disguise. Michael, Gabriel, Uriel, and Raphael 'followed me down to the fifth firmament, for they were thinking in their hearts that I was one of them' (*EpAp* 13.4). As in *AscIsaiah*, the fifth firmament marks the boundary between the upper sphere of proximity to God, inhabited by archangels, and lower angelic realms at an increasing distance from the deity. Yet in *AscIsaiah* Christ takes on the various forms of the lower realms, decreasing in glory until the plunge into the dark world of the archons. In contrast, the Christ of *EpAp* takes on a form appropriate to the upper realms, the sixth and seventh heavens: Michael and his colleagues mistakenly think that he is one of them as they accompany him to the boundary that he must cross without them. This author has adopted the motif of the descent in disguise, but he has no interest either in a carefully graded hierarchy of spheres requiring a series of transformations into ever more lowly angelic forms, or in a hostile and chaotic sphere presided over by the false god of this world. On the contrary, the disguise adopted in the upper sphere remains in place when Christ arrives in this world at the end of his downward journey. Above, he has taken a form similar to Michael, Gabriel, and other leading angelic figures. Below, he appears to Mary precisely in the form of Gabriel. Here the transformation-and-disguise motif is used to account for the role of the divine Son or Logos in his own incarnation.

In *AscIsaiah* there is a close relationship between the heavenly transformation and its earthly correlate in the circumstances of Jesus' birth. There is no annunciation in this text and no description of the event of conception: the author's account of Mary's pregnancy is indebted to *GMatthew* rather than to *GLuke* (*AscIs* 11.1–6).[23] Instead, the emphasis lies on the secrecy attending the conception, the birth, and indeed the whole of Jesus' earthly life. Just as the descending Lord takes on the form of the angels of the various heavens in order to pass through them without being recognized, so the incarnate Lord takes on a normal human form in order to pass unrecognized through this world. Thus, in an addition to the Matthean focus on Joseph's reaction to Mary's pregnancy, the Isaianic author states that Joseph 'did not reveal this matter to anyone' (11.4). The citizens of Bethlehem are puzzled by the circumstances in which Mary gave birth to her son, 'and they were all blinded concerning him – they all knew about him but they did not know where he came from' (11.15). The holy family move from Bethlehem to Nazareth to escape scandal, and there Jesus 'sucked the breast like an infant, as is usual, so that he might not be recognized' (11.17). His identity was concealed 'from all the heavens and all the rulers and gods of this world' and from 'the children of Israel, who did not know who he was' and so handed him over to be crucified (11.16, 19).[24] Only in his ascension does Jesus manifest himself in his true divine–human form:

> And I saw him, and he was in the firmament but was not transformed into their form. And all the angels of the firmament, with Satan, saw him and worshipped. And there was much sorrow there as they said, 'How did our Lord descend upon us, and we did not perceive the glory that was upon him…? (*AscIs* 11.23–24)

---

[23] For the relationship between *AscIs* and *GMatthew*, see J. Knight, *Disciples of the Beloved One*, 276–78. Knight's discussion of *AscIs*'s relationship to the New Testament in general suffers from the assumptions that the New Testament writings had already been identified as such and that they must necessarily pre-date noncanonical literature such as *AscIs* (274–314).

[24] As Darrell Hannah argues, it is not appropriate to describe this christology as 'docetic' ('The Ascension of Isaiah and Docetic Christology', *Vigiliae Christianae* 53 [1999], 165–96). For a critique of overuse of the concept of 'docetism', see Jean-Daniel Dubois, 'Le docétisme des christologies gnostiques revisité', *New Testament Studies* 63 (2017), 279 –304. On the question whether 'docetism' is a useful etic category at all, see my article, 'Pauline Reception and the Problem of Docetism', in Joseph Verheyden, et al. (eds.), *Docetism in the Early Church: The Quest for an Elusive Phenomenon*, Wissenschaftliche Untersuchungen zum Neuen Testament (Tübingen: Mohr Siebeck, 2018), 51–66. That Jesus seemed to be other than what he truly was is the general early Christian view, although there are differences of opinion about the thickness of the disguise.

Similar incredulous questions are asked all the way up to the fifth heaven (11.25–28), although in these higher realms there is no cause for sorrow.

In *EpAp* the angelic transformation motif is used to explain the event of the Logos's self-incarnation. In *AscIsaiah* it explains the non-recognition of the incarnate Son that accompanies his birth and occasions his death.[25] This is a variation on the theme of the 'messianic secret', and it can be traced back not just to Mark but also to Paul, who speaks of a mysterious divine wisdom 'which none of the archons of this age knew – for if they had known, they would not have crucified the Lord of glory' (*1 Cor* 2.8). Since the transformation is also a drastic diminution in which the divine glory is all but extinguished, it has affinities with the 'kenotic' christology of the Philippian Christ-hymn, where Christ's earthly appearance 'in human likeness' (ἐν ὁμοιώματι ἀνθρώπων, *Phil* 2.7) again suggests a disguise – in contrast to a Johannine christology in which 'the Word became flesh' and 'manifested his glory' (*GJn* 1.14; 2.11). A further parallel may be found in Ignatius, who informs his readers in Ephesus that 'hidden from the archon of this world was the virginity of Mary and her childbearing, and likewise also the Lord's death' (*IEph* 19.1). Here, the manifestation of the Lord's presence takes the form of a star which 'shone in heaven beyond all the stars', and around which the other stars, the sun and the moon 'became a chorus' (19.2) – an image perhaps suggested by Joseph's dream in *Genesis* 37.9. For the hiddenness/manifestation schema to work, the appearance of the star must signify the risen and ascended Lord rather than heralding his birth, as in *GMatthew*: Mary's childbearing cannot be both hidden

---

[25] This 'angelomorphic christology' has a functional significance for each of the two works but may also imply an inherent affinity between the pre-existent 'Son of God' (× 4 in *EpAp*) or 'Beloved' (× 20 in *AscIs*) and the angels – as argued by Jonathan Knight, *Disciples of the Beloved One*, 139–63; Jonathan Knight, *The Ascension of Isaiah* (Sheffield: Sheffield Academic Press, 1995), 79–84. In *AscIs* 9.27–42, 'the Beloved' and 'the Angel of the Holy Spirit' are simultaneously objects of worship and worshippers. While the Beloved and the Holy Spirit transcend the angels of the seventh heaven, they are located in *AscIs* 7–10 within an ontological continuum or hierarchy extending from this world to the dwelling of the 'Great Glory' (9.37), and back again. This combination of trinitarian theology and ontological continuum is paralleled in the *Apocryphon of John* 5.2–41.8, where the trinity consists in a Father, Mother, and Son (*ApocrJn* 4.2–4; 10.5–16.17), with the Mother-figure representing the Holy Spirit (12.3; 16.13; 73.18–74.2). *ApocrJn* references are to the Synopsis in Michael Waldstein and Frederik Wisse (eds.), *The Apocryphon of John: Synopsis of Nag Hammadi Codices II,1; III,1; and IV,1 with BG 8502,2*, Nag Hammadi and Manichaean Studies 33 (Leiden: Brill, 1995).

from the archon of this world and simultaneously revealed by an unprecedented astral phenomenon in the archon's own realm. Ignatius's Christ is hidden in his birth and death and manifested in the star that announces his ascension.[26]

In *EpAp* this christological myth of the descent in disguise is put to a new use, providing the back-story to the annunciation tradition which is itself reinterpreted as an account of the divine Son's self-incarnation. Although the author is aware of the credal belief that the incarnate Word was 'carried in [Mary's] womb through the Holy Spirit' (3.13), neither he nor the author of *AscIsaiah* has any place for the Spirit in their narrative accounts of the beginnings of Jesus' earthly life. The divine Son who, in willing obedience to his Father, assumes angelic form and descends through the heavens does not suddenly become the passive object of a third divine agency when he assumes flesh.

5.3   Incarnation and Virgin Birth

The substitution of the Logos for the Holy Spirit as the agent of the conception may be a peculiarity from the standpoint of later orthodoxies, but the fusion of incarnation and miraculous conception has normally been taken for granted. This linkage is, however, contingent rather than necessary or inevitable. It represents one way in which beliefs about Jesus' pre-existence, divinity and incarnation could be harmonized with narrative traditions about his earthly life, but other possibilities were also available. Might the descent of the Spirit at the river Jordan be the moment when a divine Christ, Son, or Logos is united with a human Jesus? Such a view could claim support from *GMark* or *GJohn*, where the virginal conception is not mentioned.[27] Or might the key event be the birth itself? That view is apparently shared by the authors of the *Ascension of Isaiah* and the *Protevangelium of James*, although in both cases it is expressed

---

[26] See the detailed discussion of *IEph* 19.1–3 in William R. Schoedel, *Ignatius of Antioch* (Hermeneia, Philadelphia, PA: Fortress Press, 1985), 87–94. Schoedel associates the star with Jesus' birth rather than his ascension: 'The star indicated to the powers that something threatening was afoot, but they did not assess its significance accurately since they were unaware of the startling miracles that surrounded the birth of Christ' (91). Schoedel does not adequately explain how Jesus' manifestation τοῖς αἰῶσιν by way of the star is possible at the same time as he remains hidden from 'the prince of this world'.

[27] Cf. Irenaeus, *Adv. haer.* 1.25.1; 1.26.1–2; 1.30.14; Clement, *Strom.* 1.21.146.1; *GPhil* 70,34–71,15 (NHC I, 3); *2TrSeth* 51,20–52,5 (NHC VII, 2); *TestTr* 30,18–30 (NHC IX, 3). See the final section of this chapter, below.

indirectly through the narrative and not in any explicit confessional statement.[28]

PJames includes a revised version of a Lukan annunciation scene, again without reference to the Holy Spirit. *PJames* 11.1–3 follows closely the structure of the Lukan annunciation (*GLk* 1.26–38), a dialogue in which three angelic utterances (*A1* greeting, *A2* reassurance and announcement of conception, *A3* means of conception) are each followed by a reaction or response from Mary (*B1* anxiety, *B2* question, *B3* acquiescence). In *PJames*, *A1/B1* takes place at a well, and thus at a different venue from *A2,3/B2,3*, Mary's home, where she spins purple thread for the temple veil while seated on her throne (cf. 10.2).[29] *B1*[PJas] adds the motif of incomprehension to that of anxiety: at the well, 'Mary looked right and left to see where this voice came from.' Only later is the angel identified as 'the archangel Gabriel' (12.2). When the angelic encounter is resumed in her home, Mary is told that she will 'conceive by his word' (ἐκ λόγου αὐτοῦ, 11.2).[30] Yet her question – 'Shall I conceive from the Lord the living God and give birth as every woman gives birth [καὶ γεννήσω ὡς πᾶσα γυνὴ γεννᾷ]?' (11.2)[31] – is concerned not with the miraculous conception as such but with the birth to which it will lead, in contrast to its Lukan equivalent which concerns the conception alone: 'How shall this be, since I do not know a man?' (*GLk* 1.34).[32] Mary asks whether her miraculous conception will be followed by a normal and

---

[28] Greek text of the *Protevangelium* (based on P. Bodmer V) in Émile de Strycker (ed.), *La Forme la plus ancienne du Protévangile de Jacques* (Brussels: Société de Bolandistes, 1961), 64–191; Bart Ehrman and Zlatko Pleše (eds.), *The Apocryphal Gospels: Texts and Translations* (New York: Oxford University Press, 2011), 40–71.

[29] 'While her spinning fosters her connection to the temple, indicating that she is παρθένος even in her absence from it, the fact that she spins while receiving the angel's message shows that she will remain παρθένος even in the act of conceiving a child'; Eric M. Vanden Eykel, *'But Their Faces Were All Looking Up': Author and Reader in the Protevangelium of James* (London: Bloomsbury T&T Clark, 2016), 115.

[30] As Mark Goodacre points out, the addition of 'by his word' to *GLuke* 1.31 makes it unambiguous that God is the agent of conception; 'The *Protevangelium of James* and the Creative Rewriting of *Matthew* and *Luke*', in Watson and Parkhouse, *Connecting Gospels*, 57–66; 63–64.

[31] καὶ γεννήσω is omitted in P. Bodmer V but supported by Syr[a], dated to the late fifth or early sixth century (Strycker, *Protévangile*, 35, 116). Later Greek manuscripts attest both readings: see C. Tischendorf, *Evangelia Apocrypha* (Leipzig: Avenarius and Mendelssohn, 1853), 22. The longer reading is accepted by Tischendorf and Ehrman and Pleše and seems necessary for the sense, as γεννάω means 'bear' or 'give birth' when referring to a woman, not 'conceive'. The shorter reading produces the confused question, 'Shall I conceive… as every woman gives birth?'

[32] The distinction is well brought out by E. Amann: in *PJames* 11.2, 'L'accent porte essentiellement sur γεννήσω. Dans l'Évangile, c'est avant tout la conception virginale

natural birth, and the angel's negative response indicates that the birth will be accompanied by a manifestation of the divine presence: 'Not so, Mary, for the power of God will overshadow you [ἐπισκιάσει σοι] – therefore the holy one born from you will be called son of the Highest' (*PJas* 11.3; cf. *GLk* 1.35).[33] Overshadowing by the power of God will therefore occur not at the moment of conception but at the birth, in keeping with the miracle of the conception itself.

In this text the child is born in a cave near Bethlehem, and it is there that the angel's promise of the divine overshadowing is fulfilled – not by the Holy Spirit, as in *GLuke*, but by a cloud from heaven.[34] When Joseph returns with a midwife,

> they stood in the vicinity [ἐν τῷ τόπῳ] of the cave and a bright cloud [νεφέλη φωτεινή] was overshadowing [ἐπισκιάζουσα] the cave. And the midwife said, 'My soul is magnified today, for my eyes have seen wonders [παράδοξα], for salvation has come to Israel.' And immediately the cloud began to withdraw [ὑπεστέλλετο] from the cave, and there appeared a great light in the cave so that their eyes could not bear it. And after a little while that light withdrew, until a child appeared and came and took the breast of his mother Mary. And the midwife cried out and said, 'How great is this day for me, for I have seen this new miracle [θέαμα]!'   (*PJas* 19.2).[35]

qui est visée; ici, au contraire, c'est sur l'enfantement virginal que portent les préoccupations de Marie. Consacrée au Seigneur dès avant sa naissance, elle se demande si sa virginité sera complètement respectée'; *Le Protévangile de Jacques et ses remaniements latins: Introduction, textes, traduction, et commentaire* (Paris: Letouzey et Ané, 1910), 225.

[33] The negative response confirms that Mary is not asking two questions ('Shall I conceive from the Lord the living God? And shall I give birth as every woman gives birth?') but one. The shift in 11.2 from the angel's announcement of the conception to Mary's focus on the birth is missed by Alexander Toepel, for whom Mary merely seeks clarity about the nature of her conception (*Das Protevangelium des Jakobus: Ein Beitrag zur neueren Diskussion um Herkunft, Auslegung und theologische Einordnung*, Frankfurter Theologische Studien 71 ([Münster: Aschendorff Verlag, 2014], 160–61).

[34] The author does attribute Mary's conception to the Holy Spirit, however, drawing on the Matthean rather than the Lukan presentation (*PJas* 14.2, 19.1; cf *GMt* 1.20).

[35] A 'dark cloud' in P. Bodmer V, elsewhere a 'bright cloud'. Citing *Exodus* 19.9, Strycker regards 'dark' as the original reading, the darkness understood as 'signe de la transcendance divine' (*Protévangile*, 155); so also Toepel (*Protevangelium*, 211), who suggests that νεφέλη φωτεινή is secondary and derives from *GMatthew* 17.5. Matthean influence need not be regarded as secondary, however. The cloud is bright

The 'overshadowing' announced by the angel at the time of the conception takes the form of the cloud over the cave at the moment of the child's birth. The 'new miracle' acclaimed by the midwife is the fact that 'a virgin has given birth, which her nature does not allow [ἃ οὐ χωρεῖ ἡ φύσις]' (19.3). Here φύσις is a euphemistic reference to Mary's reproductive system, which is subjected to an internal examination by the midwife's colleague, Salome, who confirms that Mary's physical virginity remains intact (20.1).[36] There has earlier been a virginal conception, but the emphasis now lies on the miracle of a 'virgin birth' – in contrast to the Lukan presentation, where the birth is narrated without reference to Mary's virginity or other miraculous accompanying circumstances (*GLk* 2.4–7).

No such shift of emphasis occurs in *EpAp* 13–14, which retells the Lukan account in a form that conflates annunciation, conception, and incarnation, but does not proceed to narrate the birth (but cf. 3.13–15). A parallel to the birth narrative of *PJames* does occur, however, in *AscIsaiah*, following an account of Mary's pregnancy with affinities to *GMatthew* rather than *GLuke* (*AscIs* 11.1–6, cf. *GMt* 1.18–25).[37] The birth is described as follows:

> And after two months of days Joseph was in the house with Mary his wife, the two of them being alone. And it happened that, as they were alone, Mary immediately looked with her eyes and saw a small child, and she was astonished. And when her astonishment ceased, her womb was found as it had been previously, before she was pregnant. And her husband Joseph said to her, 'What has made you astonished?' And his eyes were opened and he saw the child and praised the Lord, because the Lord had come into his lot. And a voice came to them: 'Do not tell this vision to anyone!' But news of the child was spread around in

because of the light shining within it which dazzles Joseph and the midwife when the cloud lifts.

[36] Mary's intact purity means that the newborn child can begin feeding immediately, without the prior maternal purification necessary for her own mother, Anna (*PJas* 5.2). On this, see Vanden Eykel, *'But Their Faces'*, 146–48.

[37] Enrico Norelli argues that *GMatthew* and *AscIsaiah* both draw from the same early traditions about the conception and birth of Jesus; the early second-century author of *AscIsaiah* is probably aware of *GMatthew* but does not attribute to it a canonical authority that would constrain his own narrative. *L'Ascensione di Isaia: Studi su un apocrifo al crocevia dei cristianesimi* (Bologna: Edizioni Dehoniane, 1994), 116–42; Enrico Norelli, 'Avant le canonique et l'apocryphe: Aux origines des récits de la naissance de Jésus', *Revue de théologie et de philosophie* 126 (1994), 305–24; 307–8.

Bethlehem. There were some who said, 'The virgin Mary has given birth before she has been married two months!' But many said, 'She did not give birth! The midwife did not go up and we did not hear cries of pain.' And they were all blinded concerning him, and none of them believed in him, and they did not know where he came from. And they took him and went to Nazareth in Galilee.   (*AscIs* 11.7–15)

In this version of the story of Jesus' birth, Joseph and Mary are at home in Bethlehem. There is no need for a cave to provide shelter and privacy on a journey there, as in the *PJames* account with its orientation here towards Luke.[38] The Matthean nativity story tells of events before and after the birth but (unlike Luke) says nothing about the birth itself. This gap is filled by *AscIsaiah*, but here the move to Nazareth occurs without the Matthean flight to Egypt to escape Herod's massacre of the innocents or the fear of Herod's successor that occasioned the relocation to Nazareth. What led to the move was not infanticide but gossip. As in *PJames* the child simply materializes outside Mary's body – though here without supernatural lighting. If the child passed through Mary's virginal birth canal at all, it did so without physical effects: in *AscIsaiah* as in *PJames*, 'her womb was found as it had been previously', although now without a midwife to verify the miracle (*AscIs* 11.9, 14).[39]

In *EpAp* it is clear that the moment of incarnation is the conception: 'I entered into her, I became flesh' (14.6). In *AscIsaiah*, in contrast, there is a disjunction between the descent narrative, which concludes with Christ's arrival in the realm of 'the angels of the air'

---

[38] The cave as Jesus' birth-place is mentioned by Justin as a fulfilment of the prophecy of *Is* 33.13–19 that exposes as a demonic distortion the legend of the birth of Mithras in a cave (*Dial.* 70.1–3). Justin and Origen also refer to the cave in connection with *GLk* 2.7b, '... because there was no room for them in the inn' (Justin, *Dial.* 78.5; Origen, *C. Cel.* 1.51). Both writers refer to an established tradition, perhaps stemming from *PJames*, a text certainly known at least to Origen (*In Matt.* 10.17).

[39] Vanden Eykel suggests the dependence of the *AscIsaiah* narrative on *PJames* (*'But Their Faces'*, 148n.). While there are common motifs – the obscure reference to Joseph as 'coming into his lot' (*AscIs* 11.3), the manifestation of the child by unknown means (11.7–8), Mary's postpartum intactness (11.9), the lack of assistance from a midwife (11.14) – these do not seem sufficient to demonstrate dependence, given the very different contexts in which they occur. The motifs of manifestation and intactness belong together, and they have their source in early Christian reflection on *Is* 7.14 LXX, where 'the virgin' identifies one who both conceives and gives birth as such: cf. *AscIsaiah* 11.13, 'Mary the virgin has given birth...' Such a birth might also be imagined as free from pain and requiring no midwife: see *Odes of Solomon* 19.7–9, *Acts of Peter* 24 (where *AscIsaiah* 11.14 is cited as a prophetic testimony).

(10.30–31), and the prophetic vision that follows of 'a woman of the house of David the prophet whose name was Mary, a virgin betrothed to a man named Joseph, a carpenter...' (11.2). Mary's pregnancy is left unexplained. In language that echoes *GMatthew*, 'she was found to be pregnant' (11.3; cf. *GMt* 1.18), but the Matthean 'by the Holy Spirit' is omitted. Instead, the role of the Spirit is conflated with that of the Matthean angel who appears to Joseph in a dream: 'The angel of the Spirit appeared in this world, and after this Joseph did not divorce Mary...' (*AscIs* 11.4; cf. *GMt* 1.19–21, 24). 'The angel of the Spirit' is distinct from Christ: Isaiah had encountered him earlier, in the seventh heaven, where his accompanying angel explains that the figure standing on Christ's left is 'the angel of the Holy Spirit who has spoken in you and also in the other righteous' (*AscIs* 9.36). The link between the appearance of the Spirit and Joseph's decision not to divorce Mary may suggest that the Spirit's role is to announce the imminent coming of Christ rather than to enable his incarnation. If so, it may be the miraculous birth that is the moment of incarnation, rather than the conception. When the child suddenly appears and Joseph 'praises the Lord because the Lord had come into his lot' (11.10), it is the birth that marks the moment of the Lord's arrival at the end of his journey of descent through the heavens – the final stage of which has been invisible to the reader. The appearance of the child coincides with its union with the Lord from heaven. Mary is the bearer of the child destined for that union with the Lord, but she is not the bearer of the Lord himself.[40]

More explicitly in *PJames*, the birth rather than the conception is the moment of incarnation. Leaving the cave in order to find a midwife as Mary is about to give birth, Joseph begins to speak in the first person about the moment of absolute stillness that occurred as time was invaded by eternity:

> And I Joseph was walking and not walking. And I looked up [ἀνέβλεψα] into the vault of heaven, and I saw it standing still [ἑστῶτα], and into the air, and I saw it stupefied [ἔκθαμβον] and the birds of heaven transfixed [ἠρεμοῦντα]. (*PJas* 18.2a)

---

[40] Compare Norelli's comments on *AscIsaiah* 11.7–11: 'On ne sait même pas si l'enfant est vraiment sorti du ventre de Marie. Ce qui importe, c'est que Marie et Joseph voient l'apparition, en ce monde, de celui qui passera pour être leur fils, mais dont ils sont les seuls à savoir qu'en réalité il est venu d'ailleurs' ('Avant le Canonique et l'Apocryphe', 308).

Joseph's first-hand account of the moment of stillness is punctuated by repetitions of the introductory formula καὶ ἀνέβλεψα... καὶ εἶδον... in the form καὶ ἐπέβλεψα... καὶ εἶδον as he turns his attention from the sky above to the world around him. Now he notices a group of workman as they share a meal, and describes in minute detail the arrested physical movements that comprise the simple act of eating out of a common bowl. One person's hand remains poised above the bowl, suspended in the act of picking up a piece of bread or some other foodstuff. Another person's hand is in the bowl, while another is conveying the food to his mouth, and another is chewing. And yet these actions require movement, and all movement has ceased:

> I looked to the earth, and I saw a bowl lying there and workmen reclining. And their hands were in the bowl, and those who chewed did not chew, and those who took did not take, and those who brought to their mouths did not bring, but their faces were all looking upwards [πάντων ἦν τὰ πρόσωπα ἄνω βλέποντα].   (18.2b)

The physical actions involved in the act of eating are being performed yet not performed, just as Joseph is walking – with one foot extended ahead of the other – yet not walking. He too has been immobilized, and all he can do is observe. He looks again and sees a flock of sheep, similarly deprived of movement together with their shepherd, who has raised his hand to strike them. He sees goats drinking yet not drinking from a stationary river – and then, 'suddenly everything was driven along by its course [ὑπὸ τοῦ δρόμου αὐτῶν ἀπηλαύνετο]' and returned to normal.

Why was time and motion suspended in this way? Before answering this question, it must be established that Joseph's vision actually belongs to the text of *PJames* in its earliest accessible form – a question raised by its absence from the oldest available manuscript, P. Bodmer V, which proceeds seamlessly from Joseph's setting out to find a midwife (18.1) to his fortunate encounter with a woman 'descending from the mountains' who just happens to be a midwife (19.1). The following factors are relevant to this question.[41]

---

[41] Details of the text-critical situation in Tischendorf, *Evangelia Apocrypha*, 33–35 and Strycker, *Protévangile*, 148–54. Examples in ancient literature of a shift from third- to first-person discourse are given by A. Toepel (*Protevangelium*, 206–7), naturally including the 'we-passages' in *Acts*.

(i)   In many manuscripts Joseph's first-person discourse continues into a well-constructed dialogue with the midwife in 19.1, switching back to third-person discourse almost imperceptibly after Joseph's explanation of Mary's unique status, with καὶ εἶπον ἐγώ giving way to καὶ εἶπεν αὐτῇ Ἰωσήφ. After the unexpected ἐγὼ δέ Ἰωσήφ in 18.1, this is a skilfully managed transition back to the text's normal mode of narration.

(ii)   Other manuscripts present Joseph's vision and the dialogue with the midwife in third-person discourse: thus at 18.2 ἐγὼ δὲ Ἰωσήφ περιεπάτουν καὶ οὐ περιεπάτουν becomes ὁ δὲ Ἰωσήφ περιεπάτει καὶ οὐ περιεπάτει. This is plausibly seen as a secondary scribal attempt to smooth over the intrusive first-person language. That this abrupt shift seemed problematic to some is confirmed by ms N's attempt to alleviate it by inserting λέγει between ἐγὼ δὲ and Ἰωσήφ.

(iii)   At 19.1 P. Bodmer V includes a poorly abridged version of the meeting with the midwife: 'And finding he led one descending from the mountains [*sic*]. And Joseph said to the midwife, "Mary is my betrothed, but she is pregnant by the Holy Spirit after being brought up in the Temple of the Lord."' Other abridgements unique to this manuscript occur at 20.1–4a (Salome's unbelief, her prayer, and her restoration) and 21.2–3a (Herod's dialogue with the Magi).[42] If the omission of Joseph's vision is of a piece with the abridgements of material that follow, then it too must be secondary. However, omission of 18.2–3 without the further abridgements is attested in the Vatican manuscripts F^b and G.

(iv)   For some early readers and scribes, Joseph's first-person narration may have been problematic not only because of its unexpectedness but also because of the tension it creates with the purported authorship of this text by his son James: ἐγὼ δὲ Ἰωσήφ... (18.2) might well seem incompatible with ἐγὼ δὲ Ἰάκωβος ὁ γράψας τὴν ἱστορίαν ταύτην... (25.1).

---

[42] See the discussion of these passages in Strycker, *Protévangile*, 377–92 ('Texte courte ou texte long aux chapitres xviii–xxi'). The third abridgement has 'stars' (plural) leading the magi to the cave, although P. Bodmer V reconnects with the majority text when it has just one of them standing over the child's head – presumably inside the cave (21.3).

The tension could be resolved either by presenting Joseph's vision in third-person form or by simply omitting it.

(v)   While the omission would result in a coherent text (18.1 + 19.1, the quest and finding of a midwife), 18.2–3 is well adapted to its context, with Joseph traversing a pastoral landscape between the cave (18.1) and his encounter with the Hebrew midwife (19.1). The use of paradox and vivid first-person discourse is consistent with the literary style of the author of Anna's lament in *PJames* 3.1–3.[43]

Having established that Joseph's vision in its first-person form is most probably integral to this text, we return to the question of its significance. Why are time and motion momentarily suspended? It is striking that the workmen's faces are all turned upwards even as their hands are still occupied with conveying food to the mouth. Likewise, the shepherd's raised hand gestures upwards. Joseph too looks up and sees the air 'stupefied', as if in the presence of an unprecedented wonder. The moment of suspended animation is caused by an event that originates from above, beyond the confines of the normal course of things, but with the earth as its goal. 'I looked up into the vault of heaven' is followed by 'I looked to the earth'. That event can only be the incarnation itself: the descent of the Son of God to enter into indissoluble union with Mary's child.[44] It is the bright cloud enveloping the cave that has conveyed him on his downward journey through the heavens, just as clouds will transport him back to heaven and bring him down again at his parousia according to other primitive Christian traditions. As depicted here, the descent of the Son of God corresponds closely to his ascent as narrated in *EpAp*, which tells how, when the risen Jesus had finished answering his disciples' questions, 'the heavens were torn asunder, and a bright cloud came and took him' (51.2). Thus his arrival in one text corresponds to his departure in the other.

---

[43] Contrast Strycker on Joseph's visionary moment: 'Il n'a certainement pas été rédigé d'une haleine avec le contexte qu'il interrompt d'une façon si bizarre et si inattendue. Nous considérons comme certain qu'il a été repris en entier à une source écrite et inséré par l'auteur du *Protévangile* dans un récit déjà achevé' (*Protévangile*, 405).

[44] The vertical emphasis in Joseph's vision seems out of step with François Bovon's suggestion that the vision is eschatological in content, announcing the dawning of a new age; 'The Suspension of Time in Chapter 18 of *Protevangelium Jacobi*' (in Birger A. Pearson [ed.], *The Future of Early Christianity: Essays in Honor of Helmut Koester* [Minneapolis, MN: Fortress Press, 1991], 393–405), 400.

5.4   The Descent of the Christ

In narratives that represent the virgin birth rather than the virgin conception as the moment of incarnation, a certain distinction is implied between Jesus' humanity as such, originating in the miraculous conception, and its role as bearer of the Saviour descended from the highest heaven, originating in the miraculous birth. The distinction takes chronological form: the Christ-child is human *before* it is divine. In other early christologies, that chronological interval is extended further: the human Jesus becomes united with the divine Saviour in the descent of the Spirit following his baptism. That view is sharply criticized by patristic heresiologists and labelled as 'adoptionist' by modern scholars. Yet there may be a shared commitment to the concept of incarnation – a union between the divine and the human uniquely embodied in a single individual – even where opinions differ as to when in the life of Jesus that union took place: at or near its beginning or following his baptism. The conventional contrast between 'high' and 'low' christology is out of place here.[45]

Affirmation both of the distinction and the union between the divine and the human in Christ is still characteristic of the Chalcedonian confession of 'one and the same Christ, Son, Lord, Only-begotten, to be acknowledged in two natures'.[46] There is no a priori reason why that distinction should not be expressed in chronological terms, as the interval between conception and birth or baptism. A chronologically defined distinction is rejected not because it is inherently flawed but because of the tradition of interpreting key Johannine and Lukan themes in the light of each other. It is this fusion of traditions that creates the platform for later christological debate, rather than any inherent logic. When post-Nicene orthodoxy proclaims that the divine Son of God, 'through whom all things were made', subsequently 'came down from the heavens and became flesh [σαρκωθέντα] by the Holy Spirit and Mary the virgin', the

---

[45] 'Adoptionist' conceptuality is said to be present in language that 'speaks of Jesus as becoming, or being begotten or being appointed to his status as the decisive intermediary between God and man during his life or in consequence of his death and resurrection' (James D. G. Dunn, *Christology in the Making: An Inquiry into the Origins of the Doctrine of the Incarnation* [London: SCM Press, 1980], 52). Such christologies are diverse, however, and there is no need to subsume them all under the single metaphor of 'adoption' or to attribute to them the view that 'Christ... was *only* a man adopted by God as Son at his Jordan baptism' (62; italics original).

[46] Greek and Latin texts in Schaff, *Creeds*, 2.62–63.

Johannine and Lukan background is clearly perceptible.[47] That is already the case when the collective apostolic authors of *EpAp* confess the Son of God as 'the Word who became flesh of Mary, carried in her womb by the Holy Spirit', born 'not by the desire of the flesh but by the will of God' and 'swaddled in Bethlehem...' (*EpAp* 3.13–15). If the Word becomes flesh in the miraculous conception, then this is the foundational event that establishes Jesus' identity once for all, rather than his birth or the descent of the Spirit.

Luke's focus on the miraculous conception is supported by Matthew, the source of the credal ἐκ πνεύματος ἁγίου (*GMt* 1.18). For Mark, however, the foundational event is the dove-like descent of the Spirit and the accompanying divine acclamation that follows Jesus' baptism (*GMk* 1.10–11). The same is true of the *Gospel of John*, when detached from its traditional Lukan linkage. In *GJohn* it is less clear than in *EpAp* that the Word became flesh in Mary's womb; no occasion is specified in *GJohn* 1.14. Indeed, the Johannine elimination of the baptism and emphasis on the testimony of John serves to heighten the Markan emphasis on the descent of the Spirit:

> And John bore witness saying, 'I saw the Spirit descending as a dove from heaven, and it remained upon him. And I did not know him, but the one who sent me to baptize in water said to me, "He on whom you see the Spirit descending and remaining is the one who baptizes in the Holy Spirit." And I have seen and borne witness that this is the Son of God.' (*GJn* 1.32–34)

GMark and *GJohn* already reflect the possibility of an incarnational christology in which the divine and the human are united in and through the post-baptismal descent of the Spirit.[48] An early account of such a christology is provided by Irenaeus, who strongly disapproves of it. In the course of his catalogue of heresies allegedly descended from Simon Magus (*Adv. haer.* 1.23–31), Irenaeus summarizes the views of Cerinthus, starting from his denial that the creator of the world is the true God: 'A certain Cerinthus, in Asia, taught that the world was made not by the first God but by a certain Power far separate and distant from the Supreme Authority [*ab ea*

---

[47] Text of the Nicene-Constantinopolitan creed in Schaff, *Creeds*, 2.57–58.

[48] On this, see Troels Engberg-Pedersen, *John and Philosophy: A New Reading of the Fourth Gospel* (Oxford: Oxford University Press, 2017), 66–73; Francis Watson, *Gospel Writing: A Canonical Perspective* (Grand Rapids, MI: Eerdmans, 2013), 507–9.

Principalitate quae est super universa], and ignorant of the God who is over all' (*Adv. haer.* 1.26.1).[49] The world is not only ruled by hostile powers, as in Paul and *AscIsaiah*, it was also created by them. If Cerinthus really held that view, he shares it with almost everyone in Irenaeus's gallery of heretics; it is also attested with greater or lesser clarity in some Nag Hammadi texts.[50] More relevant here is Cerinthus's christology, as understood by Irenaeus:

> He asserted that Jesus was not born of a virgin (for that seemed impossible to him), and that he was the son of Joseph and Mary, conceived like everyone else, but that he excelled all others in righteousness, prudence, and wisdom. And [he alleges that] after his baptism Christ descended upon him from the Supreme Authority, in the form of a dove, and that he then announced the unknown Father and performed miracles. In the end, however, Christ flew away again from Jesus. So Jesus suffered and was raised while Christ remained beyond suffering [ἀπαθῆ / *impassibilem*], as a spiritual being. (*Adv. haer.* 1.26.1)

Underlying the identification of the descending Spirit as 'Christ' is the correlation between the Spirit and anointing (cf. *GLk* 4.18, 'the Spirit of the Lord is upon me, for he has anointed [ἔχρισεν] me...'). The claim that the divine Christ 'flew away again [*revolasse iterum*]' at Jesus' passion may be intended to suggest, disparagingly, that Cerinthus's Christ retained its initial bird-like form throughout Jesus' ministry, as if perched on his shoulder.[51] In reality, the motif

---

[49] Comparison with the Latin translation shows that Irenaeus's Greek is largely preserved in the *Philophosoumena* attributed to Hippolytus, 7.33.1–2; text and notes in M. David Litwa (ed.), *Refutation of all Heresies*, Writings from the Greco-Roman World 40 (Atlanta, GA: SBL Press, 2016), 566–69. The Greek text printed in Rousseau and Doutreleau, *Irenée de Lyon: Contre les hérésies*, Sources chrétiennes 264, has been adjusted to bring it into line with the Latin translation (344–46).

[50] On Cerinthus, see Matti Myllykoski, 'Cerinthus', in A. Marjanen and P. Luomanen (eds.), *A Companion to Second-Century Christian 'Heresies'*, Vigiliae Christianae Suppl. 76 (Leiden: Brill, 2005), 213–46. Myllykoski points out that 'in the late second and early third century, Cerinthus was labelled as the progenitor of two quite different heresies – a gnostic teacher and a hedonistically-oriented chiliast' (215). Cerinthus the chiliast is probably a fictive by-product of the allegation that he is the true author of the *Book of Revelation* (Eusebius, *Hist. eccl.* 3.28.2–5; 7.25.1–2). For a positive assessment of both traditions, see Charles E. Hill, 'Cerinthus: Gnostic or Chiliast? A New Solution to an Old Problem', *Journal of Early Christian Studies* 8 (2000), 135–72.

[51] For 'flew away', Rousseau and Doutreleau propose ἀποπτῆναι (Sources chrétiennes 264, 346); *Philos.* 7.33.2 reads ἀποστῆναι, 'deserted'.

of Jesus abandoned on the cross must derive from the so-called 'cry of dereliction' attested in *GMark* and echoed in *GMatthew*: 'My God, my God, why have you abandoned me?' (*GMk* 15.34, *GMt* 27.46: ἐγκατέλιπες), or, in a Petrine variant: 'My Power, O Power, you have left me!' (*GPet* 5.19: κατέλειψας). The Markan link is later confirmed when Irenaeus admits that those who take this view of Jesus' abandonment have a particular affinity for Mark's Gospel, even though they misunderstand it:

> Those who separate Jesus from Christ and say that Christ remained beyond suffering while Jesus suffered, giving preference to the Gospel according to Mark [*id quod secundum Marcum praeferentes evangelium*], can be corrected by it if they read it with a love of the truth.   (*Adv. haer.* 3.11.7)[52]

The Christ who withdrew from Jesus on the cross is also the dove-like Christ or Spirit who descended after Jesus' baptism, the event which inaugurates the Markan account of Jesus' ministry. In this reading of Mark, the descent and ascent of the Spirit or Christ is preceded by the human existence of Jesus of Nazareth and followed by his resurrection. The christology attributed to Cerinthus is based on a Markan template, and is another version of the incarnational christology of descent and ascent attested in *AscIsaiah* and *EpAp* as well as in Paul and John. The Markan account of the descent of the Spirit is read as a narrative of incarnation, as is the Lukan annunciation story in *EpAp*. Where *GMark* is regarded as the foundational form of the gospel story, it is understandable that the virginal conception tradition is rejected as an implausible later accretion.

Close analogies to the christology attributed to Cerinthus are to be found in the *Gospel according to Philip* (NHC II,3), a miscellany of reflections on loosely connected themes that includes some more conventional gospel material and commentary on it.[53] Thus the cry of dereliction is cited in the form, 'My God, my God, why, O Lord, have you abandoned me?', followed by the comment that 'he said this on the cross, for he had departed there' (68,26–29). 'He said this'

---

[52] Echoing Irenaeus, Myllykoski states that Cerinthus 'separated the divine element (Christ) from the human being (Jesus)' and thus taught a 'separation Christology' ('Cerinthus', 236). It would be preferable to see here a construal of the union of divine and human in Jesus that only appears to advocate 'separation' because Irenaeus believes himself to hold a stronger view of that union.

[53] Text in Bentley Layton (ed.), *Nag Hammadi Codex II, 2–7*, Nag Hammadi Studies 20, 2 vols. (Leiden: Brill, 1989), 1.129–217.

refs to Jesus, while 'he had departed there' probably refers to the 'Lord' – the Cerinthian 'Christ' – who had abandoned him. Also Cerinthus-like is the rejection of the miraculous conception:

> Some say that Mary conceived by the Holy Spirit. They are in error [cερπλανεθ], they do not know what they are saying. When did a woman ever conceive by a woman? Mary is the virgin whom the Powers did not defile. She is a great anathema to the 'Hebrews', that is, to the apostles and apostolics.   (55,23–30)

The assumption that the Holy Spirit is female may reflect a Syriac background, since *ruha* is grammatically feminine and thus governs feminine verbs in the synoptic baptism narratives and the Johannine parallel.[54] Mary is a 'virgin' in the sense that the Powers did not defile her[55] – an allusion to the tradition that the virgin Eve was subjected to rape by the hostile angelic powers who created the world. Though a 'virgin' in the limited sense of avoiding the fate of Eve, Mary nevertheless became a mother in the normal way: for 'the Lord would not have said, "My Father who is in heaven" unless he had had another father, but would simply have said, "My Father"' (55,33–36). Thus, in a tradition attributed to 'Philip the Apostle', it is said that 'Joseph the carpenter' used the wood of a tree he himself had planted to make the cross on which his own 'seed' (бροс = σπέρμα) was to hang (73,8–15).

It was not in the circumstances of his birth but at the River Jordan that Jesus was revealed as 'the fullness [πλнρωма] of the kingdom of the heavens' (70,34–71,1). There, 'the one who was begotten before all things was begotten again, the one who was once anointed was anointed again...' (71,1–3). Remarkably, this divine act of (re-)anointing and (re-)begetting is itself presented as a miraculous virginal conception in which 'the Father-of-all united with the

---

[54] The neuter participles καταβαῖνον (*GMt* 3.16; *GMk* 1.10; *GJn* 1.32, 33) and ἐρχόμενον (*GMt* 3.16) are rendered by feminine verb forms in both the Old Syriac manuscripts and the Peshitta, as are καταβῆναι (*GLk* 3.22), ἔμεινεν and μένον (*GJn* 1.32, 33). Feminine forms are replaced by masculine ones in the Harklean. See George Anton Kiraz, *Comparative Edition of the Syriac Gospels, aligning the Sinaiticus, Curetonianus, Peshîttâ and Ḥarklean Versions*, 4 vols. (Leiden: Brill, 1996).

[55] So Hugo Lundhaug, *Images of Rebirth: Cognitive Poetics and Transformational Soteriology in the Gospel of Philip and the Exegesis of the Soul*, Nag Hammadi and Manichaean Studies 73 (Brill: Leiden, 2010), 179–82; Christine Jacobi, 'Jesus' Body: Christology and Soteriology in the Body-Metaphors of the *Gospel of Philip*', in Watson and Parkhouse, *Connecting Gospels*, 77–96; 80–81.

Virgin-who-descended, and a fire shone upon him' (71,4–6). The Father-of-all is most probably the Logos or Christ, and the Virgin-who-descended is the Holy Spirit.[56] The motifs of fire and begetting are already present in Justin:

> When Jesus came to the River Jordan, he was baptized by John, and when he went down into the water a fire was kindled in the Jordan. And when he came out of the water the Holy Spirit alighted upon him like a dove... and at the same time there came from the heavens a voice (in words also spoken by David, as if speaking in his [Jesus'] person what was to be said to him): 'You are my son, today I have begotten you.'   (*Dial.* 88.3, 8)[57]

What is distinctive about the *GPhilip* passage is not the fire or the begetting but the representation of the (feminine) Holy Spirit as a virgin mother.[58] What is revealed on the occasion of Jesus' baptism is thus 'the great bridal chamber', from which the reconstituted body of Jesus emerges 'as one who came into being from the bridegroom and bride' (*GPhil* 71,7–11). The original miraculous conception tradition is rejected, yet the virginal conception motif is projected onto the baptism story. The body of the human Jesus the son of Joseph and Mary is reborn as the dwelling place of the divine Christ, 'begotten before all things'. This event may also be seen as his

---

[56] So Lundhaug, *Images of Rebirth*, 182–85. Jacobi accepts the identification of the Virgin as the Holy Spirit but identifies the Father-of-all with Jesus; 'Jesus' Body', 80–82 (noting the parallel with Cerinthus).

[57] Justin's version of the divine address (= *Ps* 2.7) is also attested at *GLuke* 3.22 in D and several Old Latin manuscripts.

[58] There is a parallel to this in the combination of two fragments of the *Gospel According to the Hebrews*, preserved by Origen and Jerome: see Andrew Gregory, *The Gospel According to the Hebrews and the Gospel According to the Ebionites*, Oxford Early Christian Gospel Texts (Oxford: Oxford University Press, 2017), 69–74, 110–17. (1) The Holy Spirit is Jesus' mother, as he indicates in what may be a version of the temptation story: 'Now my mother the Holy Spirit took me by one of my hairs, and carried me to the great Mount Thabor' (Origen, *Comm. Jn.* ii.12, on *GJn* 1.3; cf. *Hom. in Jer.* xv.4, on *Jer* 15.10; three further citations of this passage in Jerome). (2) The Holy Spirit becomes Jesus' mother at the baptism, where it is she who addresses him: 'It happened that, when the Lord came up from the water, the whole font of the Holy Spirit came down and rested on him and said to him: "My son, in all the prophets I was expecting you, that you would come, and that I would rest on you. For you are my rest, you are my firstborn son who will rule for ever"' (Jerome, *Comm. Isa.* iv, on *Isa* 11.1–3). For the attribution of these fragments to the same gospel text, see Gregory, 111–12.

resurrection, so that it is an error to claim that he died before he was raised: rather, 'he rose first and then died' (*GPhil* 56,17–18).

As we have seen, the 'orthodox' account of the event of the incarnation is articulated (perhaps for the first time) in the credal formula of *EpAp* 3.13: 'the Word... became flesh of Mary, carried in her womb by the Holy Spirit.' Yet for this early Christian author and for others, the event of the incarnation required to be narrated and not simply confessed; prior gospel texts that lacked an incarnational narrative thus stood in need of supplementation and/or correction. In *EpAp* the real angel Gabriel did *not* appear to Mary, and (in spite of the earlier credal passage) there is no role for the Holy Spirit: the Logos descends through the heavens and approaches Mary *disguised* as Gabriel before incarnating himself in Mary's womb. In *AscIsaiah* a retelling of the Matthean account of Mary's pregnancy is supplemented by an original account of a miraculous birth as the moment of incarnation, with Jesus' humanity as the last in a series of disguises intended to conceal his presence from hostile spiritual powers. In *PJames* similarly, a retold Lukan annunciation proclaims not so much a virginal conception as a virgin birth as the occasion of incarnation: at the birth, time itself is momentarily suspended. In the christology of *GPhilip* the incarnational significance of Jesus' baptism and its aftermath can lay claim to deep roots within the *Gospel of Mark*, although disparaged by Irenaeus. Accompanying the well-known patristic debates and controversies about the incarnation there was also the question whether it could or should be *narrated* – and if so, how. If the Word became flesh, can this event become story?

6

PAUL AND THE APOSTOLIC MISSION

In the canonical post-resurrection narratives, Jesus appears to his disciples both to convince them that he is truly risen and to commission them for their future task as his apostles. While the apostolic mission has its antecedents within Jesus' ministry, its origins and authorization lie in the command of the risen Lord. The situation is essentially the same for the twelve (or eleven) as it is for Paul: they are apostles because they have seen and been commissioned by the risen Lord (cf. *1 Cor* 9.1; 15.5–11). They are to 'go and make disciples of all nations' (*GMt* 28.19). They are formally appointed as 'witnesses' (*GLk* 24.48; cf. *Acts* 1.8), and as such they are instructed in the prophetic scriptures which announced not only that the Christ must suffer and be raised but also that 'repentance and forgiveness of sins are to be preached in his name to all nations' (*GLk* 24.47). Their mission to the world is analogous to Jesus' mission from the Father: 'As the Father sent me, so I send you' (*GJn* 20.21). Thus, when the Longer Ending was added to *GMark*, what was felt to be lacking from the abrupt earlier ending was not just a resurrection appearance per se but a commissioning scene. In this version of *GMark*, the disciples are to 'go into all the world and preach the gospel to every creature' (16.15), their credibility validated by signs – casting out demons, speaking in new tongues, handling snakes, surviving poisoned chalices, healing the sick (16.17–18). Eternal destinies depend on whether what is heard and seen is believed (16.16).

In terms of their content, all four canonical gospels may be described as 'ministry gospels', narratives of Jesus' ministry and its culmination in Jerusalem with or without a preliminary account of his birth.[1] The twelve disciples feature fairly prominently in these

---

[1] The expression 'ministry gospels' stems from the helpful typology of Bart Ehrman and Zlatko Pleše, who differentiate between 'infancy gospels' (e.g. *PJas, IGThos*),

ministry gospels (though less so in *GJohn*), but at no point during the ministry is their future role as Jesus' witnesses 'in Judea and Samaria and to the ends of the earth' (*Acts* 1.8) even hinted at. A sudden transformation takes place in which disciples of the teacher and messianic claimant from Nazareth become the bearers of an urgent eschatologically freighted proclamation addressed to all people everywhere. Or rather, it is assumed that such a transformation *must have* taken place, following the commission although beyond the bounds of the narrative. Nothing that Jesus has said to the disciples, or that they have said to him, has indicated that he or they have designs on the whole world. Arguably, it was precisely an imperial ambition of this kind that Jesus renounced as a temptation of the devil (cf. *GMt* 4.8–10 // *GLk* 4.5–8).

In *GMatthew* the necessary transformation of disciples into apostles is implied in the risen Lord's claim that 'all authority in heaven and on earth was given to me' and in his promise that 'I will be with you always, to the end of the age' (*GMt* 28.18, 20). Making and baptizing disciples from all nations will be enabled by the unlimited authority and presence of Jesus himself. Yet these issues lie at and beyond the furthest limit of the Matthean narrative itself, which does no more than briefly gesture towards them in spite of their fundamental importance. Luke and John are more explicit, interpreting the promised presence of Jesus as mediated through the Holy Spirit or Paraclete, the effects of whose coming are impressively presented by Luke in his Pentecost narrative (*Acts* 2). Yet even in *Luke–Acts* the gulf between the disciple and the apostle remains in place, reinscribed in the division between the two books. In *GJohn*, where there is no sequel, the coming of the Holy Spirit is without perceptible effect (*GJn* 20.22–23). Among fully extant ministry gospels it is only in *GMark* (in its older form) that the problem of the transformation of disciples into apostles does not arise. At the very end of his narrative, this evangelist appears to make it impossible for any reunion with the risen Lord – and consequent commissioning of the disciples – to take place. Terrified women flee from the

---

'ministry gospels' (e.g. *GHeb, GEgyp*, the *Diatessaron*, as well as the canonical four), 'sayings gospels' (*GThos*), and 'passion, resurrection, post-resurrection gospels' (*GJudas, GMary*); *The Apocryphal Gospels: Texts and Translations* (New York: Oxford University Press, 2011), xi–xii. Ehrman and Pleše omit *EpAp*, which should be included in the fourth category. The categorization relates to a gospel's predominant emphasis and is not impaired by the presence of infancy material in *GMatthew* and *GLuke* or ministry material in *EpAp*.

empty tomb and say nothing to anybody about what they have seen or heard there (*GMk* 16.8). Unexpected though this may seem, it is in keeping with the narrative logic of a ministry gospel that it should end where Jesus' earthly life ends: at his tomb (even if empty).[2]

In contrast to the ministry gospel tradition, the *Epistula Apostolorum* is able to bring the apostolic mission from the narrative margins into the centre. It does not do so by introducing a new heavenly agency in the form of the Holy Spirit. There is here no inspirational drama of a Power sweeping down from on high in wind and fire, transforming humble fishermen, tax-collectors, and the like into fearless proclaimers of the mighty works of God. Indeed, this is a text entirely lacking in drama of any kind. When the weeping women encounter the risen Jesus at his tomb, they express neither surprise nor joy (*EpAp* 10.1–3). The disciples betray no emotion as they experience the thunder, lightning, and earthquake that accompany Jesus' ascension (51.2). From beginning to end everything in this text is prosaic, and its prosaic character is no mere stylistic limitation but belongs to the substance of its message. Here, Jesus and his disciples engage in serious and sustained conversation about the themes they must understand aright if they are to be faithful proclaimers of the word to the world. As in *GMatthew* and *GLuke*, and indeed probably deriving from them, there are indications of heavenly assistance through the ongoing presence of Jesus and the power of the Holy Spirit (*EpAp* 19.5; 30.3–5). Yet the emphasis is on instruction in key issues of faith and conduct as the primary means by which Jesus prepares his disciples for their new apostolic role – as it is also the means by which they will fulfil that role, not least in putting that instruction into writing and communicating it to the church throughout the world.[3]

The author's strategy is made clear at a point in the long dialogue where Jesus appears to become impatient with his disciples'

---

[2] Commenting on the Markan ending at 16.8, Wellhausen writes: 'Es fehlt nichts; es wäre schade, wenn noch etwas hinterher käme'; J. Wellhausen, *Das Evangelium Marci* (Berlin: G. Reimer, 1909[2]), 137.

[3] A comparable concern with preparation for mission underlies the reference in *Acts* 1.3 to the forty days during which Jesus speaks with his disciples about 'the kingdom of God'. The *Acts* passage is paraphrased by Tertullian, who states that the risen Jesus 'spent forty days in Galilee, a region of Judea, with certain disciples, teaching them what they should teach. Then he appointed them to the duty of preaching throughout the world…' (*Apol.* 21.23). The author of *EpAp* offers his readers access to that Easter teaching – delivered in two to three hours on Easter morning rather than over forty days.

questions. Following a question about eschatological reward and punishment, Jesus responds: 'How long will you question and seek?' (22.3). In slightly awkward syntax but with the sense clear, the disciples reply:

> 'Lord, it is necessary for us to question you, for you command us to preach; so that we ourselves may know with certainty through you and be useful preachers, and [that] those who will teach through us may believe in you. That is why we question you so much!' (23.1–3)

Through the collective mouth of the eleven, the author indicates that the ongoing dialogue about correct faith and conduct is both the basis of the apostolic mission and a normative pattern for those who claim to hold the apostolic faith.

In a certain sense the apostolic mission is the single theme of this text, from beginning to end. Whatever the topic of the disciples' questions and Jesus' answers – his parousia, the resurrection of the flesh, the hostility of the world, issues of wealth and poverty – the underlying theme is always preparation for and (through this text itself) exercise of the apostolic mission. Yet there are also moments when mission is more explicitly thematized. We shall follow the author as he draws from Matthean and Pauline traditions in developing this theme.

6.1 Questioning Matthew

In the so-called Great Commission, the Matthean Jesus peremptorily orders the eleven assembled on a Galilean mountain-top to 'go [πορευθέντες] therefore and make disciples of all the nations [πάντα τὰ ἔθνη]'. The syntactical combination of participle, conjunction, imperative, and object was imitated by three subsequent evangelists, the authors of the Markan Longer Ending, the *Gospel of Mary*, and the *Epistula Apostolorum* (see Table 6.1, below).[4] The Markan author uses the same participle with the same imperatival force (πορευθέντες), adding a reference to the destination absent ('into

---

[4] Coptic text of *GMary* with Greek fragments and English translation in Douglas M. Parrott (ed.), *Nag Hammadi Codices V, 2–5 and VI, with Papyrus Berolinensis 8502, 1 and 4* (Leiden: Brill, 1979), 456–71; Coptic text with French translation in Anne Pasquier, *L'Évangile selon Marie (BG 1); Texte établi et présenté*, Bibliothèque Copte de Nag Hammadi 10 (Quebec: Les presses de l'université Laval, 1983).

Table 6.1

GMt 28.19	πορευθέντες	οὖν		μαθητεύσατε	πάντα τὰ ἔθνη
GMk 16.15	πορευθέντες		εἰς τὸν κόσμον ἅπαντα	κηρύξατε τὸ εὐαγγέλιον	πάσῃ τῇ κτίσει
GMary 8, 21–22¶	πορευθέντες	οὖν		κηρύξατε τὸ εὐαγγέλιον τῆς βασιλείας	
EpAp 30.1¶	πορευθέντες			κηρύξατε	ταῖς δώδεκα φυλαῖς καὶ τοῖς ἔθνεσιν καὶ πάσῃ τῇ γῇ τοῦ Ἰσραηλ ἀπὸ ἀνατολῶν ἕως δυσμῶν καὶ ἀπὸ βορρᾶ ἕως νότου

¶ = retroversion from Coptic to Greek

all the world'), substituting 'proclaim the gospel' for 'make disciples' and 'to every creature' for 'all the nations – all within a closely similar syntactic framework (*GMk* 16.15). The Marian evangelist retains Matthew's 'Go therefore' and extends the Markan 'proclaim the gospel' while omitting any reference to addressees: 'Go therefore and proclaim [ⲃⲱⲕ ϭⲉ ⲛ̅ⲧⲉⲧⲛ̅ⲧⲁϣⲉⲟⲓⲉϣ] the gospel of the kingdom' (*GMary* 8,21–22).[5] The initial Coptic imperative probably represents the Matthean πορευθέντες in the original Greek of this gospel, for the same substitution of imperative, conjunction, and conjunctive occurs in the Sahidic translation of *GMatthew* 28.19. It also occurs in *EpAp* 30.1, though without the conjunction and with the addition of a pronoun: 'Go *ye* and proclaim" (ⲃⲱⲕ ⲛ̅ⲧⲱⲧⲛⲉ ⲧⲉⲧⲛ̅ⲧⲁϣⲉⲁⲓⲉϣ).[6] Now the emphasis lies on the objects of mission, identified in some detail:

[5] For the echoes of earlier gospels in the Saviour's farewell speech (*GMary* 8,12–9,4), see Pasquier, *L'Évangile selon Marie*, 57–58; Sarah Parkhouse, *Eschatology and the Saviour: The Gospel of Mary among Early Christian Dialogue Gospels*, Society for New Testament Studies Monograph Series 176 (Cambridge: Cambridge University Press, 2019), 143–51.

[6] Here, ⲛ̅ⲧⲱⲧⲛⲉ may be more precisely defined as an 'inflected modifier' identifying the addressee of an imperative (Bentley Layton, *A Coptic Grammar*, 2nd ed., revised and expanded, Porta Linguarum Orientalium [Wiesbaden: Harrassowitz Verlag, 2004], §152).

> Go and preach to the twelve tribes and preach also to the
> Gentiles and to the whole land of Israel from east to west
> and from south to north, and many will believe in the Son
> of God. (*EpAp* 30.1)[7]

The 'twelve tribes' are probably the 'twelve tribes who are in the
diaspora' (*Jas* 1.1) in distinction from the inhabitants of 'the whole
land of Israel'. A division of labour may be envisaged here: some will
preach to the diaspora, others to the Gentiles, others to the land of
Israel. This is a single mission, however, and there is no trace here of
the sharp distinction Paul at one point draws between an ἀποστολή
or εὐαγγέλιον τῆς περιτομῆς and a εὐαγγέλιον τῆς ἀκροβυστίας (*Gal*
2.7–8). The reference to the four points of the compass highlights the
worldwide scope of the apostolic mission, as the parallel in the
epistolary introduction indicates (*EpAp* 2.1); it is unlikely that it
refers only to the land of Israel.

These intertextual links make it clear that the evangelists who
composed *GMary* and the *Epistula* have some familiarity with
GMatthew. Yet that does not mean that *GMatthew* has attained
'canonical status' for them, if by that we might mean that a text is
put beyond the possibility of criticism. On the contrary, both texts are
rather directly critical of *GMatthew*. In *GMary*, the commission is
accompanied by a negative counterpart of the Matthean '... teaching
them to observe all that I commanded you' (*GMt* 28.20a):

> Go therefore and preach the gospel of the kingdom, and do
> not lay down any boundary [ϩⲟⲣⲟⲥ] beyond what
> I appointed for you, nor establish a law [ⲛⲟⲙⲟⲥ] like the
> Lawgiver [ⲛⲟⲙⲟⲑⲉⲧⲏⲥ], lest you be held captive
> by it. (*GMary* 8,21–9,4)

As in the Matthean parallel, these are Jesus' final words to his
disciples. 'When he had said this he departed' (*GMary* 9,5). Jesus
has evidently laid down 'boundaries' for his followers, presumably in
the form of rules of conduct analogous to the Matthean 'all that
I commanded you'. Yet the emphasis lies not on inculcating Jesus'
teaching but on avoiding the temptation to supplement it. The
disciples must not impose rules of their own devising on their future

---

[7] The command to 'go and preach' is repeated at *EpAp* 30.3, 41.1; cf. 19.1, 46.1,
where the commission is to preach and teach. On this, see Hills, *Tradition and
Composition*, 126–45.

converts, claiming like Moses that they represent divine law.[8] For the Marian evangelist, as for her Johannine counterpart, 'law came through Moses, grace and truth through Jesus Christ' (*GJn* 1.17). Grace and truth retain their integrity only if they are kept apart from law, for law leads only to an enslavement incompatible with salvation. The Marian Jesus' warning against this possibility suggests that, from the evangelist's perspective, the threat has been realized. We are not told how, but common Jewish and Christian practices such as the ones rejected by *GThomas* may be in view:

> If you fast [ⲛⲏⲥⲧⲉⲩⲉ] you will bring forth sin. And if you pray, you will be condemned [ⲕⲁⲧⲁⲕⲣⲓⲛⲉ]. And if you give alms [ⲉⲗⲉⲏⲙⲟⲥⲩⲛⲏ] you will do evil [ⲕⲁⲕⲟⲛ] to your spirits [ⲡⲛⲁ]. (*GThos* 14)[9]

As in *GMary*, practices not sanctioned by Jesus endanger one's salvation. These are, however, practices approved by the Matthean Jesus, who is concerned only that they be undertaken with pious regard for the heavenly Father rather than to gain human applause:

> When you give alms, let your left hand not know what your right hand is doing... When you pray, enter an inner room and close the door and pray to your Father who is in secret... When you fast, anoint your head and wash your face, so that your fasting may be evident not to humans but to your Father...   (*GMt* 6.3, 6, 17–18)

Whether or not the Marian evangelist disapproves of almsgiving, prayer, and fasting, the Matthean Jesus' endorsement of the letter of the Mosaic law would surely have been unacceptable to her (*GMt* 5.17–21). As the example of *GMatthew* shows, disciples of Jesus have done precisely what he forbade them to do: they have ensnared their followers in a new law, turning Jesus into a second Moses.

The Marian Great Commission occurs not at the close of the narrative, as in *GMatthew*, but at its heart.[10] In both gospels it is Jesus' last word to his disciples, but *GMary* is unique in early gospel literature in having Jesus depart in the middle of the narrative, the

---

[8] On this see Parkhouse, *Eschatology and the Saviour*, 152–54.

[9] As Simon Gathercole points out, this starkly negative view of traditional Jewish and Christian practices is not necessarily representative of *GThomas* as a whole: cf. *GTh* 27, 73, 104 (*The Gospel of Thomas: Introduction and Commentary*, Texts and Editions for New Testament Study 11 [Leiden: Brill, 2014], 269–70).

[10] The commission is repeated by Levi at the close of *GMary* (18,17–21).

second half of which is therefore dominated by the problem of his absence. Thus the narrative proceeds to recount the transition from discipleship to mission, and there is no need to refer to future transformative events lying beyond its limits. Nevertheless, that transition is difficult and painful.[11] Even after Mary has quieted their initial misgivings, the disciples *argue* [ⲅⲩⲙⲛⲁⲍⲉ] with one another about the Saviour's words (9,23–24). The instruction not to 'lay down any boundary beyond what I appointed for you' (8,22–9,2) does not resolve the question of the message the disciples are to preach and teach. Asked to communicate words of the Saviour addressed to her alone, Mary keeps scrupulously within the appointed boundary, falling silent 'because it was up to this point that the Saviour had spoken with her' (17,7–9). Yet she is accused by Andrew and Peter of having transgressed that boundary, putting her own words into the Saviour's mouth (17,10–22). Levi's intervention addresses his fellow-disciples' objections and reminds them of the Saviour's commission, and as a result 'they began to go and preach and proclaim' (19,1–2). The prospects for a single harmonious apostolic proclamation envisaged by *GMatthew* and the *Epistula* seem remote, however. Indeed, in a Greek fragment of *GMary* (*PRyl* 463) it is Levi alone who goes forth to preach.[12]

The collective apostolic authors of the *Epistula* do not share Mary's anxieties about Moses-like additions to Jesus' words, yet an important anti-Matthean moment is present here too. In the last of three occurrences of the double imperative to go and preach, Jesus speaks of the roles his disciples will take on in relation to their converts:

> 'Go, preach, and you will be good workers and servants.'
> And we said to him, 'It is you who will preach through us.'
> Then he answered us, saying, <'Will you not all be fathers?
> Will you not all be teachers?'>   (*EpAp* 41.1–3)

Here Jesus' response has been reconstructed from Coptic and Ge'ez texts that make little sense as they stand. The Coptic here reads, 'Do not all be a father, and do not all be a teacher'; Ge'ez, 'Are all

---

[11] See J. Hartenstein, *Die zweite Lehre: Erscheinungen des Auferstandenen als Rahmenerzählungen frühchristlicher Dialoge*, Texte und Untersuchungen zur Geschichte der altchristlichen Literatur 146 (Berlin: Akademie Verlag, 2000), 145–48.

[12] See Christopher Tuckett (ed.), *The Gospel of Mary*, Oxford Early Christian Gospel Texts (Oxford: Oxford University Press, 2007), 114, 132.

fathers, and are all servants, and are all teachers?' (wording perhaps influenced by *1 Cor* 12.29). The explicit or implicit rejection of the titles 'father' and 'teacher' must stem from translation errors, for the disciples immediately quote Jesus' answer in a positive version, asking how it relates to a previous prohibition of these titles in a form closely resembling *GMatthew* 23.9:

> We said to him, 'Lord, you said to us, "Do not call anyone your father on earth, for there is one who is your father who is in heaven and your teacher." Why do you now say to us, "You will be fathers of many children, and servants and teachers"?'   (*EpAp* 41.4–5)

The disciples' query cannot be a response either to the negative imperative, 'Do not all be a father...' (Coptic) or the implied negativity of the question, 'Are all fathers...?' (Ge'ez).[13] On the only other occasion in the *Epistula* where the disciples quote something Jesus has just said, they do so freely but appropriately:

> And we said to him, 'Just now did you not say to us, "I will come"? So how can you say to us, "The one who sent me will come"?'   (*EpAp* 17.3; cf. 16.3, 17.2)

At 41.3 the two versions may both have originated in an original Greek οὐκ ἔσεσθε πάντες πατέρες, οὐκ ἔσεσθε πάντες διδάσκαλοι ('Will you not all be fathers, will you not all be teachers?').[14] Following the disciples' statement, 'It is you who will preach through us' (41.2), Jesus draws attention to the future status of the disciples themselves before proceeding to explain their new roles in more detail:

> Truly I say to you that you will indeed be called fathers, because with a willing heart and love you have revealed to thcm the things of the kingdom of heaven. And you will be called servants because they will receive the baptism of life and the forgiveness of their sins by my hand through you. And you will be called teachers because you have given them the word without envy.   (*EpAp* 42.2–4)

---

[13] The problem is noted by Schmidt, *Gespräche Jesu*, 131: 'Man erwartet: "Seid ihr denn nicht alle Väter und alle Meister?"'

[14] For repeated questions with οὐκ, cf. *1 Cor* 9.1, οὐκ εἰμὶ ἐλεύθερος, οὐκ εἰμὶ ἀπόστολος...

The new roles that the disciples will assume as they engage in mission require that a former instruction of Jesus be cancelled. Although this instruction does not appear in the *Epistula*, it is evidently too well-known to be ignored; yet it has not attained the normative status that would put it beyond question. In *GMatthew* 23.8–11 Jesus demands that his disciples avoid self-aggrandizing titles:

> As for you, do not be called 'Rabbi', for there is one who is your teacher [διδάσκαλος] and you are all brethren. And do not call anyone 'Father' on earth, for there is one who is your Father, in heaven. And do not be called 'Instructor' [καθηγητής], for there is one who is your instructor, the Christ. Let the greatest among you be your servant [διάκονος].

It is this teaching that the disciples recall in the *Epistula*: 'Lord, you said to us, "Do not call anyone your father on earth, for there is one who is your father who is in heaven and your teacher."' Through the collective mouth of the apostles, the author expresses his dissent from the egalitarianism promoted by the Matthean language.[15] How would the nations hear the gospel if there were no teachers to teach them to observe all that Jesus commanded? The long question-and-answer session that comprises the bulk of the *Epistula* can be seen as a training programme in which initially ill-equipped disciples are prepared for future roles as community founders and community leaders. The risen Jesus will be with them (19.5–6; cf. 41.2), they will be assisted by the power of the Holy Spirit (30.4), but it is Jesus' answers to their persistent questioning that do most to prepare them for the future.

6.2   Paul the Jew

The author of the *Epistula* is well aware of the gulf that separates the disciple from the apostle. Thus, when given the daunting task of evangelizing the whole world, 'from east to west and from south to north' (*EpAp* 30.1), he presents the disciples as apprehensive and uncertain of success:

---

[15] As Hills notes, 'the essential point is the author's affirmation of the apostles' (and hence the community's) right to challenge a saying of the earthly Jesus' (*Tradition and Composition*, 135).

> We said to him, 'Lord, who will believe us, or who will listen to us or who will then teach the mighty works and signs that you have done, and the wonders?'   (*EpAp* 30.2)

Similar anxiety in a more extreme form is expressed in *GMary*. Following the Saviour's departure, the (male) disciples are in despair:

> And they were grieved and wept greatly, saying, 'How shall we go to the Gentiles and preach the gospel of the kingdom of the Son of man? If they did not spare him, how will they spare us?'   (*GMary* 9,5–12)

In both the *Epistula* and *GMary*, reassurance may in part be found in Jesus' own words: 'I will give you my peace' (*EpAp* 30.4), 'Receive my peace to yourselves' (*GMary* 8,14–15); 'I will be in you' (*EpAp* 30.3), 'the Son of man is within you' (*GMary* 8,18–19). In both cases, reassurance also comes in the form of a human helper, female or male – Mary, who 'turns their heart to the good' (*GMary* 9,21–22), or Paul.

In the *Epistula* the risen Jesus informs his original disciples of their future relationship with Paul by emphasizing strongly his Jewish credentials:

> And behold, you will meet a man whose name is Saul (which being interpreted is Paul), who is a Jew, circumcised by the commandment of the law, and he will hear my voice from heaven with astonishment, fear, and trembling.   (*EpAp* 31.1)

This emphasis on Paul's Jewishness is striking in a text which elsewhere shows so little interest in Jewish themes. Echoes of *Acts* and *Philippians* are perceptible in the references to Paul's double name and his Jewish ethnicity, although on closer examination it is the differences that are more significant than the similarities.

In *Acts* as in the *Epistula*, Paul has a double name: he is 'Saul who is also Paul' (*Acts* 13.9).[16] In this identification of Saul and Paul, Luke marks a change in his own usage. Up to this point he has consistently referred to Paul as 'Saul' (*Acts* 7.58–13.7, × 14). In his Saul identity, Paul is either the zealous persecutor (*Acts* 7.58–9.11) or

---

[16] On this, see D. Marguerat, *Les Actes des Apôtres*, Commentaires du Nouveau Testament, 2 vols., Va *(ch. 1–12)*; Vb *(ch. 13–28)* (Geneva: Labor et Fides, 2015), 2.31. The switch from Σαῦλος to Παῦλος occurs in the context of a reference to a Σέργιος Παῦλος, governor of Cyprus (*Acts* 13.7) and of a doubly named magus or false prophet, Βαριησοῦς whose name can somehow be 'translated' as Ἐλύμας (*Acts* 13.6, 8).

the new convert subject to the leadership of Barnabas (*Acts* 9.11–13.7). In *Acts* 13, however, the pairing of 'Barnabas and Saul' (v.7) gives way to 'those who were with Paul' (οἱ περὶ Παῦλον, v.13), and 'Paul' rather than 'Saul' is used from here onwards. For the *Epistula*, 'Pawlos' (ࡘࡘ࡚ࡘ) is not an additional name but rather a Greek translation of the Septuagintal and Hebraic name rendered here as 'Sawl' (ࡘࡘ࡚ࡘ, cf. Σαούλ).[17] Luke's hellenized Σαῦλος weakens the potential allusion to the first king of Israel, 'Saul son of Kish [τὸν Σαοὺλ υἱὸν Κίς]', although Luke is well aware of this scriptural figure (cf. *Acts* 13.21). King Saul is presented as Σαοῦλος in Josephus's *Antiquities*, however (*Ant.* vi.46, etc.), and Σαούλ does occur in all three *Acts* accounts of the words addressed to Paul by the exalted Jesus: Σαοὺλ Σαούλ τί με διώκεις (*Acts* 9.4; 22.7; 26.14; cf. 9.17; 22.13). Josephus's Σαοῦλος and Luke's Σαῦλος may make the respective Saul figures more accessible to Greek–speaking readers. In contrast, the Σαούλ form of the name, used only by the exalted Jesus, highlights the otherness of the Hebraic linguistic sphere inhabited by Jesus and his persecutor Saul. As *Acts* 26.14 explicitly states, Jesus addressed Saul 'in the Hebrew language' (τῇ Ἑβραΐδι διαλέκτῳ, cf. 21.40; 22.2).[18] The *Epistula* too uses the scriptural Σαούλ to underline Paul's Jewishness, presenting it as the Hebrew original of the more familiar Greek Παῦλος.

The *Epistula* also introduces Saul or Paul as 'a Jew, circumcised by the commandment of the law' (*EpAp* 31.1). A fuller statement of Paul's Jewish credentials is provided when the Paul of *Acts* assures the Jerusalem crowd that

> I am a Jew, born in Tarsus in Cilicia and brought up in this city at the feet of Gamaliel, instructed in the strict observance of the Law of our fathers, a zealot for God...
>
> (*Acts* 22.3; cf. 26.4–5)

---

[17] The author probably knows that the name 'Paulus' corresponds to the Latin word for 'small' and assumes that 'Saul' means the same in Hebrew. The interpretation of 'Paul' as 'paulus' = 'small' underlies the famous description of Paul's physical appearance in the *Acts of Paul and Thecla* 3, where he is 'a man small in stature' (ἄνδρα μικρὸν τῷ μεγέθει). Cf. Augustine, *De Spiritu et Littera* 7: Paul chose to be known as Paulus rather than Saulus, 'ut se ostenderet parvum, tanquam minimum Apostolorum'.

[18] Luke either has biblical Hebrew in mind here (so J. Jervell, *Die Apostelgeschichte*, Kritisch-exegetischer Kommentar über das Neue Testament [Göttingen: Vandenhoeck & Ruprecht, 1998], 593) or Aramaic (C. K. Barrett, *The Acts of the Apostles*, International Critical Commentary, 2 vols. [Edinburgh, T&T Clark, 1994–98], 2.1158, citing 21.40).

In a further parallel to the *Epistula*, the Paul of *Philippians* under-lines his Jewishness by referring to his circumcision (περιτομῇ ὀκταήμερος, *Phil* 3.5), although here – in contrast to *Acts* – markers of Jewish identity and status are apparently renounced (cf. *Phil* 3.7–9). Yet both *Acts* and *Philippians* emphasize Paul's exceptional appropriation of his Jewish identity: he has been 'instructed in the strict observance of the Law of our fathers', he is 'a zealot for God', he is 'blameless as regards the righteousness of the law' (*Acts* 22.3; *Phil* 3.6). The *Acts* passage echoes *Gal* 1.14, where Paul claims that 'I advanced in Judaism beyond my contemporaries among my own people, so exceptionally zealous was I for the traditions of the fathers.'[19] This repeated emphasis on high achievement is notably absent in the *Epistula*, where Paul is introduced as an ordinary Jew, circumcised by the commandment of the law but in no way exceptional. The effect, and probably the intention, is to show that Paul the future participant in the apostolic mission shares the Jewish identity of the eleven disciples whom Jesus here commissions. As we shall see, the author of the *Epistula* does his utmost to minimize the distinction between Paul and the eleven and to present him as a full participant in their worldwide mission.[20]

In the *Epistula* as in *Acts*, Paul hears the voice of the exalted Lord and is temporarily blinded (*EpAp* 31.1–2; *Acts* 9.4–6). In both cases, the shape of his future ministry is announced by the risen Lord. In *Acts* 9.15 Ananias receives the reassurance that Saul or Paul 'is an elect vessel of mine, to carry my name before Gentiles and kings and the sons of Israel.' Similarly, the *Epistula* envisages Paul as an 'elect vessel' (σκεῦος ἐκλογῆς) who is to preach to 'the people' (presumably the people of Israel), to kings and to the Gentiles:

---

[19] So R. Pervo, *Acts: A Commentary* (Hermeneia, Minneapolis, MN: Fortress Press, 2009), 563. Verbal links between the two passages are clear: κατ' ἀκριβείαν τοῦ πατρῴου νόμου, ζηλωτὴς ὑπάρχων… (*Acts* 22.3; cf. 21.20), περισσοτέρως ζηλωτὴς ὑπάρχων τῶν πατρικῶν μου παραδόσεων (*Gal* 1.14). Pervo also plausibly finds in the term ἀκρίβεια an echo of Josephus' descriptions of the Pharisees (563): cf. Josephus, *Vita* 191; *Bell* 1.110, 2.162; *Ant* 17.41. On *Acts*' knowledge of Paul and Josephus, and implications for dating, see R. Pervo, *Dating Acts: Between the Evangelists and the Apologists* (Santa Rosa, CA: Polebridge Press, 2006).

[20] Contra M. Hornschuh, who assumes that the author of the *Epistula* seeks to defend Paul against the Jewish Christian charge that he is an apostate from the law (*Studien zur Epistula Apostolorum* [Berlin: de Gruyter, 1965], 88).

And he will be strong among the people, and he will preach and teach many, and they will be glad to hear him, and many will be saved. And then they will hate him and deliver him into the hand of his enemy, and he will confess before transitory kings. And the fulfilment of his confessing me will come upon him, so that instead of persecuting me he confesses me. And he will preach and teach, and he will be with my elect an elect vessel and a wall that does not fall. The last of the last shall be a preacher to the Gentiles, perfected by the will of my Father. (*EpAp* 31.5–9)

It is not clear from these parallels how far the author of the *Epistula* is directly acquainted with *Acts*. There are few if any clear indications of dependence on *Acts* elsewhere in this text,[21] even in the account of the ascension with which it closes (*EpAp* 51), and the description of Paul as an 'elect vessel' and other common features may have crossed from *Acts* to the *Epistula* by way of a 'secondary orality' rather than by direct means. Since there are also significant differences between the two texts, their respective accounts of the conversion of Paul and its aftermath are best seen not as 'primary' and 'secondary' but as parallel to one another.

6.3   Paul the Persecutor

Significant differences between the *Epistula* and *Acts* may be seen in their depictions of Saul or Paul as persecutor and in the involvement of human agents in the conversion event. The persecuting Saul of the *Epistula* comes to Damascus not from Jerusalem but from Cilicia, and the apostles play a leading role in his conversion.

In the *Acts* narrative, Saul or Paul makes his first appearance at the martyrdom of Stephen, where he is introduced as a 'youth' (νεανίας) who guards the outer garments of those who are carrying out the stoning (*Acts* 7.58). As we learn later, Saul originated from Tarsus in Cilicia but was resident in Jerusalem in order to study the Torah with Gamaliel (*Acts* 22.3). In view of his youth and his minor supporting role in the death of Stephen, we might imagine that he is still Gamaliel's student. Yet Luke immediately elevates him to the role of chief instigator of the persecution that follows, which is described in dramatic terms:

---

[21] For arguments to the contrary, see Schmidt, *Gespräche Jesu*, 246–48.

> Saul was devastating the church, going from house to house
> and dragging away both men and women to commit them
> to prison.   (*Acts* 8.3; cf. 22.4)

From *Acts* 26.10–11 we also learn that Saul voted for the death penalty when charges were brought against his victims and that he visited synagogues to compel Christians he found there to 'blaspheme', perhaps by cursing Jesus. 'Breathing threats and murder against the disciples of the Lord', Saul gains high priestly support to extend his persecuting campaign to Damascus, and he journeys there in a state of 'utter fury against them' (*Acts* 9.1–2; 26.11). The youth who guarded the garments at Stephen's execution has been transformed into a demonic figure of superhuman malevolence.[22] The change of scene from Jerusalem to Damascus also serves to expand the scope of the *Acts* narrative – continuing the centrifugal movement away from Jerusalem already evident in Philip's activity in Samaria, where he is joined by Peter and John, and in his desert encounter with the Ethiopian eunuch (*Acts* 8.5–40).

The author of the *Epistula* agrees with Luke that Paul intended to persecute the church at Damascus, but he knows nothing of any state-sponsored persecuting activity in Jerusalem. In answer to the disciples' question as to when they will meet Paul, the risen Jesus informs them that

> that man will go out from the land of Cilicia to Damascus in
> Syria in order to tear apart the church that you are
> to found.   (*EpAp* 33.2)

The Ge'ez verb translated 'tear apart' (*masaṭa* / *maśaṭa*) suggests an animal-like savagery. It is used in *Ezekiel* 22.25[eth] to depict the activity of Jerusalem's princes who resemble lions tearing apart their prey,[23] and it also occurs in the characterization of Benjamin as a 'rapacious wolf' (*takʷlā maśāṭi*) in *Genesis* 49.27[eth].[24] As Darrell Hannah has argued, it is possible that the *Epistula* alludes to the early Christian understanding of *Genesis* 49.27 LXX as a prophetic

---

[22] The legendary character of this transformation is rightly emphasized by E. Haenchen, *The Acts of the Apostles,* Eng. trans. (Oxford: Blackwell, 1971), 297–98.

[23] C. F. A. Dillmann, *Lexicon Linguae Aethiopicae* (Leipzig: T.O. Weigel, 1862; repr. New York: Ungar, 1955), 162.

[24] C. F. A. Dillmann, *Veteris Testamenti Aethiopici*, I. *Octateuchus* (Leipzig: Vogel, 1855), 93.

anticipation of Paul: Βενιαμιν λύκος ἄρπαξ, τὸ πρωινὸν ἔδεται ἔτι καὶ εἰς ἑσπέρας διαδώσει τροφήν ('Benjamin is a rapacious wolf, in the morning he still devours and in the evening he gives nourishment').[25] According to Tertullian, arguing against Marcion and his followers,

> Even *Genesis* once promised me Paul. For among the figures and prophetic blessings addressed to his sons, Jacob addressed Benjamin as follows: 'Benjamin is a rapacious wolf, in the morning he still devours and in the evening he gives nourishment.' Thus he foresees that Paul would arise from the tribe of Benjamin, a rapacious wolf devouring in the morning (that is, that in his youth he would devastate the Lord's flock as a persecutor of the churches), but in the evening giving them nourishment (that is, that in his later years he would educate Christ's sheep as a teacher of the Gentiles). (*Adv. Marc.* 5.1.5)[26]

If the *Epistula* does allude to *Genesis* 49.27, it speaks of activity that Paul intends but does not actually achieve: Paul comes to Damascus '*in order to* tear apart the church...', but he does not succeed in doing so. The Paul of this text is a would-be persecutor, but there is no reference to any actual persecuting activity. Here no Christian men or women are dragged to prison from their houses or synagogues. Unlike *Acts*, this text is wholly uninterested in persecution in Jerusalem or by Jews.[27] Paul has no connection with Jerusalem, but comes to Damascus directly from his Cilician homeland.

The *Epistula* receives unexpected support at this point from the Paul of *Galatians*. As is well known, there is no indication in *Gal* 1 that Paul

---

[25] Darrell D. Hannah, 'The Ravenous Wolf: The Apostle Paul and Genesis 49.27 in the Early Church', *New Testament Studies* 62 (2016), 610–27; 622–24.

[26] 'Nam mihi Paulum etiam Genesis olim repromisit. Inter illas enim figuras et propheticas super filios suos benedictiones Iacob cum ad Beniamin direxisset, Beniamin, inquit, lupus rapax ad matutinum comedet adhuc, et ad vesperam dabit escam. Ex tribu enim Beniamin oriturum Paulum providebat, lupum rapacem ad matutinum comedentem, id est prima aetate vastaturum pecora domini ut persecutorem ecclesiarum, dehinc ad vesperam escam daturum, id est devergente iam aetate oves Christi educaturum ut doctorem nationum' (text in E. Evans, *Tertullian: Adversus Marcionem*, 2 vols. (Oxford: Clarendon Press, 1971).

[27] There is no Jewish dimension in the passing references to future persecution in *EpAp* 37.3; 38.3; 50.1.

had Jerusalem connections prior to his conversion.[28] After experiencing his divine call, Paul states that he did not 'go up' to Jerusalem but 'went away' to Arabia and then 'returned' to Damascus (*Gal* 1.17). The choice of verbs confirms the link between Damascus and Paul's conversion: he 'returned' to Damascus because that was the point from which he had started out. Paul does not say that he did not 'return' to Jerusalem, as one would have expected on the basis of the *Acts* narrative. The 'return' to Damascus implies a period of significant activity there, and Damascus and its surroundings may have been the site of the violent persecution of 'the church of God' that Paul acknowledges (*Gal* 1.13). In any case, contrary to *Acts* but in agreement with the *Epistula*, Paul did not persecute Christians in Jerusalem:

> I was not known by sight to the churches of God that are in Judea in Christ Jesus. They were only hearing that 'he who once persecuted us now preaches the faith that he then tried to destroy.' And they praised God on my account.
>
> (*Gal* 1.21–24)[29]

The 'churches of God that are in Judea in Christ Jesus' were persecuted not by Paul, who was from Cilicia, but by fellow-Judeans (cf. *1 Thes* 2.14). At the time of Paul's first visit to Jerusalem, three years after his conversion, Judean Christians were aware of his persecuting past, having heard of it from its former victims, but they were not themselves among its victims. The claim of the *Epistula*, that Paul will 'come from the land of Cilicia to Damascus in Syria in order to tear apart the church' reflects a tradition preserved in *Galatians* but significantly modified by *Acts*.

6.4   The Conversion of Paul

In *Acts* 9, the primary agent in Paul's conversion is the exalted Lord himself. As Paul or Saul approached Damascus, 'suddenly a light from heaven shone around him, and he fell to the ground and heard

[28] The absence of a Jerusalem link should therefore not be too quickly assessed as an 'apocryphal trait' in relation to canonical *Acts*, as it is by Schmidt (*Gespräche Jesu*, 248).

[29] As ever, harmonizing exegesis finds ways around this well-known discrepancy. Thus, according to F. F. Bruce, Paul was unknown in his new role as a Christian to people who knew him well as their former persecutor (F. F. Bruce, *The Epistle to the Galatians: A Commentary on the Greek Text*, New International Greek Testament Commentary [Exeter: Paternoster Press, 1982], 104).

a voice saying to him, "Saul, Saul, why do you persecute me?"' (*Acts*
9.3–4). Paul will later narrate this event in very similar terms when he
defends himself before the people of Jerusalem, adding only that it
occurred περὶ μεσημβρίαν, 'at about midday' (*Acts* 22.6). Still later, in
his defence before King Agrippa, we learn that the light was 'brighter
than the sun', that Paul's companions saw it and fell to the ground as
he did, and that the heavenly voice spoke τῇ Ἑβραΐδι διαλέκτῳ, that
is, in Hebrew or Aramaic (26.13–14).[30] It was the brightness of the
light that caused Paul's temporary blindness (22.11), although it did
not affect his companions who guided him into Damascus (9.8; 22.11).
Indeed, there is some uncertainty about what these companions did or
did not experience: they 'stood speechless [ἐνεοί], hearing the voice but
seeing no one' (9.7), they 'saw the light but did not hear the voice of
the one who was speaking to me' (22.9; cf. 26.13). Whether they hear
the voice or see the light, these anonymous companions participate in
the event of Paul's conversion and confirm its objective validity.[31]
Their role is to be witnesses; that is why they are introduced into a
narrative in which Paul/Saul otherwise carries out his violent persecuting activity single–handed (cf. 8.3; 9.1–2).

Two named individuals play a significant role in the sequel to
Paul's conversion. In Damascus, Ananias lays hands on him so that
his sight is restored (*Acts* 9.10–18); in Jerusalem, Barnabas introduces him to the apostles (9.27). We are also informed of the name
and address of the blinded Saul's host in Damascus: Ananias is told
that he will find Saul 'in the house of Judas' which is located 'in the
street called Straight' (9.11).[32] This Judas plays a more prominent
role in the Ephesus episode of the *Acts of Paul*, where Paul recounts
to his Ephesian audience 'what happened to me when I was in
Damascus, at the time when I was persecuting the faith in God'
(*AcPaul* 9.5).[33] After God revealed his Son to him, Paul joined the

---

[30] Cf. *GJn* 19.13, 17, where the place names Λιθόστρωτον and Κρανίου Τόπον are
said to render the Aramaic Γαββαθα and Γολγοθα 'in Hebrew' (Ἑβραϊστι).

[31] The effect in both cases is to place Saul's companions on the periphery of an
event intended for him alone (so Marguerat, *Actes*, 2.279). For a further variation on
this motif, cf. *Dan*10.7–8.

[32] Saul is introduced to Ananias as 'a man from Tarsus', a possible sign of a source
that does not associate Saul with Jerusalem (so Pervo, *Acts*, 243).

[33] Citations are from R. Pervo, *The Acts of Paul: A New Translation with
Introduction and Commentary* (Cambridge: James Clarke, 2014), 215; cf.
W. Schneemelcher (ed.), *New Testament Apocrypha*, vol. 2, *Writings Relating to the
Apostles; Apocalypses and Related Subjects*, Eng. trans. of 6th ed. (Cambridge: James
Clarke, 1992), 264.

church at Damascus 'through the blessed Judas, brother of the Lord, who from the beginning gave me the exalted love of faith' (*AcPaul* 9.5).[34] His new way of life as a Christian was enabled 'through the blessed prophet [i.e. Judas] and the revelation of Christ' (9.6). The obscure Judas of *Acts* 9 is identified both with the Judas named as one of Jesus' brothers (*GMk* 6.3 // *GMt* 13.55) and with the prophet Judas who plays a role in the delivery of the 'apostolic decree' (*Acts* 15.22, 27, 32).[35] In the figure of this Judas, Paul gains a more credible patron than the Ananias of *Acts*.

More significantly, perhaps, the balance between divine and human agency in Paul's conversion has shifted in the Ephesian speech of the *Acts of Paul*. Paul here has little to say about the encounter with Christ itself, recounting only that God disclosed his Son so that Paul might live in him and have no other life than that which is in Christ (*AcPaul* 9.5; cf. *Gal* 1.16, 2.20). Here there is no dazzling heavenly light to fell Paul to the ground and to blind him. What is emphasized instead is the role of Judas as introducing Paul into the Christian community in Damascus and instructing him in the faith. As Judas proclaimed Christ, 'I rejoiced in the Lord, nourished by his words', and it was on the basis of this instruction in Christian truth that Paul was enabled to become a teacher himself (*AcPaul* 9.6). In the *Acts of the Apostles*, Paul appears not to need a teacher. He spends several days with 'the disciples at Damascus', who immediately become '*his* disciples' (*Acts* 9.19b, 25),[36] and he proclaims Jesus as Son of God in the synagogues (*Acts* 9.20). The *Acts of the Apostles* exploits the apologetic potential of Paul's conversion, presenting it three times as a self–contained event in its own right. Indeed, in the speech before Agrippa Paul's conversion narrative is virtually equivalent to the gospel message itself, culminating in an appeal to Agrippa to declare himself a Christian (*Acts* 26.27–29). In the *Acts of Paul*, on the other hand, Paul's conversion simply

---

[34] As Pervo rightly notes, '[t]his account implies that Paul's host in Damascus, Judas (*Acts* 9:11), was none other than the brother of Jesus', adding that Judas' approval 'aligned Paul closely with the family and followers of Jesus' (*Acts of Paul*, 218).

[35] As a 'brother of the Lord', this Judas or Jude is also 'brother of James' (Jude 1). Hegesippus records a legend about his grandchildren appearing before the Emperor Domitian, and claims that they later became church leaders on the basis of their family relationship with the Lord (Eusebius, *Hist. eccl.* 3.19.1–20.8; 32.5–6).

[36] For the text-critical issue here, see Barrett, *Acts*, 1.466–67.

marks the necessary beginning of his career as Christian missionary rather than persecutor.

In the *Epistula Apostolorum*, it is no longer named individuals such as Ananias, Barnabas, or Judas the Lord's brother who ease the transition from persecutor to Christian but the entire group of eleven apostles named at the outset: John, Thomas, Peter, Andrew, James, Philip, Bartholomew, Matthew, Nathanael, Judas the Zealot, and Cephas.[37] According to the author, the eleven will be in Damascus to found the church there, and they will therefore be ready to meet Paul when he arrives, chastened by his encounter with the risen Lord:

> That man will go out from the land of Cilicia to Damascus in Syria in order to tear apart the church that you are to found... And that man I will turn aside so that he may not come and fulfil his evil intention, and his shall be the glory of my Father. For when I have gone and am with my Father, I will speak with him from heaven. *(EpAp 33.7–8)*

> He will hear my voice from heaven with astonishment, fear, and trembling. And he will be blinded... *(EpAp 31.1–2)*

The impact of the heavenly voice and the glory of the Father prepares Paul for the instruction in the faith that he is to receive from the eleven apostles:

> And he will be blinded, and by your hand shall his eyes be sealed with saliva. And do everything for him that I have done for you, and pass him on to others. And immediately this man's eyes shall be opened and he will praise God, my heavenly Father. *(EpAp 31.1–4)*[38]

The apostles' encounter with Paul has a clearly marked beginning, in the mysterious gesture of further sealing his blinded eyes with their saliva,[39] and an equally clearly marked end, when he is transferred to the care of others and his eyes are opened. In the intervening period, the apostles are to 'do everything for him that I have done for you' –

---

[37] On the list of apostles, see the Additional Note on *EpAp* 2.1–2.

[38] For the majority reading, 'as I have done for you', cf. *EpAp* 19.16; 27.2; 42.9. It is not clear why Hills follows MS O in reading 'as others have done for you' (*Epistle of the Apostles*, 59; cf. 7).

[39] Saliva is associated with the opening of blind eyes in *GMk* 8.23 and *GJn* 9.6. The use of saliva for sealing eyes approximates to the fish-scale-like substance which must fall from Paul's eyes for him to regain his sight (*Acts* 9.18: ὡς λεπίδες).

that is, they are to instruct him in the faith, as the risen Jesus instructed the apostles. More precisely, the apostles must teach the blinded Paul how the prophetic scriptures bear witness to Jesus and communicate to him the substance of Jesus' teaching:

> As you have learnt from the scriptures that the prophets[40] spoke about me and in me it is truly fulfilled, so you must provide guidance in them. And every word that I have spoken to you and that you write about me, that I am the Word of the Father and the Father is in me, you also must pass on to that man, as is fitting for you. Teach him and remind him[41] what is said in the scriptures about me and is now fulfilled, and then he will be the salvation of the Gentiles.   (*EpAp* 31.10–12)[42]

The instruction Paul must receive is to be based primarily on written texts, both prophetic and apostolic. The reference to Jesus as the Word of the Father, and to the presence of the Father in him, might suggest an allusion to *GJohn*,[43] a text with which the author of *EpAp* is certainly familiar (cf. *GJn* 1.1, 14; 14.10).[44] Yet it is more likely that the risen Jesus here has the present text in view, where his claim to be 'the Word' is closely correlated with references to 'the Father who is in me' (cf. 17.8–18.1; 39.11–12). The verb translated 'you write' (*ṣaḥafkəmu*) is plural, implying a text or texts for which the apostolic group as a whole is responsible, not just individual apostles.[45] The apostolic text must contain a record of 'what I have said to you', which corresponds to the core content of *EpAp* itself. It

---

[40] *Eth* here reads, 'your fathers the prophets', as in *EpAp* 27.1. The phrase probably results from a scribal misreading of 'your fathers *and* the prophets' as in 28.3 (cf. also 3.11; 19.28).

[41] Emending *maharu* ('Teach') to *maharewwo* ('Teach him'). Hills finds here a general exhortation to teach the scriptures, but its conclusion must refer to Paul and cannot mean 'then the Gentiles will have salvation' (*Epistle of the Apostles*, 60).

[42] Paul's mission to the Gentiles is not exclusively his: the eleven are ordered to '[g]o and preach to the twelve tribes [ⲫⲩⲗⲏ] and preach also to the Gentiles [ⲅⲉⲉⲛⲟⲥ] and to the whole land of Israel [ⲓⲏⲗ], from east to west and from south to north' (*EpAp* 30.1).

[43] Cf. Hannah, 'Four-Gospel "Canon"', 608–9. Hannah considers the possibility of a reference to apostolic gospels prior to *EpAp* at 1.4, 'What we have heard and remembered and written for the whole world we entrust to you, our sons and daughters...' Yet, as Hannah rightly concludes (609–10), the reference here again seems to be to *EpAp* itself. The apostolic authors entrust their text to 'sons and daughters' belonging to the churches of the east and west, north and south (2.2) so that through them this record of Jesus' teaching will extend to 'the whole world'.

[44] See Hannah, 'Four-Gospel "Canon"', 610–11; Schmidt, *Gespräche Jesu*, 218–42.

[45] See the Additional Note on 31.11, justifying the translation of *ṣaḥafkəmu* as 'we write' rather than 'we have written'.

is assumed that the apostolic testimony was put into writing so early that it could be used to instruct the newly converted Paul – in contrast to the later datings proposed by Irenaeus, for whom the gospels he attributes to Mark, Luke, and John were written after the deaths of Peter and Paul in Rome so as to ensure that the apostolic preaching was preserved after the departure of the apostles.[46] A partial analogy to the *Epistula*'s assumption of early apostolic gospel writing may be found in the *Apocryphon of James*, where 'the twelve disciples' were already 'recalling what the Saviour had said to each one of them... and putting it in books' even before Jesus' ascension (*ApocrJas* 2, 8–15). The *Apocryphon*, however, envisages individual apostolic texts rather than the collective writing presupposed in the *Epistula*, where distinct apostolic identities are virtually absent.

Paul is to receive from the eleven apostles a thorough grounding in the faith, on the basis of prophetic and apostolic texts that bear anticipatory or retrospective witness to Jesus. Thus his conversion will be complete and he will be equipped to embark on his missionary career. As Paul's instructors, the apostles play a comparable role in this text to that of Judas the Lord's brother in the *Acts of Paul*. In the *Epistula*, however, the point is to show the seamless continuity between the mission of the eleven and that of Paul. He is in effect a twelfth apostle – a replacement perhaps for Judas Iscariot. Although Judas's defection is not mentioned in this text, it is probably presupposed in the naming of eleven apostolic authors at the outset (*EpAp* 2.1). While the eleven describe themselves not as apostles but as 'his disciples' or 'we his disciples' (1.1; 5.14), the author assumes that the same individuals are 'disciples' when they are being instructed by the earthly Jesus and 'apostles' as proclaimers of the faith after his departure: thus Jesus is the one 'whom the apostles preached and the disciples touched' (3.12). Paul might seem to be an anomaly, as a disciple not of Jesus but of the apostles during the period of his blindness. Yet the content of the instruction received is the same in both cases: the apostles are to pass on everything that Jesus has told them (31.11), and it can even be said that 'it is I who will speak through you' (33.3). Instructed by the Lord through his apostles, Paul becomes an apostle in his own right, restoring the eleven to the full complement of twelve. The author of the *Epistula* would have

---

[46] Irenaeus, *Adv. haer.* 3.1.1. For analysis of this passage, see my *Gospel Writing: A Canonical Perspective*, 454–72.

agreed with the author or editor of the *Didache* who assumed that the Lord's teaching was communicated to the Gentiles 'through the twelve apostles'.[47]

In *Acts*, Paul cannot be a twelfth apostles, since the vacancy left by Judas' defection and death is immediately filled after a shortlisting process which produces two credible candidates, 'Joseph called Barsabbas, also known as Justus', and Matthias, who is the one selected (*Acts* 1.23–26). Focusing as it does on the primary figures of Peter and Paul, *Acts* leaves the relationship between Paul and the twelve undetermined.[48] The same cannot be said of *Galatians*, however, where Paul vehemently opposes the view that his conversion and apostleship derive from anyone other than Christ. It was God who 'revealed his Son in me', and that revelation was complete and sufficient in itself; there was no need to 'consult with flesh and blood', that is, go up to Jerusalem to be instructed by 'those who were apostles before me' (*Gal* 1.16–17). Paul is an apostle 'not from humans' (ἀπ' ἀνθρώπων) or 'through a human' (δι' ἀνθρώπου), but solely and exclusively 'through Jesus Christ and God the Father who raised him from the dead' (*Gal* 1.1). In the *Epistula*, the risen Jesus anticipates the moment when he will address Paul in a voice that will fill him with 'astonishment, fear, and trembling', while 'the glory of my Father will come upon him', rendering him temporarily blind (*EpAp* 31.1–2; 33.7–8). Yet Paul's conversion here takes place not only through Jesus Christ and God the Father but also from and through humans, in the form of the eleven disciples who collectively found the church in Damascus, who meet Paul after his encounter with Jesus and seal his blinded eyes with their saliva, and who instruct him in the faith as Jesus earlier instructed them. It might seem that the *Epistula* preserves the tradition of Paul's dependence on those who were apostles before him, a tradition whose existence he is forced to acknowledge precisely as he rejects it.[49]

---

[47] In the one surviving Greek manuscript, the *Didache* bears the double title, Διδαχὴ τῶν δώδεκα ἀποστόλων and Διδαχὴ κυρίου διὰ τῶν δώδεκα ἀποστόλων τοῖς ἔθνεσιν. See K. Niederwimmer, *The Didache: A Commentary* (Hermeneia, Minneapolis, MN: Augsburg Fortress, 1998), 56–57.

[48] While it is true that the Paul of *Acts* cannot be an apostle (so John Knox, *Chapters in a Life of Paul* [London: A&C Black, 1954], 117–19), the fact that he is the hero of more than half the *Acts* narrative shows that this does not detract from his status. Luke's Paul is a far more engaging character than his Peter.

[49] Markus Vinzent tries unsuccessfully to show that *EpAp* is an anti-Marcionite work directed against Paul's claim to apostolic authority (*Christ's Resurrection in*

Yet the opposition between *Galatians* and the *Epistula* is not straightforward. It seems likely that, with their demand for circumcision and submission to the Law of Moses, Paul's opponents claim to be completing the process of conversion that he had initiated in Galatia. That would account for the sarcastic allusion in *Gal* 3.3 to the position his readers have adopted: ἐναρξάμενοι ἐν πνεύματι νῦν σαρκὶ ἐπιτελεῖσθε. From the opponents' standpoint, however, they are not opponents at all but fellow–workers.[50] Their relationship to Paul is analogous to Paul's own account of his relationship to Apollos: 'I planted, Apollos watered, and God gave the growth' (*1 Cor* 3.6). From the new teachers' point of view, what Paul had planted in Galatia needed to be watered by instruction in the Torah in order to grow and flourish. The teachers may have claimed some kind of commission from the apostles, like the 'people from James' Paul disparages in *Gal* 2.12, and they probably attributed a similar commission to Paul: for Paul has to argue strenuously in *Gal* 2.1–10 that the three Jerusalem 'pillars' recognized the divine origin of his apostleship to the Gentiles – rather than bestowing a commission on him themselves and thereby 'adding' something to his existing position (cf. *Gal* 2.6). In this context, the claim to an apostleship bestowed directly and exclusively by Jesus Christ serves to establish Paul as an equal partner in the work of proclamation. Paul is called to preach to Gentiles, Peter to Jews, and the two missions are to coexist in parallel, with neither subordinated to the other. In reality there is a fine line between recognizing and bestowing a commission, and the 'right hand of fellowship' (*Gal* 2.9) could signify either. In asserting an authorization independent of any human mediation,

---

Early Christianity and the Making of the New Testament [Farnham: Ashgate, 2011], 128–42). Vinzent finds in *EpAp* a downgrading of Paul's status in relation to *Acts*, directed 'presumably against Marcion's "overstatement" of Paul' (142). An author who devotes so much space to a prophetic account of Paul's future career can hardly be trying to downgrade him.

[50] If Paul's account of his criticism of Peter in *Gal* 2.11–21 is a self–defence against the charge of insubordination, then the new Galatian teachers would indeed see themselves as Paul's opponents. J. L Martyn puts into their mouths the following case against Paul: 'The man called Paul spent a significant amount of time in Jerusalem receiving accurate instruction in the gospel-tradition from the apostles in the mother church. Later, pursuing a pseudo-mission among Gentiles... he deviated seriously from that true line of tradition, and he continues to do that to this day' (*Galatians: A New Translation with Introduction and Commentary*, Anchor Bible [New York: Doubleday, 1998], 178). While it is plausible that the teachers appealed to the practice of Cephas/Peter and James, Paul does not suggest that his own conduct had been criticized.

Paul's major concern is to deny the Galatian teachers' right to water what he has planted.

Written over a century later,[51] the *Epistula Apostolorum* does not directly participate in this old controversy. In giving the eleven such an important role in instructing the newly converted Paul, the intention is not at all to subordinate his authority to theirs, which is the issue in *Gal* 1–2. The opposite is the case: the Paul of the *Epistula* will hear from the eleven at Damascus exactly what they hear from the risen Lord throughout this dialogue, the voice of the risen Lord is mediated through their instruction, and the effect is to integrate Paul into the original apostolic group and not to subordinate him to it.[52] In spite of the tension between this depiction and the denial of human mediation in *Gal* 1–2, the *Epistula* is in essential agreement with the Paul of *1 Corinthians* 15 that, although he is 'the least of the apostles' (v. 9), he is nevertheless one of them, carrying out his ministry on the same basis as they do: 'Whether it is I or they, so we preach and so you believed' (v. 11).

As he begins the fifth and final book of his great work *Against Marcion*, Tertullian reflects on the strangeness of the position ascribed to the apostle Paul. Why was Paul called so belatedly? Can his claim to full apostolic status really be substantiated? Imagining that he is hearing about Paul for the first time, Tertullian finds that his suspicions are aroused

> when I am told that someone is an apostle whom I do not find mentioned in the list of apostles in the Gospel. Indeed, when I hear that he was chosen by the Lord only after he had attained his rest in heaven, it almost seems a lack of foresight if Christ did not know beforehand that he was necessary to him, but thought of adding him only when the apostles had already been appointed to their office and sent forth for their labours...   (*Adv. Marc.* 5.1.1–2)[53]

---

[51] For discussion of factors relating to the dating of this text, see Schmidt, *Gespräche Jesu*, 361–402.

[52] The same is true when the Paul of *3 Corinthians* writes that 'I delivered to you first of all what I received from the apostles before me who were always with Jesus Christ' (*3 Cor* 3.4).

[53] '... cum is mihi affirmatur apostolus quem in albo apostolorum apud evangelium non deprehendo. Denique audiens postea eum a domino allectum, iam in caelis quiescente, quasi inprovidentiam existimo si non ante scivit illum sibi necessarium Christus, sed iam ordinato officio apostolatus et in sua opera dimisso... adiciendum existimavit.'

The role assigned to Paul as the twelfth or thirteenth apostle cannot easily be harmonized with the gospel portrayal of Jesus' calling of his disciples and his sending them out to preach the gospel to the world.

It is precisely Tertullian's issue that the *Epistula* seeks to address. The author is concerned to show that there was no lack of foresight on the part of Jesus when Paul was called so belatedly to join the eleven. His call was not an afterthought, improvised to meet some unforeseen deficiency in the structure already established. On the contrary, Jesus planned the circumstances of Paul's conversion and its aftermath long in advance, and communicated his plans to the original disciples after he rose from the dead. Nothing was fortuitous: 'All that I have predicted to you about him will take place' (*EpAp* 33.9).

7

VINDICATING DIVINE JUSTICE

The author of the *Epistula Apostolorum* is neither a profound speculative thinker nor a gifted story-teller. The narrative components of this text – the miracle cycle, the Easter narrative, the Ascension – exist purely in the service of the creed-like items of belief that constitute the author's model of apostolic orthodoxy, from creation by the Word through to the resurrection of the flesh (cf. *EpAp* 3). Allusive and speculative language is largely confined to a single passage where Jesus provides an obscure gloss on his identity as the Logos: he is 'the thought fulfilled in the type', who 'came into being on the eighth day, which is the Lord's Day' and who will bring about 'the fulfilment of all fulfilment' (*EpAp* 18.1–3).[1] What this author does possess is a certain ability to synthesize the themes he touches on, demonstrating their coherence. In his own way, he is a systematic thinker.

In earlier gospel literature, Jesus' rising on Easter morning issues in apostolic mission but is otherwise an isolated, one-off event with no explicit connections forward to the events of the eschaton or backward to Jesus' earthly career. Post-Markan gospels recognize the imbalance between Mark's passion narrative and his brief and inconclusive empty tomb story and seek to remedy it by adding narratives of appearances that may include an act of commissioning, but the fact that such narratives were evidently unknown to the earliest tradition seems to inhibit their development.[2] Symptomatic of their belatedness is the fact that in two cases secondary Longer Endings have been provided to fill out the otherwise sparse picture (*GMk* 16.9–20; *GJn* 21.1–25). The canonical Easter narratives are not so much the culmination of the main story as appendices to it. In

---

[1] On this passage see the Additional Notes.
[2] See R. Bultmann, *The History of the Synoptic Tradition*, Eng. trans. (Oxford: Blackwell, 1963), 284–91.

contrast, in *EpAp* the story of Easter morning *is* the main story – although events of Jesus' earlier ministry are also noted as a prelude to it.

In *EpAp* Jesus' resurrection is the basis and precedent for the future resurrection and salvation of his followers. It is the key soteriological event:

> Truly I say to you, as my Father raised me from the dead, so you too will rise and they will take you up above the heavens to the place of which I spoke to you in the beginning, to the place prepared for you by the one who sent me. (*EpAp* 21.1)

A future resurrection is also envisaged in the synoptic tradition, where it ushers in an angelic heavenly life in which there is no marrying or giving in marriage (*GMt* 22.23–33 + pars.). In this synoptic passage the future post-resurrection life lacks any distinctively Christian basis. Responding to sceptical Sadducees, Jesus appeals to the power of God and the testimony of Moses, but there is no suggestion that he himself will shortly demonstrate the reality of resurrection. The resurrection life is also defined negatively in *EpAp*, where it is located 'not in the lower creation but in that which is incorruptible', a sphere 'where there is no eating or drinking and no anxiety or grief and no corruption for those who are above' (*EpAp* 19.14–15). Here, however, the link between the resurrection life and Jesus himself is made explicit. The heavenly realm is Jesus' original place of residence with his Father, to which he will shortly return, and it is accessible to others only on the basis of their relationship to him: 'As I am always in him, so are you in me' (19.16).[3] The analogy between the two relationships (the Father and Jesus, Jesus and his disciples) extends to the events in which these relationships are consummated:

> Truly I say to you, as my Father raised me from the dead, so you too will rise and they will take you up above the heavens to the place of which I spoke to you in the beginning, to the place prepared for you by the one who sent me. (21.1)

On the synoptic Jesus' reading of *Exodus* 3.6, God shows himself to be 'the God of the living not the dead' when he identifies himself

---

[3] Cf. *GJn* 17.23, 'I in them and you in me'. The Johannine Jesus prays that the disciples 'may be with me where I am', that is, in the sphere of his pre-existent glory (17.24), but there is no explicit reference here to resurrection.

to Moses as 'the God of Abraham, Isaac, and Jacob' (*GMt* 22.32 + pars.). Elsewhere Jesus speaks of these same patriarchs as reclining at table in the kingdom of God (*GMt* 8.11) together with the prophets (*GLk* 13.28). There is no indication that their presence there has anything to do with Jesus. In *EpAp*, Jesus is 'the Saviour' (10.5) and even patriarchs and prophets must look to him for their salvation. Securing that salvation by descending to their post mortem residence was, indeed, the reason why he had to die:[4]

> For this is why I descended to the place of Lazarus and preached to your fathers and the prophets that they would go forth from the rest below and ascend to that which is in heaven. And with my right hand I poured over them the baptism of life and forgiveness and deliverance from all evil... For what I have promised you I shall also give them, so that they may come forth from the prison and chains of the rulers and the terrible fire.   (*EpAp* 27.1–2a, 28.2)[5]

The reference to Lazarus presumably alludes to Jesus' parable in *GLuke* 16.19–31, where Lazarus is comforted 'in the bosom of Abraham' after his earthly sufferings (vv. 22, 25). In the Lukan parable as in Jesus' debate with the Sadducees, it is the testimony of scripture that establishes the existence of this post mortem life (vv. 29–31). Neither Lazarus nor Abraham needs to be rescued from it by Jesus, following his own death and in consequence of his resurrection. In contrast, *EpAp* has removed the impassable gulf between

---

[4] Jesus' crucifixion is an article of faith (*EpAp* 9.1) and is remembered each year at the Feast of the Pascha (15.1), but his death is subordinated to his incarnation: 'Behold, I have put on your flesh, in which I was born and in which I was crucified...' (19.18); 'I am the Word who became flesh and suffered' (39.12). In contrast with another post-resurrection dialogue, the *Apocryphon of James*, Jesus nowhere tells the disciples to expect to suffer as he has suffered (cf. NHC I, cf. esp. 4,23–6,18, but n.b. *EpAp* 15.8–9). In *EpAp* the incarnate Jesus lives for the sake of the living and dies for the sake of the dead.

[5] In this version of the *descensus ad inferos* tradition, Jesus descends to Hades in order to preach to the dead, providing them with the same opportunity to believe and be saved that he bestows on the living: cf. *GPet* 10.41–42, where, as the risen Jesus emerges from the tomb with two angelic assistants and the cross, the guards 'heard a voice from the heavens saying, Did you preach to those who sleep?, and an answer was heard from the cross: Yes!' On this and related passages, see Paul Foster (ed.), *The Gospel of Peter: Introduction, Critical Edition and Commentary*, Texts and Editions for New Testament Study 4 (Leiden: Brill, 2010), 423–31. Jesus' preaching in Hades does not secure immediate release and salvation for the righteous dead, as in Ignatius (*Magn.* 9.2) and the later *Gospel of Nicodemus* (24.1–2, part of an extended scene inspired by *GMt* 27.52–53).

Lazarus's place of refuge and the rich man's place of torment (cf. *GLk* 16.26); Abraham needs Jesus as his Saviour no less than the disciples. From the proto-orthodox standpoint of the *Epistula*, the older synoptic traditions seem surprisingly casual and ad hoc in their testimony to what came to be viewed as core Christian beliefs.

7.1   Judgement: Scope and Criterion

According to the *Epistula*, Jesus' resurrection is integral to his role as Saviour but salvation will only be finally attained at his coming again as judge of all. Here too this text holds together items of belief that are often isolated from each other in early Christian literature. Elsewhere Jesus' parousia can be seen as itself the occasion for the salvation of the elect, without reference to judgement (cf. *GMt* 24.30–31; *1 Thes* 4.16–18). Conversely, a judgement according to works can be announced without reference to the parousia (cf. *Rom* 2.5–16). The two themes are reunited in the image of the Son of man coming in his glory and taking his seat to judge the nations (*GMt* 25.31), but even here there is little or no sense of a spatial movement from one location (heaven) to another (earth) by way of a created entity that mediates the distance between the two (the clouds). In contrast, *EpAp* asserts the logical connection between Jesus' spectacular descent from heaven and his role as judge of all:

> Truly I say to you, I shall surely come like the rising sun, shining seven times more than it in my glory. On the wings of clouds I shall be borne in glory, the sign of the cross before me. And I will come down to the earth and judge the living and the dead.   (*EpAp* 16.3–5)[6]

Jesus' resurrection, ascension, and return are necessary preconditions for his role as Saviour, together with his descent into Hades, but those who wish him to be their Saviour must first encounter him as their Judge. That is the message that comes increasingly to the

---

[6] Similar motifs and language occur in the *Apocalypse of Peter* 1.6–7[eth]. Text in Dennis D. Buchholz, *Your Eyes Will Be Opened: A Study of the Greek (Ethiopic) Apocalypse of Peter* (Atlanta, GA: Scholars Press, 1988), 166, 168. Cf. also the *Didache*'s reference to a 'sign of extension' (σημεῖον ἐκπετάσεως) as the first of three signs heralding the Lord's coming in the clouds – the other two being the sound of the trumpet and the resurrection of the righteous dead (*Did* 16.6–8). On the σημεῖον ἐκπετάσεως as the cross, see Kurt Niederwimmer, *The Didache: A Commentary* (Minneapolis, MN: Augsburg Fortress, 1998), 223–25.

fore during this long Easter question-and-answer session, and it is here that the emphasis finally lies rather than on themes such as resurrection and mission that are prominent earlier.[7] Even for believers there is no possibility of bypassing the judgement, for it is all too possible to believe in Jesus while failing to observe his commandments. One commandment in particular is singled out: the demand that the wealthy and powerful within the Christian community should not be exempted from necessary criticism and correction.

While the theme of Jesus as judge first occurs in connection with his parousia (*EpAp* 16.3–5), its first extended development arises out of the lengthy discussion of the resurrection of the flesh (*EpAp* 19.17–25.9). Jesus has announced the hope of salvation (12.4; 19.5–16), and that hope has been enthusiastically acclaimed by the disciples: 'Lord, in everything you have become to us salvation and life, proclaiming such a hope to us!' (19.12). Yet that hope will be realized in an incorruptible heavenly sphere where normal bodily functions such as eating and drinking are absent (19.14), so the disciples ask about the form of that future redeemed existence. Will it be fleshly, a perfected version of the present life, or will we be transformed into angels, possessing a rarefied spiritual body better suited to heavenly existence than the present carnal one (19.17)? Jesus' answer seems to evade the question:

> Behold, I have put on your flesh, in which I was born and in which I was crucified and raised by my heavenly Father, that the prophecy of David the prophet might be fulfilled, concerning what was proclaimed about me and my death and my resurrection...   (*EpAp* 19.18–19)

This is followed by a citation of the whole of *Psalm* 3 LXX, a complaint about the speaker's enemies that is not particularly apposite apart from the words 'I lay down and slept, I was raised' (*Ps* 3.6 = *EpAp* 19.24).[8] The implication may be that, as Jesus was born, crucified, and raised in flesh, so we too will retain our flesh in the

---

[7] The fundamental importance of future eschatology to this text is rightly noted by Schmidt: 'Die christliche Gemeinde verehrt in Christus nicht so sehr den gegenwärtigen, nach der Himmelfahrt zur Rechten des Vaters sitzenden κύριος, sondern im Anschluss an die regula den zukünftigen, vom Himmel herabkommenden Richter der Lebendigen und der Toten' (*Gespräche Jesu*, 337).

[8] In *EpAp* scriptural citations real or alleged occur on seven occasions (11.8; 19.19–26; 33.5–6; 35.5–8; 43.4; 47.6; 49.2).

resurrection – but if so this is not spelled out here.[9] It turns out that the psalm citation has an additional function, which is to confirm the veracity of Jesus' statements about the eschaton: 'If all the words spoken by the prophets are fulfilled in me – for I was in them – then how much more what I say to you!' (*EpAp* 19.28). So the disciples ask permission to repeat their question about the nature of the risen life (20.2), and they finally get to do so only after another digression – with the addition of a reference to the judgement:

> Lord, is the flesh really to be judged with the soul and the spirit? And will some find rest in the kingdom of heaven and other be condemned for ever while living?   (*EpAp* 22.1–2)[10]

Jesus's contrasting responses to this question – first impatient, then conciliatory – create further delays (22.3–25.3), but at last a full and unambiguous answer is forthcoming:

> Truly I say to you that the flesh will rise with the soul alive, so that they may be judged on that day for what they have done, whether good or evil, so that there may be a selection of believers [ⲉⲕⲗⲟⲅⲏ ⲛ̄ⲛ̄ⲡⲓⲥⲧⲟⲥ] who have performed the commandments of my Father who sent me. Thus the judgement will take place in severity. For my Father said to me, 'My Son, on the day of judgement you shall neither be ashamed before the rich nor pity the poor, but according to the sin of each you shall deliver them to eternal punishment.' But to my beloved, who have performed the commandments of my Father who sent me, I will give rest of life in the kingdom of my Father in heaven.   (*EpAp* 26.1–5)[11]

Here the connection is made between the fleshly resurrection of the dead and the event to which it leads, the divine decision about each

---

[9] In *1 Clement* 26.2, *Psalm* 3.6 is applied to the general resurrection of the righteous, while in Justin and later writers it is applied specifically to the resurrection of Jesus (Justin, *1Apol* 38.5; *Dial. Try.* 97.1, citing vv. 5–6). It is possible that the author of *EpAp* also has a traditional more general application in mind as he reads the psalm christologically.

[10] On the textual problems here see the Additional Notes. The question about resurrection is repeated at *EpAp* 24.2, though without the reference to judgement: 'Lord, is it possible for what is dissolved and destroyed to be saved?' Schmidt notes that Jesus' angry response characterizes the disciples as ὀλιγόπιστοι (24.4), suggesting that the issue with the resurrection of the flesh is that it is generally counter-intuitive and is not occasioned by dualistic heretical distortions (*Gespräche Jesu*, 348–49).

[11] See *Additional Notes* for the textual problems at *EpAp* 26.1.

individual's ultimate destiny based on the conduct of their earthly life. While the concept of a judgement according to works is commonplace in early Christian texts, there are two notable features of this passage.

First, the passage seems to be concerned only with 'believers'. Believers and unbelievers alike will experience the cosmic and earthly catastrophes that announce the imminence of the eschaton (34.7), but it is not clear that unbelievers are subject to fleshly resurrection and judgement. It may be the author's view that only those who are united to the risen Jesus by faith will be raised as he was – a view shared with Paul, the 'apostle of resurrection' (ἀναστάσεως ἀπόστολος).[12] According to Paul, the risen Christ is 'the first-fruits [ἀπαρχή] of those who sleep', and his resurrection will be followed at his 'coming' (παρουσία) by the resurrection of 'those who are Christ's' (οἱ τοῦ Χριστοῦ) (*1 Cor* 15.23). Here, as perhaps in *EpAp*, resurrection is contingent on belonging to Christ. Resurrection seems to be synonymous with salvation in *1 Corinthians* 15, where there is no mention of judgement, yet Paul will later warn the same Corinthian readership that 'we must all appear before the judgement seat of Christ, so that each may receive their due for what they did through the body, whether good or evil' (*2 Cor* 5.10; cf. *EpAp* 26.1, '. . . so that they may be judged on that day for what they have done, whether good or evil').[13] If it is only those who are in Christ who will be raised, it is only those who are in Christ who will be judged. Elsewhere, however, Paul envisages a universal judgement according to works in which rewards and punishments are meted out 'to the Jew first and also the Greek', that is, to the whole of humanity as Paul conceives it (*Rom* 2.9–10); that judgement will be executed by 'Christ Jesus', and Paul insists that this belief is integral to 'my gospel' (*Rom* 2.16). There is no reference to resurrection here. As we have seen, the author of *EpAp* is concerned about the consistency and coherence of Christian beliefs, and it is possible that he does believe in a universal resurrection and judgement (cf. 16.4, 'I will come down to the earth and judge the

---

[12] Clement of Alexandria, *Exc. Theod.* 23.2.

[13] Commenting on *2 Cor.* 5.10 in its relation to *1 Cor* 15, Margaret Thrall suggests that 'Paul's convictions about judgement and about resurrection, though firm, were not correlated chronologically with any degree of precision' (*The Second Epistle to the Corinthians*, 2 vols., International Critical Commentary [London: T&T Clark, 1994–2000], 1.296). Arguably, it is characteristic of Pauline discourse in general that it omits to synthesize ostensibly related themes.

living and the dead') but chooses to focus primarily on implications for believers.

Second, according to *EpAp*'s resurrection-and-judgement scenario the goal of the judgement is 'a selection [ἐκλογή] of believers who have performed the commandments of my Father who sent me' (26.2). Here selection or election occurs not 'before the foundation of the world' (*Eph* 1.4) or 'before they were born or had done anything good or evil' (*Rom* 9.11) but after and on the basis of their completed good or evil actions as disclosed at the judgement. The elect are elected on merit, and they are a subset of the broader category of 'believers'. Towards the end of this text the disciples will put to Jesus the question: 'Lord, among the believers, those among them who truly believe the preaching of your name, will there really be division and strife and jealousy and quarrelling and hatred and slander among them?' (49.5). The answer has to be yes. Jesus replies that the purpose of the judgement is 'that the wheat may be put into its barns and its chaff put onto the fire' (49.7–8). As in the Matthean parable alluded to here, the judgement effects a final and irrevocable division between members of the Christian community, even though they all believe and confess Jesus (cf. *GMt* 13.36). The elect are those believers 'who have performed the commandments of my Father who sent me' (26.2), and it is their obedience that ensures their election and not their faith alone.

What are these commandments that must be obeyed? There is no trace of the Decalogue in this text, nor is there any reference to sexual sins. The author draws from both Johannine and Matthean traditions to characterize the life of the disciple as a life of love for those within and without the Christian community:

> Behold, I give you a new commandment: love one another, and that there may be continual peace among you. Love your enemies, and what you do not wish them to do to you, do not do to another, or that one to you.
>
> (*EpAp* 18.5–6; cf. *GJn* 13.34; *GMt* 5.44, 7.12)

There is little emphasis on such general principles, however, for the author is preoccupied with a single specific issue: the duty to challenge inappropriate conduct within the community and not to be intimidated from doing so by wealth and social status. 'Those who desire to see the face of God, and who do not show partiality to rich sinners, and who are not ashamed before the men who go astray but rebuke them, these will be crowned in the presence of the Father'

(*EpAp* 38.1). More succinctly: 'Those who rebuke their neighbour will be saved' (38.2). Underlying this requirement is the disciplinary procedure outlined in *GMatthew* 18.15–17: 'If your brother sins against you, go and tell him his fault, between you and him alone...' The Matthean procedure is repeated in *EpAp*, with the significant difference that all sin must be challenged, not just the sin directed against oneself:

> If you see a sinner, reprove him between yourself and him. But if he does not listen to you take up to three others with you and teach your brother. If he again does not listen to you, set him before you as a gentile and a tax-collector. (*EpAp* 48.1–2)[14]

This duty to challenge must be carried out impartially, with a particular focus on 'the rich' who 'do not do my commandments but delight in their wealth' (46.1). Every member of the community is obliged not only to observe its norms themselves but also to ensure their observance by others. One must even be willing to challenge one's 'benefactor',[15] on whom one is dependent for material and social support, for what is at stake here is the salvation not only of the sinner but also of the challenger. Conversely, failure to rebuke sin is complicity in sin and merits the same punishment:

> If one should fall, bearing a burden because of the sins he has committed, let his neighbour reprove him for what he did to his neighbour. And when his neighbour has reproved him and he returns, he will be saved and the one who reproved him will be awarded eternal life. But if a man who is in need sees his benefactor sinning and does not reprove him, he will be judged with an evil judgement. And if a blind man leads a blind man, both will fall into a pit. And whoever shows partiality and whoever receives partiality will both be judged with a single judgement. (*EpAp* 47.1–5)[16]

---

[14] The Matthean passage has also shaped *GLuke* 17.3–4 (cf. *GMt* 18.15, 21–22), where it is assumed that reproof will normally lead to repentance and forgiveness, and *Didache* 15.3, where reproof is to be carried out ὡς ἔχετε ἐν τῷ εὐαγγελίῳ – i.e. the *Gospel of Matthew*, though Niederwimmer is unduly sceptical about this (*Didache*, 204). On Luke's use of material in *GMatthew* 18, see my *Gospel Writing: A Canonical Perspective*, 210–12.

[15] Probably εὐεργέτης in the original Greek, as in *GLuke* 22.25.

[16] The themes of partiality towards the rich and rebuking sin both occur within the *Epistle of James*, but separately from one another (*Jas* 2.1–9; 5.19–20). As in *EpAp*, showing preferential treatment to the rich is a serious matter: 'If you show partiality,

That judgement, enacted by Jesus himself, will exemplify precisely the impartiality that was lacking when the sinner remained unchallenged and uncorrected. Jesus the future judge models the practice that must be observed here and now within his community: 'Consider how it is with the judgement! For truly I say to you, in that day I will neither fear the rich nor have pity on the poor' (*EpAp* 47.7–8). In this he observes the commandment of the Father who sent him:

> For my Father said to me, 'My Son, on the day of judgement you shall neither be ashamed before the rich nor pity the poor, but according to the sin of each you shall deliver them to eternal punishment.'   (*EpAp* 26.4)

Like Jesus, his followers must not be influenced by wealth and status as they enforce communal norms. Nor should they be influenced in the opposite direction, by lack of wealth or status as though poverty were virtuous in itself. The communal practice that determines salvation or condemnation on the Day of Judgement coincides with that final and decisive act of judgement itself.

If the Son of God himself needs to be warned by his Father not to show partiality, the existence of a status differential within the Christian community must be a major and pressing problem for the author of the *Epistula*. The problem arises from the fact that the rich 'do not do my commandments but delight in their wealth' (46.1). This deficiency is also noted in the *Shepherd of Hermas*, which speaks of believers (πιστοί) who become rich (πλουτήσαντες) and who are said to remain in the faith without doing the works of the faith (*Sim.* 8.9.1). The context here is an elaborate judgement scene in which each person is given a stick cut from a gigantic willow-tree, which is planted and watered to see if there is still life in it (*Sim.* 8.1–11). This judgement is presided over by the Angel of the Lord rather than the Son of God (*Sim.* 8.1.2), and it seems to take place here and now rather than at the eschaton, for there is still opportunity to repent. The rich who fail to perform the works of faith receive back sticks partly green but mostly dry. Elsewhere they are depicted as round stones useless for the construction of the Tower that represents the Church until they become square: for 'those who are rich in this world, except their wealth be cut away from them, cannot

---

you commit sin and are convicted by the law as transgressors' (*Jas* 2.9). Both texts are hostile to the rich, though the author of *EpAp* cannot match Ps-James's prophetic rhetoric (cf. *Jas* 2.6–7, 5.1–6; *EpAp* 46.1).

be useful [εὔχρηστοι] to the Lord' (*Vis.* 3.6.6).[17] They possess faith but nothing else of any worth, for they are 'preoccupied with business matters and wealth and heathen friendships [φιλίαις ἐθνικαῖς] and many other of the concerns of this world' (*Mand.* 10.1.4). Although they are citizens of the heavenly city, they fail to live by its laws and devote themselves instead to 'fields and expensive furnishings and buildings and superfluous rooms' (*Mand.* 10.1.1). Thus they place themselves at severe risk of being stripped of their heavenly citizenship.[18]

Hermas and the author of the *Epistula* are agreed in their condemnation of the rich who possess faith without works.[19] The difference is that the *Shepherd* is concerned with the problem that wealth poses for individual salvation whereas the *Epistula* is concerned with its threat to the well-being of the entire community. If the rich are not challenged when they 'delight in their wealth' and neglect the laws of the heavenly city, their conduct is normalized. The believing community acquiesces in the proposition that status differentials within the wider society also have their legitimate place within the church. Indeed, it may be proud of the fact that it numbers powerful and influential people among its members. Wealth, then, is a trial and temptation not just for the individuals who possess it but for the community as a whole, and the individual and communal response to this problem will determine nothing less than the outcome of the final judgement.

The Christian community views its wealthy members as a problem, but it also needs them and the resources they can provide to support its disadvantaged and impoverished members. On one occasion when Hermas is walking in the country, the angelic Shepherd appears to him as he contemplates an elm-tree around which a vine is

---

[17] Carolyn Osiek notes that the 'story about the cosmic willow and the fate and meaning of its branches given to various sorts of people... is a recasting with different images of the building of the tower. As there each kind of stone represents some class of believers, so here each kind of branch rendered corresponds to some group of believers' (*The Shepherd of Hermas: A Commentary* [Minneapolis, MN: Fortress Press, 1999], 290).

[18] On rich and poor in *Hermas*, see M. Dibelius, 'Der Hirt des Hermas', in M. Dibelius, et al., *Die Apostolischen Väter*, IV, Handbuch zum Neuen Testament Ergänzungsband (Tübingen: J.C. B. Mohr (Paul Siebeck), 1923), 555–56, where *Hermas*'s view is compared with that of *James*.

[19] On Hermas as an individual and his social context, see Peter Lampe, *From Paul to Valentinus: Christians at Rome in the first two Centuries*, Eng. trans. (Minneapolis, MN: Fortress, 2003), 218–36.

growing, and explains that 'these two trees are put there as a type for the servants of God' (*Sim.* 2.1–2). The vine is dependent on the elm, for if it grows along the ground its fruit will rot; yet the elm is also dependent on the fruitbearing vine to counteract its own sterility.[20] This is an image of the mutually beneficial partnership between the rich man (the elm) and the poor man (the vine). The rich man provides material support to the poor man, but his concern for this-worldly affairs impoverishes his own spiritual life; his prayer and confession are infrequent and ineffectual. In contrast, the poor man is rich in spiritual resources; his thankful prayers on behalf of his wealthy benefactor are acceptable to the Lord. It is an ideal partnership: each side receives from the other what it lacks in itself. 'The poor, interceding with the Lord for the rich, complement their riches, and again the rich, supplying the needs of the poor, complement their prayers' (*Sim.* 2.8).

The author of the *Epistula* is more critical of wealth than the author of the *Shepherd*, but he too acknowledges in passing the role of the benefactor and the reciprocal nature of the relationship with the beneficiary. Hermas's emphasis on prayer for the benefactor is replaced by 'reproof', a willingness to criticize a benefactor's inappropriate conduct. Otherwise the relationship of the benefactor to the beneficiary would be a case of the blind leading the blind, so that both fall into a pit (*EpAp* 47.4; cf. *GMt* 15.14b). If the beneficiary is willing to reprove his benefactor and if the reproof is accepted, the result will be a mutually beneficial relationship analogous to the one in Hermas's parable; the benefactor 'will be saved and the one who reproved him will be awarded eternal life' (*EpAp* 47.2). Also noteworthy here is the recognition that the role of benefactor requires only that one should have enough to spare, not that one need necessarily be rich: 'If one who is not rich, having a little property, gives to the poor and needy, people will call him a benefactor' (46.3).[21] The demand that every member of the community should play an active role in enforcing communal norms has its context within an economy that aims at the salvation of all. Every time correction is impartially given and received, the likelihood

---

[20] On the agricultural background to this image, see Osiek, *Shepherd*, 162.

[21] As Justin Meggitt notes (with particular reference to Phoebe, *Rom* 16.1–2), 'patronage ties extended throughout the different strata of Roman society and its language could be applied to relationships between a wide variety of classes' (*Paul, Poverty and Survival*, Studies of the New Testament and Its World [Edinburgh: T&T Clark, 1998], 147).

diminishes of falling victim to the final and definitive act of impartial judgement.

7.2   Justice or Mercy?

After the lengthy preview of Paul's future ministry in *EpAp* 31–33, the disciples express their satisfaction with everything they have so far heard:

> And we said to him again, 'Lord, what great things you
> have spoken to us and announced to us and revealed to us,
> things never yet spoken, and in everything you have com-
> forted us and been gracious to us! For after your resurrec-
> tion you revealed all this to us, so that we might truly
> be saved.'   (*EpAp* 34.1–2)

The author here asserts the crucial importance of the post-resurrection setting for the revealed knowledge that leads to salvation, thereby enhancing the importance of his own text in relation to gospel literature focusing primarily on Jesus' earlier ministry. The *Epistula* includes a selection of miracle stories from the period of the ministry (*EpAp* 5), but Jesus' teaching activity is ignored – except to contrast its parabolic obscurity with Easter clarity (32.2–3) and to cancel the requirement not to 'call anyone your father on earth' (41.4; cf. *GMt* 23.9).

The Easter revelations have not yet concluded. The disciples now request that another gap in their understanding be filled: 'You have told us only that there will be signs and wonders in heaven and on earth before the end of the world comes – so teach us, that we may know' (*EpAp* 34.3). In response, Jesus speaks of unprecedented and catastrophic events that will disrupt the regular order of the heavens, heralded by the blast of an angelic trumpet: stars appearing during the day or falling like fire, sun and moon fighting with each other, thunder, lightning, and fiery hailstones (34.7–9). The author does not dwell on these cosmic fantasies, choosing to emphasize an event closer to home – a plague or epidemic that early readers in Asia Minor may have experienced at first hand (*EpAp* 34.10–13; 36.1–12).[22] The

---

[22] The reference is probably to the Antonine plague (165 onwards), which in combination with Jesus' announcement of a parousia after 150 years (*EpAp* 17.2ᵉᵗʰ) suggests that *EpAp* may be dated to *c*.170. See the Introduction to this volume and literature cited there.

plague will be heralded by an earthquake in which 'cities shall fall and people shall die in their ruins' (*EpAp* 34.10), but there will be many who survive that catastrophe only to succumb to the next.[23] The plague will kill so many that it becomes impossible to mark their passing with the customary funeral rites (34.9–13). These events express the divine wrath against human wickedness, and there is more to come (35.1): deceivers and enemies of righteousness (35.5–9), universal warfare (37.2), a breakdown of social order (37.3–5).

All this will be experienced by 'believers and unbelievers' alike (34.7). There is no encouragement to believers to see these trials as a sign of hope, in contrast to the Lukan Jesus' exhortation, 'When these things begin to take place, look up and raise your heads because your redemption draws near' (*GLk* 21.28). As this scenario for the Last Days develops, the disciples become increasingly concerned. The lack of differentiation between believers and unbelievers is the topic of their first intervention: 'Lord, what then of those who hope in you?' (35.2). When this fails to elicit a satisfactory response, they point out that a deity who neglects to care for his own exposes himself to reputational damage: 'Lord, will the Gentiles not say, "Where is their God?"' (36.1). A series of further questions express mounting anxiety that the last generation of believers will be subjected to extreme suffering in this world and may even be deprived of salvation in the next:

> And we said to him, 'Will their departure from the world be through the plague that torments them?' (36.3)

> And we said to him, 'Lord, will they be like those who do not believe? And will you punish those who survive the plague in the same way?' (36.9)

---

[23] Aelius Aristides refers to 'the many severe earthquakes' that devastated cities in Asia Minor during the proconsulship of Albus (*Or.* 49.38), and G. W. Bowersock has argued convincingly that these earthquake events are to be dated to the year 161 ('The Proconsulate of Albus', *Harvard Studies in Classical Philology* 72 [1968], 289–94). One such event is the subject of a recently published inscription in which Antoninus Pius commends the citizens of Ephesus for their recovery from 'the earthquakes that befell your city [ἐπὶ τοῖς συμβᾶσι τῇ ὑμετέρᾳ πόλει σεισμοῖς]'. For the text and analysis, see Christopher Jones, 'A Letter of Antoninus Pius and an Antonine Rescript concerning Christians', *Greek, Roman, and Byzantine Studies* 58 (2018), 67–76; 68. Charles Hill assembles evidence of earthquakes in Asia Minor from earlier in the second century ('The *Epistula Apostolorum*: An Asian Tract from the Time of Polycarp', *Journal of Early Christian Studies* 7 [1999], 1–53; 41–43). While this evidence makes it possible for Hill to date *EpAp* 'somewhere in the period 117–48' (51), the correlation of earthquake and plague fits the 160s particularly well.

> And we said to him again, 'Lord, so this is the fate of those
> who survive, that they fail to attain life?'   (36.11)

Jesus is unmoved by these protests. When believers are tormented
by the plague, they are being tested: 'If there is faith within them
and if they remember these words of mine and obey my commandments, they will be raised' (36.5). On the other hand, 'If they believe
in my name but acted as sinners, they have behaved like
unbelievers' (36.10). In these exchanges between Jesus and his
disciples, the *Epistula* dramatizes the tradition that, faced with the
stresses of the Last Days, 'the love of many will grow cold' and that
'the one who endures to the end will be saved' (*GMt* 24.12–13). In
EpAp this love grown cold is interpreted as love turned to hatred;
endurance means enduring that hatred (cf. 38.4–5). Those who
believe and obey will be a minority, persecuted by those who also
believe yet acquiesce in the anti-Christian norms promoted by
'rich sinners':

> There are some of those who believe in my name but follow
> evil and vain teaching. And people will follow them and obey
> their wealth, their wickedness, their drunkenness, and their
> bribery; and there will be partiality among them.
>
> (*EpAp* 37.4–5)
>
> Woe to those who walk in arrogance and boasting! For their
> end is perdition.   (*EpAp* 38.7)

At this point the disciples' increasingly agitated questions give way
to open protest: 'Lord, it is in your power not to allow these things to
befall them!' (39.1). 'These things' probably refers not just to the
sufferings of the elect among the believers but to the entire community's sufferings in the plague and other disasters – a test of obedience that will divide the community, separating those who endure
from those whose love turns to hate. Why must the final generation
of believers be tested in this way, causing this fatal division?
Unusually, Jesus responds by way of a question:

> He answered and said to us, 'How will the judgement take
> place for either the righteous or the unrighteous?'
>
> (*EpAp* 39.2)

If Jesus were to intervene as his disciples have demanded, sparing the
believing community the trial that would divide it, what need would
there be for a final judgement in which the righteous are

differentiated from the unrighteous?[24] Here too it is the judgement of the community that is in view. It has already been established that at the judgement it is only 'a selection of believers' who will be saved, elected for salvation on the basis of their steadfast obedience to the divine commandments, whereas the rest will be delivered up to eternal punishment (26.2, 4). If the division within the community is to be finally exposed at the judgement, then it must have manifested itself during its existence on earth. Influential teachers will arise, transgressors of the commandments 'teaching with different words those who believe in me rightly' and causing some to fall away and to incur eternal punishment (29.1). It is necessary for this to happen,

> so that those who do evil and those who do good may be revealed. And in this way the judgement will reveal those who do these works, and according to their works they will be judged and delivered to death. (*EpAp* 29.3–4)

All this takes place within the divine plan, which will not be emended to secure the happy outcome for all that the disciples have demanded, entailing the cancellation of the final act of separation between the righteous and the unrighteous.

A further objection follows, however, and it is put into the mouths of those whom the judgement will condemn to everlasting punishment:

> We said to him, 'Lord, in that day they will say to you, "You did not separate righteousness and unrighteousness, light and darkness, evil and good!"' (*EpAp* 39.3)

Separating righteousness and unrighteousness, light and darkness, evil and good is precisely the point of the judgement. The objection asks why righteousness and unrighteousness, light and darkness, evil

---

[24] The argument recalls *Romans* 3.5–6, where Paul refutes the objector he has just invented, arguing that it is false to claim that a God who inflicts his wrath on sinners would show himself unjust, since that would call into question the non-negotiable fact of the future impartial divine judgement. The similarity to *EpAp* is generic, for both authors exploit diatribal conventions in simulating a 'dialogue of questions and answers between the author and an imaginary interlocutor' (Stanley Stowers, *A Rereading of Romans: Justice, Jews, and Gentiles* [New Haven, CT and London: Yale University Press, 1994], 162). In both cases the author (or Jesus as his proxy) responds to an objection (*Rom* 3.5; *EpAp* 39.1) with a counter-question (*Rom* 3.6; *EpAp* 39.2, cf. 39.3 + 9–10), a characteristic feature of diatribe style (so R. Bultmann, *Der Stil der Paulinischen Predigt und die kynisch-stoische Diatribe* [Göttingen: Vandenhoeck & Ruprecht, 1910], 11, 85–86).

and good were allowed to mingle in the first place, in such a way as to expose righteousness, light, and goodness to corruption by unrighteousness, darkness, and evil. The condemned challenge the justice of the judge who placed them in a world where sin was an ever-present possibility and then held them solely responsible for succumbing to it. Jesus – for he is the future judge – has his answer ready. No one is compelled to sin, for to be human is to be free to choose and thus to be accountable for one's choice:

> Then he said, 'I will answer them, saying: "Adam was given the power to choose one of the two. And he chose the light and stretched out his hand for it, but the darkness he rejected and cast it from him. So all people have the power to believe in the light, which is the life of the Father who sent me."'   (*EpAp* 39.4–6)

That human freedom to choose good or evil derives from Adam was earlier noted by Ben Sira in a similar context, in response to an allegation of divine complicity in human sin (*Sir* 15.11–20). We are not to attribute our failure to keep to the right way to the Lord, for in Adam he endowed us with freedom to choose: 'He has placed before you fire and water; stretch out your hand for whichever you wish' (*Sir* 15.16). In *EpAp* light and darkness take the place of fire and water, but the image of stretching out the hand is common to both texts. Also common to both is the assumption that every human being starts from the same situation as Adam at the time of his creation. There is no suggestion that an original act of disobedience has fundamentally altered the situation of Adam's descendants. The difference is that Ben Sira remains within the bounds of the *Genesis* story, where Adam chooses death rather than life (cf. *Sir* 15.17), whereas the author of *EpAp* has him making the correct choice – light rather than darkness, good rather than evil, righteousness rather than unrighteousness (cf. *EpAp* 39.3). The idea seems to be that, though expelled from paradise, Adam takes with him the knowledge of good and evil and must henceforth live on the basis of that knowledge, choosing good and rejecting evil.[25]

---

[25] On *EpAp*'s positive view of Adam, cf. M. Hornschuh, *Studien zur Epistula Apostolorum*, Patristische Texte und Studien 5 (Berlin: de Gruyter, 1965), 68–70. Hornschuh notes Tertullian's belief that Adam would be saved and Irenaeus's outrage at Tatian's rejection of that belief (69n.), but (more questionably) discusses this topic under the heading of 'Jewish influences' on *EpAp*.

A similar idea occurs in the *Vita Adae et Euae*, an early Christian text that recounts the story of Adam and Eve after their expulsion from the Garden of Eden.[26] An important role is assigned to Seth, whose birth is announced not by Eve, as in *Genesis* 4.25 ('God has raised up for me another seed in place of Abel, whom Cain killed') but by Adam: 'And Adam said to Eve, "Behold, I have begotten a son in place of Abel, whom Cain killed"' (*Vita* 24.2). While Adam will later beget thirty more sons and thirty daughters (24.3–4), it is to Seth alone that he recounts a vision received while at prayer with Eve, in which he was taken up into the presence of God by the archangel Michael and pleaded for restoration to the divine favour. In response, he receives a promise of godly offspring, a reference to Seth and his descendants:

> Because your days are numbered you have become one who loves knowledge [*factus es diligens scientiam*], and therefore there shall never be taken away from your seed one to serve me. (*Vita* 27.3)

Eating from the Tree of knowledge has caused Adam's days to be numbered, yet he is commended here for valuing the knowledge he received, presumably by pursuing the good and rejecting evil. The forbidden fruit has brought gain as well as loss. In gratitude, Adam acclaims God as 'the true light shining above every light [*super omne lumen fulgens vera lux*], living life...' (*Vita* 28.2). In the language of the *Epistula*, Adam 'chose the light and stretched out his hand for it, but the darkness he rejected and cast it from him' (*EpAp* 39.5). The 'power to choose one of the two' (39.4) was bestowed on him by the fruit of the Tree of knowledge, not by the earlier prohibition.

That power has been passed on to Adam's descendants: 'All people have the power to believe in the light, which is the life of the Father who sent me' (*EpAp* 39.6). Thus,

---

[26] For introductions to this text, see M. D. Johnson, 'Life of Adam and Eve', in James H. Charlesworth (ed.), *The Old Testament Pseudepigrapha*, 2 vols. (London: Darton, Longman & Todd, 1985), 249–95; 249–57; Simon J. Gathercole, 'The Life of Adam and Eve (Coptic Fragments)', in Richard Bauckham, James R. Davila, and Alexander Panayotov (eds.), *Old Testament Pseudepigrapha: More Noncanonical Scriptures*, vol. 1 (Grand Rapids, MI: Eerdmans, 2013), 2.22–27. In the present context, the discussion is confined to the Latin form of this text rather than the (perhaps earlier) Greek, otherwise know as the *Apocalypse of Moses*.

> everyone who believes and does the works of light will live
> through them. But if there is someone who confesses that he
> belongs to the light while doing the works of darkness, such
> a person has no defence, nor will he lift up his face to look at
> the Son of God, which is I myself. For I shall say to him, 'As
> you sought you have found, and as you asked you have
> received! Why did you condemn me, O man? Why did you
> proclaim me and deny me? And why did you confess me and
> deny me?' Therefore every person has the power to live or to
> die, and so the one who keeps my commandments will
> become a son of light, that is, of the Father who is
> within me.   (*EpAp* 39.7–11)

As in the earlier judgement scenario in *EpAp* 26, the author is
preoccupied here with the fate of those who believe or confess yet
fail to obey and who thus 'deny'. The disciples imagine that such
people will accuse Jesus of placing them in an environment in which
righteousness, light, and good are undermined by the presence of
unrighteousness, darkness, and evil (39.3). Jesus has his answer
ready. Like Adam, the objectors were free to choose; unlike Adam,
they chose wrongly. Now they must face the eternal consequences,
for Jesus became flesh and suffered in order to teach 'that those who
are called will be saved and that those who are lost will be lost
eternally and tormented alive and punished in their flesh and their
soul' (*EpAp* 39.13).

Jesus' imagined refutation of objectors who question his right to
punish them fails to silence his disciples. In their collective advocacy
role on behalf of the condemned, they even succeed in extracting
from Jesus a double concession. The prayer of the righteous for the
unrighteous is legitimate and effective, and it may be addressed
directly to Jesus himself and not just to his more distant Father:

> We said to him, 'Lord, truly we are concerned for them!'
> And he said to us, 'You do well, for the righteous are
> concerned for sinners and pray for them, interceding with
> my Father.' Again we said to him, 'Lord, so does no one
> intercede with you yourself?' And he said to us, 'Yes, and
> I will hear the prayer the righteous make for them.'
>   (*EpAp* 40.1–4)

The dialogue on the fate of the unrighteous breaks off at this
point, but it will shortly be resumed and the issue of intercession

on behalf of the unrighteous is again to the fore. Will it still be possible for the righteous to intercede effectively for the unrighteous on the Day of Judgement? How can the righteous enjoy the promised eternal life while aware that others are excluded from it? These questions arise from Jesus' Parable of the Wise and Foolish Virgins (*EpAp* 43.1–10; cf. *GMt* 25.1–12). Remarkably, the message that Jesus intends to communicate through the parable is quite different from what the disciples actually hear.

Initially, Jesus provides only a brief summary of the parable as a sequel to his previous outline of the disciples' future ministry as fathers, servants, and teachers (*EpAp* 41.1–42.7). As they exercise this ministry, they

> will be like the wise virgins who watched and did not sleep but went out to meet the Lord and entered with him into the wedding-chamber. But the foolish ones were unable to watch but slept. (*EpAp* 43.1–2)

In this version of the parable the wise are those who are kept awake as they waited for the bridegroom, the foolish, those who fell asleep. There is no reference to lamps or oil.[27] In the Matthean version all ten virgins sleep, and the wise are those who have brought extra oil for their lamps in case the bridegroom is delayed – which he is, in both versions.[28] Sleep here represents death, now regarded as inevitable in view of the indefinite delay to the parousia, and waking from sleep represents the resurrection of the dead. In the *EpAp* version, wakefulness and sleep are correlated with the presence and absence respectively of virtues necessary for effective leadership within the community. This is broadly in line with the close of the Matthean parable, with its exhortation, 'Watch therefore. . .' (*GMt* 25.13), out of place in its own context where sleep is identified with death rather than spiritual negligence.[29] While it is possible that *EpAp* is

---

[27] References to lamps in *EpAp* 43.1[eth] are clearly due to secondary Matthean influence.

[28] In neither version of the story is there a role for a bride. This is disputed by Hornschuh, who sees here a major difference from the Matthean version: 'Dort [in *GMt*] sind die Jungfrauen nichts als Gespielinnen der Braut, hier [in *EpAp*] sind sie die Bräute des Bräutigams' (*Studien*, 21). See Additional Notes on 43.1 for linguistic arguments against this interpretation.

[29] The incongruity that *GMatthew* 25.13 fits better with *EpAp* 43.1 than with its Matthean context is noted by Hills, *Tradition and Composition*, 150. The exhortation has been taken over from the conclusion of the Markan eschatological discourse, of which the Matthean parable is an extension (cf. *GMk* 13.33–37; *GMt* 24.42).

dependent on the Matthean parable, eliminating the lamps and reverting to a metaphorical rather than euphemistic use of the sleep-motif, it is at least equally likely that it preserves features of an alternative, pre- or non-Matthean version of the parable.[30]

> And we said to him, 'Lord, who are the wise and who are the foolish?' He said to us, 'There are five wise. Of them the prophet said, "They are children of God." Hear their names!... The five wise are Faith and Love and Grace, Peace and Hope. Those who possess these among those who believe will be guides to those who believe in me and in the one who sent me.'   (*EpAp* 43.3–4, 6–7)

Who then are the foolish?

> He said to us, 'Hear their names: Knowledge, and Wisdom, Obedience, Patience, and Mercy. For it is these that slept among those who believe and confess me. Since those who slept did not fulfil my commandments, they will remain outside the kingdom...'   (*EpAp* 43.16–44.1)

These are the virtues that 'slept' (i.e. that were lacking) in those who will be excluded from the kingdom when subjected to scrutiny at the judgement.[31] The message Jesus intends the parable to communicate is straightforward. The ten qualities he seeks in his followers are faith, love, grace, peace, hope, knowledge, wisdom, obedience, patience, and mercy.[32] It is the presence or absence of these qualities that will determine the outcome of the judgement that leads either to life eternal or everlasting torment.[33] Thus the sleepers in the parable are said to represent both those who lack crucial virtues and those

---

[30] Cf. Hills's source-critical analysis of *EpAp* 43–45, *Tradition and Composition*, 146–68.

[31] The author's point is that virtues such as knowledge and wisdom were lacking in the foolish, not that these qualities are to be judged negatively as marks of heretical opponents – as implausibly argued by Hornschuh, *Studien*, 21–29.

[32] Cf. Hermas, *Vis.* 3.8.3–8, where the tower under construction (the church) is supported by seven women who personify Faith, Restraint, Simplicity, Knowledge, Innocence, Reverence, and Love, each of which gives birth to the next. In *EpAp* the ten are sisters (43.11, 13; 45.5, 7), daughters of God (45.6, cf. 43.4).

[33] Like its Matthean equivalent, the parable has to do with eschatological judgement, not with disciplinary procedures within the community as argued by Schmidt, *Gespräche Jesu*, 380–82. It is sexual sin or apostasy that could lead to exclusion from an early Christian community, not lack of knowledge or wisdom.

who neglect Jesus' commandments; and these two groups are one and the same.[34]

The disciples' reaction to this parable is not at all what was intended. Even as Jesus announces that the ten virgins represent virtues, the disciples continue to regard them as people. Between the appeal, 'Hear their names!', and the naming of the wise a parenthetical note is inserted: 'But we were weeping and distressed at heart about those who slept' (*EpAp* 43.5). The disciples' distress anticipates that of the foolish, as becomes clear when Jesus resumes the retelling of the parable:

> For I am the Lord and I am the bridegroom whom they received, and they entered the bridegroom's house and reclined with me in my wedding-chamber and rejoiced. But as for the five foolish ones who slept, they awoke and came to the door of the wedding-chamber and knocked, for it had been shut against them. Then they wept and grieved that they did not open to them. (*EpAp* 43.8–10)

In the Matthean version it is the bridegroom who refuses to admit the foolish virgins, denying all knowledge of them when they appeal to him to 'open to us' (*GMt* 25.11–12). In the *Epistula* they weep because '*they*' – their wise sisters – 'did not open to them.' When the great separation takes place on the Last Day, the unrighteous can expect no help from the righteous. There is a corresponding lack of solidarity in the Matthean parable: the wise turn down the request to share their spare oil in case they no longer have enough for themselves, and recommend a visit to the shops – which turns out to be futile (*GMt* 25.8–10). By refusing to share their oil or open the door, the wise show no sympathy for their sisters' predicament. The disciples find this implausible and unacceptable:

> We said to him. 'Lord, those wise sisters of theirs who were in the bridegroom's house, did they fail to open to them? And did they not grieve for them or did they not plead with

---

[34] Hills argues that the sleepers are 'false teachers' and those influenced by them, characterized by their failure to observe the commandments; parallels are cited from *1 John* (*Tradition and Composition*, 155–65). The problem of 'other teachings' that go 'beyond what you have told us' and lead people astray is associated with transgression of Jesus' commandments in *EpAp* 29.1–4, but there is no sign of a specific group of teachers in the discussion of the parable in ch. 43–45. The 'other teachings' of ch. 29 evidently have to do with conduct rather than beliefs. In spite of the double reference to Simon and Cerinthus (1.2; 7.1–3), this text seems unconcerned about heresy.

> the bridegroom on their behalf to open to them?' He
> answered, saying to us, 'They were not yet able to find grace
> on their behalf.' We said to him, 'Lord, when will they enter
> for their sisters' sake?' Then he said to us, 'Whoever is shut
> out is shut out.' And we said to him, 'Lord, is this matter
> decided?...'   (*EpAp* 43.11–15)[35]

After identifying the foolish with the qualities they lack, Jesus
issues yet another threat of dire and irrevocable punishment for the
unrighteous, and the disciples now seem to acquiesce: 'And we said
to him, "Lord, you have revealed all things to us well"' (45.1). Yet
those five excluded virgins still weigh heavily on their minds:

> 'Those who watched and were with you, the Lord and
> bridegroom, surely they do not rejoice over those who
> slept?' And he said to us, 'They indeed rejoice that they
> entered with the bridegroom, the Lord, and they grieved
> over those who slept, for they are their sisters. For the ten
> are daughters of God the Father.'   (*EpAp* 45.3–6)

So Jesus is forced to concede that there is enduring solidarity
between the wise and the foolish, the righteous and the unrighteous,
in spite of the eschatological act that divides them by assigning them
to opposing categories and destinies. The joy of the saved will be
tempered by their grief over the unsaved, since they all belong to the
same family. Surely some resolution is needed to ensure an unam-
biguously happy ending to the story of salvation? But the authors of
that story – Jesus and his Father – think not:

> We said to him, 'Lord, it is in your power to be gracious to
> their sisters!' He said to us, 'That is not your affair but his
> who sent me, and I myself agree with him.'   (*EpAp* 45.7–8)

---

[35] The disciples' persistent questioning of Jesus' rigorous view of divine justice
recalls Ezra's dialogue with the angel Uriel on the same issue in *4 Ezra* 7. On this
passage, see my *Paul and the Hermeneutics of Faith* (London: T&T Clark, 2015²),
450–64. The issue of intercession for the unrighteous is featured in both texts (*4 Ezra*
7.102–15; *EpAp* 40.1–4, 43.11, 45.2–8).

Part III

Additional Notes on Text and Translation

ABBREVIATIONS

For details of manuscripts, see Chapter 2.

Bick–Hauler	Josef Bick, 'Wiener Palimpseste' (1908), Edmund Hauler, 'Zu den neuen lateinischen Bruchstücken' (1908)
Cop	Coptic version of *EpAp*, Coptic language
Cop^{ly}	Coptic, Lycopolitan (= Subakhmimic)
Cop^{sa}	Coptic, Sahidic
Crum	W. E. Crum, *A Coptic Dictionary*
Dillmann	C. F. A. Dillmann, *Lexicon Linguae Aethiopicae* (1865)
Duensing 1925	Hugo Duensing, *Epistula Apostolorum* (1925)
Duensing 1959	Hugo Duensing, 'Epistula Apostolorum', in Hennecke–Schneemelcher, *Neutestamentliche Apokryphen*³ (1959)
Duensing	Duensing 1925 and Duensing 1959
EpAp	*Epistula Apostolorum*
EpAp^{cop}	*Epistula Apostolorum*, Coptic version (in cases where *Cop* is ambiguous)
EpAp^{eth}	*Epistula Apostolorum*, Ethiopic (Ge'ez) version (in cases where *Eth* is ambiguous)
EpAp^{gk}	*Epistula Apostolorum*, underlying Greek version (in cases where *Gk* is ambiguous)
Eth, Eth	Ethiopic version of *EpAp*, Ethiopic language (Ge'ez)
(Eth), (Eth)	Ethiopic MSS other than the one(s) cited or under discussion
GD	*Galilean Discourse* (Guerrier's *Testament en Galilée*, chapters 1–11, as enumerated in Appendix)

Gk	Original Greek version, reconstructed, Greek language
Guerrier	Louis Guerrier (with Sylvain Grébaut), *Le Testament en Galilée de Notre-Seigneur Jésus-Christ* (1912)
GMt[eth-A]	Old Ge'ez gospel translation of *Gospel of Matthew* (see Zuurmond)
GMt[eth-B]	Revised Ge'ez translation of *Gospel of Matthew* (see Zuurmond)
GMt[sah], *GMk*[sah] . . .	Sahidic New Testament (see Horner)
Hauler	Edmund Hauler, 'Zu den neuen lateinischen Bruchstücken' (1908)
Hills	Julian V. Hills, *The Epistle of the Apostles* (2009)
Horner	G. W. Horner, *Coptic Version of the New Testament in the Southern Dialect*, 7 vols. (1911)
James	M. R. James, *The Apocryphal New Testament* (1924)
Lambdin	Thomas O. Lambdin, *Introduction to Classical Ethiopic (Ge'ez)*
Lampe	G. W. H. Lampe, *A Patristic Greek Lexicon*
Lat	Latin version (partially extant only in *EpAp* 12.1–13.7, 17.2–5)
Layton	B. Layton, *A Coptic Grammar*[2]
Leslau	*Comparative Dictionary of Ge'ez*
Müller	C. Detlef G. Müller, 'Epistula Apostolorum' (said to be a revision of the translation by Duensing), in Hennecke–Schneemelcher, *Neutestamentliche Apokryphen*[6] (1990) = *New Testament Apocrypha*, vol. 1, Eng. trans., ed. R. McL. Wilson (1991) = J. K. Elliott (ed.), *The Apocryphal New Testament* (2004[2]) = C. Markschies and Jens Schröter (eds.), *Antike christliche Apokryphen in deutscher Übersetzung*, vol. 1. *Evangelien und Verwandtes*, 2 (2012)
Müller/Taylor	Müller's German translation translated into English (see Taylor, below)
Pérès	Jacques-Noël Pérès, *L'Épître des Apôtres* (1994, Ethiopic only)

PG	Migne, Patrologia Graeca
Schmidt	Carl Schmidt, *Gespräche Jesu mit seinen Jüngern* (1919)
Schmidt-Wajnberg	Carl Schmidt (with Isaak Wajnberg), *Gespräche Jesu mit seinen Jüngern* (1919)[1]
Taylor	English translation of Duensing's German translation of *Epistula Apostolorum* as revised by Müller (Hennecke–Schneemelcher, *Neutestamentliche Apokryphen*[6] [1990]), in *New Testament Apocrypha*, vol. 1 (1991), J. K. Elliott, *The Apocryphal New Testament* (2004[2])
TestDom[eth]	*Testamentum Domini éthiopien* (cited by chapter enumeration, with line numbers in the edition by R. Beylot)
TestDom[syr]	*Testamentum Domini nostri Iesu Christi* (Syriac version: I. Rahmani)
Thompson	Sir Herbert Thompson, *The Gospel of St. John According to the Earliest Coptic Manuscript* (1924)
Trr, trr	most or all previous translators
Wajnberg	Isaak Wajnberg (translation of Ethiopic), in Schmidt, *Gespräche* (above)
Wechsler	Michael G. Wechsler, *Evangelium Iohannis Aethiopicum* (2005)
Zuurmond I, II	Rochus Zuurmond, *Novum Testamentum Aethiopice* I–II (1989)
Zuurmond III	Rochus Zuurmond, *Novum Testamentum Aethiopice* III (2001)

1.1 *What Jesus Christ revealed to his disciples <the book> and <how Jesus Christ revealed a book through {about} the company of the apostles, disciples of Jesus Christ* Eth> *to all]*

(1) *What Jesus Christ revealed to his disciples.* C G S omit the first occurrence of 'the book', read by A B K L and followed by trr: 'What Jesus Christ revealed to his disciples, the book.' This has been taken to mean either 'What Jesus Christ revealed to his disciples *as a*

---

[1] Used where the reference is to Wajnberg's work on the Ethiopic text within the Schmidt volume.

letter' (Duensing, Müller), or as a title: 'The Book of the Revelation of Jesus Christ to his Disciples' (Hills). Neither option is satisfactory: Jesus Christ did not present his revelation 'as a letter'. The word-order and the use of the verb *kaśata* rather than the noun *rə'əy* seems to rule out 'the Book of the Revelation. . .,' for which one would expect *maṣhafa rə'əy*.

(2) The addition of <the book> is best understood as one of two scribal attempts to turn the opening words into a title, the other of which is represented by S, assimilating to the title and opening of *GD* (see Appendix): '<The Testament of> what Jesus Christ <spoke and> revealed to his disciples.' The text-critical issue is ignored by Duensing, who follows Guerrier's L text without reference to the variants listed by Guerrier himself and by Wajnberg.

(3) *and* <*how Jesus Christ revealed a book through the company of the apostles, disciples of Jesus Christ*> *to all.* This appears to be a secondary attempt to improve on an earlier version of the opening ('What Jesus Christ revealed to his disciples, [the book]'). The two phrases have five items in common and in a similar sequence: the relative pronoun *za*-, 'revealed', 'Jesus Christ', 'disciples', and 'book', with the last two items reversed in the second phrase and with an expansion of 'to his disciples' into 'through the company of the apostles, disciples of Jesus Christ.' While the secondary phrase was apparently modelled on the first and probably intended to replace it, the manuscript tradition has combined them. If the secondary phrase is omitted, the prepositions that introduce the beneficiaries of the revelation match each other: *la-'ardā'ihu* and *la-kʷəllu* ('to his disciples' and 'to all'). This corresponds to the way in which, elsewhere in *EpAp*, Jesus addresses himself to his disciples but adds a reference to 'those who believe in me' (19.6, 29; 27.2; 35.4).

(4) There is no basis for translating *la-kʷəllu* as 'to the Catholics' ('den Katholischen'). See Dillmann 814–16, where 'catholic' is associated with *kʷəllu* only in a few references to 'the Catholic Church' (815). This egregious translation error stems from Duensing, who originally translated the phrase, 'den für alle (bestimmten)', glossing this in a footnote as 'katholischen' (Duensing 1925, 5). In the 1959 edition of the Hennecke–Schneemelcher collection this gloss is incorporated into the main text of the Duensing translation, where it persists in the 'careful revision' of C. D. G. Müller published in the 1990 edition of Hennecke–Schneemelcher and in the collections of New Testament apocrypha edited by Wilson, Elliott, and Markschies–Schröter.

(5) *Gk* may perhaps have read: ὃ ἀπεκάλυψεν Ἰησοῦς Χριστὸς τοῖς μαθηταῖς αὐτοῦ καὶ πᾶσιν. Cf. *1 Jn* 1.1–3, where the text opens with a series of ὅ-clauses.

1.2 *for there is in them a venom by which they kill people]*
For G's 'venom' (*ḥamz*) other MSS read 'deceit' (*ḥabl*). Cf. *EpAp* 35.6, 'Swift are their feet to shed blood, and their tongue weaves deceit [*ṣalḥut*], and the venom [*ḥamz*] of snakes is on their lips' (citing *Is* 59.7 and *Ps* 140.3; cf. *Rom* 3.15, 13bc). For evidence of the comparative reliability of G in relation to *(Eth)*, see Chapter 1 n. 89, and the *Additional Note* on 6.3.

1.3 *From what you have heard, the word of the gospel]*
Cf. *Acts* 15.7: Peter reminds his hearers how ἀφ᾽ ἡμερῶν ἀρχαίων ἐν ὑμῖν ἐξελέξατο ὁ θεὸς διὰ τοῦ στόματός μου ἀκοῦσαι τὰ ἔθνη τὸν λόγον τοῦ εὐαγγελίου καὶ πιστεῦσαι.

1.4 *What we have heard and remembered and written for the whole world we entrust to you, our sons and daughters, in joy.]*
An echo of *1 Jn* 1.3 is perceptible: ὃ ἑωράκαμεν καὶ ἀκηκόαμεν ἀπαγγέλλομεν καὶ ὑμῖν. Hills divides the text into two unconnected sentences, passing over *wa-* ('and') before 'written' and preferring 'greet' (*'amāḥnākamu*) to 'entrust'(*'amānḍanākamu*): 'What we have heard and remembered we have written for the whole world. We greet you in joy, our sons and daughters. . .' The Ge'ez is best taken as a single sentence, as above.

1.5 *In the name of God, ruler of the whole world, and of Jesus Christ, grace be multiplied to you]*
The epistolary greeting formula, 'In the name of God. . . and of Jesus Christ, grace. . .' is equivalent to the Pauline 'Grace and peace to you from God the Father and the Lord Jesus Christ' (*Rom* 1.1). 'God, ruler of the whole world' must render ὁ θεὸς ὁ παντοκράτωρ (cf. *Rev* 16.14). Dillmann 769 cites *1 Chron* 11.9; 17.7, etc., where *'agzi'abaḥer 'aḥāze kʷallu* renders κύριος παντοκράτωρ. In a Christian context θεός is more likely than κύριος. B L S read 'God <the Father>, ruler of the whole world', but the reference to 'the Father' may be an addition influenced by the Nicene Creed (ἕνα θεὸν πατέρα παντοκράτορα, cf. Irenaeus *Adv. haer.* 1.10.1), breaking the older link between θεός and παντοκράτωρ (cf. *Adv. haer.* 4.33.7). For 'grace be multiplied to you', *Gk* would have been χάρις πληθυνθείη ὑμῖν (cf. *1 Pet* 1.2; *2 Pet* 1.2; *Jude* 2). The closest parallels to the *EpAp* greeting are the incipits of *1 Clement* (χάρις ὑμῖν καὶ

εἰρήνη ἀπὸ <u>παντακράτορος</u> θεοῦ διὰ Ἰησοῦ Χριστοῦ <u>πληθυνθείη</u>) and Polycarp's letter to the Philippians (ἔλεος ὑμῖν καὶ εἰρήνη ἀπὸ θεοῦ <u>παντοκράτορος</u> καὶ Ἰησοῦ Χριστοῦ τοῦ σωτῆρος ἡμῶν <u>πληθυνθείη</u>).

2.1–2 John and Thomas and Peter and Andrew and James and Philip and Bartholomew and Matthew and Nathanael and Judas the Zealot and Cephas* to the churches of the east and the west, to those in the north and the south]

(1) '(We), John, Thomas… and Cephas, we have written (*or,* write) to the churches' (trr). The omission of *Eth* 'we have written/ write' brings the text into line with standard Greek epistolary formulations such as *Rev* 1.4, Ἰωάννης ταῖς ἑπτὰ ἐκκλησίαις ταῖς ἐν τῇ Ἀσίᾳ, which may here be echoed (Ἰωάννης καὶ Θωμᾶς… ταῖς ἐκκλησίαις…). It is hard to see how the senders' names could coexist with ἐγράψαμεν or γράφομεν. While an explicit reference to writing was probably also present here in *Cop*, this would have taken third person rather than first person form (cf. ⲉⲅⲅ̅ⲁⲓ, *1 Thes* 1.1, etc.).

(2) *Eth* mss differ slightly in the list of eleven apostles (see Hills), most significantly in the promotion of Peter over Thomas. The sequence followed here is already present in G, and may be compared with the lists of disciples in *GMt* 10.2–4, *GMk* 3.16–19, *GLk* 6.14–16, *Acts* 1.13, and Papias (Eusebius, *Hist. eccl.* 3.39.4). In spite of variations in order, the first eight names (John to Matthew in *EpAp*) are the same in all five cases, with the exception that Papias fails to mention Bartholomew. In *EpAp* John and Thomas are promoted from their fourth and seventh place in *GMatthew* to first and second place, but from Peter to Matthew the list otherwise follows the Matthean order. The sequence is almost entirely different in the parallel passage from Papias (enumeration = position in Matthean sequence): *2* Andrew, *1* Peter, *5* Philip, *7* Thomas, *3* James, *4* John, *8* Matthew. In ninth to eleventh place of full lists of the Twelve, it is the names themselves that differ: *9* James the son of Alphaeus (*GMt, GMk, GLk, Acts*), but Nathanael (*EpAp*, cf. *GJn* 1.45–51), compare Aristion (Papias); *10* Thaddaeus, also known as Lebbaeus = Levi in some mss (*GMt, GMk*), or Judas son of James (*GLk, Acts*; cf. *GJn* 14.22), Judas the Zealot (*EpAp*); *11* Simon the Cananaean (*GMt, GMk*), Simon the Zealot (*GLk, Acts*), Cephas (*EpAp*, cf. *GJn* 1.42). In *EpAp* the number of apostles is restored from eleven to twelve by the inclusion of Paul (see *EpAp* 31–33), although this text at no point makes the numerical issue explicit ('we the twelve' at 19.12 *Eth* is secondary).

(3) '... to those in the north and the south', following E G K (*la-'əlla*) rather than 'above' (*lā'la*). Trr '... *towards* the North and the South' is unlikely. Without knowledge of E G K, Guerrier emends *lā'la* to *la-'əlla*, 'à celles du Nord...'

2.3 ... *as we heard so have we written; and we touched him after he was raised from the dead, when he revealed to us what is great and wonderful and true]*
(1) The reading in G ('as we heard so have we written') seems preferable to that of A B E K L S ('as we have written so we have heard him'). The C reading ('as we have seen so we have written and we have heard him') may represent a conflation of the two.
(2) '... things great, astonishing, real' (Müller/Taylor). For *həlləw* as rendering ἀληθής, see Dillmann 6, citing *Wis* 1.17, 2.17; *Prov* 22.21; etc. For the first two attributes, cf. *Rev* 15.3, μεγάλα καὶ θαυμαστὰ τὰ ἔργα σου, κύριε ὁ θεὸς ὁ παντοκράτωρ.

3.1 *This we declare, that our Lord Jesus Christ is God, the Son of God]*
Trr, 'This we know', rendering the basic G-form of the verb (MSS A B C L), although Dillmann 728 gives *monstrare, ostendere, significare*, etc. for the G-form and *cognoscere, percipere* for the CG-form (MSS E G). The verb recurs in its G-form in an equally credal context in 9.1, where *Cop* reads ⲡⲉⲓ [ⲉⲧⲚ̄ⲣ̄]ⲘⲚ̄ⲧⲣⲉ ⲁⲭⲱϥ ϫⲉ (*Gk* perhaps τοῦτο μαρτυροῦμεν ὅτι).

3.3 *who is above all authorities, Lord of lords and King of kings, Power of the heavenly powers]*
Hills takes 'heavenly' (*samayāwi* = ἐπουράνιος) as a substantive to introduce the statement that follows: 'the Heavenly One who sits upon the cherubim [and seraphim]' (so also Müller/Taylor). While Hills rightly breaks with the practice of formatting this passage as a piece of unstructured prose, it is preferable to preserve the sequence of statements introduced by 'who' and to use this to determine the verse-divisions (3.3–12). ἐπουράνιος is only rarely used as a substantive with reference to God (cf *Ps* 67.15) but is frequent with reference to angels. For 'heavenly powers', cf. *GMt* 24.29 (αἱ δυνάμεις τῶν οὐρανῶν), Theodoret on *Phil* 2.10 (ἐπουράνια καλεῖ τὰς ἀοράτους δυνάμεις, cited by Lampe 542). While in *Eth* 'heavenly' is singular and 'powers' plural, this does not rule out the translation 'heavenly powers': plural nouns that do not refer to human beings 'may have either singular or plural verbs and modifiers, with no clear preferences' (Lambdin 27).

3.4 *who sits over the Cherubim <and Seraphim> at the right hand of the throne of the Father]*
This passage is drawn not only from *Ps* 109.1 LXX (Κάθου ἐκ δεξιῶν μου) but also from *Ps* 79.2 (ὁ καθήμενος ἐπὶ τῶν χερουβιν), a text understood christologically by Irenaeus (*Adv. haer.* 3.11.8). This phrase also occurs in *4 Kgdms* 19.15 = *Is* 37.16, *1 Chr* 13.6, *Ps* 98.1. The explicit reference to Christ here indicates that he rather than the Father is the subject of all the *who*-clauses in 3.3–12 (cf. 3.2). The omission of 'and Seraphim' is attested only in A but is likely to represent *Gk*, as the pairing of Cherubim and Seraphim appears to be relatively late (Lampe 1230, citing Athanasius and Dionysius the Areopagite; 'Seraphim and Cherubim' occurs in Origen). The reference in *1 Enoch* 14.11 to 'fiery Cherubim' (χερουβὶν πύρινα) suggests that the Cherubim are identified with the Seraphim of *Is* 6.2 (from Hebrew *śāraph*, 'burn').

3.5 *who by his word commanded the heavens and founded the earth and what is in it, and established the sea, and it did not cross its boundary, and depths and springs to gush forth and flow into the earth day and night]*
(1) For the sequence here, cf. Irenaeus, *Adv. haer.* 1.10.1: τὸν πεποιηκότα τὸν οὐρανὸν καὶ τὴν γῆν καὶ τὰς θαλάσσας καὶ πάντα τὰ ἐν αὐτοῖς (*Gk* in Epiphanius, *Pan.* 31.30.3). As in *EpAp*, this is the faith received παρὰ τῶν ἀποστόλων καὶ τῶν ἐκείνων μαθητῶν (ibid.). The *Eth* relative clauses probably represent *Gk* participles.
(2) In the E G reading selected here ('he established the sea and it did not cross its boundary'), 'established' rather than 'restrained' *(Eth)* represents *'aqama* rather than *'āqama*. The E G reading avoids repetition ('bounded... boundary') and views Christ as the creator of the sea rather than its controller. The change of subject from Christ/God ('he established') to the sea ('it did not cross') recalls *Jer* 8.22, τὸν τάξαντα ἄμμον ὅριον τῇ θαλάσσῃ, πρόσταγμα αἰώνιον καὶ οὐχ ὑπερβήσεται αὐτό.

3.11–12 *who spoke with the forefathers and prophets in parables and in truth; whom the apostles preached and the disciples touched]*
(1) *who spoke]* Less likely, 'of whom the patriarchs and the prophets spoke...' (Hills). For *tanāgara* as *colloqui*, speaking-with, cf. Dillmann 689–90.
(2) *in parables and in truth]* The translation follows Wajnberg in assuming a reference to parabolic and literal discourse within the Son's converse with the patriarchs and prophets. Trr generally link

'in truth' to the sequel: 'who spoke in parables through the patriarchs and prophets and in truth through him whom the apostles declared and the disciples touched' (cf. the S reading). *Eth* does not support the parallel here between 'through the patriarchs...' (*ba-*) and 'through him...' (*za-*, 'who[m]'): hence the emendation in Duensing 1925, 'Vor *zaḥawārjāt* [whom the apostles] ist *ba* [through] ein-zuschieben.' The emendation has been followed by subsequent trans-lators, and has the added disadvantage that it introduces a distinction between the one who spoke to the fathers (God) and the one proclaimed by the apostles (Christ). It is clear from *EpAp* 3.4 that Christ is the subject of the whole passage.

3.13 *And God the Son of God do we confess, the Word who became flesh of Mary,* <the virgin E G K, from the holy virgin* (Eth)>, *carried in her womb through the Holy Spirit]*

(1) *confess]* The verb *'amna* can mean 'believe' or 'confess' (Dillmann 735), but the latter is more likely in the absence of the preposition *ba-*. *Gk* may have been ὁμολογοῦμεν + acc. (cf. *1 Jn* 2.23; 4.2, 3; *2 Jn* 7).

(2) *the Word who became flesh]* This corresponds to the wording of *GJn* 1.14[eth] apart from the addition of the relative pronoun. If the *Gk* verbs in this credal passage were participles such as τὸν σαρκωθέντα (Irenaeus, *Adv. haer.* 1.10.1) or τὸν σαρκοποιηθέντα (Justin, *1 Apol.* 66.2), the proximity to *GJn* 1.14 would not be quite so clear.

(3) *Cop* probably lacked *the virgin* or *from the holy virgin* (cf. the reference to Mary in 14.5, where *Eth* adds 'the virgin' or 'the holy virgin'). 'Mary' appears without the addition of 'the virgin' in Ignatius *Eph* 7.2, 18.2; *Trall* 9.1; cf. *Smyr* 1.1. Trr overlook the syntactical differentiation between the construct 'flesh-of-Mary' and 'from the holy Virgin' ('das Wort, welches aus der heiligen Jungfrau Maria Fleisch wurde' [Duensing], 'the word which became flesh through the holy virgin Mary' [Müller/Taylor]). The reference to Mary belongs to the echo of *GJn* 1.14, and should not be separ-ated from it as it is by Wajnberg: '... dass er das Fleisch gewordene Wort ist, in Mariä, der heiligen Jungfrau, Leib getragen').

(4) The phrase translated 'carried in her womb' has caused unnecessary confusion. Guerrier proposes '(qui) a été porté dans son sein', although *māḥdan* translates μήτρα, 'womb', rather than 'breast' (Dillmann 138). 'Of Mary the holy virgin he took a body' (James) is at best a free paraphrase. The correct translation, 'in

ihrem Schosse getragen' (Duensing) is undone by Müller's misplaced emendation, 'in ihrem Geburtsschmerzen geborgen', 'hidden in her birthpangs'. The verb-form *taḍwra* derives from *ṣwr*, 'carry', not *sawwara* (*śawwara*), 'hide' (Dillmann 1297, 384). Substitutions of *ḍ* for *ṣ* are frequent (examples in Leslau 542, 543 [× 3], 544 [× 3], etc.), but not for *s* or *ś*. 'Birthpangs' does not seem to be attested for *māḫḍan* ('womb').

(5) There is a close parallel to the *EpAp* passage in Ignatius *Eph* 18.2: ὁ γὰρ θεὸς ἡμῶν Ἰησους ὁ Χριστὸς ἐκυοφορήθη ὑπὸ Μαρίας κατ̓ οἰκονομίαν [θεοῦ] ἐκ σπέρματος μὲν Δαυείδ πνεύματος δὲ ἁγίου. Cf. also Athanasius: ἐκυοφορήθη ἐννεαμηνιαῖον χρόνον ἐν τῇ μήτρᾳ τῆς παρθένου (*Serm. in nat. Chr.*, PLG 28.961). *Gk* may have read: τὸν λόγον τὸν σαρκωθέντα ἐκ Μαρίας, κυοφορηθέντα ἐν τη μητρᾷ αὐτῆς ἐκ πνεύματος ἁγίου.

3.14 *And not by the desire of the flesh but by the will of God was he born]*

(1) If participial constructions continued in *Gk* (cf. notes 3.5 (1) and 3.13 (2) above), this may originally have read: οὐκ ἐξ ἐπιθυμίας σαρκὸς ἀλλ᾽ ἐκ θελήματος θεοῦ γεννηθέντα. The echo of *GJn* 1.13 is clear: οἳ οὐκ... ἐκ θελήματος σαρκὸς οὐδὲ ἐκ θελήματος ἀνδρὸς ἀλλ᾽ ἐκ θεοῦ ἐγεννήθησαν. Similar language also occurs in the singular and in connection with the miraculous conception in Irenaeus (*Adv. haer.* 3.16.2, 19.2; 5.1.7). The singular reading of the Johannine passage is defended by Tertullian (*De car. Chr.* 19.1–5, 24.2) and attested in *Codex Veronensis* (b), where *GJn* 1.12–13 reads: ... *in nomine eius, qui non ex sanguine neque ex voluntate carnis nec ex voluntate viri sed ex deo natus est* (cf. also *Codex Fossatensis*, where an original singular reading has been corrected to a plural). The singular reading may have arisen from a popular adaptation of *GJn* 1.13 to serve as commentary on the miraculous birth traditions, subsequently read back into the Johannine text. Alternatively and perhaps equally likely, the plural reading may have adapted a pre-Johannine singular, echoed in *EpAp*. The *EpAp* passage indicates that the singular reading is not generated solely by the ambiguity of the Latin *qui* (= ὅς or οἵ).

(2) The E reading ('by the will of God was God born') arises from a double occurrence of the word for 'God' (*'ǝgzi'abǝḥer*) at the bottom of one page and the top of the next, and may be a scribal error.

3.15 *and he was swaddled in Bethlehem and manifested and nourished and grew up as we saw]*

After 'Bethlehem', many MSS read 'he was killed who was nourished'; B L S 'and manifested and nourished' (followed by trr). 'Killed' seems out of place here. If 'manifested' is part of the original text, the reference is probably to the Matthean star that guided the magi. 'As we saw' presumably refers only to Jesus' arrival at adulthood.

5.1 *and they invited him with his mother and brothers]*
'They invited him' (*ṣawwəʿəwwo*) probably renders a Greek passive, as in *GJn* 2.2 (ἐκλήθη δὲ καὶ ὁ Ἰησοῦς καὶ οἱ μαθηταὶ αὐτοῦ) where the Ethiopic translation has *ṣawwəʿəwwomu* ('they invited them').

5.2 *And the dead he raised, and paralytics {the paralytic* E K S} *he made to walk, and the man whose hand was withered he restored]*
While the third part of this summary passage refers to a specific individual (cf. *GMt* 12.9–14), the plural reading 'paralytics' is probably correct. In the second miracle summary, four classes of people are mentioned, without individual instances: 'Then the deaf he made to hear and the blind to see and those with demons he exorcized and those with leprosy he cleansed' (5.9). Here too some MSS introduce a singular: 'the one with leprosy' (G K). General statements are probably individualized because scribes recall individual stories (cf. *GMt* 9.1–8 for 'the paralytic', 8.1–4 for 'the one with leprosy').

5.6 *And he answered and said to us, 'I felt that power came forth upon me* B {*from me* L, *from upon me* (Eth)}.' *]*
Like *GLk* 8.46, *EpAp* explains how Jesus knows that the hem of his garment has been touched. The Lukan Jesus experiences power 'going out from me'. In *EpAp* the correct reading is probably 'upon me' (B), suggesting that the power to heal is from God and channelled through Jesus, rather than proceeding directly from Jesus. L's 'from me' assimilates to *GLuke*, and 'from upon me' (or 'from above me') is a conflation of the two earlier readings.

5.8 *Your faith has made you well]*
For 'has made you well' *EpAp*[eth] has *ʾaḥyawataki*, in agreement with *GMt*[eth-A] 9.22 against *GMt*[eth-B] which reads *ʾadḫanataki* ('has saved you'). *GMt*[eth-A] is the early Geʿez translation of *GMatthew*, revised in *GMt*[eth-B] to conform more closely to the Greek (see Zuurmond I-II, III); compare the relationship of the Old Syriac to the Peshitta, or the *Vetus Latina* to the Vulgate. The 'B' revision

applies to *GMatthew* alone, however, so it is in this gospel that a distinction between older and more recent readings may best be observed. *GMt*[eth-A] may date from the fourth century and is attested in MSS probably dating from *c.* 600;[1] *GMt*[eth-B] may have followed shortly afterwards. At *GMt* 9.22 both A and B translations are reasonable renderings of σέσωκέν σε, and *EpAp*'s agreement with *GMt*[eth-A] might be coincidental, as perhaps when it agrees with *GMt*[eth-B] 9.21 in selecting *lakafat* for 'touched' rather than the synonymous *gasasat(o)* (*GMt*[eth-A]). Yet other agreements between *EpAp* and *GMt*[eth-A] against *GMt*[eth-B] might establish a pattern, suggesting an Ethiopic translator influenced by a *Versio Antiqua* of *GMatthew* that was superseded in the latter part of the first millenium. This would confirm what is in any case highly probable, that *EpAp*[eth] is a relatively early translation directly from the original Greek rather than a medieval translation from a hypothetical Arabic – a view that has been unthinkingly repeated by successive scholars over the past hundred years. See the Notes on 5.10, 17, 19, below.

5.10 Before the day of our destruction arrives, have you come to drive us out?]

At *GMt* 8.29 most *Gk* MSS read, ἦλθες ὧδε πρὸ καιροῦ βασανίσαι ἡμᾶς (with some variation in the word-order), although ℵ* replaces 'torment' with 'destroy' (ἀπολέσαι) and W conflates the two readings. *GMt*[eth-B] renders πρὸ καιροῦ as 'before its time' (*za-'ənbala gizehu*), whereas *GMt*[eth-A] reads, 'before its time arrives' (*za-'ənbala yəbṣāḥ gizehu*). The added verb *yəbṣāḥ* also occurs in *EpAp*. Thus *EpAp*[eth] here agrees with *GMt*[eth-A] against both *GMt*[eth-B] and *GMt*[gk].

5.15–16 Let one of you cast a hook* into the deep and draw out a fish, and he will find denarii in it. Give them to the tax-collector for myself and for you.]

(1) *Eth* glosses the term 'hook' (*maqātən* = ἄγκιστρον [*GMt* 17.27]) with 'a snare of the throat' (*maśgərta 'anqār*), presumably for the benefit of readers not familiar with this form of fishing.

(2) *Denarii* renders *Eth dinār*, to be understood as a plural ('Give them...'). Taxes are to be paid by Jesus and all of his disciples, and

---

[1] See the defence of this dating (exceptionally early for *Eth* MSS) in Judith S. McKenzie and Francis Watson, *The Garima Gospels: Early Illuminated Gospel Books from Ethiopia* (Oxford: Manar al-Athar, 2016), 205–9.

not just by Jesus and Peter (as in *GMt* 17.27). There must have been a small hoard of coins in this fish's mouth.

5.17 *he commanded the men to recline]*
Here *EpAp*^eth agrees with *GMt*^eth-A 14.19 against *GMt*^eth-B in the reading *'azazomu la-sab'ə* rather than *'azaza sab'a.* The sense is not affected.

5.19 *twelve basketfuls of pieces]*
'Baskets' is rendered as *maśāyəmt* in *EpAp*^eth and *GMt*^eth-A 14.20 and as *mazār'ə* in *GMt*^eth-B. In conjunction with the similar pattern of agreement in *EpAp* 5.8, 10, 17 (see above), the *EpAp* translator's familiarity with the Old Geʻez gospels would seem to be established. See also the Note on 41.4, below.

6.2 *our ministry and our praise]*
'Our praise' is preferable to 'glory' (Duensing, Müller/Taylor) as a rendering of the plural *səbḥatina* ('hymns of praise'). On the basis of a single ms, Hills opts here for 'preaching' (*səbkatəna*).

6.3 *he will be merciful and gracious and save constantly, to the end of the age]*
(1) G reads *yəməḥḥər* (he will be merciful), misread in other mss as *yəmhar* or *yəmehher* (he will teach). 'He will be merciful and gracious' alludes to *Ex* 34.6 and *Ps* 102.8 (οἰκτίρμων καὶ ἐλεήμων).
(2) E G preserve the correct reading ('to the end of the age', cf. ἕως τῆς συντελείας τοῦ αἰῶνος [*GMt* 28.20]). This was amended to 'and to the age of the age without end' (B L S), and the two readings were conflated as 'and to the end of the age, the age without end' (A C).

7.1 *Cerinthus and Simon have gone out, they go around the world]*
(1) On folio 1 of *Cop* (**I, II**) a steep diagonal break has destroyed the endings of ll. 1–9 recto and the beginnings of ll. 1–9 verso, with up to 10 letters missing at the top of the page, diminishing to 1–3. There are also lacunae of 3–5 letters at the endings (recto) and beginnings (verso) of ll. 11–15.
(2) *Eth* 'gone out' corresponds to *Gk* ἐξῆλθον, and *Cop* should be restored as ⲁⲅⲉⲓ ⲁⲃ[ⲁⲗ]. Schmidt reads the doubtful letter before the lacuna as ⲛ, but the surviving traces seem to represent the upper half of a ⲃ (cf. ⲁⲃⲁⲗ, **I** 5). Similar language occurs in *2 Jn* 7, πολλοὶ πλάνοι ἐξῆλθον εἰς τὸν κόσμον. *Eth* 'go around' = *Gk* διοδεύουσιν (Dillmann 1000) = *Cop* [ⲥⲉⲙⲁ]ⲅⲉ ⲛ̄ (Crum 203b, 204b). Trr unnecessarily insert a purpose clause: '… sind gekommen, die Welt zu

durchwandeln' (Duensing) = '... have come to go through the world' (Müller/Taylor). The passage differentiates the heretics' departure from the Christian community (cf. *1 Jn* 2.19, ἐξ ἡμῶν ἐξῆλθαν) from their present wide-ranging missionary activity.

7.2 Cop *they pervert the wo[rd]s and the work, that is, Jesus Christ*, Eth *they pervert <utterly those who believe in the true> word and the work, that is, Jesus Christ]*

Here and elsewhere *Eth* shows a tendency to expansiveness and redundancy, but the underlying text appears to be similar to *Cop*. For the formula 'that is, Jesus Christ', cf. Ignatius *Eph* 17.2: διὰ τί δὲ οὐ πάντες φρόνιμοι γινόμεθα λαβόντες θεοῦ γνῶσιν, ὅ ἐστιν Ἰησοῦς Χριστός. In *EpAp*, Jesus Christ is identified with the divine speech and action.

7.3 *So beware of them]*

Eth 'Take heed and beware of them' (*'uquke wata'āqabəwommu*) may be an expansion of *Gk*, as the lacuna in *Cop* allows space for only a single imperative verb. *Gk* exemplars might here have read προσέχετε ἀπ' αὐτῶν (cf. *GMt* 6.1; 7.15; 10.17; 16.11) or ὁρᾶτε καὶ προσέχετε ἀπ' αὐτῶν (cf. *GMt* 16.6; *GMt*[eth-A] *'uqu wata'aqabu* [Zuurmond III, 168]). Ignoring *Eth* as usual, Schmidt fills the *Cop* lacuna with a personal pronoun: ⲛⲉⲓ ϭⲉ ⲛ̅[ⲧⲱⲧ]ⲛⲉ ⲛ̅ⲧⲏⲛⲉ ⲁⲃⲁⲗ ⲛ̅ⲙⲁⲩ. It is hard to see how this can mean '<Ihr> nun haltet euch ferne von diesen'. Given that the first letter (ⲛ according to Schmidt) is actually illegible, a better reconstruction would be: ⲛⲉⲓ ϭⲉ [ϯϩⲧⲏ]ⲛⲉ ⲛ̅ⲧⲏⲛⲉ ⲁⲃⲁⲗ ⲛ̅ⲙⲁⲩ, 'Beware of them'; cf. *GMt* 10.17[sah], ϯϩⲧⲏⲛ ⲉⲣⲱⲧⲛ ⲉⲃⲟⲗ ϩⲛ̅ ⲛ̅ⲣⲱⲙⲉ, 'But beware of men'. For *EpAp*'s warning to avoid heretics, cf. Ignatius *Trall* 7.1, φυλάττεσθε οὖν τοὺς τοιούτους.

7.4 *Their end will be judgement and eternal perdition]*

A *Cop* lacuna can better be filled by [ⲧⲟⲩ]ϩⲁⲉⲓ ('their end') than by Schmidt's [ⲙⲛ̅ ⲧ]ϩⲁⲉⲓ ('and the end'); cf. *Eth daḥārihu* ('his end').

9.1 *This we confess, that the Lord {Eth he} was crucified by {Eth in the days of} Pontius Pilate and Archelaus <Eth the Judge> between the two thieves <Eth he was crucified and with them <he was numbered, C> they took him down from <the tree of B L> the {his G} cross>, and he was buried in a place called 'Skull'.]*

(1) Taking the demonstrative as personal ('He') rather than impersonal ('This') results in a nonsensical sentence without a main verb ('He concerning whom we bear witness that this is the Lord who was crucified...' [Müller/Taylor]) and another unnecessary difference

from *Eth* ('He of whom we are witnesses we know as the one crucified...' [Müller/Taylor]).

(2) *Cop* 'by' and *Eth* 'in the days of' Pontius Pilate are probably alternative renderings of the Greek formula ἐπὶ Ποντίου Πιλάτου (*1 Tim* 6.13; Ignatius *Trall* 9.1; Justin, *1 Apol.* 46.1, *Try.* 30.3). The addition of Archelaus may be an attempt to identify the Herod associated with Jesus' crucifixion (Ignatius *Smyr* 1.3, ἐπὶ Ποντίου Πιλάτου καὶ Ἡρώδου τετράρχου; cf. *GLk* 23.6–12, *Acts* 4.27, *GPet* 1.1–2.5). The correct name, Antipas, would be known only to readers of Josephus; Archelaus is named in *GMt* 2.22.

(3) The reference to the deposition is one of the rare instances where the *Eth* tradition as a whole adds substantial content to *Cop*. The secondary character of this passage is already indicated by the redundant repetition of 'he was crucified'. C's 'and with them he was numbered...' probably stems from the secondary allusion to *Is* 52.12 in *GMk* 15.28, attested in Greek manuscripts from the sixth century onwards and present throughout the Ethiopic gospel tradition (Zuurmond II, 285).

9.2 *There came to that place three women* {Cop *a third woman*}, *Mary* {Eth *Sarah*} *and* {Cop *[sister] of*} *Martha and Mary Magdalene]*

Cop reads 'a third woman, Mary [sister] of Martha, and Mary Magdalene'. Here only two women are named: ⲙⲁⲣⲓⲁ ⲧⲁⲙⲁⲣⲑⲁ (Schmidt, Duensing: 'Maria, die zu Martha gehörige') and Mary Magdalene. Müller/Taylor misinterpret Duensing's 'die zu Martha gehörige' as a second individual, 'the daughter of Martha', impossible in view of the lack of a conjunction in *Cop*. An anonymous 'third woman' is oddly mentioned first; contrary to trr, the Coptic numeral is ordinal (ⲙⲁϩ[ϣⲁⲙⲧⲉ ⲛ̄ⲥ]ϩⲓⲙⲉ) rather than cardinal (cf. Layton §112). In the narrative that follows, Martha and Mary are present at the tomb (10.3, 8; 11.1), and they must therefore both have been named at 9.2, along with Mary Magdalene. That there were three women at the tomb is also clear from 'Mary and her sisters' (11.1). Most probably, 'Mary and Martha' was changed to 'Mary [sister] of Martha' in order to differentiate her from Mary Magdalene (cf. the substitution of 'Sarah' in *Eth*). Mary is similarly identified through Martha in *GJn* 11.5[sah] (ⲙⲁⲣⲑⲁ ⲙⲛ̄ ⲙⲁⲣⲓⲁ ⲧⲉⲥⲥⲱⲛⲉ, 'Martha and Mary her sister', *Gk* Μάρθαν καὶ τὴν ἀδελφὴν αὐτῆς). Identifying Mary by way of Martha reduces the named women at the tomb from three to two, and the anonymous 'third woman' seems to be a scribal attempt to restore the number to three.

9.3 *They took ointment to pour over his body]*
Cop 'they poured it' is obviously in error in having the women actually pouring their ointment over the body, doing so before they reached the tomb. There is no reason to render synonymous Coptic and Geʻez verbs by different German or English ones (Duensing, Müller/Taylor: *carried/took, pour out/pour*).

9.4 *But when they reached the tomb*, Cop *they looked inside*, <Eth *they found the stone where it had been rolled from the tomb and they opened the door {and the door opened* A} *and* > *they did not find the body]*
As in 9.1, where the reference is to the crucifixion, *Eth* has additional substantive material that may derive from a different *Gk* exemplar or from the translator's recollection of canonical gospel narratives. Since the stone *is* the door, the A reading is likely to be correct. Cf. *GLk* 24.2–3, εὗρον δὲ τὸν λίθον ἀποκεκυλισμένον ἀπὸ τοῦ μνημείου, εἰσελθοῦσαι δὲ οὐχ εὗρον τὸ σῶμα τοῦ κυρίου Ἰησοῦ.

10.1 *And as they were grieving and weeping. . .]*
There is no need to find an adversative sense in *Cop* and to contrast it with *Eth*: 'And (*Copt.*: But) as they were mourning and weeping. . .' (Müller/Taylor, Duensing).

10.4 *We said to her, 'What do you want with us, O woman? One who died and is buried, can he live?']*
(1) *Eth* 'What to us and to you, O woman?' reflects *Gk* τί ἡμῖν καὶ σοί, γύναι, echoing *GJn* 2.4, whereas *Cop* paraphrases exactly as at *GJn* 2.4[sah] (Horner iii.22). These are probably different renderings of the same underlying *Gk*.
(2) *Eth* 'One who died and is buried, can he live?' refers to the impossibility of resurrection in general, whereas *Cop* 'The one who died is buried, and can he live?' refers specifically to Jesus. The difference lies in the position of the conjunction. *Eth* is probably original: cf. 24.2 for the disciples' incredulity about the possibility of resurrection in general.

10.6 (1) On folio 2 of *Cop* (**III, IV**), 2–12 letters have been lost from ll. 10–15 of the recto, and 2–5 letters from ll. 9–14 of the verso.
(2) *the Lord]* Here and elsewhere, agreements of G and *Cop* suggest that *Eth* divergences from *Cop* may have entered the manuscript tradition at a relatively late stage. 'Our Lord' (A C E L) is unattested in *Cop* but repeated at 10.10[eth] and linked to 'our Saviour' at 6.1, 8.1, 12.2, cf. 3.1[eth]. The Pauline 'our Lord Jesus Christ' does,

however, occur at 7.1^{cop}. *Eth* shows a general tendency to add a first plural suffix to christological titles.

10.8 *we disbelieved her]*

Cop ⲛ̄ⲡⲛ̄ⲣ̄ⲡⲓⲥⲧⲉⲩⲉ ⲛⲉⲥ and *Eth* *'akḥadnāhā* (Dillmann 824) may both derive from *Gk* ἠπιστήσαμεν αὐτῇ (cf. *GLk* 24.11). Rendering *Eth* as 'we accused her of lying' (Müller/Taylor, Duensing, Pérès) creates an unnecessarily sharp difference from *Cop*.

11.2 Cop *he found us within*, Eth *he found us fishing {veiled}]*

In *Gk*, 'within' will have been ἔσω (cf. *GJn* 20.26, πάλιν ἦσαν ἔσω οἱ μαθηταὶ αὐτοῦ). *Eth* has Jesus finding his disciples 'fishing' or 'veiled'. The two Ge'ez terms are similar, and *nəgelləb* (= *nəgalləb* S, 'we were fishing' [Dillmann 1138–39]) has evidently been misread as *nətgalabbab* ('we were veiled'). 'Fishing' suggests the Galilean setting of *GJn* 21.1–5 and *GPet* 14.60, and is in keeping with the Galilean setting of the Ethiopic *GD* (cf. *GD* 1.1, Appendix). There is no justification for the composite reading, 'found us inside, veiled' (Müller/Taylor, reproducing an error in Duensing).[2]

11.3 Cop *He called us forth, but we thought it was a phantasm*, Eth *And we doubted and did not believe, he seemed to us a phantasm]*

Cop 'we thought it was', *Eth* 'he seemed to us' may both represent *Gk* ἐδόκει ἡμῖν (so Hills). Cf. *GLk* 24.37, ἐδόκουν πνεῦμα θεωρεῖν.

11.4 *I am your teacher]*

The *Cop* lacuna should be filled from *Eth* (so Hills): ⲁⲛⲁⲕ [ⲡⲉ ⲡⲉⲧⲛ̄ⲥⲁϩ] = ἐγώ εἰμι ὁ διδάσκαλος ὑμῶν. Jesus' self-disclosure corresponds to the message previously entrusted to Martha and Mary but disbelieved: 'Come, the Teacher has risen from the dead' (10.1). While Schmidt's translation follows Wajnberg ('ich bin euer Meister'), his original conjecture ⲁⲛⲁⲕ [ⲅⲁⲣ ⲡⲉ ⲡⲭⲁⲓⲉⲥ] ('For I am the Lord') remains uncorrected in his Coptic text (Schmidt 41, 3*). It is also too long for the space available. Duensing renders *Eth* as 'Lehrer', the non-existent *Cop* as 'Meister', and the unnecessary distinction remains predictably intact in Müller/Taylor.

---

[2] Duensing 1925, 'fand us drinnen *verhüllt*' (italics incorrectly assign 'veiled' to *Cop*); Duensing in Hennecke–Schneemelcher 1959, 'fand us drinnen verhüllt' (incorrectly assigning 'veiled' to both *Cop* and *Eth*).

11.7 *That you may know that it is I, Peter, put your fingers into the nail-marks of my hands, and you, Thomas, put your hands into the spear-wounds in my side...]*

(1) *put your fingers into the nail-marks of my hands]* The Coptic verb here translated 'put' corresponds to βάλλειν (Crum 403b), confirming the close relationship between this passage and *GJn* 20.25 (cf. v.27): ἐὰν μὴ ἴδω ἐν ταῖς χερσὶν αὐτοῦ τὸν τύπον τῶν ἥλων καὶ βάλω τὸν δάκτυλόν μου εἰς τὸν τύπον τῶν ἥλων. The relationship is so close that the *Gk* instruction to Peter may be reconstructed: βάλε τοὺς δακτυλούς σου εἰς τὸν τύπον τῶν ἥλων ἐν ταῖς χερσίν μου.

(2) 'Put your fingers *Cop* E G {your hand A L S, your hand and your fingers B K, and your fingers C} into the nail-marks of my hands.' The reading 'your hand' rather than 'your fingers' presumably arose through late assimilation to the instruction to Thomas; E G preserve the earlier reading corresponding to *Cop*. As occurs routinely in the *Eth* manuscript tradition, the B scribe has incorporated both variants into his text. There is no need to perpetuate a manifestly false reading by translating *Eth* as '... lay your hand, Peter, (and your finger) in the nail-print of my hands' (Müller/Taylor; Taylor's sing. 'finger' mistranslates Müller's pl.).

(3) *and you, Thomas, put your hands into the spear-wounds in my side]* Again, the relationship to *GJohn* is unmistakable. In *GJn* 20.27 (cf. v.25) Jesus instructs Thomas: φέρε τὴν χεῖρά σου καὶ βάλε εἰς τὴν πλευράν μου. *EpAp*[gk] here can be reconstructed: βάλε τὴν χεῖρά σου εἰς <τὰ τραύματα τῆς λόγχης> ἐν τῇ πλευρᾷ μου.[3] The reference to the spear-wounds (pl.) recalls *GJn* 19.34: ἀλλ' εἷς τῶν στρατιωτῶν λόγχῃ αὐτοῦ τὴν πλευρὰν ἔνυξεν.

12.1 *And we touched him, that <Cop we might know> truly <Cop that> he had risen in flesh.]*

At this point fragmentary *Lat* text is also available, reconstructed as follows by Bick–Hauler (16): *Nos enim temptantes / quo̦<d ve>r̦e i̦n <car>ne̦ / r̦eșur̦e̦<xerat>*, 'we testing that truly he had risen in flesh', suggesting agreement with *Eth* in connecting 'truly' to Jesus' resurrection in flesh rather than to the disciples' knowledge of it. If the reading is reliable, *Lat* 'we testing that truly he had risen in flesh' avoids the awkwardness of *Eth* 'we touched him that truly he had risen in flesh.' In contrast, the few doubtful letters in the phrase that

---

[3] For τὰ τραύματα λόγχης, cf. *Ezk* 32.29: εἰς τραύμα μαχαίρας.

follows (reconstructed probably incorrectly as *ora<mus>* /
Iustorum. . .) do not seem to correspond to *Cop Eth* 'and we fell on
our face'.

12.1–3 *And we touched him, that we might know that he had truly
risen in flesh. And we fell on our faces, confessing our sins, because we
had been unbelieving. Then the Lord our Saviour said to us, 'Rise. . .'*
This passage is echoed at the opening of the *Testamentum Domini*,
a manual of church order with a post-resurrection setting that may
date from the mid-fourth century. It is attributed to Clement of
Rome in the Syriac tradition and to John, Peter, and Matthew in
the text itself (*TestDom*[syr] ii.27 = *TestDom*[eth] 60). In Ethiopic manuscripts the text now known as the *Epistula Apostolorum* is usually
found as a supplement to this longer and later text, together with the
introductory chapters with a Galilean setting (see Appendix: The
Galilean Discourse [*GD*]). *TestDom*[eth] opens as follows:

> And it came to pass after our Lord Jesus Christ was raised
> from the dead that he appeared to us and was touched by
> Thomas, Matthew, and John. And we, rejoicing that our
> Teacher had been raised, fell on our faces and blessed the
> One who saved us through Jesus Christ our Lord, the
> Father who sanctified the world. Great fear seized us and
> we lay prostrate on the ground like supplicants. And laying
> his hand on each one of us our Lord Jesus Christ raised us
> saying, 'Why is your heart so downcast and you so
> troubled. . .?'   (*incipit* ll. 1–10)

Here as in *EpAp* the risen Lord is touched by three disciples (Peter,
Thomas, and Andrew in *EpAp* 11.7, Thomas, Matthew, and John in
TestDom), after which all of the disciples fall on their faces (cf. *EpAp*
12.2) and are raised up by Jesus (cf. *EpAp* 12.3). In *TestDom*[syr] it is
said that, as a result of the touching, 'we were persuaded that our
Teacher had truly risen from the dead' (in place of the reference in
the Ethiopic to the disciples 'rejoicing', which is anyway textually
uncertain); cf. *EpAp* 12.1, 'And we touched him, that we might know
that he had truly risen in flesh.' On the relationship between *EpAp*
and *TestDom*, see the further discussion in the Appendix to
this volume.

12.3 *Then the Lord our Saviour said to us, 'Rise **V** and I will reveal
to you what is above the heavens and what is in the heavens and your
rest in the kingdom of the heavens]*

(1) *said to us]* *Cop* omits 'to us', as at 13.1 and 39.4 where *Eth* again reads 'said to us'. As 'said to us' is standard usage throughout the dialogue, *Eth* is likely to be correct.

(2) Folio 3 of *Cop* (**V**, **VI**) is relatively well preserved, with most line beginnings and endings intact.

(3) *Cop* 'what is above the heavens and what is in the heavens', *Eth* 'what is of the heavens and what is above the heavens.' *Eth* here transposes and omits a preposition but is otherwise close to *Cop*. This is overlooked by Müller/Taylor, who reproduce the L S variant in which the Saviour promises to reveal 'what is on earth and what is above the heavens,' even though Duensing rightly notes the proximity of the alternative reading to *Cop*. In view of the references to 'heavens' and 'firmaments' in 13.1–5, the plural 'heavens' should be retained in translating 12.3, even in the phrase 'kingdom of the heavens.'

12.4 *For my Father gave me authority to take you up and those who believe in me]*

(1) Here *Cop* agrees with *Eth* A in opening this statement with 'For' (γάρ) rather than the barely intelligible 'concerning which' (L, followed by trr).

(2) The extant *Lat* of *EpAp* 12.1 opens the first of two columns on fol. 67r of the palimpsest Codex Vindobonensis 16. Since col. II begins at 13.1, col. I must have contained the equivalent of 12.1–4. Although Hauler identifies a maximum of just 21 letters in lines 5–18 of col.I, line 13 (*in c<aelis>..... in*) may approximate to *Cop* 'what is *in the heavens* and your rest *in* the kingdom of the heavens' (12.3). In line 18, *et...* may represent *Cop Eth* 'and with those who believe in me' (*et qui in me credunt*, Hauler 16; *EpAp* 12.4).

13.1a *And what he revealed <Eth to us> are these things that he said <Eth Lat: to us>]*

Bick–Hauler reconstruct *Lat* as *<Quae il>le <manifes/tavit sunt quae> di<cit | nobis> Dum...* Fragmentary *Lat* is available for *EpAp* 13.1–17.5 but with 14.1–17.1 omitted.

13.1b *... when I came from the Father of all and passed through the heavens, I put on the wisdom of the Father and clothed myself in the power of his might]*

(1) Here and elsewhere, the Ge'ez syntax ('when' + imperfect × 3) suggests underlying Greek participles (Dillmann 778). *Cop* here opens with an imitation of the Septuagintal καὶ ἐγένετο, two variants

('when I came, coming') and a dittography, followed by finite verbs ('I passed, I put on'). The past reference of the *Eth* subordinate clauses is established by the main verb, 'I was [in the heavens]' (13.2; so Wajnberg), and the Ge'ez imperfects should not be translated as presents ('lorsque je viens..., alors que je traverse les cieux...' [Guerrier]). Differences between *Eth* and *Cop* here probably represent translators' decisions rather than Greek variants.

(2) Bick–Hauler reconstruct *Lat* on the basis of *Cop*: *Ḍum ve̦ni̦o̦ <per / patrem omni>po̦<tente(m) / transie>ns caelos, <sa/pientia ind>utu̦<s su(m) / patris et t>um vi̦r<tute / sp(iritu)s s(an)c(t)i pe>r̦ vi̦rt<ute(m) / patris>* Several elements here are questionable, notably *Ḍum ve̦ni̦o̦ <per>, <et t>um vi̦r<tute sp(iritu)s s(an)c(t) i>*, and the second *patris*. The double reference to 'power' (*virtus*) suggests a Greek exemplar closer to *Eth* than to *Cop*, where 'I clothed myself in the power of his might' echoes *Eph* 6.10.

13.2 *I was in the heavens]*
Eth 'I was *to* the heavens' is emended by Wajnberg to 'in the heavens'. There is no basis for 'I was like the heavens' (Müller/ Taylor). *Lat* omits 'I was in the heavens' but otherwise approximates to *Cop* and *Eth* wording and word-order, reading (as reconstructed by Bick–Hauler): *Et <cora>m <arch/angelis et> angelis p<er/trans->iens in simil<i/tudinem> effigies il<lo>/rum quasi unus ex <il>li̦s.*

13.3 Cop *Among the rulers and authorities I passed, having the wisdom of the one who sent me*, Eth *Orders and authorities and rulers I passed, having <put on* A C*> the measure of the wisdom of the Father <and clothed with the power of the one* G*> who sent me*, Lat (Hauler): *vir<tutes> e̦t pot<es>/ta̦tes et p̦rincipes <su(m) / transgressus> e<t ei/us qui me misit p>oș<se/di sapientiam>.*]
Lat resembles *Eth* in the absence of an initial preposition and in the presence of an order of angels prior to 'authorities and rulers' (the reverse of *Cop* ⲚⲀⲢⲬⲎ ⲘⲚ ⲚⲈⲌⲞⲨⲤⲒⲀ [cf. *Eph* 6.12]). However, *virtutes* corresponds to δυνάμεις (cf. *Rom* 8.38), whereas the Ge'ez term might represent τάξεις (Dillmann 262; Lampe 1372b–1373a). The *Cop* sequence is perhaps to be preferred, as it preserves the original *Gk* terms.

13.4 Cop *The commander of the angels is Michael, with Gabriel and Uriel and Raphael, and they followed me*, Eth *The archangels Michael and Gabriel, Raphael and Uriel {Seraphim and Cherubim* G*} followed me – such was the power given me by the Father]*

(1) *Cop* here differentiates the role of Michael as ⲁⲣⲭⲓⲥⲧⲣⲁⲧⲏⲅⲟⲥ of the angels from that of the archangels (ⲁⲣⲭⲁⲅⲅⲉⲗⲟⲥ) of 13.2. The distinctive role is absent in *Eth*, as it is in *Lat* (Bick–Hauler): *Aṛ<chlang>elus Michael et / <G>abriel et Uriel et Ra/<f>ael palam comitati / <s>unt mihi usque ad / quintum caelum / <p>utantes me esse unu(m) / ẹx eis.*While the use in *Eth* and *Lat* of 'archangel' rather than 'commander' may stem from a variant in *Gk*, use of the sing. *archangelus* in spite of the naming of three further archangels (plural in *Eth*) suggests that the necessarily singular ἀρχιστράτηγος is likely to be original.

(2) Cop *thinking in their hearts that I was one of them*, Eth *as it {I} seemed to them one of them*, Lat *<p>utantes me esse unu(m) ẹx eis*] The translation variants might all be accounted for by *Gk* δοκοῦντες με εἶναι εἷς ἐξ ἑαυτῶν (cf. Crum 199b, Dillmann 171).

13.5 Cop *And on that day {Eth Then} I prepared the archangels, in a voice of wonder, so that they might go {Eth to wonder at the voice and to go} to the altar of the Father and serve and fulfil {Eth <the Father L S> in} their ministry until I returned to him.* Lat (Bick–Hauler): *ẹt tunc feci archan/gelos iṇ stuporem / ỵocis ducẹrẹ ipsos / ad / <a>ltarẹụṃ patris mei / <s>ervientes et replen/<t>es ministratione(m) / <u>sque quo irem ad eu(m).]*

(1) *Cop* reads ⲁⲣⲭⲉⲁⲅⲅⲉⲗⲟⲥ, corrected or mistranscribed by Schmidt as ⲁⲣⲭⲁⲅⲅⲉⲗⲟⲥ

(2) *Eth* and *Lat* agree in reading 'then' rather than *Cop* 'on that day'. *Cop* and *Lat* agree in referring to 'serv[ing] and fulfil[ling] their {Lat the} ministry'. *Cop* and *Eth* agree against *Lat* that the archangels were to 'go' to the altar rather than being 'led' there by Christ.

(3) In spite of minor differences, the three versions are agreed that the 'voice' is Christ's, and that it creates astonishment among the archangels whom he calls to serve as his deputies while he is away. To translate *Cop* as 'In that day I adorned the archangels with a wondrous voice' and *Eth* as 'Then I made the archangels to become distracted with the voice' (Müller/Taylor, following Duensing) is to mistake an adverbial phrase for an indirect object in the case of *Cop* and to reduce *Eth* to nonsense.

13.6 *This is what I did in the wisdom of the likeness {Eth likeness of his wisdom}, for I became all in all <Eth with them> so that I might fulfil the {Eth having fulfilled the merciful} will of the Father of glory {Eth and the glory of him} who sent me and return to him.* Lat (Bick–Hauler): *<s>ic feci per sapientia(m) / <s>imilitudinis. Ego eni(m) /*

*<i>n̪ omnib̪us̪ omnia / fac[u]tus sum, sim/ul̪ ut voluntatem / patris̪
me̪i laudem / qu̪ia̪ mis̪it̪ me̪ i̪[n]ta̪.]*

(1) *Cop* and *Lat* agree on 'the wisdom of the likeness' against the
transposition in *Eth*. If the Coptic conjunctive (translated 'I might
fulfil') is not a scribal error, a verb has dropped out: 'so that the will
[ⲟⲓⲕⲟⲛⲟⲙⲓⲁ] of the Father of glory who sent me [I might...] and fulfil,
and return to him.' In *Eth* the construction 'having fulfilled the
merciful will' suggests an underlying Greek participle. A possible
Gk original for *ut voluntatem patris mei laudem qui[a] misit me*
would be ἵνα τὴν οἰκονομίαν τοῦ Πατρὸς δοξάσω τοῦ πεμψάντός
με. *Cop Eth* might reflect a variant τοῦ Πατρὸς τῆς δόξης τοῦ
πεμψάντός με.

(2) The phrase, 'For I became all in all' occurs here and in *Cop*
14.3 in slightly different forms: *Cop* literally 'For I became in all in
everything' (13.7), 'I was all in everything' (14.3), *Lat* 'For I was
made in all all' (13.7), *Eth* 'I was in all all' (13.7 B L). *Eth* lacks the
repetition at *Cop* 14.3. The origin of this phrase in its christological
sense may lie in *Eph* 1.23, where the church is the fullness τοῦ τὰ
πάντα ἐν πᾶσιν πληρουμένου (cf. also *1 Cor* 15.28).

(3) At this point *Lat* omits 14.1–17.1, which may suggest an
exemplar with a missing bifolium in the middle of a quire.

14.5 *I appeared to Mary <the (holy S) virgin L>]*

Since *Eth* as attested in A B C G agrees with *Cop* here in referring
simply to 'Mary', it is misleading to include the full expression 'the
Virgin Mary' in modern translations, even with the addition of 'not
in all manuscripts' (Müller/Taylor).

14.6 Cop *she believed, sh[e moul]ded me*, Eth: *she believed and she laughed]*

(1) There is a lacuna in *Cop* after 'she believed', and only the
letters ⲁ....ⲁⲥⲥⲉ are clearly legible. The third letter is probably ⲣ̄,
from the verb 'to do' used in conjunction with verbs taken over from
Greek (cf. the preceding word, ⲁⲥⲡ̄ⲓⲥⲧⲉⲩⲉ, 'she believed'), and in this
context the second letter is likely to be either ⲓ or ⲥ (representing
respectively a first sing. or third sing. fem. pronoun). While Schmidt
reconstructs the phrase as ⲁ[ⲓⲣ̄ⲡⲗ]ⲁⲥⲥⲉ ⲛ̄ⲙⲁⲓ, 'ich formte mich' (= trr),
the third sing. fem. reading ⲁ[ⲥⲣ̄ⲡⲗ]ⲁⲥⲥⲉ is a better fit for the space in
the lacuna. Schmidt's reading requires a reflexive sense for ⲛ̄ⲙⲁⲓ, i.e.
'myself' (thus ἔπλασα ἐμαυτόν), but a reflexive pronoun is rendered
differently two lines below (ⲛⲉⲓ ⲟⲩⲁⲉⲧ, 'to myself' [14.7]), and ⲛ̄ⲙⲁⲓ /
ⲙ̄ⲙⲁⲓ is elsewhere 'me' (39.10 × 5). *Gk* here was most probably

ἔπλασέν με (cf. *Gen* 2.7 LXX). Thus the moment of incarnation is depicted by way of two pairs of verbs, the first pair referring to Mary ('she believed, she formed me'), the second to Jesus ('I entered into her, I became flesh').

(2) It has been suggested that *Eth* 'she laughed' might derive from a *Gk* variant (ἐγέλασεν). At *SibOr* 7.463–69 a fulsome account of Mary's emotional response to the annunciation includes her laughter (467). Yet the reading 'she laughed' is more likely to have arisen within the *Eth* tradition. In *Eth* MSS the correct word is regularly replaced by a similar-sounding word with a different meaning, and that is probably the case here: *wasaḥaqat* ('she laughed') has been substituted for *walaḥak^wat* ('and she formed') or *walaḥak^watəya* ('and she formed me'). The *Eth* letters *l* and *s* are easily confused, and a scribe might have assumed that *k^w* was simply a variant spelling and replaced it with *q*, perhaps with Sarah's laughter in mind (cf. *Gen* 18.12). Thus *Eth* indirectly supports *Cop* as reconstructed above and as rendering *Gk* ἔπλασέν με. Cf. *Is* 29.16^{eth} *yəbəloni ləhək^wət lalaḥāk^wihu* = μὴ ἐρεῖ τὸ πλάσμα τῷ πλάσαντι αὐτό (Dillmann 31–32). For other examples of the same common scribal tendency, see the Notes on *EpAp* 1.2, 1.4, 2.2, 6.3, 11.2, 16.3, etc.

14.7 Eth *For I became my own servant,* <Cop *to Mary*> *in the appearance of the likeness of an angel]*

'My own servant' is literally 'a servant to myself'. *Eth* gives a clear sense consistent with the rest of the passage. *Cop* 'to Mary' seeks to differentiate who Christ is for himself and who he is for Mary, although he has previously appeared as an angel to descending ranks of angels (*EpAp* 13.2–7), and not just to Mary. In 14.8, 'I will do likewise...' implies that 14.7 refers to a singular action, repeated after the Ascension in the liberation of the disciple from prison (15.4).

15.1 *And as for you, celebrate the memorial of my death when the Feast of the Pascha comes** {Eth *which is the Pascha*}*]

The Coptic text links the reference to the Passover with the sentence that follows, thereby detaching it from the reference to Jesus' death:

> And as for you, celebrate the memorial of my death. And when [ⲟⲧⲁⲛ ϭⲉ] the Feast of the Pascha comes, then [ⲧⲟⲧⲉ] one of you will be thrown into prison for the sake of my name.

(So trr, with the exception of Hills). ⲟⲧⲁⲛ ϭⲉ may correspond to *Gk* ὅταν δέ, which would normally mark the beginning of a sentence. Indeed ⲟⲧⲁⲛ ⲇⲉ occurs in just this form in *EpAp* 15.7 (the only other use of ⲟⲧⲁⲛ in this text). Nevertheless, there are grounds for thinking that the ϭⲉ may not correspond to anything in *Gk* (cf. Crum 802a). τότε most often begins a new sentence, in *EpAp* as in the canonical gospels, and it would be redundant after ὅταν δέ. The partial parallel in *GJn* 12.16 (ἀλλ' ὅτε ἐδοξάσθη Ἰησοῦς τότε ἐμνήσθησαν κτλ) in fact proves the point, for here τότε is added for emphasis: Jesus' disciples did not understand his triumphal entry at the time, but when he was glorified, *then* they recalled the relevant scriptural passage. In the *EpAp* context there is no question of any such emphasis. Most probably a Coptic scribe assumed that the ⲟⲧⲁⲛ he found in his exemplar opened a new sentence and added the connective ϭⲉ for stylistic reasons. *Gk* may have read: ὑμεῖς δὲ ποιεῖτε τὴν ἀνάμνησιν τοῦ θανάτου μου ὅταν ἡ ἑορτὴ τοῦ πάσχα γενήται. *Eth*'s identification of the memorial of Jesus' death with the Pascha might be viewed as a paraphrase of some such statement.

15.8 Cop *Lord, is it again necessary for us to take the cup and drink,* Eth *Lord, have you not completed drinking the Pascha, for us to do it again?*]

Eth is apparently thinking of the metaphorical cup of suffering (cf. *GMt* 20.22, δύνασθε πιεῖν τὸ ποτήριον ὃ ἐγὼ μέλλω πίνειν). In *Cop* the reference is probably to the cup of the paschal eucharist, which is to be celebrated each year 'until the day when I come with those who were put to death for my sake' (15.9; cf. *1 Cor* 11.26).

16.1 *Lord, great indeed are the things you have now revealed to us!*]

The translation follows *Eth* word-order (though not wording) in presenting this as an acclamation opening with 'great' (the final word in *Cop*). Cf. *Rev* 15.3, μεγάλα καὶ θαυμαστὰ τὰ ἔργα σου. 'Now' (*Cop* only, literally 'before') refers to the revelation delivered thus far (cf. *EpAp* 12.4–15.9). This and similar acclamations at *EpAp* 20.1 and 34.1–2 mark significant turning-points in the narrative.

16.2 *But in what power or likeness will you come?*]

(1) More literally translated, 'In what power or in what sort of likeness…?' *Cop* duplication of almost synonymous interrogative expression (ⲛⲉϩ ⲛⲙⲓⲛⲉ, ⲛⲉϩ ⲛ̄ϩⲉ) recurs in *Eth* manuscript B (*ba-'ay ḥayl waba-'ay 'ar'ayā*). *Gk* perhaps ἐν ποίᾳ δυνάμει ἢ ἐν ποταπῇ ὁμοιότητι μέλλεις ἔρχεσθαι.

(2) *likeness]* *Cop* has ⲁⲓⲥⲑⲏⲥⲓⲥ, normally 'perception' in *Gk* but here meaning 'perceptible form', thus 'likeness' (*Eth ʼarʼayā*). This is a case where a loanword does not necessarily reproduce *Gk* (here perhaps ὁμοιότης) but may reflect general *Cop* usage.

(3) *will you come?]* Here, *Eth təmaṣāʼ hallawaka* reflects the *Gk* idiom μέλλει... ἔρχεσθαι (cf. *GMt* 16.27, μέλλει γὰρ ὁ υἱὸς τοῦ ἀνθρώπου ἔρχεσθαι) whereas *Cop* ⲕⲛ̅ⲛⲏⲩ does not. The *Eth* equivalent to μέλλειν + inf. is, however, well-established and can even render a simple *Gk* future tense (Dillmann 4–5). Its presence suggests translation directly from *EpAp*[gk], but does not require it.

16.3 *And he answered and said to us, 'Truly* [ⲅⲁⲙⲏⲛ ⲅⲁⲣ] *I say to you, I will come like the rising sun']*

(1) In spite of the ⲅⲁⲣ, *Gk* must here have been ἀμὴν λέγω ὑμῖν. While ἀμὴν γὰρ λέγω ὑμῖν is attested in *GMt* 5.18, 13.17, 17.20, it serves there to explain or reinforce the preceding statement rather than initiating a saying or series of sayings, as here and in *EpAp* 21.1, 25.2, 28.4. The conventional explanatory usage occurs in *EpAp* 41.7, 47.8, and ⲅⲁⲙⲏⲛ alone (19.14) and ⲅⲁⲙⲏⲛ ⲇⲉ (26.1) are also attested. In these instances it is more likely that *Gk* is accurately represented. The *Cop* translator can use ⲅⲁⲣ to add emphasis to the preceding word, as in 20.3, 25.2 (†ⲥⲁⲩⲛⲉ ⲅⲁⲣ, 'I know indeed'). The important methodological point here is that loanwords in *Cop* do not necessarily correspond either to the underlying *Gk* or to conventional *Gk* usage.

(2) The variant 'shining in humanity' for 'shining seven times more' stems, as so often, from a deliberate or accidental change from the correct Geʻez word [*masbəʼito*, 'seven times more'] to a similar-sounding word with a different meaning [*ba-tasbʼət*, 'in humanity'].

17.2 *He said to us, 'When the hundred and ~~twentieth~~* fiftieth year is completed, between Pentecost and the Feast of Unleavened Bread, the coming of my Father will take place.']*

The text as reconstructed here draws on all three available versions of Jesus' answer to the disciples' question about the date of the parousia. From 'between Pentecost' to 'will take place', the versions are in close agreement, but the crucial first part of Jesus' answer to the question of the date of the parousia is more problematic.

(1) In *Lat* (as noted above, on 13.6), *EpAp* 14.1–17.1 is missing, perhaps owing to a damaged exemplar, and the reference to 'the Father who sent me' (13.6) is followed by: '... year being completed, between Pentecost and Unleavened Bread, the coming of my Father will take place' (*anno implente inter pentecosten et azyma erit adventus patris mei*). Assuming that an intact Latin translation once existed, the singular *anno implente* must have been preceded by an ordinal rather than a cardinal figure: 'When the ...eth year is completed.'

(2) *Cop* 'When the hundredth part and the twentieth part are completed...' If *Gk* here used an ordinal number as *Lat* suggests, and if that number was 'the hundred-and-twentieth', it might have been expressed either as τὸ ἑκατοεικοστόν ('the hundred-twentieth')[5] or, in an alternative usage attested in LXX, as τὸ ἑκατοστὸν καὶ εἰκοστόν ('the hundredth and twentieth').[6] The alternative form would account for *Cop* as it stands: the translator seems to have taken the single ordinal number as a mysterious pair of fractions ('the hundredth part and the twentieth part'). In *Gk* an ordinal without the necessary addition of μέρος can express a fraction, whereas *Cop* requires ογωⲛ (ογⲛ), 'part'. Thus in *Rev* 6.8 τὸ τέταρτον τῆς γῆς is correctly rendered as ⲡογⲛ ⲛ̄ϥⲧⲟⲟⲩ ⲙ̄ⲡⲕⲁϩ, 'the fourth part of the earth', essentially the construction found in *EpAp* 17.2, ⲡⲟγⲱⲛ ⲛ̄ϣⲉ ⲙⲛ̄ ⲡⲟγⲱⲛ ϫⲟγⲱⲧ (further examples in Crum 483ab). The translator either fails to recognize the sequential usage, though it is present in the term ⲡⲉⲛⲧⲏⲕⲟⲥⲧⲏ which he takes over from his Greek exemplar, or deliberately converts an ordinal number into a mysterious fraction because he realizes that 120 years has long since elapsed. *EpAp*[gk] may here have lacked 'year' (absent in *Cop* though present in *Lat* and *Eth*). In answer to the question, 'After how many years...?', the response, 'When the hundred and twentieth is completed...' is entirely intelligible.

---

[5] *Moulton's Grammar*, ii.174 cites an occurrence of ἑκατοπεντηκοστόν (no reference given), while noting a tendency to replace higher ordinals with cardinals.

[6] Cf. *4 Kgdms* 13.10, ἐν ἔτει εἰκοστῷ καὶ τρίτῳ ('in the twentieth and third year'); 25.27, ἐν τῷ τριακοστῷ καὶ ἑβδόμῳ ἔτει ('in the thirtieth and seventh year'). An ordinal in exactly this format for a figure over a hundred is found in *1 Macc* 1.20, ἐν τῷ ἑκατοστῷ καὶ τεσσαρακοστῷ καὶ τρίτῳ ἔτει ('in the hundredth and fortieth and third year'), and with minor variations in *1 Macc* 3.27; 6.20; 10.1, 57, 67; *2 Macc* 13.1; 14.4 (ascending rather than descending sequence); *2 Macc* 1.7; 11.21, 33, 38 (omission of 'and').

(3) *Eth*, 'When the hundred and fiftieth year is completed.' In view of the singular noun and verb, the *Eth* figure too should be regarded as ordinal rather than cardinal. Jesus here gives a straightforward answer to the disciples' question, 'In how many years...?', which arises out of the answer to the previous question about the parousia. There are several possible explanations for the additional 30 years beyond the 120 of *Cop*, and they are not necessarily mutually exclusive. First, it may reflect a later adjustment to the parousia's non-occurrence at the expected time (cf. *Dan* 12.11, 12). Second, the difference might reflect a variant in *EpAp*[gk], where τὸ ἑκατοστὸν καὶ πεντηκοστὸν ἔτος may have been suggested by the reference to πεντηκοστή (Pentecost, the Fiftieth Day) that follows: *Gk* was perhaps ἐν τῷ μεταξὺ τῆς πεντηκοστῆς καὶ τοῦ πάσχα. The parousia will occur in the hundred and fiftieth year, between the Fiftieth Day and the Pascha. Third, as suggested in the Introduction, the change from '120th' to '150th' may be the result of a more accurate assessment of the interval between the end of Jesus' ministry and an actual time of composition in *c.*170 CE.

(4) All three versions agree that the parousia will take place at some point between Pentecost and Unleavened Bread (*Cop, Lat*) or Pascha (*Eth*). This order – rather than the expected 'between Unleavened Bread and Pentecost' – is probably original, given the agreement of all three versions. While it might suggest an author who believes that Pentecost precedes Unleavened Bread rather than following it, it is more likely that the intention is to emphasize the beginning of the fifty-day period. In delimiting the time of the parousia from the fiftieth day to the first, it is implied that Pascha/ Unleavened Bread is the critical moment (cf. 15.1–7).

17.4, 8a *I am wholly in my Father and my Father is in me]*
Misled by the repetition of this statement, the *Cop* scribe mistakes 17.8a for 17.4 and omits 17.5–7. *Lat* confirms that this passage belongs to the text and is not an *Eth* supplement. Jesus' repeated claim echoes *GJn* 14.10, 11: οὐ πιστεύεις ὅτι ἐγὼ ἐν τῷ πατρὶ καὶ ὁ πατὴρ ἐν ἐμοί ἐστιν... πιστεύετέ μοι ὅτι ἐγὼ ἐν τῷ πατρὶ καὶ ὁ πατὴρ ἐν ἐμοί. The identification of Jesus and the Father is still more strongly emphasized by the addition of 'wholly'.

18.1–2 Cop *'I am the Logos, I became a reality to him – that is, [I am the thou]ght fulfilled in the type, I came into being on the eighth day, which is the Lord's Day*, Eth *And I am his perfect Word, that is, when he was crucified and died and rose, as he said, and the work that was accomplished in flesh, when he had been crucified {killed* G}, *and his ascension]*

(1) Both versions offer an explanatory gloss on 'I am the Logos' or 'I am his perfect Word', but diverge here more widely than usual. *Eth*'s third person discourse here is out of place in *EpAp*: unusually, the gloss views Jesus' being as the Word as fulfilled in his earthly career. Trr allow the lacuna in *Cop* to stand, although Schmidt's reconstruction is plausible [ⲁⲛⲁⲕ ⲡⲉ ⲡⲙⲉⲟ]ⲩⲉ ('[I am the thou]ght').[7]

(2) *Cop* suggests a distinction between what Jesus *is* (the Logos, the thought) and what he *becomes* (a reality, a ⲧⲩⲡⲟⲥ fulfilling the thought). There may be a parallel here with Tertullian's distinction between a *ratio* that is eternally in God and the *sermo* that God puts forth in creation (*Adv. Prax.* 5–6): the 'completed birth of the Word' (*nativitas perfecta sermonis*) occurs when God says, 'Let there be light' on the first day of creation (*Gen* 1.3). In *EpAp*, however, Jesus 'came into being on the eighth day' rather than the first. There is probably an allusion here to the day of his resurrection (cf. *Barn* 15.8–9), and *EpAp* may here anticipate the view of Basil of Caesarea that the ἡμέρα μία, 'one day' of *Genesis* 1.5 is τὴν ἁγίαν κυριακὴν τὴν τῇ ἀναστάσει τοῦ κυρίου τετιμημένην (*Hex.* 2.66 [PG 29.52]). The divine 'thought' is fulfilled in the 'type', i.e. the first day as the type of the day of Jesus' resurrection (the ⲕⲩⲣⲓⲁⲕⲏ), in which his original coming into being is re-enacted.

(3) The identification of [ⲡⲙⲁϩ]ϩⲙⲟⲩⲛ ('eighth') with the ⲕⲩⲣⲓⲁⲕⲏ is understood in spatial rather than temporal terms by Schmidt (275–81), followed by Hornschuh (*Studien*, 35–37), on the basis of Clement of Alexandria's *Excerpta ex Theodoto* 63. This is unlikely, as the feminine κυριακή assumes a reference to ἡμέρα. The Theodotus passage explains the feminine as referring to Sophia, mother of the Demiurge, but these characters have no place in the thought-world of *EpAp*.

18.3 Cop *And the fulfilment of all fulfilment you will see through the redemption which has come to pass in me*, Eth *And <this is> the fulfilment of <the number, and wonders and his likeness and> all fulfilment you will see <in me> through the redemption which <is> in me]*

---

[7] [ⲡⲙⲉ]ⲩⲉ according to Schmidt, but the space available makes [ⲡⲉⲙⲉⲟ]ⲩⲉ more likely. Both spellings of this word are attested in the *EpAp*^{cop} manuscript.

In the expanded *Eth* version of 18.3, 'the fulfilment of the number' may reflect the reference to 'the eighth day' preserved in 18.2 *Cop*. The expansion obscures the eschatological statement still perceptible in *Cop*.

19.7 *Truly I say to you, such and so great a joy has my Father prepared, which angels and authorities longed to behold,* and it will not be permitted them]*

The passage recalls *1 Pet* 1.12, εἰς ἃ ἐπιθυμοῦσιν ἄγγελοι παρακύψαι. Several characteristic tendencies of *Eth* scribes are illustrated in the variants here; so too is the possibility of reconstructing a reasonably satisfactory text in spite of them.

(1) *Eth* '... which angels and authorities longed <and long B G L> to behold and see.' By analogy with the shorter A reading ('longed' without 'and long'), 'to behold and see' is probably another of the redundant doubling of synonyms typical of *Eth*. Other doublings here ('such and so great', 'angels and authorities') are more likely to be original: cf. 'in what power and in what sort of likeness' in 16.2^{cop}, 'archangels and angels..., rulers and authorities' in 13.2–3^{cop}.

(2) Assuming another reference to 'my Father who sent me', C replaces *fatawu wa-yəfattəw* ('longed and will long') with *fannawani wa-yətfennawu*, 'sent me and are sent'), producing the reading, '... has my Father *who sent me* prepared – angels and authorities *are sent*, they behold and see.' This reading must postdate the doubling of the verb, 'long'.

(3) The blunt A reading, 'and it will not be permitted them' appears to set the redeemed above the angels, and is omitted by C and mitigated by *(Eth)*. According to E G K L S (followed by trr), the angels 'will not be permitted to see the greatness of my Father', although the theme here is or should be eschatological salvation rather than divine ineffability. B rejects the idea that angels are denied anything, and reads: 'What angels and authorities longed and long to behold and see, they saw.'

19.10 *(And the Son will be perfected by the Father, the light – for the Father who perfects is perfect... death and resurrection, and the perfection will surpass perfection)]*

The fragmentary *Cop* at the start of **XI** corresponds to 19.9, 11 *Eth* but has no room for 19.10 – probably a gloss on *EpAp* 19.9 ('You will see a light brighter than that which shines and more perfect than perfection').

19.11 *I am wholly the right hand of the Father, in the one who is the fullness* {Eth *who fulfils*} *]*

Cop and *Eth* are closer in the second half of this statement than appears in trr: e.g. *Cop* '... me *[sic]*,[8] which is the fullness', *Eth* 'I am in him who accomplishes' (Müller/Taylor). The *Eth* verb *faṣṣama* and adjective *faṣṣum* can be used to translate both τελειοῦν / τέλειος and πληρῶσαι / πλήρης (Dillmann 1387–88), and *Cop* indicates a distinction between the two word-groups within *EpAp* 19.9, 11 *Gk* that is concealed in *Eth* (Crum 761a ϫⲱⲕ, 208a ⲙⲟⲩϩ). It is most probably τελειοῦν / τέλειος that underlies 'the perfect perfected i[n the perfe]ct' (19.9 *Cop*)[9] = 'the perfect from the perfect' (19.9 *Eth*), and πλήρωμα that underlies 'the one who is the fullness' (19.11 *Cop*). Contrast 19.11 *Eth*, 'the one who fulfils', where the selection of the verbal form is twice anticipated in the interpolated 19.10.

19.14 *such will be your rest, where there is no eating or drinking and no anxiety or grief* <Eth *and no earthly clothing*> *and no corruption* <Cop *for those who are above*> *]*

Following Duensing, Müller/Taylor translate *Eth* as, 'Such a rest will be yours where there is no eating and drinking and no mourning and singing (*or* care) and neither earthly garments nor perishing', and *Cop* as, 'Your rest will be in heaven, in the place where there is neither eating nor drinking, neither rejoicing nor mourning nor perishing of those who are in it'. Trr fail to note that two of the differences – *Cop* 'in heaven', *Eth* 'Such a...', *Cop* 'rejoicing', *Eth* 'singing (*or* care)' – arise from Schmidt's reconstructions of the damaged *Cop* text, carried out without reference to *Eth*: [ⲛ̄ⲧⲡ]ⲉ,'in heaven', and [ⲧⲉ]ⲗⲏ[ⲗ] 'rejoicing'. In the light of *Eth*, [ⲛ̄ⲧⲡ]ⲉ should be read as [ⲛ̄ⲧϩ]ⲉ, 'in this way', 'such' (so rightly Hills). [ⲧⲉ]ⲗⲏ[ⲗ] should be abandoned, as its two doubtful letters occur on a detached papyrus fragment the placement of which within **XI** is entirely uncertain. A denial of joy in heaven would contradict *EpAp* 19.7 and would be odd in itself. Equally odd would be the absence of 'singing'. The *Eth* term might be read as *halǝy*, from *halaya*, 'sing', but more probably as *hallǝy*, from *hallaya*, 'care' (Dillmann 577–78), the verb that represents *Gk* μεριμνᾶν in *GMt* 6.31[eth-A] and elsewhere. As for 'grief', *Eth* makes Schmidt's conjectural ⲗ[ⲩⲡ]ⲉⲓ plausible,

---

[8] Schmidt's ⲁⲣⲁⲓ ('to me') is doubtful and would be better read as ⲁⲣ[ⲁϥ], ('to him'), corresponding to *Eth botu* ('in him').

[9] Restoring ϩ......ⲟⲛ as ϩⲛ̄ ⲡⲧⲉⲗⲉⲓⲟⲛ (cf. Hills, *Epistle*, 43).

though one would expect λγπн. There will be no lack of rejoicing or singing in heaven, but there will be 'no grief or anxiety' (*Eth*), 'no anxiety or grief' (*Cop*).

19.20–27 *Lord, how many are those who afflict me. . . Deliverance is the Lord's, and his love is for his people]*
In response to the disciples' question about the nature of the resurrection body, Jesus cites the whole of *Psalm* 3. Several of the differences between the two versions reflect the assimilation of *Eth* to *Ps* 3 *Eth*.[10] Allowing for dialectal differences, *Cop* is generally close to the earliest extant Sahidic version of the psalm.[11]

(1) 21 (*Ps* 3.3) Cop *Many there are who say of my soul, 'There is no salvation for you with God'*, Eth *Many there are who say to my soul, 'There is no salvation of his God'] Ps* 3.3 LXX: πολλοὶ λέγουσιν τῇ ψυχῇ μου, οὐκ ἔστιν σωτηρία αὐτῷ ἐν τῷ θεῷ αὐτοῦ. *Cop* 'for you' (ꞏɴмо) refers to the (feminine) soul. In *Eth*'s 'of his God', a preposition (*'əm*, 'from') may have dropped out through haplography.

(2) 23 (*Ps* 3.5) *With my voice I cried to the Lord, and he heard me* <Eth *from the mountain of his sanctuary*>] The additional phrase in *Eth* renders *Ps* 3.5 LXX, ἐξ ὄρους ἁγίου αὐτοῦ. This phrase, present in *Ps* 3.5[eth.sah], was probably already absent in *EpAp*[gk]: God's 'holy mountain' is unnecessary in a context where the psalm is applied to Jesus' resurrection.

(3) 24 (*Ps* 3.6) Eth *I was raised, for God raised me*, Cop. . . *I rose, for you, Lord, are my support]* The *Eth* passive renders LXX ἐξηγέρθην (*Ps* 3.6). Lacking a passive, *Cop* does not differentiate between 'was raised' and 'rose' (cf. *1 Cor* 15.4[sah]), and *Eth* here is undoubtedly closer to *Gk*. On the other hand, 'for God raised me' assimilates to *Ps* 3.6[eth], where it is a christologically oriented gloss that specifies the nature of God's 'support' of Jesus.

(4) 25 (*Ps* 3.7) Cop. . . *I will not be afraid of tens of thousands of people who oppose me round about* {*Eth who surrounded me and rose against me*}] *Cop* = LXX, οὐ φοβηθήσομαι ἀπὸ μυριάδων λαοῦ τῶν κύκλῳ συνεπιτιθεμένων μοι. *Eth* = *Ps* 3.7[eth].

---

[10] Hiob Ludolf, *Psalterium Davidis aethiopice et latine* (Frankfurt am Main: J. D. Zunner and N. W. Helwig, 1701), 4.
[11] E. A. Wallis Budge, *The Earliest Known Coptic Psalter* (London: Kegan Paul, Trench, Trübner, 1898), 2.

(5) 26 (*Ps* 3.8) Cop *Rise, Lord, save me, my God*, Eth *Rise, Lord my God, and save me*] *Cop* = LXX, ἀνάστα, κύριε, σῶσόν με, ὁ θεός μου. *Eth* = *Ps* 3.8[eth].

(6) 27 (*Ps* 3.9) Cop *Salvation is the Lord's, and his love is upon his people* {Eth *and upon your people be your blessing*}] LXX τοῦ κυρίου ἡ σωτηρία καὶ ἐπὶ τὸν λαόν σου ἡ εὐλογία σου. *Eth* = *Ps* 3.9[eth] and is closer to LXX than *Cop* both in word-order and vocabulary. *Cop* = *Ps* 3.9[sah].

21.1 ... *so you too you will rise and they will take you up above the heavens to the place of which I spoke to you in the beginning...*]
There is no need to differentiate *Eth* 'taken up above the heavens' from *Cop* 'taken up to heaven', as Hills does: *Cop* ⲁⲡⲣⲣⲉ ⲛ̄ⲛ̄ⲡⲏⲅⲉ = *Eth mal'əlta samāyāt*. Since *Eth* as well as *Cop* employs a third pl. active verb, the active sense ('they will take you up') should be retained, a reference probably to angels (cf. *GMt* 24.31). Since final salvation (ⲁⲛⲁⲡⲁⲅⲥⲓⲥ, 'rest') is to be found in 'the kingdom of heaven' (*EpAp* 12.3, 22.1; cf. 26.5, 27.1), and not above it, 'above the heavens' must refer to the uppermost heaven (cf. 13.1–5 on the multiple heavens through which Christ passes on his way to incarnation). *Gk* perhaps ἐπάνω τῶν οὐρανῶν, as in *Ps* 107.5.

21.6–7 *He answered and said to us, 'Do you believe* that everything I say to you will come to pass?' And we answered him and said to him, 'Yes, Lord!'*]
The *Eth* imperative, 'Believe that everything...' is probably a misunderstanding of the ambiguous *Gk* πιστεύετε (so Hills). Elsewhere, 'Yes' responds to a question (*EpAp* 14.2, 4; 16.9; 40.4; 45.3). Cf. *GJn* 14.1, 16.31 for indicative, imperative, and interrogative uses of πιστεύετε.

21.8 ... *so that those in darkness I may turn to light*]
In a fragment from the bottom of **XV–XVI** *Cop*, 'in darkness I...' indicates that *Cop* continues to keep in step with *Eth* throughout this passage. The fragment appears to have suffered further damage since being transcribed by Schmidt.

22.1–2 *And when he said this to us, we said to him, 'Lord, is the flesh really to be judged with the soul and the spirit? And will some find rest in the kingdom of heaven and others be condemned for ever while living?*]
(1) The translation is based on *Eth*, with the exception of the contrast between 'some' and 'others' which is clear in the surviving

fragment of **XVI** *Cop*: [ⲅⲁⲉⲓⲛⲉ] ⲙⲉⲛ ⲅⲉⲛⲕⲉ[ⲕⲉⲅⲉ] ⲇⲉ = *Gk* οἳ μέν... οἳ δέ..., *Eth manfaq... manfaq* (part... part, cf. Dillmann 712, citing *Rom* 9.21, ὃ μὲν εἰς τιμὴν σκεῦος ὃ δὲ εἰς ἀτιμίαν). *Eth* reads: 'Lord, is the flesh really to be judged with the soul and the spirit [*wa-manfas*]? Will it find rest in the kingdom of heaven and part [*wa-manfaq*] be condemned for ever while living?' It is likely that the partitive construction found in *Cop* also occurred in *Eth*, and that the first *wa-manfaq* dropped out accidentally because of confusion with *wa-manfas* at the end of the preceding question: 'Lord, is the flesh really to be judged with the soul and the spirit? Will part [= some] find rest in the kingdom of heaven and part [= others] be condemned for ever while living?'

(2) Schmidt's translation of *Cop* may respond to Wajnberg's *Eth*, even though his edition of *Cop* remains uncorrected. Drawing from *Eth*, Schmidt reconstructs and translates *Cop* as follows:

> \<O Herr, ist es wahr, dass gerichtet wird das\> Fleisch (σάρξ) \<und die Seele (ψυχή) und der Geist (πνεῦμα), und dass die einen\> zwar (μέν) werden \<ruhen in dem Reich der Himmel\>, die andern aber (δέ) \<werden bestraft (κολάζειν) werden ewiglich\> (noch) lebend?   (Schmidt 75, 77)

As Schmidt rightly notes, the *Cop* plurals [ⲅⲁⲉⲓⲛⲉ] ⲙⲉⲛ, 'die einen', ⲅⲉⲛⲕⲉ[ⲕⲉⲅⲉ] ⲇⲉ, 'und die andern') indicate that a second question is here being posed, related to but differentiated from the first. The disciples ask first about the presence of the flesh at the judgement along with the soul and the spirit, and second about the division between the saved and the condemned.

(3) In contrast, Duensing's rendering of *Eth* ignores the *Cop* plurals:

> O Herr, steht es wirklich dem Fleisch bevor, mit der Seele und dem Geist (zusammen) gerichtet zu werden, und wird (die eine Hälfte davon) (K. zwar) im Himmelreich ruhen und die andere (K. + aber) ewiglich, indem sie (noch) leben, gestraft werden?[12]

In the Müller/Taylor version this reads:

> O Lord, is it really in store for the flesh to be judged (together) with the soul and spirit, and will (one of these)

---

[12] K = Koptisch.

(*Copt.:* really) rest in heaven and the other (*Copt:* however) be punished eternally while it is (still) alive?

By conflating the two distinct questions, Duensing has replaced a division of the human race (one part destined for heaven, the other for condemnation) with an anomalous division into two halves of the three constituents of the human person (flesh, soul, spirit). Müller/Taylor render Duensing's two halves as 'one of these' and 'the other', which makes equally little sense in the context of a tripartite rather than bipartite anthropology. An eschatology in which the body endures eternal punishment while the spirit rests in heaven would, of course, be highly unusual.

(4) These problems are perpetuated in the most recent translation, that of Hills (2009), where the reconstruction of *Cop* is based on Schmidt while the unlikely eschatology is Duensing's:

> [O Lord..., will the] *flesh* (σαρξ) [be judged with the *soul* (ψυχη) and the *spirit* (πνα)? And will one], then, [rest in the kingdom of heaven,] (and) the other [(be) eternally *punished* (κολαζε) while still li]ving? (Hills 49)

Incidentally, σάρξ, read by Schmidt, is no longer extant in the fragment of **XVI**.

23.1–2 Cop *Lord, it is necessary for us to question you, for you command us to preach; so that we ourselves may know with certainty through you and be useful preachers, and [that] those who will teach through us may believe in you,* Eth *Lord, it is necessary, for you commanded us to preach and proclaim and teach, so that having heard with certainty from you we may be useful preachers and teach them that they may believe in you]*

The main differences between the two versions are *(i)* the absence from *Eth* of 'to question you', redundant in view of Jesus' preceding question; *(ii)* the typical *Eth* addition of two near-synonyms to 'preach'; *(iii)* *Cop* future knowing, *Eth* past hearing; *(iv)* *Cop* 'those who will teach through us', *Eth* 'them', not further specified. The emphasis on ongoing transmission is stronger in *Cop*, with its link between what is to be known 'through you' and those who will later believe and teach 'through us'.

24.6 Cop *But without delay or shame (that we are asking you so much and are wearying you. Then he answered) or partiality, serve in the way that is straight and narrow and difficult]*

The Coptic scribe has accidentally inserted the beginning of the next question and answer, his eye having wandered from one reference to 'shame' (24.6) to another a few lines below (25.1). Realizing his mistake, he places the incorrect words in parentheses and returns to the correct point in his exemplar.

25.1 Cop *Lord, we are now ashamed that we are asking you so much and are wearying you*, Eth *Lord, behold, with so many questions we are talking foolishly to you]*

The *Eth* verb translated 'talk foolishly' (*zangəʻa*) gives an acceptable sense here, and there is no need to follow Wajnberg's emendation to a dubious causative form that supposedly means 'enrage' (Schmidt-Wajnberg 80, cf. Hills 51), or Duensing's emendation to 'mock' (*zangʷagʷa*), reproduced by Müller/Taylor. See Dillmann 1055–56; Leslau 640. Assuming *Cop* to remain closer to *Gk* here, the slight semantic shift in *Eth* is typical of this version of *EpAp*. The translator or a later scribe may have wished to avoid the impression that the risen Lord could become weary.

25.6 Eth *Which is it that perishes, the flesh or the spirit?*, Cop *Does the flesh perish that is in the Spirit?]*

The apparent reference to the Holy Spirit is not relevant here, and *Eth* makes better sense of the disciples' answer: 'It is the flesh that perishes!' (25.8).

26.1 *Truly I say to you that the flesh will rise with the soul alive, so that they may be judged on that day for what they have done, whether good or evil]*

(1) *the flesh will rise with the soul alive]* 'Alive' is derived from *Eth*, filling a lacuna in *Cop*. Correspondence with *Eth* makes ⲉⲩⲁⲛ = *həyāw* ('alive', cf. 39.11) preferable to Schmidt's ⲙⲛ̄ ⲡⲛⲁ̄ ('and the spirit', cf. 22.1; 24.1). Hills accepts Schmidt's conjecture in his translation of *Cop* and then transfers it to *Eth*: '... the flesh will arise alive with the soul and the spirit'.

(2) *so that they may be judged]* *Cop* might more literally be translated, 'so that their ⲁⲡⲟⲗⲟⲅⲓⲁ might take place', with the loanword here used to mean not so much 'defence' (Schmidt, Hills) as 'trial' or 'judgement.' *Eth* 'so that they may confess and be judged in righteousness' suggests an original *Gk* ἵνα κριθῶσιν, subjected to typical *Eth* expansions.

(3) *on that day]* This phrase represents Schmidt's restoration: [ⲛ̄ϥⲟⲟⲩⲉ] ⲉⲧⲙ̄ⲙ̣ⲟ The phrase is attested in *EpAp*ᶜᵒᵖ 13.5, 14.5, 39.3

(cf. *EpAp*^{eth} 39.3, 47.8), and surviving ink-traces at the upper edge of the lacuna make ⲉⲧⲏⲙⲟ highly probable. *Eth* substitutes 'in right-eousness' for 'in that day.'

26.6 Cop *And they will see what he has granted me: he has given me authority to do as I will, and to give what I promised and what I willed to give them and grant them,* Eth *Behold, see what authority he has granted me: he has given me what I will and what I willed for those to whom I promised]*

Where possible, the translations of the two versions use the same vocabulary so that their relationship can be analysed. In both, a bestowal by the Father to the Son is first asserted and then (following the colon) defined in two further stages. Underlinings below repre-sent words or verbal forms present in one translation only, at points indicated by empty square brackets in the other. Angled brackets indicate a transposition:

(1) Cop *And [ ] they will see what he has granted me: he has given me authority to do as I will,* Eth *Behold, [ ] see what <authority> he has granted me: he has given me [ ] what I will]* The *Eth* imperative, 'see', is probably a corruption of an earlier *Eth* 'they will see', which the context requires; the imperative was then reinforced by the addition of 'Behold'. In *Cop*, 'authority to do as I will' is 'what he has granted me'. In *Eth*, it is unclear how the 'authority' granted relates to the vague 'what I will'.

(2) Cop *and to give what I promised and what I willed to give them and grant them,* Eth *and [ ] what I willed <for those to whom I promised>]* In *Cop* Jesus asserts the identity of the salvation he will finally bestow with what he intended and promised all along. *Eth*'s abbreviation of *Gk* (if that is what it is) produces a more confused sense.

27.1 *This is why I descended* Cop *to the place of Lazarus and preached to your fathers and the prophets* {Eth *and conversed with Abraham, Isaac, and Jacob*}, *that they would go forth from the rest below and ascend <–Eth> to that which is in heaven]*

There are some textual uncertainties in *Eth*, but it seems clear that 'the place of Lazarus' (cf. *GLk* 16.20, 23) has been deleted, that 'conversed with' has been substituted for 'preached to', and that 'Abraham, Isaac, and Jacob' is a gloss on 'your fathers' in the phrase that follows. As regards *Cop*, there is no justification for Schmidt's conjectural [ⲛ̄ⲛ̄ⲇⲓ]ⲕⲁ[ⲓⲟⲥ ⲙⲛ̄] ('to the righteous and', accepted by

Hills) rather than [ⲛⲉⲧ]ⲛ̄[ⲉⲓⲁⲧⲉ ⲙⲛ̄], 'to your fathers and. . .', as suggested by *Eth* and by a possible trace of the letter ⲛ rather than ⲕⲁ.

27.2 *And with my right hand I poured* over them the baptism of life*, Cop. . . *right [ha]nd over them. . . of life* Eth *And I gave them the right hand, the baptism of life]*

(1) In view of *Eth* here and the phrase 'the baptism of life' in 42.3, *Cop* **XXII** 2 should be restored as [ⲡⲃⲁⲡⲧⲓⲥⲙⲁ] ⲛ̄ⲱⲛϩ. *Eth* 'And I gave them the right hand' corresponds to *Cop* '[. . . . . .] right hand over them' (**XXII** 1), and 'over them' and the following reference to baptism indicate that the missing *Cop* verb is likely to be not 'give' but 'pour': perhaps [ⲁⲓⲡⲁϩⲧ ϩⲛ̄ ⲧⲁϭⲓ]ϫ ⲛ̄ⲟⲩⲛⲉⲙ ⲁϩⲣⲏⲓ ⲁϫⲱⲟⲩ [ⲡⲃⲁⲡⲧⲓⲥⲙⲁ] ⲛ̄ⲱⲛϩ, 'I poured with my right hand over them the baptism of life'. For ⲡⲱϩⲧ ⲉϩⲣⲁⲓ ⲉϫⲛ, 'pour over', cf. *GMt* 26.7[sah], *Acts* 10.44[sah]. For 'with my right hand', cf. *EpAp* 42.3, where 'the baptism of life' is again carried out ϩⲛ̄ ⲧⲁϭⲓϫ, 'by my hand.'

(2) In previous translations the passage is unintelligible. Schmidt's tentative translation is correct as far as it goes: '<Und ich habe ausgegossen? mit? meiner> rechten <Hand> über sie / <. . . . .> des Lebens und Vergebung und Erretung <vor> allem <Bösen>' (Schmidt-Wajnberg 87). Yet, here as elsewhere, Schmidt's failure to fill the remaining lacuna on the basis of *Eth* is remarkable. Duensing leaves the lacunae unfilled: '. . . rechte <Han>d auf sie. . . des Lebens.' Müller offers '(indem ich ausstrecke) meine rechte Hand über sie. . . des Lebens,' accepting Schmidt's original conjectural ⲉⲓⲡⲱⲣϩ (Schmidt-Wajnberg 13*, cf. Crum 269b) which he failed to correct when he proposed reconstructing the text as, 'Und ich habe ausgegossen' (87). Hills rightly fills the second lacuna with '[the baptism] of life', but the resulting translation ('. . . them the right hand of the baptism of life', etc.) introduces further confusion by identifying Christ's right hand with baptism.

28.3 Cop (reconstructed): *Lord, you have surely given us rest [of life] and you have given us joy with signs to [confirm] faith. Will you now preach to us what you preached to our fathers and the prophets?*, Eth (A): *Lord, in everything you have given us joy and rest in faith and truth, you have preached to our fathers and the prophets <and likewise to us and to all –A>]*

(1) The reconstruction of 28.3 *Cop* is uncertain. Schmidt's 'rest [of life]' is plausible in view of 26.5, although *Eth* suggests that this is given 'to us' rather than 'to them' (i.e. the righteous in Hades) as Schmidt proposes. 'Joy' derives from *Eth*, as *Cop* at this point is

seemingly unintelligible. *Cop* and *Eth* both refer to 'faith', and Schmidt's conjecture 'confirm' (ⲧⲁϫⲣⲟ) might correspond to *Eth* 'truth' (*'amin*) and is elsewhere closely associated with 'signs' (cf. *GMk* 16.20[sah]; *Heb* 2.3–4[sah]).

(2) The disciples draw a parallel between Jesus' preaching to the dead and to the living. The versions refer to the two audiences in reverse order, and *Eth* extends the living audience into the future. The *Cop* request is more appropriate to the context than the *Eth* assertion.

29.1 Cop *But those who transgress my commandments and teach teachings other [than] what is written, and who add to th[em]...]*
'Teaching other teachings' may represent *Gk* ἑτεροδιδασκαλέω, attested by Ignatius as he warns Polycarp against οἱ δοκοῦντες ἀξιόπιστοι εἶναι καὶ ἑτεροδιδασκαλοῦντες (Ignatius *Pol* 3.1). 'Adding' to the commandments derives ultimately from Moses' warning to the Israelites: οὐ προσθήσετε πρὸς τὸ ῥῆμα ὃ ἐγὼ ἐντέλλομαι ὑμῖν (*Deut* 4.2; cf. *Barn* 19.11; *GMary* 8,22–9,2, 18,19–21). The corresponding warning not to remove commandments is present only in *Eth*. This passage recalls the warnings against Simon and Cerinthus (*EpAp* 1.2; 7.1), but the concern is with improper conduct – transgressing Jesus' commandments – rather than doctrines.

30.3 *Go and preach the mercy of my Father...]*
Eth MSS here demonstrate their tendency to progressive expansion of *Gk*. B originally shared with E K the reading, 'Go and preach about the mercy of my Father', an equivalent of *Cop* which must therefore correspond closely to *Gk*. After 'preach' a sign indicates the insertion of additional words located at the head of the column, 'and teach about my coming and'. Thus the corrector wishes the passage to read: 'Go and preach <and teach about the coming and> about the mercy of my Father.' The insertion causes an unidiomatic repetition of 'about' which confirms that the short text is not the result merely of a scribal error; the stylistic awkwardness is smoothed over when the second 'about' is omitted in L. The insertion itself consists of two distinct elements, however, for A C include only 'and teach': 'Go and preach <and teach> about the mercy of my Father.' The passage thus exists in short (B* E K), intermediate (A C), and long (B[1] G L) forms. The long form has probably arisen through an earlier substitution of 'the [his] coming' (*maṣ'atu*, with anticipatory pronominal suffix) for 'the [his] mercy' (*maḥratu*) and the subsequent

combination of the two variants. The long form is further refined in S: 'Go and preach and teach about the coming *as of* the mercy of my Father.' Since the B* E K reading = *Cop*, it most probably preserves the original *Eth* reading, suggesting that many *Eth* deviations from *Cop* may be secondary and do not reflect a different *Gk* text.

30.5 Cop *And to others also I will give my power, and they will teach the rest of the Gentiles* {Eth... *so that they may give it to the Gentiles*} *]*

Cop should be translated 'the rest of the Gentiles' (Hills) rather than 'the rest of the nations', i.e. in addition to the nation of Israel (Müller/Taylor). While the apostles preach primarily to the people of Israel but also to the Gentiles (30.1; 36.7), others are needed – of whom Paul is the foremost (31.9, 12) – if the Gentile mission is to be completed. *EpAp* appears not to know the tradition that the Twelve evangelized the whole world, apparently without help from Paul (cf. *GMt* 28.19–20; *AcThos* 1).

31.10 Eth *As you have learnt from the scriptures that your fathers the prophets spoke about me and in me it is fulfilled, so you must provide guidance in them.]*

(1) The phrase, 'your fathers the prophets' is attested in *Eth* MSS at *EpAp* 27.1, where it is a conflation of 'your fathers and the prophets' (E K, cf. *Cop*). Most probably, 'your fathers' should be deleted here and the text should read: 'As you have learnt from the scriptures that the prophets spoke about me...' (cf. 19.29^{cop}, 'And if all the words spoken by the prophets are fulfilled in me...').

(2) 'So you must provide guidance in them' might be more literally translated, 'so you, be in/to them a guide', where 'in them' would refer to 'the scriptures' and 'to them' to unspecified persons. The former is more probable in this context, as 'to them' would lack an antecedent. The apostles here are told to provide Paul with the guidance in the scriptures that the Ethiopian eunuch received from Philip (cf. *Acts* 8.31, πῶς γὰρ ἂν δυναίμην ἐὰν μή τις ὁδηγήσει με;).

31.11 *And every word that I have spoken to you and that you write about me, that I am the Word of the Father and the Father is in me, you also must pass on* to that man]*

'That you write' is literally 'that you have written'. While it is not impossible that the author believes that the apostles have already written about Jesus on Easter Day, it is preferable to suppose that a future perfect sense is intended: they are to communicate to

Saul/Paul what they will have written when they encounter him, although they have not written it yet. The essential content of that future writing – 'that I am the Word of the Father and the Father is in me' – might suggest an allusion to *GJohn* but is more likely to refer to the present text, where Jesus' claim to be 'the Word' is closely correlated with references to 'the Father who is in me' (cf. 17.8–18.1; 39.11–12). The plural verb (*ṣaḥafkəmu*) implies that collective rather than individual apostolic authorship is in view. If *EpAp* refers here to itself, the apostles write their letter at a time before Jesus' prophecy of the conversion of Saul/Paul has been fulfilled.

33.3 Eth *It is I who will speak through you, and it will happen soon]*
In place of 'It is I who will speak through you' (cf. Wajnberg, Duensing, Müller/Taylor, Pérès), Hills translates 'that is, I through you', and connects the reference to Christ's speech with the statement that follows: 'What I say will be accomplished quickly.' The conjunction in *wa-yəbaṣṣəḥ* ('and it will happen') makes this translation unlikely. 'And it will happen soon' might alternatively be translated 'and he will come quickly'. For *baṣḥa* (happen, occur, arrive) with a personal subject, cf. *Isa* 60.1, 'he who comes [*za-baṣḥa*] from Edom' (Dillmann 545). The impersonal sense seems more appropriate to this context, however.

33.4–5 *so that what the prophetic voice said might be fulfilled: 'Behold, from the land of Syria I will begin to call a new Jerusalem, and Zion I will subdue to myself and it will be captured.']*
EpAp includes genuine scriptural quotations at 19.20–26 (*Ps* 3.2–7 LXX) and 35.6–8 (*Pss* 13.3, 49.18–20 LXX) and largely or entirely invented ones here and at 11.1 ('For it is written in the prophet, "As for the appearance of a demon, its foot is not in contact with the ground"'); 43.4 ('Of them the prophet said, "They are children of God"'); 49.2 ('For as it is written, "Let not your ear listen to anything against your brother"'). In 47.6 ('As the prophet said, "Woe to those who show partiality, who justify the sinner for a bribe, whose stomach is their god"'), the second phrase derives from *Isa* 5.22–23, the third from *Phil* 3.19.

34.4 Eth A S: *I will teach you what will happen not only to you but also to those whom you teach and who believe <and those who hear this man and believe* (Eth)*> in me]*
The longer text here seems to include a further reference to Paul ('this man', cf. 33.1, 2; see Wajnberg's comments [Schmidt-Wajnberg

101n.] on translation issues here). A distinction between the disciples' converts and Paul's is in line with 32.1–2, and is probably original to the present context. The omission would be a straightforward case of haplography.

34.10 *and a great earthquake and widespread death and many trials]*
The translation follows *Eth* in differentiating three noun + adjective pairings by way of the conjunction *wa-*. 'Many trials' (or 'much testing') takes *maftani* as a variant spelling of *maftani*, 'testing' rather than 'quick' (trr). Such minor spelling variants are common in the *Eth* manuscripts. Duensing's rendering, 'eine grosse Pest und ein ausgebreitetes und häufiges schnelles Sterben' (followed as usual by Müller/Taylor) requires an unlikely translation of *bəzuḥ* as 'häufig', 'frequent'. Hills translates, 'severe and prolonged plague; so much death, and so sudden', which ignores the placement of the *Eth* conjunctions, as does Guerrier's 'peste grande et étendue, et la mort fréquente et rapide'. For 'widespread death', cf. *EpAp* 34.13 ('there will be a plague everywhere'), and for 'many trials', cf. 36.4 ('such an affliction will be to test them').

34.12 *And those who are bereaved will rise up and see those who had departed from them being carried out]*
Or, 'And those who are forsaken will rise up and see those who forsook them being carried out.' It is difficult to make sense of this except in terms of bereavement. The sense may be that one family member recovers from the plague only to see the corpse of another being carried out.

35.6–8 (1) *Swift are their feet to shed blood,* (2) *and their tongue weaves deceit,* (3) *and the venom of snakes is under their lips.* (4) *And I see you go about as a thief, and with an adulterer is your portion.* (5) *While you sit you slander your brother and set a stumbling-block for your mother's son. What do you think, that I am like you?]*
This passage is derived in part from the composite scriptural citation in *Rom* 3.13–18 as interpolated into *Ps* 13.3 LXX. The opening of the Pauline catena is drawn from *Ps* 13.1–3 (cf. *Rom* 3.10–12), and a Christian interpolator added the remainder of the catena to the psalm text on the mistaken assumption that Paul was citing a single passage, subsequently truncated in the manuscript tradition. The interpolation was already recognized as such by Origen, and it occurs throughout the LXX tradition with the

exception of the Lucianic recension.[13] The *EpAp* passage is thus drawn from two sources (*Pss* 13.3, 49.18–20) rather than the multiple sources underlying the original Pauline passage (noted in Duensing 1959, contra Duensing 1925). The reference to Davidic authorship (*EpAp* 35.5) may stem from a Greek exemplar in which *Ps* 49 was attributed to David (rather than Asaph) in addition to *Ps* 13, as in Codex Alexandrinus. References below are to the ten lines of *Ps* 13.3 LXX as printed in the Rahlfs edition.

(1) The *Eth* word-order follows that of *Ps* 13.3g LXX (=*Rom* 3.15): ὀξεῖς οἱ πόδες αὐτῶν ἐκχέαι αἷμα. The Pauline sources are *Isa* 59.7a: οἱ δὲ πόδες αὐτῶν ἐπὶ πονηρίαν τρέχουσιν ταχινοὶ ἐκχέαι αἷμα, and/or *Prov* 1.16: οἱ γὰρ πόδες αὐτῶν εἰς κακίαν τρέχουσιν καὶ ταχινοὶ τοῦ ἐκχέαι αἷμα.

(2) *Ps* 49.19b: καὶ ἡ γλῶσσά σου περιέπλεκεν δολιότητα (*var.* κακίαν). Cf. *Ps* 13.3d (*Rom* 3.13b = *Ps* 5.10d): ταῖς γλώσσαις αὐτῶν ἐδολιοῦσαν. The close relationship between these two passages probably underlies the decision to combine other material from *Pss* 13.3 and 49.18–20.

(3) *Ps* 13.3e (*Rom* 3.13c = *Ps* 139.4b): ἰὸς ἀσπίδων ὑπὸ τὰ χείλη αὐτῶν.

(4) *Ps* 49.18: εἰ ἐθεώρεις κλέπτην, συνέτρεχες αὐτῷ, καὶ μετὰ μοιχῶν [*var.* μοιχοῦ] τὴν μερίδα σου ἐτίθεις.

(5) *Ps* 49.20–21b: καθήμενος κατὰ τοῦ ἀδελφοῦ σου κατελάλεις καὶ κατὰ τοῦ υἱοῦ τῆς μητρός σου ἐτίθεις σκάνδαλον. ταῦτα ἐποίησας, καὶ ἐσίγησα. ὑπέλαβες ἀνομίαν ὅτι ἔσομαί σοι ὅμοιος.

36.4–5 *... when they are tormented such an affliction will be to test them. If there is faith within them and if they remember these words of mine and obey my commandment, they will be raised.*]

(1) The translation follows Guerrier in assuming that 'if there is faith within them...' begins a new sentence: 'Si la foi fut en eux, s'ils sont souvenus de ma parole, et ont accompli ma volonté, ils ressusciteront...' The expression translated 'if there is' (*'əmmabo*) recurs in *EpAp* 48.1 at the opening of a sentence.

(2) In contrast, Wajnberg attaches the conditional clauses to the preceding statement: '... aber wenn sie solche Schmerzen leiden, wird dies ihnen zur Prüfung, ob sie Glauben haben und ob sie dieser meiner Worte gedenken und meine Gebote erfüllen. Diese werden

---

[13] See A. Rahlfs, *Psalmi cum Odis*, Vetus Testamentum Graecum X (Göttingen: Vandenhoeck & Ruprecht, 1979³), 30–31.

auferstehen...' (cf. Duensing, Müller). This translation results in an abrupt beginning to the new sentence and overlooks the author's fondness for opening sentences with conditional clauses (cf. 19.29; 27.3; 38.4; 39.7).

(3) A further possibility is to divide the two conditional statements, as does Hills: the affliction of the elect 'will be a test for them, whether they have faith. If they remember this word of mind and keep my commandments they will arise...' (cf. Pérès). The translation overlooks the co-ordination of the two conditional clauses: *'əmmabo... wa-'əmma...* (if there is... and if...).

36.6–7a *And their situation will be for a few days, so that the one who sent me may be glorified and I with him, for he sent me to you. This I tell you, and you must tell it to Israel and to the Gentiles...]*

(1) 'Their situation' (*nəbtratomu*) probably refers to the suffering to be endured by the elect, not to their pre- or post-mortem 'waiting' (Müller, cf. Duensing, Wajnberg).

(2) Hills again punctuates differently: 'For he sent me to you that I might tell this to you, and that you tell Israel and the Gentiles...' The purpose clause reduces slightly the redundancy caused by the double reference to sending, but it is not clear that the Ge'ez can bear this sense.

36.7b-8 *... and be saved and believe and depart out of the affliction of the plague. And whoever survives the affliction of death will be taken and kept in prison, punished like a thief]*

Confusingly, the same verb (*waḍ'a / waṣ'a*) is used both of the elect who 'depart' from the world (36.2–3) or from the plague (36.7) and of unbelievers or false believers who 'survive the affliction of death' (36.8) and yet are punished (cf. 36.9, 11). The distinction may have been clearer in *Gk* than it is in *Eth*. Thus in 36.3, 'their departure' (*ḍa'ātomu*) may represent *Gk* ἡ ἔξοδος αὐτῶν, an echo of *Wis* 3.2. Or *Gk* may be better reflected by the variant 'their coming out of the world' (A C), a possible echo of *Rev* 7.14 (οἱ ἐρχόμενοι ἐκ τῆς θλίψεως τῆς μεγάλης).

36.11 *Lord, so this is the fate of those who survive, that they fail to attain life?]*

While the syntax of the disciples' statement or question is difficult, a reference to 'fate' is more probable than Hills's proposal, 'In that case, have those who survive no life?' Müller/Taylor's 'Have they who escaped this destiny no life?' (= Duensing) makes little sense in this context.

36.12 *Whoever glorifies my Father will dwell* with my Father]*
Eth here reads: 'Whoever glorifies my Father is the dwelling-place of/with my Father.' The variant 'with' (A C E G K) may stem from a reading in which it was preceded not by a verbal noun but by a finite verb in the imperfect. Salvation as a future dwelling with the Father is more in keeping with the soteriology of this text than a present indwelling of the Father (cf. *EpAp* 12.3–4; 19.1–3, 14; 28.4; 42.6).

38.1 *And those who desire to see the face of God, and who do not show partiality to rich sinners, and who are not ashamed before the men who go astray but rebuke them, these will be crowned* in the presence of the Father.]*
'Crowned' ($q^w a\d{s}ul\bar{a}n$) is Guerrier's emendation of *Eth* 'wounded' ($q^w asul\bar{a}n$). Thus, instead of 'these will be crowned in the presence of the Father', Hills's translation of *Eth* reads, 'they, the wounded, will be with the Father'. The case for the emendation is strong. The tendency of *Eth* MSS to substitute similar words with different meanings can be illustrated from this same passage, where B C read 'who [*ʾəllā*] rebuke them' rather than 'but [*ʾāllā*] rebuke them' (A G L).

39.1 *Lord, it is in your power* [lit. *it is yours*] *not to allow these things* to befall them!]*
This is probably a statement not a question, as the Lord's response takes the form of a question. The translation and the sense are uncertain, however, and the rendering here requires an emendation of *Cop* ϫⲉⲕⲁⲁⲥ ⲛⲉⲕⲕⲁⲁⲛⲉ (that you may not allow us) to ϫⲉⲕⲁⲁⲥ ⲛⲉⲕⲕⲁⲁ ⲛⲉⲓ (that you may not allow these things). As *Cop* stands, it may be translated, 'O Lord, what is yours is this, that you do not let us come upon them' (Müller/Taylor), which is almost meaningless. In favour of emending ⲛⲉ to ⲛⲉⲓ is the *Eth* reading, 'Lord, will this befall all of them?', which may be understood as an attempt to dilute what is actually the disciples' protest against the coming disasters of which Jesus has spoken. That the *Cop* scribe or his source is capable of such an error is evident from the next line (**XXVIII** 3), where, in the stock phrase, 'he answered and said', ⲁϥⲟⲩⲱϣⲃⲉ ('he answered') is copied without the final syllable as ⲁϥⲟⲩⲱϣ ('he wished').

39.3 Cop *You did not separate righteousness and unrighteousness, light and darkness, evil and good.* Eth *You showed righteousness and sin and you separated darkness and light and evil and good]*

Trr 'you did not pursue righteousness. . .', taking ⲡⲱⲧⲥⲉ as 'pursue after' (Sahidic ⲡⲱⲧ ⲛ̄ⲥⲁ) rather than the more probable 'divide, separate, split' (= ⲡⲱⲧⲥ, Crum 276a; addition of a final *epsilon* is very common in *EpAp*^cop). That this is the correct reading is confirmed by *Eth* 'you separated' (*falaṭka*, Dillmann 1343), although *Eth* has removed the negative and added a verb, transforming the complaint of the unrighteous into a confession of divine justice. In *Cop* the unrighteous complain that clear moral guidance was not provided in their earthly lives.

40.1–2 *We said to him, 'Lord, truly we are concerned for them.' He said to us, 'You do well, for the righteous are concerned for sinners]*

(1) In the disciples' expression of concern over the fate of sinners, trr tend to differentiate *Cop* from *Eth*: thus Hills, 'Truly we are concerned about them' (*Cop*), 'Truly we are sad about them' (*Eth*). Yet *Cop* and *Eth* may represent the same *Gk*, perhaps ἀληθῶς μέλει ἡμῖν περὶ αὐτῶν. The *Cop*^ly and *Eth* verbs are, respectively, ϥⲓⲣⲁⲅⲱ (Crum 307b) and *ḥazana* (Dillmann 123: *ḥazana*), and they coincide again in the *Cop*^ly and *Eth* translations of *GJn* 10.13, οὐ μέλει αὐτῷ περὶ τῶν προβάτων (Thompson 20; Wechsler 61).

(2) In Jesus' response *Eth* selects a different verb, *takkaza*, which like *ḥazana* can mean either 'grieve' or 'be concerned' (Dillmann 567). A reference to grief might suggest *Gk* λυπεῖσθαι, but this is unlikely as *Cop* elsewhere takes over this term as a loanword (ⲣ̄ⲗⲩⲡⲉⲓ: *EpAp* 15.3; 43.11; 46.5) but does not do so here.

40.3 *Eth Lord, so does no one intercede with you yourself?*, Cop *Lord, why then is no one ashamed before you?]*

The sequel, in which Jesus confirms that he himself will hear the intercession of the righteous for the unrighteous, shows that the *Eth* reading here is correct. It is possible that, at some point in the *Cop* manuscript tradition, ϣⲓⲡⲉ ⲅ̄ⲏⲧⲕ (ashamed before you) has replaced ϣⲓⲛⲉ (ask) + prepositional phrase. This would give a sense close to *Eth*, though with a superfluous 'why' added: 'Lord, why then does no one ask you?' The disciples' question arises from the previous reference to intercession addressed to the Father, leading them to ask whether Jesus himself will hear intercession.

41.4 *Lord, you said to us, Do not call anyone your father on earth {Eth Do not say, <We have a A> father on earth and teacher}, for there is one who is your Father who is in heaven and your teacher {Eth your teacher who is in heaven}]*

As the disciples quote back to Jesus something he said to them earlier, before his passion, so *EpAp* quotes from an earlier gospel text, *GMt* 23.9, supplemented by a contrast between the earthly and heavenly teacher drawn from *GMt* 23.8, 10. *Cop* is closer to *GMt* than *Eth*, and variants within the *Eth* manuscript tradition make it impossible to identify an alignment with *GMt*$^{\text{eth-A}}$ or *GMt*$^{\text{eth-B}}$ (see the *Additional Notes* on *EpAp*^{eth} 5.8, 10, 17, 19). Thus for 'father on earth' different *Eth* MSS attest both *'aba ba-mədr* (=*GMt*$^{\text{eth-A}}$) and *'aba ba-diba mədr* (=*GMt*$^{\text{eth-B}}$).

43.1–2 Cop *And you will be* {Eth *And be*} *like the wise virgins who watched* {Eth *lit their lamps*} *and did not sleep but went out* <Eth *with their lamps*> *to the lord* <Eth *the bridegroom and entered with him*> *into the wedding-chamber. But the foolish ones* <Eth *who spoke with them*> *were unable to watch but slept]*

(1) The *Eth* virgins 'made light' (*'abrəhā*), i.e. they lit their lamps; they did not themselves 'shine' (Hills), as the following *Eth* reference to 'their lamps' (*maḥatwihon*) makes clear (cf. *GMt* 25.3–4). In *Cop* the Matthean lamps are absent. *Cop* '... went out to the Lord into the wedding-chamber' seems to require the second verb ('and entered') supplied by *Eth* here and echoed by 43.8^{cop}. In *GMt* 25 likewise, the wise virgins go out (v.6) and enter (v.10): *Gk* 'entered with him into the wedding-chamber' would correspond closely to *GMt* 25.10, εἰσῆλθον μετ' αὐτοῦ εἰς τοὺς γάμους (*Sah* ⲁⲩⲃⲱⲕ ⲉⲅⲟⲩⲛ ⲛⲙⲙⲁϥ ⲉⲡⲙⲁ ⲛϣⲉⲗⲉⲉⲧ).

(2) The five wise virgins are admitted either to a wedding feast (γάμος) or a 'bride-chamber' (νυμφών), i.e. a bedroom, as at *Tobit* 6.13, 16. *Cop* is ambiguous here. The Coptic term ϣⲉⲗⲉⲉⲧ, 'bride', also means 'wedding' (Crum 560b), and ⲡⲙⲁ ⲛϣⲉⲗⲉⲉⲧ ('the place of the bride/wedding') may render either γάμος (*GMt* 22.8, 9; 25.10) or νυμφών (*GMt* 9.15 + pars.).

(3) In *EpAp* 43.1^{eth}, the virgins enter the *ṣərḥa mar'āwi*, the upper room of the bridegroom, i.e. the bride-chamber (Dillmann 310, 1273), perhaps suggesting that *Gk* νυμφών rather than γάμος underlies both *Eth* and *Cop* here; for γάμος one would expect *kabkāb*, 'wedding[-feast]' as at *EpAp* 5.1. Yet *GMt* 25.10$^{\text{eth-A}}$ has the wise virgins entering the *ṣə<r>ḥa mar'āwi*, whereas in a later revision they enter the *kabkāb*, 'wedding' (Zuurmond III, 252, 253), and it is probable that *Eth* here reflects familiarity with the Matthean parable in the vernacular rendering and that *Gk* here read γάμος rather than νυμφών. Matthean influence is clear from the double reference to lamps in *EpAp* 43.1^{eth}.

43.8 Cop... *and they reclined with me in my wedding-chamber*, Eth... *and they reclined with the bridegroom]*

'Reclined' represents *Cop* ⲁⲩⲧⲏⲕⲟⲩ, from ⲧⲱⲕ,'throw', thus literally 'they threw them[selves]'. Cf. *GMt* 22.10,11[sah], where those who recline at the wedding feast (οἱ ἀνακειμένοι) are ⲛⲉⲧⲛⲏⲝ, literally 'the thrown' (from ⲛⲟⲩϫⲉ).

43.11–12 Cop '*... And did they not grieve for them or did they not plead with the bridegroom on their behalf to open to them?' And he answered, saying to us, 'They were not yet able to find grace on their behalf'*, Eth (–A): '*... And did they not grieve for them?' And he said to us, 'Yes, they were sorrowful and they grieved for them, (+A) and they pleaded with the bridegroom, and they were not <yet B K> able to prevail on their behalf]*

(1) The *Cop* negatives (ⲙⲡⲟⲩ-) and the use of ⲏ = ἤ ('or') suggest *Gk* questions introduced by οὐ[κ] or οὐχί, expecting and appealing for an affirmative response and implying incredulity towards a potential negative one. (Cf. *GMt* 20.13, 15: οὐχὶ δηναρίου συνεφώνησάς μοι... ἢ οὐκ ἔξεστίν μοι ὃ θέλω ποιῆσαι ἐν τοῖς ἐμοῖς.) The disciples here put pressure on Jesus to revise the parable's scenario of inclusion and exclusion.

(2) By shifting back the introductory formula ('And he said to us'), *Eth* ᴍss here present Jesus as repeating and amplifying the disciples' appeal on behalf of the excluded. The point may be to reduce the gap that opens up here between the disciples and Jesus.

43.15 *And we said to him, Lord, is this matter decided? <And he said to us, Yes! And we said to him G>, Who then are the foolish?]*

According to *Cop* and *(Eth)*, the disciples ask a pair of questions without a break between them ('Is this matter decided? Who then are the foolish?'). G alone has Jesus answer the first question with a curt affirmative, requiring an additional introductory phrase for the second question.

44.1 Eth *Since {Cop And} those who slept did not fulfil my commandments, {Cop so} they will remain outside the kingdom and the fold of the shepherd of the {Cop and his} flock]*

Eth 'since' may represent *Gk* ὅτι (cf. *GJn* 1.50; 20.29). *Cop* 'And... so' represents ⲇⲉ and ⲅⲁⲣ, in contrast to Hills's translation where ⲅⲁⲣ serves to identify the grounds rather than the consequence of the preceding statement: 'But my commandments were not done by those who slept, *for* they will remain outside the kingdom...' Yet remaining outside the kingdom is the consequence of failing to observe the commandments (i.e. of 'sleeping'), not its precondition. There are other instances in *EpAp* where the usage of ʀⲁⲡ is unlikely to reflect *Gk*, for example, when used at the beginning of utterances where there is no previous statement to reinforce or explain (*Cop* 14.5; 15.4; 16.3; 20.2; 21.1; 23.1; 25.2, 3; 26.1; 28.4; 41.7; 47.8).

44.2 *And whoever remains outside the sheepfold the wolves will eat, and he will hear them, dying in much suffering, and distress and endurance shall come upon him]*

(1) *and he will hear them]* There is a lacuna in *Cop* where *Eth* MSS have 'hear', and *Cop* 'and he will hear them' ϥⲛⲁ[ⲥⲱⲧⲙⲉ ⲛ̄ⲙⲁⲩ] is a possible reconstruction. According to Schmidt, the penultimate letter of the missing phrase is ⲁ (although no clear trace of this is now visible).

(2) *dying in much suffering, and distress and endurance shall come upon him]* Following Schmidt's reconstructed *Cop* rather than *Eth*, trr read here: '. . . neither [res]t nor endurance shall come upon him'. Here '[res]t' represents the conjectural ⲟⲩ[ⲙⲁⲧⲛ]ⲉⲥ (Crum 195a). While this term does not occur elsewhere in *EpAp*, it may be used here as an alternative to the loanword ⲁⲛⲁⲡⲁⲩⲥⲓⲥ (12.3; 19.14; 26.5; 27.1; 28.5). *Eth*, however, refers here not to 'rest' but to 'distress' (*ḍāmā*). Schmidt's 'neither. . . nor' represents ⲙⲛ̄,. . . ⲙⲛ̄ which might be understood as an alternative to *Gk* terminology used elsewhere, ⲟⲩⲧⲉ. . ., ⲟⲩⲧⲉ. . . (26.4; 47.8), n.b. ⲙⲛ̄. . . ⲟⲩⲧⲉ. . . ⲟⲩⲧⲉ (19.14). More commonly, however, ⲙⲛ̄ is used used synonymously with ⲁⲩⲱ ('and').

47.6 (Eth) *As the prophet said and he said to them* {Cop L S *Woe to those*} <B *Woe to those*>]

In most *Eth* MSS *wa-yəbelomu* ('and he said to them') has been substituted for *'ale lomu* ('woe to those'). Here, as so often, the *Eth* variants arise from deliberate or unconscious replacement of a word or phrase by a similar-sounding word or phrase though with a quite different sense. Equally characteristic of *Eth* is the conflation of the two variants in B, with the first now attached to the preceding sentence:

> 'And likewise whoever shows partiality and whoever receives partiality will both be judged with a single judgement, as the prophet said.' And he said to them, 'Woe to those who show partiality. . .'

48.1 *If you see a sinner, reprove him between yourself and him* {Eth *you* [*sing., pl.* A] *alone*}. <*If he listens to you, you have gained him.* B K L S>

(1) The language here echoes *GMt* 18.15: Ἐὰν δὲ ἁμαρτήσῃ ὁ ἀδελφός σου, ὕπαγε ἔλεγξον αὐτὸν μεταξὺ σοῦ καὶ αὐτοῦ μόνου. *Cop*... ϫ[ⲡⲓⲁϥ ⲟⲩ]ⲧⲱⲕ ⲟⲩⲧⲁⲩϥ ('reprove him between yourself and him') corresponds to *GMt* 18.15^sah, ⲃⲱⲕ ⲛ̄ⲭⲡⲓⲟϥ ⲟⲩⲧⲱⲕ ⲟⲩⲧⲁⲩϥ ⲙⲁⲩⲁⲁⲕ ('go and reprove him between yourself and him alone'). In the *Eth* version (MS A), *babāḥtitkəmu gaśəṣṣo* ('between you [pl.] alone reprove him') reflects the early A-text of *GMt* 18.15^eth, *gaśəṣṣo babāḥtitkəmu* ('reprove him between you [pl.] alone'), rather than the revised B-text which reproduces the *Gk* idiom more precisely: *gaśəṣṣo babāḥtitkəmu 'anta wa-wə'ətu* ('reprove him between you and him alone'): see Zuurmond III, 186–87.

(2) *Cop* and *Eth* A C E G lack the reference that follows to the positive outcome, reproduced in B K L S: ἐάν σου ἀκούσῃ ἐκέρδησας τὸν ἀδελφόν σου. Where *Cop* and *Eth* MSS agree against other *Eth* MSS this should normally be taken as an indication of priority, and trr are therefore at fault in following the Matthew-derived longer reading.

48.2–3 *But if he does not listen to you take up to three others with you and teach your brother. If he again does not listen to you, set him before you as a gentile and a tax-collector*]

Cf. *GMt* 18.16–17: ἐὰν δὲ μὴ ἀκούσῃ, παράλαβε μετὰ σοῦ ἔτι ἕνα ἢ δύο, ἵνα ἐπὶ στόματος δύο μαρτύρων ἢ τριῶν σταθῇ πᾶν ῥῆμα. ἐὰν δὲ παρακούσῃ αὐτῶν εἰπὲ τῇ ἐκκλησίᾳ. ἐὰν δὲ καὶ τῆς ἐκκλησίας παρακούσῃ ἔστω σοι ὥσπερ ὁ ἐθνικὸς καὶ ὁ τελώνης. In *GMatthew* a negative response to the initial private warning is followed by two further warnings, one from a more formal delegation of two or three, the other in the presence of the whole congregation. In *EpAp* the maximum size of the delegation is four rather than three, and there is no third warning.

49.8 *So that the wheat may be put into its barns and its chaff put onto the fire*]

There is an echo here of *GMt* 3.12b, καὶ συνάξει τὸν σῖτον αὐτοῦ εἰς τὴν ἀποθήκην τὸ δὲ ἄχυρον κατακαύσει πυρὶ ἀσβέστῳ (cf. *GLk* 3.17b). The eschatological separation of wheat and chaff is seen as the solution to division and dissension within the church (*EpAp* 49.5–6) in a manner that also recalls the Matthean parable of the wheat and the chaff (*GMt* 13.24–30). The plural 'barns' occurs in *GMt* 13.30$^{\text{eth-A}}$ (13.30^{gk} sing., 13.30$^{\text{eth-B}}$ 'house').

50.1 *So shall it be with those who hate. And the one who loves me and the one who reproves those who do not observe my commandments will be hated and persecuted and despised and mocked.*]

(1) *So shall it be with those who hate*] The translation and the link with what precedes is uncertain. Duensing assumes a lacuna here ('... die also hassen').

(2) *those who do not observe my commandments*] The negative occurs in E K S but is lacking in G and the four MSS on which Guerrier's edition of *EpAp*^{eth} is based. The latter read, '... and the one who reproves those who observe my commandments', which agrees neither with 'the one who loves me' nor with the positive evaluation of 'reproof' throughout this passage (*EpAp* 47.1, 2, 3; 48.1; 49.3; 50.3, 4).

APPENDIX: THE *GALILEAN DISCOURSE*

Cop	Coptic manuscript of *Epistula Apostolorum (EpAp)*
GD	*Galilean Discourse* (= *TG-G* 1–11, see below)
GD/EpAp	*Galilean Discourse* + *Epistula Apostolorum*, i.e. *EpAp* in its longer Ethiopic form = *TG-G*
TestDom[eth]	*Testamentum Domini éthiopien* (cited by chapter enumeration with line numbers, from the edition by R. Beylot)
TestDom[syr]	*Testamentum Domini nostri Iesu Christi* (Syriac version: I. Rahmani)
TG-G	*Testament en Galilée-Guerrier* (= *GD/EpAp*)
underlining	material overlapping with *EpAp* 34 or the *Testamentum Domini* (specified in Apparatus); gaps in underlining = material in parallel text absent or occurring in different sequence

****

Absent from the Coptic but present in the Ethiopic textual tradition is a later introduction with a post-resurrection Galilean setting (*GD*), usually opening with the title *Testament of our Lord and Saviour Jesus Christ*, which stands over the entire work (*GD/EpAp*). In reality, the title belongs to the longer account of Easter instructions that precedes it in most Ethiopic manuscripts, a text also extant in Syriac and generally known as the *Testamentum Domini*. Thus the modern edition of the Ethiopic *GD/EpAp* was entitled *Le Testament en Galilée de Notre-Seigneur Jésus-Christ* (Guerrier), with 'en Galilée' added to differentiate this work from the *Testamentum Domini*, which it follows in the manuscripts Guerrier collated.[1] In

---

[1] While *TestDom* is absent from the relatively old and reliable MS G (not known to Guerrier), *GD/EpAp* still bears its title here – an indication that the link between the two texts has already been established.

my usage, *Galilean Discourse* (*GD*) refers only to the later introduction to *EpAp* (chapters 1–11 of Guerrier's *Testament en Galilée*). Guerrier's chapter 1 is a later addition and has been transferred here to the critical apparatus. My *GD* 1 corresponds to the opening of Guerrier's chapter 2; chapter enumeration in *GD* otherwise follows Guerrier. Verse enumeration is my own.

At two extended passages in *GD* there are close verbal connections with continuous sections of *EpAp* and *TestDom* respectively, indicated in the translation by underlining. As will be seen, there are significant overlaps between *GD* 4.1–16 and *EpAp* 34.3–36.7 and between *GD* 5.1–7.3 and *TestDom* 5, 4–6, 10. Literary dependence is beyond question, but there are several ways in which the three texts might be correlated. To take the relationship of *GD* and *EpAp* first, the main options would seem to be:

(1)   *GD* → *EpAp* → *GD*/*EpAp*, or
(2)   *EpAp* → *GD* → *GD*/*EpAp*, or
(3)   *EpAp* → *GD*/*EpAp*

According to the first two options, one text derives material from another and the two texts are later combined. In the third and most likely option, *GD* was never a separate document. It was composed as an introduction to *EpAp*, highlighting and extending the more limited discussion of the 'signs and wonders' presaging the end in *EpAp* 34–36. The second and third options agree in regarding *GD* as secondary to *EpAp*. While it may be unusual for an extension to an existing work to include an additional version of material already present in it, it seems that this is what has happened here.[2]

GD 4.1 opens with the formula, 'And our Lord said to us...', even though Jesus is already the speaker, followed by, 'And we said to our Lord...' This piece of dialogue is an anomaly within *GD*, which is otherwise a monologue. It derives from *EpAp* 34.3, where the disciples say, 'You have told us only that there will be signs and wonders in heaven and on earth before the end of the world comes'. This reference to earlier teaching has no antecedent within *EpAp*. In spite of what the disciples say, Jesus has not in fact spoken previously of signs and wonders (cf. *EpAp* 41.4 for a similar case). Aware of this

---

[2] Not considered here is the possibility that *EpAp* is a secondary and abbreviated version of *GD*/*EpAp*. *EpAp* 1–2 clearly mark the beginning of a text, and the shift between the Galilean setting of *GD* and the (implied) Jerusalem setting of *EpAp* also rule out an originally unified document.

absence, *GD* 4.1 emends the passage to read, 'And the Lord said to us, "There will be signs and wonders in heaven and on earth before the end."' As a result, *EpAp* 34.3 now refers back to *GD* 4.1:

> And our Lord said to us, 'There will be signs and wonders in heaven and on earth before the end comes.' (*GD* 4.1)

> ... And we said to him again, 'Lord, what great things you have spoken to us and announced to us and revealed to us... But you have told us only that there will be signs and wonders in heaven and on earth before the end of the world comes – so teach us, that we may know.' (*EpAp* 34.1, 3)

Formulaically expressed, this suggests *EpAp* → *GD*/*EpAp* (the third option, above), rather than the two-stage *EpAp* → *GD* → *GD*/*EpAp* (the second option). The *GD* passage has been composed to provide the antecedent missing from *EpAp*.

The dependence of *GD* 4.1 on *EpAp* 34.3 would eliminate *GD* → *EpAp* → *GD*/*EpAp* (the first option), and there are two further reasons why *GD* → *EpAp* is unlikely. First, introducing the new eschatological teaching, *EpAp* 34.4 reads, 'It is not only to you that this will happen, but [also] those whom you teach and who believe', whereas *GD* 4.3 reads, 'It is not to you that this will happen, but those whom you have taught and who believe in me.' The omission of 'only' creates a sharp distinction between the age of the apostles and the end-time with its signs and wonders. Second, *EpAp* 36.7 explains that the purpose of mission to Israel and the Gentiles is 'that they may hear and be saved and believe in me and depart out of the affliction of the plague'. *GD* 4.15 replaces the last phrase with, '... and escape from the wrath that is coming with flaming fire'. The reference to a specific event – probably an actual historical occurrence, as argued in the Introduction to this volume – has been replaced by a stereotypical reference to fiery divine wrath.

What then of the relationship between *GD*/*EpAp* and *TestDom*? The encounter between the risen Jesus and his disciples that opens *TestDom* shows clear evidence of acquaintance with *EpAp* 12.1–3. In both cases the risen Lord is touched by three named disciples, who fall on their faces and are raised up by him. Correlating this with our previous results, the options are now either *EpAp* → *GD*/*EpAp* → *TestDom* or *EpAp* → *TestDom* → *GD*/*EpAp*. On the second option, which is the more likely, *GD* has added to *EpAp* an introductory section on signs of the end to match the extended treatment of the same topic in *TestDom*. Thus *GD* assimilates *EpAp* to *TestDom*, and it does so in part with material culled from each of them, introduced in both cases by shorter passages opening with the appeal, 'Hear me, children of light!' (*GD* 2.1–3.2, followed by 4.1–16 // *EpAp* 34.3–36.7) and 'Hear this, children of light' (*GD* 4.17–20, followed by 5.1–7.3 // *TestDom* 5, 4–6, 10). There is, then, a symmetry between *GD*'s use of the two passages, one of which derives from the text it now introduces, the other from the text that provides the model for a discourse on signs of the end as a prelude to Jesus' Easter instructions to his disciples. As *GD* assimilates *EpAp* to *TestDom*, so *GD*/*EpAp* becomes an adjunct to *TestDom* in the Ethiopic manuscript tradition, even sheltering under the same title. *GD* may well be an original Ethiopic composition, and the link it creates with *TestDom* may help account for *EpAp*'s survival in its Ethiopic guise.

The Fate of the Wicked

<ETH> 1 *GD* 1 The discourse that Jesus Christ spoke to his twelve disciples in Galilee after he was raised from the dead, saying:

GD 2.1 'Hear me, children of light, and listen to the voice of your Father, and I will reveal to you what is coming to the world, 2 so that when they hear it those who believe in me shall fear. 3 And those sinners who do not believe in me will not understand my signs. 4 They will persecute my beloved, they will be given up to a

---

1 [*TG-G* 1 Testament of our Lord and Saviour Jesus Christ. I looked from its outside to within, its appearance and its reality; strange and hard (are) its two sides, judgement according to one's works.]

Testament... works] –B E K (K *attaches* I... works *to preceding text, TestDom*) | Testament... Christ] Our Saviour Jesus Christ A, –K | hard C L] closed G S | its... sides] doubly S | according... works G] <each L S> according to their works A K L S

GD 1 Cf. *TestDom*[eth] incipit, 1–2: 'And it came to pass that after our Lord Jesus Christ was raised from the dead he appeared to us...' | The discourse] The covenant S | Jesus Christ G K] our Lord <and our God and our Saviour S> Jesus <Christ A B C S> L | his... disciples] the twelve A, his eleven disciples G L

GD 2.1 Cf. *TestDom*[eth] 1, 28: 'And now hear me, children of light...' | me E G K S] –(*Eth*)

2 those... fear] those may fear who believe in me S | fear] + greatly C

3 those... understand] those who do not believe A K | understand] believe C G

4 They... conscience] but my beloved. They will be pursued to a flame of judgement and be given up to the fire, their conscience is convicted L | judgement of flame] flame of judgement K L

judgement of flame, and fire will convict their conscience. 5 For Gehenna has opened her mouth and longs to fill her bosom. 6 For her root is spread and her fruit is the destruction of the children of men, for their disobedience leads to destruction. 7 Their transgression is hidden at present, but at the last it shall be manifested, for his voice will be heard and it will rebuke them. 8 For by it the world will be oppressed for some days, and I myself will provide no helper.

GD 3.3 'There will be slaughter in the kingdom of the east and it will put on mourning, and the west will prepare itself, the south will be dismayed, and the north will hear and despair. 4 And so it shall be with those who survive when the judgement approaches and when the scriptures are fulfilled and the day draws near.'

The Last Days

GD 4.1 And our Lord said to us, 'There will be signs and wonders in heaven and on earth before the end comes.'

2 And we said to our Lord, 'Tell us and show us!'

3 And he said to us, 'I will indeed tell you and teach you! 4 It is not to you that this will happen, but those whom you have taught and who believe in me. 5 At that time believers in me and those who do not believe will perceive the sound of a trumpet from heaven that reaches the earth, and stars falling like fire, and great stars that appear during the day. 6 And a star will appear from the east like fire, the sun and moon will fight together, and [there will be] constant fear and terror of thunder, lightning and thunderbolt and constant earthquakes. 7 And cities shall fall, and people shall die in their ruins, and the earth will quake continually as the waters vanish, the springs fail, the rivers disappear, and the sea dries up. 8 And there will be a great plague and death for many so that funerals will

---

5 bosom] child K S
6 is spread] –C, is uprooted B L
7 his] their E G K S
8 I... helper] in me a helper A C E

GD 4.1 Cf. *EpAp* 34.3 | our Lord] again the Lord S | before] for S
2 Cf. *EpAp* 34.2 | show us] + a sign C
3 us] them E G | and teach you] –A
3–4 Cf. *EpAp* 34.4
5 Cf. *EpAp* 34.7–8 | believe] + you E K S
6 Cf. *EpAp* 34.9 | thunder B L] constant thunder *(Eth)*
7 Cf. *EpAp* 34.10 | dries up] departs B L
8 Cf. *EpAp* 34.10 | many] + people B K

cease for those who die. 9 And the passing of children with their parents shall be on one bed, and kin will abandon kin, and one person will not turn to another. 10 And those who are bereaved will rise and see those who had departed from them being carried out. 11 For there will be a plague, suffering and envy, and they will take from one and give to another in hatred, and they will mourn those who did not hear my commandment. 12 And then my heavenly Father will become angry because of human evil, for in the corruption of their uncleanness the transgressions they devised have multiplied, so that the prophecy may be fulfilled that says, 13 "I see you as you go about with a thief, and with an adulterer is your portion, and while you sit you slander your mother's son, and your tongue weaves iniquity, and for your mother's son you set a great stumbling-block. 14 What do you think, that I am like you? But I shall be a witness to your impure deeds." 15 Behold, this is what I say to you! 16 And as for you, you must tell it to Israel and to the Gentiles, that they may hear and believe and be saved and escape from the wrath that is coming with flaming fire.

17 'Hear this, children of light! 18 When God is coming and draws near, the angels will take away the fruits, the rivers, the deeps, and the trees, and their fruits will be scorched. 19 And whoever survives the heat the locust will consume, and whoever survives the locust the caterpillar will consume, and whoever survives the caterpillar the grasshopper will consume. 20 And when the Contemptible One

9 Cf. *EpAp* 34.11 | passing A C G] strife *(Eth)* | children] the child G | their] his G | abandon] not abandon A

10 Cf. *EpAp* 34.12 | bereaved] buried A, anointed K | being... out] –A, not being carried out L

11 Cf. *EpAp* 34.13 | suffering] + and hatred C | they... hatred] he will take from one and give another a share K | my] his L

12 Cf. *EpAp* 35.1 | the corruption of] –A

13 a thief and with] –A | your portion] you return your portion E | mother's son (× 2)] brother's son G | weaves] + arrogance and A

13–14 Cf. *EpAp* 35.6–8

14 like you] like him A | your impure deeds] all your deeds L

16 Cf. *EpAp* 36.7 | and believe] –E | and be] so as to be L

17 this] now S

18 the fruits] –C

19 the locust... the grasshopper will consume G] the locust will consume and the caterpillar and whoever survives the caterpillar <locust C> the grasshopper will consume A B C K, the grasshopper will consume and whoever survives the grasshopper the caterpillar will consume E, the locust will consume him and the grasshopper and the caterpillar will consume him L

20 oppress*] *yəḥeḥḥi* A, *wa-yəḥeḥḥi* C E (unknown word), sing *(Eth)*

approaches (that is, Satan), he will oppress* the four corners of the world.'

The Fate of the Nations

GD 5.1 'Then Syria will be captive and will bewail her children; 2 Cilicia will crane her neck until her judge appears. 3 Arise, you who sit upon a throne and rest in your glory, daughter of Babylon, drink what is poured out for you! 4 Cappadocia and Phrygia and Lycaonia, bend your backs to your ground, for many peoples will trample upon you! 5 Then the camps will open and the armies will come forth and cover all the earth, and they will destroy the sanctuaries of the heathen. 6 Pontus and Bithynia, your youth will fall by the sword, your sons and your daughters will be made captive, 7 and the walls of Pontus will lament, the rivers of Lycaonia will be mixed with blood! 8 Great Pisidia who trusts in her riches, you will be trampled into the ground because of the evil of your deeds. 9 Therefore I will raise up against you kings for destruction, and they will mingle your blood, and your soul shall be with those who go down to Gehenna. 10 Pamphylia and all her coastlands, gird yourself with brass and iron, conceal the alien things, and prepare your ships for escape! 11 And for those who remain within you the sea will be their grave. 12 As for Phoenicia, the sword shall come upon her, for they are children of corruption! 13 Judah, put on

GD 5.1 = *TestDom*[eth] 5, 4

2 = *TestDom*[eth] 5, 4–5

3 Cf. *TestDom*[eth] 5, 5–7: The daughter of Babylon shall arise from the throne of her glory to drink the cup mixed for her.

4 Cf. *TestDom*[eth] 5, 7–8: Cappadocia and Phrygia and Lycaonia will bend their backs, for many peoples are corrupted by their sins. | trample upon] cover K

5 Cf. *TestDom*[eth] 5, 8–10: Then the camps of the enemy will be opened and armies will come forth and torment the earth. | cover] cleave S | all] –A

6 Cf. *TestDom*[eth] 5, 10–12: [As for] Armenia, Pontus, and Bithynia, their youth will fall be the sword, their sons and their daughters will be made captive. | the sword] the hand of the sword B E K L | your sons] –C | walls] rivers C

7 Cf. *TestDom*[eth] 5, 12.

8 Cf. *TestDom*[eth] 5, 12–13: Great Pisidia who trusts in her riches will be cast down to the ground. | Great A] proud *(Eth)* | you] –S | the evil of B E K] –*(Eth)* | your] her S

10 your G K] –*(Eth)*

12 Cf. *TestDom*[eth] 5, 13–15: As for the land of Phoenicia, the sword shall come, for they are children of corruption!

13 Cf. *TestDom*[eth] 5, 15–15: The land of Judah will put on mourning and prepare for the day of destruction, because of her impurity. | put on] + the strength of C G | open... courts] open your courts, extend {open E} your gates E G, extend your courts,

mourning, raise your walls and open your gates, extend your courts, adorn yourself with the adornment of your youth, beautify yourself for your beloved and prepare your throne for your king and prepare for the day of destruction, when your sorrow comes!'

The False Christ

GD 6.1 And then he spoke about the Deceiver: 2 'He will come as if he were Christ, by the number of his sufferings, and how he will show still further sufferings. 3 For his coming is for destruction, and the Unclean One has drawn near and come forth, and the east is open to him and they will prepare for him his way. 4 A burning sword is in his hand, his anger and fury are fire. 5 He is a shield of judgement, born for destruction, an enemy, a spiller of blood, 6 for his strength is error and his hand is deception, his right hand is sorrow and his left hand is darkness. 7 And these are his marks: his head is like a flame of fire, his right eye is bloodshot and his left is dead, both the pupils of his eyes are white in his eyelids, 8 his lower lip is enlarged, his feet are deformed, and his fingers and the joints of his feet are twisted. 9 He

open your gates K S | beautify... and] –E | beloved G S] beloved ones *(Eth)* | for... prepare] –K | destruction] your destruction B S

GD 6.1 And... spoke] –A, + again C K, And then it was said B E

2 He will come] –A C G L | by... his sufferings C E] whose number is in {as K} his sufferings A G K, who numbers us in his sufferings B L

3 Cf. *TestDom*[eth] 5, 17: The east is open to him, and his ways will be opened. | For... Unclean One] For his coming <has drawn near E K S> for impure destruction E G K S | come forth L] completed *(Eth)* | the east... way C E G] the east is open to him and they will prepare for him the way A K S, the way is open to him B L. Cf. *TestDom*[eth] 5, 17: The east is open to him, and his ways will be opened.

4 Cf. *TestDom*[eth] 5, 17–19: Sword and flame are in his days <hands *TestDom*[syr]>, anger and torment are fire.

5 Cf. *TestDom*[eth] 5, 19–20: This is the shield <weaponry *TestDom*[syr]> of judgement, which is for the destruction of creation | He... shield] this is the generation S, he is a son C G | enemy A C G] eradicator E S, legislator K L | a spiller of blood] spilling E G, doubly K

6 Cf. *TestDom*[eth] 5, 21–22: his strength is for blasphemy, his hands are for error, his right hand for sorrow, <his left hand for darkness *TestDom*[syr]> | error] errors G

7 Cf. *TestDom*[eth] 6, 1–3: And these are his marks: his head is like a flame of fire, his right eye is bloodshot and his left eye is joyful, the pupils of his eyes two of them, his eyelids white. | in] and the pupil of B L

8 Cf. *TestDom*[eth] 6, 3–5: his lower lip is enlarged, his right arm is thin, his feet are deformed, his joints are twisted | the... feet] joints A

9 Cf. *TestDom*[eth] 6, 5–8: He is the sickle of destruction. About this I make known to you, children of light, that his time has come, he has risen for the harvest so that those destined for judgement should be harvested.

is the sickle of destruction, and his time has come, his harvest has drawn near, and he will reap those destined for judgement. 10 And to the many he will present himself as the Christ, and he will praise his works and establish the desires of his heart.'

The Salvation of the Elect

GD 7.1 'And then God will appear to those who trust in him. 2 And when he shall come, a great sign will appear so that only my beloved will recognize it, 3 those who keep my Father's commandments and who hate gold and silver and the wealth of this world and the good things of this earth. 4 These I shall receive on that day, and their face will shine seven times more than the sun. 5 I will be their God and they will be my people, 6 I will be their father and they will be my sons and daughters, 7 I will be their altar and they will be my temple, 8 and I will reveal to them the will of my Father and the judgement of this world. 9 I will set them with my angels, and they shall rejoice for thousands of years without number, 10 for they have been found among those who love my name more than themselves. 11 For they suffered from the world that leads astray, and they hated all ease of life.'

The Sacrifices of the Unrighteous

GD 8.1 'But many are those who reject and hate the commandments of God and persecute the righteous, who are tormented by those who love this world. 2 And they will be delivered up to the judgement of burning flames of fire, and the desire of their heart will be consumed. 3 For there are many who think that I desire sacrifices and drink offerings of animals, and who pour out blood in my name as an

---

10 Cf. *TestDom*[eth] 6, 8–9: To the many he will appear as good and he will praise their works | praise] + himself and B C L

GD 7.1 And... appear] God A | trust] believe A
2 –3 Cf. *TestDom*[eth] 6, 9–11: And it shall come to pass that when he approaches a sign will be given to the elect, those who keep my Father's mysteries
3 hate] despise L | earth] world B K
5 God] a Father C
6 daughters] my daughters B K
9 with G K L] as *(Eth)*

GD 8.1 and hate E G K] –*(Eth)*
3 drink offerings] and books C

offering for their sins. 4 By doing so they treat me as though I were an idol! 5 Through the prophets I told their fathers not to eat the flesh of a corpse or to drink the blood of what has died. 6 They are flesh, and they think fleshly things of me.

GD 9.1 'But judgement will come upon bishops and priests, for they have led my people astray in their desire for their own pleasure. 2 Through Isaiah the prophet I have spoken to them and said, "I commanded weeping and lamentation and putting on sackcloth, but they rejoiced, slaughtering cattle and sacrificing sheep, saying, "Let us eat and drink, for tomorrow we die." 3 And this is revealed in the ears of God, ruler of all the world, and their sin will not be forgiven them until they die. 4 For "the sacrifice of God is a gentle spirit, and a heart gentle and sorrowful God will not despise." 5 So turn to me, all of you, and I will turn to you, says God, ruler of all the world. 6 Do not be like your fathers, to whom the prophets spoke and who ate manna and did not understand, not knowing the grace of God, 7 and who desired flesh and ate and satisfied the desire of their evil heart. 8 And as he said, "My people ate flesh and drank wine, they have become fat and heavy, they kicked against my beloved, 9 for priest and prophet are stupefied with wine. 10 Jonadab and his descendants are blessed for ever, because they drank no wine and kept the commandment of their fathers."

GD 10.1 'Therefore I say to you, continue in the fear of God and in righteousness, for you have brought nothing into this world and you can take nothing out. 2 Naked you came into this world and naked you will leave this world, 3 therefore acquire only righteousness and the love of God.'

5 the prophets] my prophets G K
6 They] For they L

GD 9.1 judgement] my judgement A | upon] against B | my people] the people S
2 I commanded] + them B K, and commanded E | slaughtering... sheep E K] sacrificing cattle and slaughtering sheep *(Eth)*
3 ears of God] + Sabaoth A
4 gentle and sorrowful] gentle and pure L, gentle and pure and sorrowful C, pure and gentle S
5 So] –B
6 manna] + in the wilderness B L
7 and who] but S | and ate] –B K L
8 My people] the people E | heavy] broad L
9 for G L] until A B C | stupefied] strong K
10 and... blessed S] son of {brought forth K} blessed ones *(Eth)*

GD 10.2 leave this world] + again C

The End

GD 11.1 'For when the days come to an end, the wicked will rise up
and persecute those who fear God and the righteous, 2 for they will
accuse them of whatever they wish, for their mind is blinded. 3 And
the sinners will strive against the righteous and persecute them and
hate them and speak evil words against them. 4 Therefore God will
cast them into the inextinguishable fire where the worm does not die.
5 Then all creation shall enter the heat of the fire, for the sun and the
moon will not give their lights, the waters will be scattered and the
rivers will dry up, the heavens will be rolled up and the earth will be
split. 6 For God will arise to judge his people and to render to each of
them according to their works and according to the words they have
spoken against the way of righteousness. 7 And as for the righteous
who have walked on the way of righteousness, they will inherit the
glory of God and his power, and there shall be given them what eye
has not seen and ear has not heard, and they shall rejoice in my
kingdom.'

GD 11.1 the days... end E G K] the days draw near A, it comes to an end
{approaches C} and the days draw near **B** C **L**

3 evil A G] all evil *(Eth)* | against them] + and abuse them G

4 where... die **B** G K] –A, where the worm does not sleep L, + and the {his C G}
inextinguishable fire C E G

5 fire A K] man **B** C E **L** | lights G K] light *(Eth)*

7 the righteous] my righteous ones E | and his power] –A E | my kingdom] the
kingdom of heaven **B** K S

BIBLIOGRAPHY

Aasgaard, Reidar, *The Childhood of Jesus: Decoding the Apocryphal Gospel of Thomas*, Eugene, OR: Cascade, 2009.

Amann, E., *Le Protévangile de Jacques et ses remaniements latins: Introduction, textes, traduction, et commentaire*, Paris: Letouzey et Ané, 1910.

Ashton, John, *Studying John: Approaches to the Fourth Gospel*, Oxford: Clarendon Press, 1994.

Attridge, Harold W. (ed.), *Nag Hammadi Codex I (The Jung Codex): Introductions, Texts, Translations, Indices*, Nag Hammadi Studies 22, Leiden: Brill, 1985.

Barrett, C. K., *The Gospel According to John: An Introduction with Commentary and Notes on the Greek Text*, London: SPCK, 1978[2].

The Acts of the Apostles, International Critical Commentary, 2 vols., Edinburgh, T&T Clark, 1994–98.

Bauckham, Richard, James R. Davila, and Alexander Panoyotov (eds.), *Old Testament Pseudepigrapha: More Noncanonical Scriptures*, vol. 1, Grand Rapids, MI: Eerdmans, 2013.

Bauer, Walter, *Das Johannes-Evangelium*, Handbuch zum Neuen Testament 6, Tübingen: J. C. B. Mohr (Paul Siebeck), 1925[2].

Beavis, Mary Ann, and Allysin Kateusz (eds.), *Rediscovering the Marys: Maria, Mariamne, Miriam*, Library of New Testament Studies, London: T&T Clark/Bloomsbury, 2020.

Bettiolo, Paulo, et al. (eds.), *Ascensio Isaiae*, Corpus Christianorum, Series Apocryphorum, vol. 7, Turnhout: Brepols, 1995.

Beylot, Robert, *Testamentum Domini éthiopien: Édition et traduction*, Louvain: Peeters, 1984.

Bick, J., 'Wiener Palimpseste, I. Teil: Codex Palat. Vindobonensis 16 olim Bobbensis', *Abhandlungen der Sitzungsberichte der k. Akademie der Wissenschaften in Wien: Phil.-hist. Klasse* 159 (1908), 90–99.

Bihlmeyer, P., 'Un texte non interpolé de l'Apocalypse de Thomas', *Revue bénédictine* 28 (1911), 270–82.

Bockmuehl, Markus, *Ancient Apocryphal Gospels*, Louisville, KY: WJK Press, 2017.

Bonwetsch, G. Nathanael (ed.), *Methodius*, Griechische Christliche Schriftsteller, Leipzig: J. C. Hinrichs, 1917.

Bouriant, Urbain, 'Les Papyrus d'Akhmim: Fragments de manuscrits en dialectes bachmouriques et thébain', in *Mémoires publiées par les membres de la Mission archéologique française au Caire*, vol. 1/2, Paris: Leroux, 1885, 243–304.

'Fragments Grecs du livre d'Énoch et de quelques écrits attribués à saint Pierre', in *Mémoires publiées par les membres de la Mission archéologique française au Caire*, vol. 9/1, Paris: Leroux, 1892, 91–147.

Bovon, François, 'The Suspension of Time in Chapter 18 of *Protevangelium Jacobi*', in Birger A. Pearson (ed.), *The Future of Early Christianity: Essays in Honor of Helmut Koester*, Minneapolis, MN: Fortress Press, 1991, 393–405.

Bowersock, G. W., 'The Proconsulate of Albus', *Harvard Studies in Classical Philology* 72 (1968), 289–94.

Brakke, David, 'A New Fragment of Athanasius's Thirty-Ninth Festal Letter: Heresy, Apocrypha, and the Canon', *Harvard Theological Review* 103 (2010), 47–66.

Brown, Raymond E., *The Gospel According to John*, Anchor Bible Series, 2 vols., New York: Doubleday, 1966.

Bruce, F. F., *The Epistle to the Galatians: A Commentary on the Greek Text*, New International Greek Testament Commentary, Exeter: Paternoster Press, 1982.

Bruun, Christer, 'The Antonine Plague and the "Third Century Crisis"', in O. Heckster, G. de Kleijn, and Daniëlle Slootjes (eds.), *Crises in the Roman Empire*, Leiden: Brill, 2007, 201–17.

Buchholz, Dennis D., *Your Eyes Will Be Opened: A Study of the Greek (Ethiopic) Apocalypse of Peter*, Atlanta, GA: Scholars Press, 1988.

Budge, E. A. Wallis, *The Earliest Known Coptic Psalter*, London: Kegan Paul, Trench, Trübner, 1898.

By Nile and Tigris: A Narrative of Journeys in Egypt and Mesopotamia on Behalf of the British Museum between the Years 1886 and 1913, vol. 1, London: Murray, 1920.

Bultmann, Rudolf, *Der Stil der Paulinischen Predigt und die kynisch-stoische Diatribe*, Göttingen: Vandenhoeck & Ruprecht, 1910.

The History of the Synoptic Tradition, Eng. trans., Oxford: Blackwell, 1963.

The Gospel of John: A Commentary, Eng. trans., Oxford: Blackwell, 1971.

Burkitt, Francis Crawford, *Jewish and Christian Apocalypses: The Schweich Lectures 1913*, London: British Academy, 1914.

Burton, P. H., J. Balserak, H. A. G. Houghton, and D. Parker (eds.), *Vetus Latina, The Verbum Project: The Old Latin Manuscripts of John's Gospel* (2007), www.iohannes.com/vetuslatina.

Chaîne, M., *Catalogue des manuscrits éthiopiens de la collection Antoine d'Abbadie*, Paris: Imprimerie Nationale, 1912.

Charles, R. H., *The Ascension of Isaiah*, London: A&C Black, 1900.

Charlesworth, James H. (ed.), *The Old Testament Pseudepigrapha*, 2 vols., London: Darton, Longman, and Todd, 1985.

Cooper, James, and Arthur John Maclean, *The Testament of our Lord, Translated into English from the Syriac with Introduction and Notes*, Edinburgh: T&T Clark, 1902.

Corcoran, Simon, and Benet Salway, 'A Newly Identified Greek Fragment of the *Testamentum Domini*', *Journal of Theological Studies* 62.1 (2011), 118–35.

Crawford, Matthew R., 'Ammonius of Alexandria, Eusebius of Caesarea, and the Beginnings of Gospel Scholarship', *New Testament Studies* 61 (2015), 1–29.

The Eusebian Canon Tables: Ordering Textual Knowledge in Late Antiquity, Oxford Early Christian Studies, Oxford: Oxford University Press, 2019.

Crum, Walter Ewing, 'Inscriptions from Shenoute's Monastery', *Journal of Theological Studies* 5 (1904), 552–69.

d'Abbadie, Antoine, *Catalogue raisonnée de manuscrits éthiopiens*, Paris: Imprimerie Impériale, 1859.

Dibelius, Martin, 'Der Hirt des Hermas', in M. Dibelius, et al., *Die Apostolischen Väter*, IV, Handbuch zum Neuen Testament Ergänzungsband, Tübingen: J. C. B. Mohr (Paul Siebeck), 1923.

Dillmann, C. F. A., *Veteris Testamenti Aethiopici*, I. *Octateuchus*, Leipzig: Vogel, 1855.

Lexicon Linguae Aethiopicae, Leipzig: T.O. Weigel, 1862; repr. New York: Ungar, 1955.

Dochhorn, Jan, 'Ascensio Isaiae', in G. Oegema (ed.), *Jüdische Schriften aus hellenistisch-römischer Zeit*, vol. 6, part 1, *Unterweisung in erzählender Form*, Gütersloh: Gütersloher Verlagshaus, 2005, 1–45.

Dubois, Jean-Daniel, "Le Docétisme des christologies gnostiques revisité", *New Testament Studies* 63 (2017), 279–304.

Duensing, Hugo, review of C. Schmidt and I. Wajnberg, *Gespräche Jesu*, *Göttingische Gelehrte Anzeigen* 184 (1922), 241–52.

Epistula Apostolorum nach dem äthiopischen und koptischen Texte herausgegeben, Bonn: A. Marcus & E. Weber, 1925.

Duncan-Jones, R. D., 'The Impact of the Antonine Plague', *Journal of Roman Archaeology* 9 (1996), 108–36.

'The Antonine Plague Revisited', *Arctos* 52 (2018), 41–72.

Dunderberg, Ismo, *The Beloved Disciple in Conflict? Revisiting the Gospels of John and Thomas*, Oxford: Oxford University Press, 2006.

Dunn, James D. G., *Christology in the Making: An Inquiry into the Origins of the Doctrine of the Incarnation*, London: SCM Press, 1980.

Edwards, Mark, 'The *Epistle to Rheginus*: Valentinianism in the Fourth Century', *Novum Testamentum* 37 (1995), 76–91.

Ehrman, Bart, and Zlatko Pleše (ed.), *The Apocryphal Gospels: Texts and Translations*, New York: Oxford University Press, 2011.

Elliott, J. Keith (ed.), *The Apocryphal New Testament: A Collection of Apocryphal Christian Literature in an English Translation based on M. R. James*, Oxford: Clarendon Press, 1993[1], 1999[2].

Emmel, Stephen, and Cornelia Eva Römer, 'The Library of the White Monastery in Upper Egypt', in Harald Froschauer and Cornelia Eva Römer (eds.), *Spätantike Bibliotheken: Leben und Lesen in die frühen Klöstern Ägyptens*, Vienna: Phoibos, 2008, 5–14.

Engberg-Pedersen, Troels, *John and Philosophy: A New Reading of the Fourth Gospel*, Oxford: Oxford University Press, 2017.

Evans, Ernest (ed.), *Tertullian's Treatise on the Resurrection*, London: SPCK, 1960.

Tertullian: Adversus Marcionem, 2 vols., Oxford: Clarendon Press, 1971.

Fortna, Robert T., *The Gospel of Signs: A Reconstruction of the Narrative Source Underlying the Fourth Gospel*, Society for New Testament Studies Monograph Series 11, Cambridge: Cambridge University Press, 1970.

The Fourth Gospel and its Predecessor: From Narrative Source to Present Gospel, Edinburgh: T&T Clark, 1989.

Foster, P. (ed.), *The Gospel of Peter: Introduction, Critical Edition and Commentary*, Texts and Editions for New Testament Study 4, Leiden: Brill, 2010.

Fuller, R. H., *The Formation of the Resurrection Narratives*, London: SPCK, 1980².

Gathercole, Simon J., 'The Life of Adam and Eve (Coptic Fragments)', in Richard Bauckham, James R. Davila, and Alexander Panayotov (eds.), *Old Testament Pseudepigrapha: More Noncanonical Scriptures*, vol. 1, Grand Rapids, MI: Eerdmans, 2013, 22–27.

The Gospel of Thomas: Introduction and Commentary, Texts and Editions for New Testament Study 11, Leiden: Brill, 2014.

Goodacre, Mark, *The Case against Q: Studies in Markan Priority and the Synoptic Problem*, Harrisburg, PA: Trinity Press International, 2002.

'The *Protevangelium of James* and the Creative Rewriting of *Matthew* and *Luke*', in Francis Watson and Sarah Parkhouse (eds.), *Connecting Gospels: Beyond the Canonical/Non-Canonical Divide*, Oxford: Oxford University Press, 2018, 57–66.

'The Magdalene Effect: Misreading the Composite Mary in Early Christian Works', in Mary Ann Beavis and Allysin Kateusz (eds.), *Rediscovering the Marys: Maria, Mariamne, Miriam*, London: T&T Clark/Bloomsbury, 2020.

Grafton, Anthony, and Megan Williams, *Christianity and the Transformation of the Book*, Cambridge, MA: Harvard University Press, 2006.

Grébaut, Sylvain, 'Littérature éthiopienne pseudo-clémentine', *Revue de l'orient chrétien* 12 (1907), 139–51.

'Littérature éthiopienne pseudo-clémentine: Texte et traduction du *mystère du jugement des pecheurs*', *Revue de l'orient chrétien* 12 (1907), 285–97, 380–92; *Revue de l'orient chrétien* 13 (1908), 166–80, 314–20.

'Littérature éthiopienne pseudo-clémentine: Texte et traduction du traité, "La seconde venue du Christ et la résurrection des morts"', *Revue de l'orient chrétien* 15 (1910), 198–214, 307–23, 425–39.

Sargis d'Aberga: Controverse judéo-chrétienne, Patrologia Orientalis 3.4, 13.1, Paris: Firmin-Didot, 1909–19.

Gregory, Andrew, *The Gospel According to the Hebrews and the Gospel According to the Ebionites*, Oxford Early Christian Gospel Texts, Oxford: Oxford University Press, 2017.

Guerrier, Louis, 'Le Testament de Notre-Seigneur Jésus-Christ: Essai sur la partie apocalyptique', unpublished PhD thesis, Lyons, 1903.

'Un "Testament (éthiopien) de Notre-Seigneur et Sauveur Jésus-Christ" en Galilée', *Revue de l'orient chrétien* 12 (1907), 1–8.

Guerrier, Louis (with Sylvain Grébaut), *Le Testament en Galilée de Notre-Seigneur Jésus-Christ*, Patrologia Orientalis, Paris: Firmin-Didot, 1912; repr. Turnhout: Brepols, 2003.

Haenchen, Ernst, *The Acts of the Apostles*, Eng. trans., Oxford: Blackwell, 1971.

Hall, Robert G., 'The Ascension of Isaiah: Community Situation, Date, and Place in Early Christianity', *Journal of Biblical Literature* 109 (1990), 289–306.

Hall, Stuart George (ed.), *Melito of Sardis, On Pascha and Fragments: Texts and Translations*, Oxford: Clarendon Press, 1979.

Hannah, Darrell D., 'The Ascension of Isaiah and Docetic Christology', *Vigiliae Christianae* 53 (1999), 165–96.

'Isaiah's Vision in the Ascension of Isaiah and the Early Church', *Journal of Theological Studies* 50 (1999), 80–101.

'The Four-Gospel "Canon" in the *Epistula Apostolorum*', *Journal of Theological Studies* 59 (2008), 598–633.

'The Ravenous Wolf: The Apostle Paul and Genesis 49.27 in the Early Church', *New Testament Studies* 62 (2016), 610–27.

Hartenstein, Judith, *Die zweite Lehre: Erscheinungen des Auferstandenen als Rahmenerzählungen frühchristlicher Dialoge*, Texte und Untersuchungen zur Geschichte der altchristlichen Literatur 146, Berlin: Akademie Verlag, 2000.

Hartenstein, Judith, and Uwe-Karsten Plisch, 'Der Brief des Jakobus', in Hans-Martin Schenke, Hans-Gebhard Bethge, and Ursula Ulrike Kaiser (eds.), *Nag Hammadi Deutsch*, I, Berlin and New York: de Gruyter, 2001, 11–26.

Hauler, Edmund, 'Zu den neuen lateinischen Bruchstücken der Thomasapokalypse und eines apostolischen Sendschreibens im Codex Vind. Nr. 16', *Wiener Studien* 30 (1908), 308–40.

Heckster, O., G. de Kleijn, and Daniëlle Slootjes, *Crises in the Roman Empire*, Leiden: Brill, 2007.

Heekerens, H.-P., *Die Zeichen-Quelle der johanneischen Redaktion. Ein Beitrag zur Entstehungsgeschichte des vierten Evangelium*, Stuttgart: Katholisches Bibelwerk, 1984.

Helmbold, Andrew K., 'Gnostic Elements in the "Ascension of Isaiah"', *New Testament Studies* 18 (1972), 222–27.

Hennecke, Edgar (ed.), *Neutestamentliche Apokryphen: in Verbindung mit Fachgelehrten in deutscher Übersetzung und mit Einleitungen*, 2 vols., Tübingen: J. C. B. Mohr (Paul Siebeck), 1904[1], 1924[2].

Hennecke, Edgar (with W. Schneemelcher) (eds.), *Neutestamentliche Apokryphen in deutscher Übersetzung*, vol. 1, *Evangelien*, Tübingen: J. C. B. Mohr (Paul Siebeck), 1959[3], 1990[6].

Hill, Charles E., 'The *Epistula Apostolorum*: An Asian Tract from the Time of Polycarp', *Journal of Early Christian Studies* 7 (1999), 1–53.

'Cerinthus: Gnostic or Chiliast? A New Solution to an Old Problem', *Journal of Early Christian Studies* 8 (2000), 135–72.

The Johannine Corpus in the Early Church, Oxford: Oxford University Press, 2004.

Hills, Julian V., *Tradition and Composition in the Epistula Apostolorum*, Cambridge, MA: Harvard University Press, 2008[2].

The Epistle of the Apostles, Early Christian Apocrypha 2, Santa Rosa, CA: Polebridge Press, 2009.

Hornschuh, Manfred, *Studien zur Epistula Apostolorum*, Patristische Texte und Studien 5, Berlin: de Gruyter, 1965.

Hoyland, Robert G., *Seeing Islam as Others Saw It: A Survey and Evaluation of Chrstian, Jewish and Zoroastrian Writings on Early Islam*, Princeton, NJ: Darwin Press, 1997.

Jacobi, Christine, 'Jesus' Body: Christology and Soteriology in the Body-Metaphors of the *Gospel of Philip*', in Francis Watson and Sarah Parkhouse (eds.), *Connecting Gospels: Beyond the Canonical/Non-Canonical Divide*, Oxford: Oxford University Press, 2018, 77–96.

'"Dies ist die geistige Auferstehung": Paulusrezeption im Rheginusbrief und im Philippusevangelium', in Jens Schröter, Simon Butticaz, and Andreas Dettwiler (eds.), *Receptions of Paul in Early Christianity: The Person of Paul and his Writings through the Eyes of his Early Interpreters*, Berlin: de Gruyter, 2018, 355–75.

James, Montague Rhodes, *Apocrypha Anecdota: A Collection of Thirteen Apocryphal Books and Fragments*, Cambridge: Clay and Co., 1891.

'A New Text of the Apocalypse of Peter', *Journal of Theological Studies* 12 (1910), 36–54.

'The Epistola Apostolorum in a New Text', *Journal of Theological Studies* 12 (1910), 55–56.

'A New Text of the Apocalypse of Peter, II', *Journal of Theological Studies* 12 (1911), 362–83.

'A New Text of the Apocalypse of Peter, II', *Journal of Theological Studies* 12 1911), 573–83.

James, Montague Rhodes, (ed.), *The Apocryphal New Testament*, Oxford: Clarendon Press, 1924.

Jervell, Jacob, *Die Apostelgeschichte*, Kritisch-exegetischer Kommentar über das Neue Testament, Göttingen: Vandenhoeck & Ruprecht, 1998.

Johnson, M. D., 'Life of Adam and Eve', in James H. Charlesworth (ed.), *The Old Testament Pseudepigrapha*, 2 vols., London: Darton, Longman & Todd, 1985, 2.249–95.

Jones, Christopher, 'A Letter of Antoninus Pius and an Antonine Rescript concerning Christians', *Greek, Roman, and Byzantine Studies* 58 (2018), 67–76.

Jülicher, Adolf (ed.), *Itala: Das Neue Testament in altlateinischer Überlieferung*, IV. *Johannes-Evangelium*, Berlin: de Gruyter, 1963.

Junod, Eric, and Jean-Daniel Kaestli (eds.), *Acta Iohannis*, Corpus Christianorum Series Apocryphorum, 2 vols., Turnhout: Brepols, 1983.

Kiraz, George Anton, *Comparative Edition of the Syriac Gospels, aligning the Sinaiticus, Curetonianus, Peshîṭtâ and Ḥarklean Versions*, 4 vols., Leiden: Brill, 1996.

Klauck, Hans-Josef, *Apocryphal Gospels: An Introduction*, London and New York, T&T Clark, 2003.

Knibb, Michael A., *The Ethiopic Book of Enoch: A New Edition in the Light of the Aramaic Dead Sea Fragments*, 2 vols., Oxford: Clarendon Press, 1978.

'Martyrdom and Ascension of Isaiah', in J. H. Charlesworth (ed.), *The Old Testament Pseudepigrapha*, 2 vols., London: Darton, Longman, and Todd, 1985, 2.143–76.

Translating the Bible: The Ethiopic Versions of the Old Testament, Oxford: British Academy/Oxford University Press, 1999.

Knight, Jonathan, *The Ascension of Isaiah*, Guides to Apocrypha and Pseudepigrapha, Sheffield: Sheffield Academic Press, 1995.

Disciples of the Beloved One: The Christology, Social Setting and Theological Content of the Ascension of Isaiah, Sheffield: Sheffield Academic Press, 1996.

Knox, John, *Chapters in a Life of Paul*, London: A&C Black, 1954.

Kraus, Christina S., *The Limits of Historiography: Genre and Convention in Ancient Narrative Texts*, Leiden: Brill, 1999.

Kühn, C. G. (ed.), *Galeni Opera Omnia*, vol. 19, Leipzig: Car. Cnoblochii, 1830.

Lampe, Peter, *From Paul to Valentinus: Christians at Rome in the First Two Centuries*, Eng. trans., Minneapolis, MN: Fortress, 2003.

Layton, Bentley, *The Gnostic Treatise on Resurrection from Nag Hammadi*, Harvard Dissertations in Religion 12, Missoula, MT: Scholars Press, 1979.

The Gnostic Scriptures, New York: Doubleday, 1987.

Layton, Bentley, (ed.), *Nag Hammadi Codex II, 2–7*, Nag Hammadi Studies 20, 2 vols., Leiden: Brill, 1989.

A Coptic Grammar, 2nd ed., revised and expanded, Porta Linguarum Orientalium, Wiesbaden: Harrassowitz Verlag, 2004.

Lehtipuu, Outi, *Debates over the Resurrection of the Dead: Constructing Christian Identity*, Oxford Early Christian Studies, Oxford: Oxford University Press, 2015.

Lindars, Barnabas, *The Gospel of John*, New Century Bible Commentary, London: Marshall, Morgan & Scott, 1972.

Littman, R. J., and M. L. Littman, 'Galen and the Antonine Plague', *American Journal of Philology* 94 (1973), 243–55.

Litwa, M. David (ed.), *Refutation of all Heresies*, Writings from the Greco-Roman World 40, Atlanta, GA: SBL Press, 2016.

Logan, Alastair H. B., *The Gnostics: Identifying an Early Christian Cult*, London: T&T Clark, 2006.

Ludolf, Hiob, *Psalterium Davidis aethiopice et latine*, Frankfurt am Main: J. D. Zunner and N. W. Helwig, 1701.

Lührmann, Dieter, *Die apokryph gewordenen Evangelien: Studien zum Neuen Texten und Neuen Fragen*, Leiden: Brill, 2004.

Lundhaug, Hugo, *Images of Rebirth: Cognitive Poetics and Transformational Soteriology in the Gospel of Philip and the Exegesis of the Soul*, Nag Hammadi and Manichaean Studies 73, Leiden: Brill, 2010.

Lundhaug, Hugo, and Lance Jennott, *The Monastic Origins of the Nag Hammadi Codices*, Studies and Texts in Antiquity and Christianity 97, Tübingen: Mohr Siebeck, 2015.

McKenzie, Judith S., and Francis Watson, *The Garima Gospels: Early Illuminated Gospel Books from Ethiopia*, Oxford: Manar al-Athar, 2016.

Marcovich, Miroslav (ed.), *Iustini Martyris Apologiae pro Christianis, Dialogus cum Tryphone*, Berlin and New York: de Gruyter, 2005.

Marguerat, Daniel, *Les Actes des Apôtres*, Commentaires du Nouveau Testament, 2 vols., Va *(ch. 1–12)*; Vb *(ch. 13–28)*, Geneva: Labor et Fides, 2015.

Marincola, John, 'Genre, Convention, and Innovation in Greco-Roman Historiography', in C. S. Kraus (ed.), *The Limits of Historiography: Genre and Convention in Ancient Narrative Texts*, Leiden: Brill, 1999, 281–324.

Marjanen, Antti, and Petri Luomanen, *A Companion to Second-Century Christian 'Heresies'*, Vigiliae Christianae, Suppl. 76, Leiden: Brill, 2005.

Markschies, Christoph, *Valentinus Gnosticus? Untersuchungen zur valentinianischen Gnosis mit einem Kommentar zu den Fragmenten Valentins*, Wissenschaftliche Untersuchungen zum Neuen Testament 65, Tübingen: J. C. B. Mohr (Paul Siebeck), 1992.

'Carl Schmidt und kein Ende: Aus großer Zeit der Koptologie an der Berliner Akademie und der Theologischen Fakultät der Universität', *Zeitschrift für Antikes Christentum* 13 (2009), 5–28.

Markschies, Christoph, and Jens Schröter (eds.), *Antike christliche Apokryphen in deutscher Übersetzung*, vol. 1. *Evangelien und Verwandtes*, 1–2, Tübingen: J. C. B. Mohr (Paul Siebeck), 2012.

Martyn, J. L., *Galatians: A New Translation with Introduction and Commentary*, Anchor Bible, New York: Doubleday, 1998.

Maspero, Gaston, 'Fragments de Manuscripts Copte-Thébains provenants de la bibliothèque du deir Amba-Shenouda', in *Mémoires publiées par les membres de la Mission archéologique française au Caire*, vol. 6/1, Paris: Leroux, 1892, 1–160.

Meggitt, Justin J., *Paul, Poverty and Survival*, Studies of the New Testament and Its World, Edinburgh: T&T Clark, 1998.

Ménard, Jacques É., *Le Traité sur la résurrection*, Bibliothèque Copte de Nag Hammadi 12, Quebec: Les presses de l'université Laval, 1983.

Moulton, James Hope, et al., *Moulton's Grammar of New Testament Greek*, 5 vols., Edinburgh: T&T Clark, 2019.

Myllykoski, Matti, 'Cerinthus', in A. Marjanen and P. Luomanen (eds.), *A Companion to Second-Century Christian 'Heresies'*, Vigiliae Christianae Suppl. 76, Leiden: Brill, 2005, 213–46.

Nau, F., and P. Ciprotti., *La Version syriaque de l'Octateuque de Clément*, Milan: Giuffrè, 1967.

Nickelsburg, George W. E., *1 Enoch 1: A Commentary on the Book of Enoch, Chapters 1–36; 81–108*, Mineapolis, MN: Fortress Press, 2001.

Niederwimmer, Kurt, *The Didache: A Commentary*, Hermeneia, Minneapolis, MN: Augsburg Fortress, 1998.

Norelli, Enrico, *L'Ascensione di Isaia: Studi su un apocrifo al crocevia dei cristianesimi*, Bologna: Edizioni Dehoniane, 1994.

'Avant le canonique et l'apocryphe: Aux origines des récits de la naissance de Jésus', *Revue de théologie et de philosophie* 126 (1994), 305–24.

Oegema, G. (ed.), *Jüdische Schriften aus hellenistisch-römischer Zeit*, vol. 6, part 1, *Unterweisung in erzählender Form*, Gütersloh: Gütersloher Verlaghaus, 2005.

Osiek, Carolyn, *The Shepherd of Hermas: A Commentary*, Hermeneia, Minneapolis, MN: Fortress Press, 1999.

Parkhouse, Sarah, *Eschatology and the Saviour: The Gospel of Mary among Early Christian Dialogue Gospels*, Society for New Testament Studies Monograph Series 176, Cambridge: Cambridge University Press, 2019.

Parrott, Douglas M. (ed.), *Nag Hammadi Codices V,2–5 and VI, with Papyrus Berolinensis 8502, 1 and 4*, Nag Hammadi Studies 11, Leiden: Brill, 1979.

—— (ed.), *Nag Hammadi Codices III,3–4 and V,1*, Nag Hammadi Studies 27, Leiden: Brill, 1991.

Pasquier, Anne, *L'Évangile selon Marie (BG 1): Texte établi et présenté*, Bibliothèque Copte de Nag Hammadi 10, Quebec: Les presses de l'université Laval, 1983.

Peel, Malcolm L., 'The Treatise on the Resurrection', in Harold Attridge (ed.), *Nag Hammadi Codex I (The Jung Codex)*, Nag Hammadi Studies 22–23, 2 vols., Leiden: Brill, 1985, 1.123–57, 2.137–215.

Pérès, Jacques-Noël, *L'Épître des Apôtres et le testament de notre sauveur Jésus-Christ: Présentation et traduction de l'éthiopien*, Turnhout: Brepols, 1994.

Pervo, Richard, *Dating Acts: Between the Evangelists and the Apologists*, Santa Rosa, CA: Polebridge Press, 2006.

—— *Acts: A Commentary*, Hermeneia, Minneapolis, MN: Fortress Press, 2009.

—— *The Acts of Paul: A New Translation with Introduction and Commentary*, Cambridge: James Clarke, 2014.

Rahlfs, Alfred, *Psalmi cum Odis*, Vetus Testamentum Graecum X, Göttingen: Vandenhoeck & Ruprecht, 1979[3].

Rahmani, Patriarch Ignatius Ephraem II, *Testamentum Domini Nostri Iesu Christi*, Mainz: Kirchheim, 1899, repr. Hildesheim: Georg Olms, 1968.

Rauer, Max (ed.), *Origenes Werke*, vol. 9, *Die Homilien zu Lukas in der Übersetzung des Hieronymus und die griechischen Reste der Homilien und des Lukas-Kommentars*, Griechische Christliche Schriftsteller, Berlin: Akademie-Verlag, 1959[2].

Refoulé, R. F., and P. de Labriolle (eds.), *Tertullien: Traité de la prescription contre les hérétiques*, Sources chrétiennes 46, Paris: Éditions du Cerf, 1957.

Riley, Gregory J., *Resurrection Reconsidered: Thomas and John in Controversy*, Minneapolis, MN: Fortress Press, 1995.

Rothschild, Clare K., *New Essays on the Apostolic Fathers*, Wissenschaftliche Untersuchungen zum Neuen Testament 375, Tübingen: Mohr Siebeck, 2017.

Rousseau, Adelin, and Louis Doutreleau (eds.), *Irenée de Lyon: Contre les hérésies*, 10 vols., Sources chrétiennes, Paris: Éditions du Cerf, 1965–92.

Schaberg, Jane, *The Resurrection of Mary Magdalene: Legends, Apocrypha, and the Christian Testament*, London and New York: Continuum, 2004.

Schaff, Philip (ed.), *Creeds of Christendom*, 3 vols., New York: Harper & Brothers, 1877; repr. Grand Rapids, MI: Baker, 1977.

Schenke, Hans-Martin, Hans-Gebhard Bethge, and Ursula Ulrike Kaiser (eds.), *Nag Hammadi Deutsch*, 2 vols., Berlin and New York: de Gruyter, 2001–3.

Schmidt, Carl, 'Eine bisher unbekannte christliche Schrift in koptischer Sprache', *Sitzungsberichte der Königlich Preussischen Akademie der Wissenschaften zu Berlin*, June–Dec. 1895, 705–11.

'Ein vorirenäisches gnostisches Originalwerk in koptischer Sprache', *Sitzungsberichte der Königlich Preussischen Akademie der Wissenschaften zu Berlin*, July–Dec. 1896, 839–47.

'Der 1. Clemensbrief in altkoptischer Übersetzung', *Sitzungsberichte der Königlich Preussischen Akademie der Wissenschaften zu Berlin*, Jan.–June 1907, 154–64.

Der erste Clemensbrief in altkoptischer Übersetzung, Leipzig: J. C. Hinrichs, 1908.

'Eine Epistola apostolorum in koptischer und lateinischer Überlieferung', *Sitzungsberichte der königlich Preussischen Akademie der Wissenschaften zu Berlin*, 1908, 1047–56.

Schmidt, Carl (with Isaak Wajnberg), *Gespräche Jesu mit seinen Jüngern nach der Auferstehung: Ein katholisch-apostolisches Sendschreiben des 2. Jahrhunderts*, Leipzig: J. C. Hinrichs, 1919; repr. Hildesheim: Georg Olms, 1967.

Schmidt, Carl (with Violet Macdermot), *Pistis Sophia*, Nag Hammadi Studies 9, Leiden: Brill, 1978.

Schneemelcher, W. (ed.), *Neutestamentliche Apokryphen*, vol. 1, *Evangelien*, Tübingen: J. C. B. Mohr (Paul Siebeck), 1990[6].

Schneemelcher, W. *New Testament Apocrypha*, vol. 1, *Gospels and Related Writings*, Eng. trans., rev. ed., ed. R. McL. Wilson, Louisville, KY: WJK, 1991.

New Testament Apocrypha, vol. 2, *Writings Relating to the Apostles; Apocalypses and Related Subjects*, Eng. trans. of 6th ed., ed. R. McL. Wilson, Cambridge: James Clarke, 1992.

Schoedel, William R., *Ignatius of Antioch*, Hermeneia, Philadelphia, PA: Fortress Press, 1985.

Schrader, Elizabeth, 'Was Mary of Bethany Added to the Fourth Gospel in the Second Century?', *Harvard Theological Review* 110 (2017), 360–92.

Schröter, Jens, Simon Butticaz, and Andreas Dettwiler (eds.), *Receptions of Paul in Early Christianity: The Person of Paul and his Writings through the Eyes of his Early Interpreters*, Berlin: de Gruyter, 2018.

Schürer, Emil, *The History of the Jewish People in the Age of Jesus Christ*, 3 vols., rev. and ed. G. Vermes, F. Millar, and M. Goodman, Edinburgh: T&T Clark, 1987.

Sider Hamilton, Catherine, with Joel Willitts (eds.), *Writing the Gospels: A Dialogue with Francis Watson*, London: T&T Clark, 2019.

Sim, David C., 'Matthew's Use of Mark: Did Matthew Intend to Supplement or Replace his Primary Source?', *New Testament Studies* 57 (2011), 176–92.

Smith, David L., and Zachary L. Kostopoulos, 'Biography, History, and the Genre of Luke–Acts', *New Testament Studies* 63 (2017), 390–410.

Stowers, Stanley, *A Rereading of Romans: Justice, Jews, and Gentiles*, New Haven, CT and London: Yale University Press, 1994.

Strycker, Émile de, *La Forme la plus ancienne du Protévangile de Jacques*, Brussels: Société de Bolandistes, 1961).

Swanson, Reuben (ed.), *New Testament Greek Manuscripts: Variant Readings Arranged in Horizontal Lines against Codex Vaticanus: John*, Sheffield and Pasadena, CA: Sheffield Academic Press/William Carey International University Press, 1995.

New Testament Greek Manuscripts: Variant Readings Arranged in Horizontal Lines against Codex Vaticanus: Mark, Sheffield and Pasadena, CA: Sheffield Academic Press/William Carey International University Press, 1995.

Thompson, Sir Herbert (ed.), *The Gospel of St. John According to the Earliest Coptic Manuscript*, London: British School of Archaelogy in Egypt, 1924.

Thrall, Margaret E., *The Second Epistle to the Corinthians*, International Critical Commentary, 2 vols., London: T&T Clark, 1994–2000.

Tischendorf, Constantin, *Evangelia Apocrypha*, Leipzig: Avenarius and Mendelssohn, 1853.

Toepel, Alexander, *Das Protevangelium des Jakobus: Ein Beitrag zur neueren Diskussion um Herkunft, Auslegung und theologische Einordnung*, Frankfurter Theologische Studien 71, Münster: Aschendorff Verlag, 2014.

Tuckett, Christopher (ed.), *The Gospel of Mary*, Oxford Early Christian Gospel Texts, Oxford: Oxford University Press, 2007.

Uhlig, Siegbert, and Alessandro Baussi (eds.), *Encyclopaedia Aethiopica*, 5 vols., Wiesbaden: Harrasowitz, 2003–14.

Vanden Eykel, Eric M., *'But Their Faces Were All Looking Up': Author and Reader in the Protevangelium of James*, London: Bloomsbury T&T Clark, 2016.

VanderKam, James C., *Textual and Historical Studies in the Book of Jubilees*, Missoula, MT: Scholars Press, 1977.

Verheyden, Joseph, et al. (eds.), *Docetism in the Early Church: The Quest for an Elusive Phenomenon*, Wissenschaftliche Untersuchungen zum Neuen Testament, Tübingen: Mohr Siebeck, 2018.

Vinzent, Markus, *Christ's Resurrection in Early Christianity and the Making of the New Testament*, Farnham: Ashgate, 2011.

Waldstein, Michael, and Frederik Wisse (eds.), *Apocryphon of John: Synopsis of Nag Hammadi Codices II,1; III,1; and IV,1 with BG 8502,2*, Nag Hammadi and Manichaean Studies 33, Leiden: Brill, 1995.

Watson, Francis, *Gospel Writing: A Canonical Perspective*, Grand Rapids, MI: Eerdmans, 2013.

Paul and the Hermeneutics of Faith, London: T&T Clark, 2015[2].

The Fourfold Gospel: A Theological Reading of the New Testament Portraits of Jesus, Grand Rapids, MI: Baker Academic, 2016.

'How Did Mark Survive?', in K. A. Bendoraitis and N. K. Gupta (eds.), *Matthew and Mark across Perspectives: Essays in Honour of Stephen C. Barton and William R. Telford*, Library of New Testament Studies, London: T&T Clark/Bloomsbury, 2016, 1–17.

'A Gospel of the Eleven: The *Epistula Apostolorum* and the Johannine Tradition', in Francis Watson and Sarah Parkhouse (eds.), *Connecting Gospels: Beyond the Canonical/Non-Canonical Divide*, Oxford: Oxford University Press, 2018, 189–215.

'Pauline Reception and the Problem of Docetism', in Joseph Verheyden, et al. (eds.), *Docetism in the Early Church: The Quest for an Elusive Phenomenon*, Wissenschaftliche Untersuchungen zum Neuen Testament, Tübingen: Mohr Siebeck, 2018, 51–66.

'A Reply to my Critics', in Catherine Sider Hamilton with Joel Willitts (eds.), *Writing the Gospels: A Dialogue with Francis Watson*, London: T&T Clark, 2019, 227–48.

Watson, Francis, and Sarah Parkhouse (eds.), *Connecting Gospels: Beyond the Canonical/Non-Canonical Divide*, Oxford: Oxford University Press, 2018.

Wechsler, Michael (ed.), *Evangelium Iohannis Aethiopicum*, Corpus Scriptorum Christianorum Orientalium, Leuven: Peeters, 2005

Wellhausen, Julius, *Das Evangelium Johannis*, Berlin: Georg Reimer, 1908.

Wilhelm, Friedrich, *Deutsche Legenden und Legendare: Texte und Untersuchungen zu ihrer Geschichte im Mittelalter*, Leipzig: J. C. Hinrichs, 1907.

Wright, William, *Catalogue of Ethiopian Manuscripts in the British Museum Acquired since the Year 1847*, London: British Museum, 1877.

Zuurmond, Rochus (ed.), *Novum Testamentum Aethiopice: The Synoptic Gospels, General Introduction/Edition of the Gospel of Mark*, Stuttgart: Franz Steiner, 1989.

Novum Testamentum Aethiopice, Part III: The Gospel of Matthew, Wiesbaden: Harrassowitz Verlag, 2001.

AUTHOR INDEX

SUBJECT INDEX

Acts of the Apostles 118, 154, 165, 166, 174–83, 186, 219, 220
Acts of John 116–17
Acts of Paul 130, 152, 181–5
Acts of Peter 8
Adam 69, 206–7
Akhmim/Panopolis 19–21
Akhmimic dialect 1, 21
angels 23, 41, 51–2, 112–13, 135–48, 222, 236
Antichrist, physical appearance of 274–5
Antonine plague 9–11
apocrypha 6–7, 15, 16–17, 94
apostles 92–3
  named 44, 220
  unbelief of 113–15
ascension 77, 166
Ascension of Isaiah 140–8, 151–3
Asia Minor 7–8
Athanasius 6, 190

baptism 60, 252

Cerinthus 7–8, 19, 44, 48, 86–7, 158–60
church 44, 47
christology 45, 54, 83, 96–7, 242–3
crucifixion 48, 192
Clement, First Letter of 20–1, 40, 219–20
Clement of Alexandria 148, 195, 196, 243
Corinthians, Paul's First Letter to the 120, 123, 128, 147, 164, 196, 252–7
Corinthians, Paul's Second Letter to the 196
Corinthians, Paul's Third Letter to the 130

descent into hell 60–1, 192, 252
Dialogue of the Saviour 7, 92, 111
Didache 5, 186, 193, 198

Ephesians, Paul's Letter to the 131, 136
Epistle to Rheginus, see *Treatise on the Resurrection*
epistolary genre 2–3, 22, 26–8
Ethiopic gospels, *see* gospels in Ethiopic
Ethiopic manuscripts, *see* manuscripts, Ethiopic
Eusebius 99, 159, 182, 220

Galatians, Paul's Letter to the 180, 186–7
gospel genre 4–5, 83–93, 164–5
gospels in Ethiopic 41, 216, 225–8, 260

Hermas, Shepherd of 199–202, 210
Holy Spirit 32, 46, 47, 123, 135, 150, 158, 161–2, 166

Ignatius of Antioch 148, 192, 223, 224, 228, 229, 253
incarnation 50–2, 57, 89, 127, 134–63
  'adoptionism' 157
  'docetism' 117–18, 127, 146
Irenaeus 18, 81, 88, 94–7, 103–4, 119, 123, 127, 128, 134, 148, 158–60, 163, 185, 206, 217, 222, 223, 224

James, Apocryphon of 7, 83–4, 92, 119, 185, 192
James, First Apocalypse of 7, 84
James, Protevangelium of 4, 148–56
John, Apocryphon of 4, 85, 92–3, 147
John, First Letter of 89, 105, 107, 219, 223, 228
John, Gospel according to 4, 81–2, 89–90, 94, 104–6, 120–3, 242
  prologue 45, 89, 158, 170, 223–4
  descent of Spirit/Christ 158, 161
  water into wine 46, 97–9, 225
  'new commandment' 54, 121, 197

295

CPSIA information can be obtained
at www.ICGtesting.com
Printed in the USA
BVHW041656021122
650988BV00001B/9

9 781108 794619